The Minister's Annual Manual
for Preaching and Worship Planning
2014-2015

Logos Productions Inc.
6160 Carmen Avenue
Inver Grove Heights, MN 55076-4422
1-800-328-0200
www.LogosProductions.com

First Edition
Twenty-eighth Annual Volume

Compiled and edited by Suzanne L.H. Olson

Published in the United States by Logos Productions Inc.
6160 Carmen Avenue
Inver Grove Heights, Minnesota 55076-4422
Phone: 800-328-0200
Fax: 651-457-4617
www.LogosProductions.com

ISBN: 978-1-885361-33-2
ISSN: 0894-3966

Contents

Children's Time

Appendices

FREE Children's Sermon Index

Your paid subscription now includes FREE access to the *Children's Sermon Index* – a database of children's sermons based on the Revised Common Lectionary for each Sunday of the year. You can search by theme, season of the church year, or keyword.

* **Your activation code is MA620.**
* **Visit www.logosproductions.com** and click on activate my complimentary "Children's Sermon Index" under "online resources."
* Follow the instructions to receive FREE access to the *Children's Sermon Index* for as long as you subscribe to *The Minister's Annual Manual*.

How to Use This Book

Dear Readers of *The Minister's Annual Manual,*

This book contains planning resources for 62 worship occasions from August 2014 through July 2015. In addition, there are Monthly Prayers for Church Meetings (see pp. 445-457) and a helpful article for preachers, entitled "Sermon Making" (see pp. 13-17).

Please make good use of the materials here over the course of the coming church year.

Order of Worship Materials

Each week contains the following resources:

- Lessons assigned for liturgical preaching
- Speaker's introductions for the lessons, which may be read aloud during worship or printed as notes in the bulletin
- Worship theme
- Thought for each day, related to the theme
- Sermon summary
- Call to Worship
- Pastoral prayer for the worshiping community
- Prayer of Confession and Assurance
- Prayer of Dedication of Gifts and Self for the offering
- Hymn of the day with background information
- Children's message related to the sermon theme, which can be used by pastors and others who lead this time in worship or children's education
- Sermon based on one of the day's texts
- Hymn suggestions for opening, sermon, and closing songs

Sermon Use

The sermons in this book are best used as thought starters, devotional reading, and a source for anecdotes or illustrations. While they are not intended to be used verbatim, if you do choose to preach a sermon included in this edition or quote extensively from it, please give proper attribution for the source. Both your congregation and the writers of these works deserve the acknowledgment.

Lectionary Guidelines

If you are accustomed to using the lectionary lessons, you will find these materials especially suited for your worship planning. If you don't typically base worship on the lectionary, these materials will still be useful in planning liturgy and sermons based on specific texts related to the church season.

Many denominations now follow the Revised Common Lectionary, the organizing basis for the resources in *Minister's Annual Manual*. You can easily adapt these materials to your own church calendar.

For Sundays from the Second Sunday after Pentecost through Reign of Christ, the Revised Common Lectionary provides two distinct patterns for readings from the Hebrew Scriptures. One pattern uses a series of semicontinuous readings from the Hebrew Scriptures over the course of these Sundays. The Presbyterian Church USA, United Church of Christ, and United Methodist Church elected to use these readings. Corresponding lections are labeled (SC).

The other pattern, used primarily by Lutherans, offers complementary readings in which the Hebrew Scriptures and Gospel reading for each Sunday are closely related. These lections are labeled (C).

The Epistle and Gospel lections are common to both streams of the Revised Common Lectionary.

Hymn Resources

Many of the hymns suggested may be reproduced if your congregation obtains a license. A copyright-cleared music license for churches is available through LicenSing at www.licensingonline.org.

More Planning Resources

You will also find a four-year church year calendar in the appendices (see p. 460) and calendars for 2014 and 2015 (see p. 461).

Please enjoy the materials in this book; our hope is that they enrich your worship preparation and experience.

Suzanne L.H. Olson, Editor
January 2014

Using the CD-ROM

Although the book may be the easiest way to read weekly material, if you wish to reprint prayers or worship material in your Sunday bulletin, using the CD-ROM will save you time and effort. As a purchaser of *The Minister's Annual Manual 2014-2015,* you have permission to use and reprint the entire contents of this book. (When quoting portions from the sermons, please credit the author.) Following are some simple hints for using the CD-ROM:

- This CD can be used in both IBM-compatible and Macintosh computers.
- Insert the CD into your computer's CD-ROM drive and select your preferred word-processing application. Click on "File" and then "Open." Be sure the "List Files of Type" drop-down menu says "All Files (*.*)." For additional help, refer to your software manual.
- Select the week of materials you are interested in viewing or copying and double-click on that file.
- Once the file has opened, you will see a plain text version of the manuscript. You may highlight any or all of the information, then copy and paste it into another document – for example, into your worship bulletin.
- Once the material is in place, change the type font and size to match the document.

Sermon Making
By Charles Somervill

I have an eight-year-old granddaughter, Samantha, who surprised me – as grandchildren often do. For the past 14 years, in addition to serving as a pastor, I've taught business and professional speaking as an adjunct professor at Texas Christian University (yea, Horned Frogs). My granddaughter wanted to know what I taught, so I told her about speaker's notes on three-by-five-inch cards. She said, "I can do that. Give me a three-by-five-inch card." Later she came back and presented me with the following card in large print:

Anivesiry (*sic*)
Wife   Love
Nice   Sweet
Pretty
Siceley (*sic*) Charlie

"That looks right," I said, "but why are you giving me your card?"

"It's a speech I made for you to give to Nana (her grandmother)," Samantha answered.

"But these are your words," I said. "I don't know how to give your speech. Speaker notes are known only to the person who wrote the speech. They are like clues for giving your speech."

"Okay," she took the card back, "I'll give you the speech and you give it to Nana."

She looked at the card and gave the following speech keeping good eye contact: "I want to say something to my wife on our anniversary. I love you. I think you are very nice and sweet. You are very pretty too. Sincerely, Charlie."

Then she gave the card back to me and instructed me to give the speech to Nana. I complied and made it through the speech. I thought Samantha did a good job with the speaker's notes and told her so. "Only next time," I said, "please use it as a code for your speech, not mine."

Alternatives

Speaker's notes that come from extemporaneous speaking have the great advantage of eye contact, vocal variety, a sense of spontaneity, and at least some movement toward the audience. The preparation in advance of speaker's notes dealing with content takes time, especially when it comes to sermon making. Sermon making incorporates the dynamics of good speech making, but it's different from just giving a speech. Sermon making is something the Lord inspires with our cooperation. Even so, as Paul told Timothy (I like the KJV on this one): "Study to shew thyself approved unto God, a workman that needeth not to be ashamed, rightly dividing the word of truth (2 Tim 2:15)." I doubt that Paul would have approved of speaking impromptu or "off the cuff" Sunday after Sunday.

Some time ago, I was asked by our local ministerial alliance to talk about sermon making. Few people understand the private world of preachers who take a breath after one Sunday only to be faced with another. What's worse, as far as the congregation is concerned, we're only as good as the next one! It sounds terrible and it is, but for a preacher it's kind of enjoyable – don't you think?

My journey as a preacher started with manuscripts. I read them and they sounded read. My head bobbed up and down trying to make eye contact and keep my place at the same time. I felt like I was losing my audience, and I probably was.

So next I tried memorizing my manuscripts and ended up spending more time on delivery than content. As every actor knows, it takes lots of practice to memorize and deliver lines so that they don't sound memorized. I had heard somewhere that an audience will respond more positively to a well-delivered sermon with poor content than a poorly delivered sermon with great content. For a while, I found that truth comforting as I took the stage with the content of my sermon getting less attention than my delivery. Distractions, of course, were a problem. Actors go ballistic with a crying baby.

I was still memorizing sermons when I pastored a congregation that required copies of the sermon for the following week. I edited the manuscript on Monday and had the advantage of making corrections. However, I became bored with my own sermons. That happens with a steady diet of pabulum where content has been short changed.

I then went back to school and finished my doctorate in communication at the University of Oklahoma. I learned the fine points of extemporaneous speaking and wound up sharing them at the local ministerial alliance in Granbury. Here's my take on it:

Start with One Point, Not Three

My father was an attorney who grew up on a Tennessee farm. He was not happy with one of our ministers. He said, "That minister starts out hunting rabbits, then squirrels, then quails. He's in the air, on the ground, and then in the trees. You don't know what point he's trying to make."

So how can we avoid the foregoing problem? Narrow down the topic. Think about cutting an apple in half and then cut it again. Get it down to a fine point – not three points, but one. For example, the general topic might be about love. Cut it in half – maybe talk about how hard it is to love those closest to you, especially when betrayed. Or talk about a particular act of love that changed someone's life (for example, "Today's Good Samaritan"). Love can be subdivided into many good sermons. Don't preach them all at once.

Preparation

I think it helps to use a carefully thought-out plan, such as a lectionary, with scripture readings for the entire year – it provides variety and increases the congregation's knowledge of the Bible. Of course, if you have a great inspiration during the week, go with that and come back to the scripture plan next time.

Start your preparation on Monday or Tuesday – no later. Spread out your materials and start reading from at least five to seven commentaries and preaching journals. Think of them as an advisory committee. At that point, your brain should start processing, perhaps buffering like the circle whirling around on a computer. A little bell may ring when reading a particular commentary. Give it time, keep the buffering going overnight. The Spirit may be at work within you, but don't assume you've finished. It's tempting to say "Amen" and stop right there, especially when there's something fun you're planning on a Saturday night.

On Wednesday, go back and read your advisors again, but this time use a red pencil and underline key thoughts. I'm often surprised to discover new insights I didn't see before. There's an extra benefit to starting early this way. You are not only preparing your sermon but you are allowing time for meditation. When the weather permits, I take my study books out on the back porch, breath in the fresh air, look for gems in my sermon materials and meditate. It's refreshing and renewing – something I very much need. It only works when I start early. If I wait until Saturday (and sometimes that happens with emergencies), it's crunch time and I'm left with the desperate prayer of a panicked preacher.

Do something else on Thursday to clear your mind and pray that God will connect the dots on Friday. Write out your ideas on Friday; I usually have about six to eight pages of notes. Then start cutting them in half. The last stage is a final cut with no more than seven three-by-five-inch cards with just a few phrases to keep you on track. (I usually wind up with too many cards and have to cut them down again.) Make a special note of transitional phrases; those are the glue that holds your sermon together. Don't write a completed manuscript. You'll get sucked into your own verbiage and you'll end up reading it.

There are two exceptions for writing out complete sentences: (1) Quotations, especially longer ones, should be written out on a card with credit given. No one expects you to memorize a quotation and it looks more natural to read it. (2) You may want to write out the last two or three sentences of your conclusion. An awkward conclusion that does not tie up things tightly can ruin a sermon. If you suddenly remember something you should have said, forget it. No one will know the difference except you. Don't end your sermon with an anticlimax.

Communication studies suggest that the average attention span is no more than ten minutes. You can go a little longer if you have a wonderful story to regain interest, but the best advice is simple. If you've made your point, wrap it up and sit down.

Once you get used to speaker's notes, it's like a light and a voice that comes on in an airplane: "You are now free to move about the plane." You are now free to engage the audience with eye contact, movement, a sense of spontaneity, vocal variety, and an occasional joke that you just thought of. Distractions are not going to be a problem. When a cell phone goes off you can give your favorite reply without losing your place. Some of my favorites are: "If that's for me, tell them Monday is my day off." "Is that a time signal? I'm not ready to quit yet." "Oh, I'm so glad. I thought that was my phone."

Presentation

Introduce your sermon by gaining our attention with a story or a surprising fact, then tell us where you are going with it (orientation), and how we would benefit from hearing it. In other words, give us a map and make us interested in going there. If you are a new minister or a guest minister, you need to tell us why we should listen to you. In other words, say something to establish your credibility. It's best when someone else gives you a good introduction; if not, then it's your responsibility to tell us why we should listen. It's not bragging. Your qualifications are needed to open the door for a fair hearing.

Everyone has their own style. Pick one that's comfortable for you, but please don't use a stained-glass voice that drones on like a TV evangelist. Don't "preach" but talk to people in a conversational way. Movement is sometimes good, but don't pace like a tiger or violate the personal space of others (stay nine to twelve feet away from people depending of the size of your audience).

Once in a while you might try something different. Some preachers will have a congregational member walk up and play the devil's advocate. It takes rehearsal for that to work, but it creates interest when not over-used. In smaller churches, I know one minister who successfully preaches while sitting on a stool in the middle aisle. Others use visuals. If you use PowerPoint, don't lose eye contact using too many slides. Limit your slides to 15 and use phrases, not sentences, with lots of white space and colorful graphics. But please don't do it every Sunday. The same principle applies to acting, dancing, and singing. Especially creative sermons are like spice. Seasoning is good, but too much spoils the soup.

Exceptions

There are always exceptions to the rules. Ronald Reagan, contrary to popular opinion, read his speeches from a teleprompter, and they never sounded read. Bill Clinton can give a good speech impromptu – just point him in the direction of a podium and he's ready. I've heard Fred Craddock read an entire sermon and it sounded read, but it was still great. Professional speakers will memorize a speech they give over and over and some of them can do it without sounding memorized.

The best speeches, however, are usually extemporaneous. These speeches come from hard study, note taking, and finally speaker's notes. When it's done right, as with the great musician or athlete, it looks easy and holds our attention from start to finish.

On a Monday, if a manuscript is required, the speaker's notes are still fresh and you will have little trouble writing out a sermon. With the con-fidence of preparation and the freedom of speaker's notes, there is nothing like the engagement you have with the congregation. It's the best kind of preaching enjoyment.

August 3, 2014

8th Sunday after Pentecost (Proper 13)
RC/Pres/UCC: 18th Sunday in Ordinary Time

Lessons

Semi-continuous (SC)	Complementary (C)	Roman Catholic (RC)
Gen 32:22-31	Isa 55:1-5	Isa 55:1-3
Ps 17:1-7, 15	Ps 145:8-9, 14-21	Ps 145:8-9, 15-18
Rom 9:1-5	Rom 9:1-5	Rom 8:35, 37-39
Mt 14:13-21	Mt 14:13-21	Mt 14:13-21

Speaker's Introduction for the Lessons
Lesson 1
Genesis 32:22-31 (SC)

Some believe that Jacob wrestles with God, and others say he wrestles with demons that haunt him. Either way, Jacob's experience shows that in our wrestling, we can prevail and find ourselves blessed.

Isaiah 55:1-5 (C); 55:1-3 (RC)

Written after the time of exile, this passage reminds us that God offers us the sustaining word as a free gift – no strings attached. All are invited to celebrate the feast of God's promise.

Lesson 2
Psalm 17:1-7, 15 (SC)

In David's prayer to God, he is asking God to look at the secrets of his heart, and he asks to be tested. David believes he will see God's face.

Psalm 145:8-9, 14-21 (C); Psalm 145:8-9, 15-18 (RC)

This final psalm from David expresses David's commitment to worship God. God's goodness brings praise.

Lesson 3
Romans 9:1-5 (SC/C)
These verses begin a long "sermon" from Romans 9–11, wherein Paul struggles with the reality that his own people have not come to experience the new life that Christ offers.
Romans 8:35, 37-39 (RC)
Paul summarizes the gospel with a series of rhetorical questions and concludes with the ultimate truth: absolutely nothing can separate us from the love of God.

Gospel
Matthew 14:13-21 (SC/C/RC)
Comparing God's reign to a huge banquet was an important image for people who struggled with hunger every day. Many see this story of Jesus feeding the crowd as a precursor to the last supper.

Theme
With the grace of God there is enough for everybody.

Thought for the Day
It's not necessary to feed the 5000 in our time as long as you are willing to tell them to their faces.

Sermon Summary
Two thousand years ago Jesus put a possible task – feeding the multitudes – in the lap of the apostles, but ended up taking care of things himself. The task is still ours, and still doable.

Call to Worship
One: Hey there! Everyone who thirsts, come to the waters; and you that have no money, come and eat. Do not labor anymore for that which does not satisfy. Listen carefully to what is good. God is making us a witness to the world. Receive God's steadfast love!

All: Come, let us praise the Holy One, who has made an everlasting covenant with us. Let us receive God's holy word, and witness to all who are starving for that word!

Pastoral Prayer

God of great blessing, God of abundance, God of all, we lift up your name in praise, and ask that you hear the prayers of our hearts. There are great concerns and wonderful joys that we lift up to you. Most of all, we praise you because you are God, and worthy of all praise simply for creating us. We are thankful beyond words that you are more than creator. You are actively involved in our lives as individuals and as a worshiping people. Bless us this day. Guide us in your way. May your will be done. Amen.

Prayer of Confession and Assurance

Though we live in a world of abundance, we confess, God of all, that we cultivate the fear of scarcity. We hoard our blessings, earthly and heavenly, concerned that if we benefit others we might suffer want and need. We are afraid of feeling the least bit hungry so we are always stuffed. We are afraid of trusting you, so we gather and garner and store far more than we could ever use. We use words of faith, but we live lives of mistrust. May we, with your help, hear your call, Jesus who fed the multitudes, and in blessing our bread share it. May we trust that there is enough for everyone around the world. May we cease to worship borders and boundaries and instead recognize your spirit, your spark, in everyone. This we pray with your people, as your people. Amen.

Prayer of Dedication of Gifts and Self

We offer you thanksgiving and praise, now and always, for the gift of your steadfast and eternal love, and your endless bounty, which you invite us to share with all. In receiving we are committed to giving. In giving we are engaged in praising you! Bless us as your people in this time of offering. Multiply and magnify these gifts to your work, so that as we give in your name and in your spirit, we may receive a hundredfold your blessings, which are so abundant there is enough for all! Amen.

Hymn of the Day
If You Will (But) Trust in God to Guide You

Georg Neumark, after an incident where he was attacked, robbed of all his possessions, and left without employment, wrote this text "to the honor of my beloved Lord." It is considered his finest hymn. The text is a blend of two translations by Catherine Winkworth and Jaroslav Vajda. In times of anguish or despair this text serves as a reminder that God affirms our beliefs and helps us live these beliefs in our daily lives. This hymn is suitable for use as an opening hymn or during confirmation or commissioning services. Neumark composed the commonly used tune, NEUMARK. The accompaniment can be enriched with the addition of brass quartet.

Children's Time: Having Enough

(Talk with the children about money. You might show them some coins and ask them if they know how much the amount will buy. Perhaps some of them receive an allowance. What do they like to do with their money? Have any of them ever tried to save for something big? Perhaps you can share a story of your own about saving up for something when you were younger. Talk about the offering at church and how people put in what they can. Perhaps the children contribute themselves; be sure to affirm them.)
Once Jesus told the disciples to feed a crowd of people. They didn't think they could do it because they only had a small amount of food. But Jesus told them to try, and they found that when they shared it together, everybody had enough. Whether we are rich or poor, we all have gifts to share. When we share our money together through the offering, we are able to do great things. Talk about some of the ministries the offering in your church supports. Share in the amazement that probably none of us could do those things alone, but like the disciples, when we share our gifts together, we are able to do some of the things that Jesus wants us to do.

The Sermon: The Unnecessary Miracle
Scripture: Matthew 14:13-21

In 1973 the science fiction writer Ursula K. LeGuin wrote *The Ones Who Walk Away from Omelas* and won a Hugo Award for the best science fiction story of the year. The story concerned the magical city of Omelas, where all lived charmed lives, safe from danger, free from want.

But there was a price for this security; a child was isolated and imprisoned, ill-fed and ill-clothed. Moreover, the residents of Omelas had to walk by the cell where the child was kept once a year and see this for themselves.

How absurd! Who could live with themselves, and stay happy, if their prosperity depended on the suffering of others, especially children?

Which is, of course, exactly what we in the richer countries do, at the expense of those in poorer countries. Or poorer counties.

Of course we don't think of it that way. We talk about what is ours, as if we created the land and the seeds. We treat our good fortune as if it were not a matter, as it is so often, of an accident of birth. We take credit for things that are gifts of God.

Most of all, we do our best not to look our sisters and brothers in the face. We do not, as they did in Omelas, walk past those who suffer and admit that our prosperity depends on their misery.

The familiar story of the miracle of the loaves and fishes seems to get us off the hook. Jesus blesses and breaks bread, and feeds over 5000 people. We can stand back and admire Jesus, knowing we are not capable of stretching five loaves and two fishes among 500 people, or even 50, much less 5000.

Hooray Jesus! Way to go, Jesus! Wow! That was really something.

But there's something so obvious about this scripture, especially in its cultural context, that we don't see it.

Matthew's account begins right after the execution of John the Baptist. Jesus, having heard about this terrible injustice, looked for a deserted place to get away by himself. However, the crowds found him.

How did Jesus respond? Torn between what he wanted to do and the needs of those who were suffering, the scripture says Jesus had compassion for the crowds.

Now that compassion was gutty. The word has as its roots the Greek word *splagknos*, which means nothing less than entrails, or guts. In Jesus' time, that's where people believed true feeling took place. Love, compassion, any strong emotion had its seat in one's guts. For Jesus they seem to have churned, and he responded by healing the suffering and feeding the hungry.

At first the apostles advised Jesus to "send the crowds away so that they may go into the villages and buy food for themselves" (Mt 14:15). That was not unreasonable. Hospitality lies at the heart of the Middle-Eastern culture, then and now. People looked on unexpected guests who were total strangers as a blessing, not an inconvenience. They were not bothered by the opportunity. They rejoiced! If Jesus had sent the people into the nearby villages they would have been received and fed and sheltered overnight.

But Jesus invites his disciples to find a way to feed them. Their response – what are these five loaves and two fishes among so many – indicates they could not see their way to the task. Jesus responded by blessing and breaking bread, with language reminiscent of the communion language of the last supper, and feeding the multitudes miraculously.

So yes, there is a miracle at the heart of this story, but why was the miracle necessary? Lack of vision. Lack of excitement at the opportunity at hand. Lack of faith.

The demand of scripture is we treat each other equitably. But we in the Western world take credit for our relative prosperity compared to the rest of humanity. We credit our initiative and smugly believe there is something superior about us that the rest of the world is lacking. But is that true? Author and anthropologist Jared Diamond was once asked by a friend of his who was a hunter-gatherer, "Why do you people have all the cargo?" By that his friend meant how did the Western world come to invent and possess high technology while other parts of the world seem to have lacked it? Diamond spent decades researching the question and discovered that hunter-gatherers are actually more intelligent and resourceful than those who live in societies with technology.

In his book *Guns, Germs, and Steel* Diamond suggested that the real reason for scientific development, and therefore prosperity as we measure it, in some countries and not in others was geography, not genetics. Simply put, Eurasia had the appropriate geography for advancements in agriculture and technology to spread rapidly east and west, whereas other continents had physical barriers that prevented such a spread in a north-south direction.

Whether or not this is true, the fact remains that much of the world struggles, whereas in a few places a few people control most of the world's wealth. Jesus expects us to see the suffering of others and to have a gutty kind of compassion that compels us to develop miracles of our own in order to share.

Oh, and remember that story I mentioned at the outset? *The Ones Who Walk Away from Omelas*, the people mentioned in the title, those who see the suffering child and refuse to live at the expense of others, those who refuse false prosperity travel to a place that others cannot imagine.

Which is what happens when we witness the suffering of others and as a result make changes in our lives and in other lives in the name of

Jesus, at the command of Jesus. When we realize we don't need a miracle, we don't need Jesus to feed the multitudes, because we have the power to do so if we are willing to make the sacrifices necessary, we too enter into a place that most people cannot imagine – the kingdom of God.

– Frank Ramirez

Hymns
Opening: Here, O Lord, Your Servants Gather
Sermon: O Let All Who Thirst
Closing: Move in Our Midst

August 10, 2014

9th Sunday after Pentecost (Proper 14)
RC/Pres/UCC: 19th Sunday in Ordinary Time

Lessons

Semi-continuous (SC)	Complementary (C)	Roman Catholic (RC)
Gen 37:1-4, 12-28	1 Kings 19:9-18	1 Kings 19:9, 11-13
Ps 105:1-6, 16-22, 45b	Ps 85:8-13	Ps 85:9-14
Rom 10:5-15	Rom 10:5-15	Rom 9:1-5
Mt 14:22-33	Mt 14:22-33	Mt 14:22-33

Speaker's Introduction for the Lessons
Lesson 1
Genesis 37:1-4, 12-28 (SC)
> The story of Joseph and his brothers combines two sources, which might explain some of the oddities and contradictions. But the power of the story shines through, full of intrigue, tragedy, and, ultimately, forgiveness and reconciliation.

1 Kings 19:9-18 (C); 1 Kings 19:9, 11-13 (RC)
> To attempt to run away from God is futile. Efforts to avoid God's call tend to fail. Yet, when we seek God's voice, sometimes we have to be open to surprises.

Lesson 2
Psalm 105:1-6, 16-22, 45b (SC)
> This psalmist calls upon us to make known the deeds and works of God, in particular those that delivered Joseph from peril and into power.

Psalm 85:8-13 (C); Psalm 85:9-14 (RC)
> This is a salvation oracle that promises God's covenant gifts of steadfast love, faithfulness, and righteousness.

25

Lesson 3
Romans 10:5-15 (SC/C)
Through this reading shines Paul's primary focus: it is not living by the law that makes us righteous with God, but faith in Jesus Christ.
Romans 9:1-5 (RC)
These verses begin a long "sermon" wherein Paul struggles with the reality that his own people have not come to experience the new life that Christ offers.

Gospel
Matthew 14:22-33 (SC/C/RC)
Life is full of storms. When we focus on our immediate situation, we can falter and fall. Trust in God, however, can calm the stormiest of seas.

Theme
Reach out in the name of Jesus to receive help and to give help.

Thought for the Day
The best way to survive the storms of life is to trust in Jesus and in each other.

Sermon Summary
Peter did the right thing when he stepped out of the boat: he obeyed Jesus. And when he started to sink he did the right thing again. He called out, then reached out, for help! In our individualistic culture we should obey Jesus, and if necessary reach out for help.

Call to Worship
One: O give thanks to the Lord, call on his name, make known his deeds among the peoples.
All: Sing to God, sing praises to God; tell of all the wonderful works we have seen!
One: Glory in God's holy name; let the hearts of those who seek the Lord rejoice. Seek the Lord, seek the strength of the Lord; seek God's presence continually.

All: Remember, too, all those wonderful works of Jesus, the miracles and the wisdom of his words.

One: Come, let us seek God's will for our lives together!

Pastoral Prayer

Hear our prayer, God who acts. In the storms of our lives we reach out to you. In danger of being overwhelmed by the pressures, the distractions, even the gadgets that inundate our lives, may we find peace, clarity, and simplicity in Jesus. Reveal your will for our lives in the words spoken in this service, as well as in the songs and in the silences that we share. Trusting in your presence, we base our hope in you. Amen.

Prayer of Confession and Assurance

God of the universe, God of all things great and small, who guides your creatures in their great migrations, tends to the cicadas who dwell beneath the earth for many long years, who shepherds the stars and galaxies in the heavens, and delights in the wildly spinning and swirling subatomic particles beyond our imagining. We confess that we have little faith, that we doubt, that in the storms of life we falter, though we say we trust in you. Hear our hope, even in our doubting, that you will answer. Command us, in the storm, to come to you. Hear our cry, as we sink: Jesus, save us! Truly you are the one foretold by the prophets: Emmanuel, God among us! Save us! Redeem us! Make us whole! Amen.

Hear the words of the one who saves: Take heart, it is I; do not be afraid.

Prayer of Dedication of Gifts and Self

Our gifts of our wealth, our gifts of our time and energy, our gifts of our talents we bring to you this day. We bring forward with these the gifts of who we are – our doubting, our stressing, our fussing over small things when you call us to great things! Receive us as we are, transform us according to your will, and through us accomplish the great thing you have planned for the universe. This we pray in your name. Amen.

27

Hymn of the Day
Here, O God, Your Servants Gather/*Sekai no tomo*
This hymn was composed for the 14th World Council of Christian Education in 1958. It is a remarkable statement of the strength found in ecumenical ministry. The unfamiliar (to most North Americans) beauty of both the text and the tune require careful introduction and presentation. Explore a number of presentation possibilities. The use of a wind ensemble for accompaniment will greatly enhance the beauty of the music. Make sure that the melody, TOKYO, is presented with sensitivity and freedom. Allow the text to dictate a speech rhythm. If you have the availability of Japanese traditional instrumentation (such as *koto* or *shakuhachi*), use this hymn as a way to introduce new and spiritually exciting sounds into worship.

Children's Time: Sink or Float?
(Bring a large clear plastic container filled halfway with water and an assortment of small objects, some that sink and some that float. For example: coin, rock, crayon, paper clip, feather, candy wrapper.)
What is in this tub? Yes, water. What floats on water? *(Boats, balls, and so on.)* What sinks? *(Stones, coins, and so on.)* Do you think this coin will sink or float? *(Have a child drop the coin in the water and call out the result. Repeat for all objects.)*

In our Bible story, Jesus' disciples were floating in a boat, sailing across the lake. Jesus stayed behind to pray. There was a terrible storm that night. Early in the morning, Jesus set out across the water toward the boat. Do you think Jesus sank or floated? *(Accept responses.)* The Bible tells us that Jesus walked right on top of the water, all the way to the boat. No ordinary person can walk on water. But this was Jesus. Jesus walked on the water to help the disciples believe that he was God's Son and to trust that he would help them, no matter what.

Let's pray together: Help us, Lord Jesus, to grow in our faith and love for you. Amen.

The Sermon: Reach Out a Hand in Two Directions
Scripture: Matthew 14:22-33

In 1995 a killing heat wave left 739 people dead in Chicago. Recently
scientists studied that natural disaster to see if there were any lessons to be
learned that might save people in future climatological disasters. Though
one of the largest cities in the world, Chicago is often called a town
because it consists of many small neighborhoods where people of various
economic and ethnic backgrounds congregate. One thing was obvious
after the disaster. Many of the deaths took place in the poorest neighborhoods, where there was little or no air conditioning. Air conditioning
saved lives. But did this mean that those who were poor were automatically doomed to suffer more?

As it turned out, two communities, Englewood and Auburn Gresham, side by side in Chicago's South Side, which had similar poverty and
similar ethnic backgrounds. Nevertheless, Englewood had one of the
highest death rates, while Auburn Gresham one of the lowest. Further
study showed that even without taking the storm into account, Auburn
Gresham's residents lived five years longer than Englewood's.

What was going on? Simply this, people were out on the sidewalks
of Auburn Gresham. There were stores in their community and local
people shopped there. There were restaurants, community centers, and
– very important – churches. All this meant that people went to places
where they recognized each other, knew each other, and, if someone wasn't
there, missed them! As a result, during the heat wave people in places like
Auburn Gresham checked on each other. Church members looked in on
other church members. If folks in the community had no air conditioning, required fresh water, or were struggling medically, someone else knew
about it and took action.

By contrast people who lived in places like Englewood had no stores
or restaurants or community centers. Their neighborhoods had been abandoned by businesses. People stayed at home, and they did not know each
other. No one checked on those who were really suffering.

The implication is that being church, being community, being
concerned and caring about each other saves lives! ("Adaptation: How
Can Cities Be 'Climate-Proofed'?" in *The New Yorker,* January 7, 2013, pp
32-37)

When someone reached out a hand for help, there was someone there to lift them up! As was the case, for instance, with the apostle Peter in stormy waters, sinking beneath the waves, with Jesus close at hand.

Last's week Gospel passage involved the feeding of the 5000. You may remember that the apostles seemed to grasp there was a larger community available to help in times of emergency. They were quick to point out to Jesus that the impending disaster of feeding a multitude could be handled by the people of faith! Just send the hungry folks to the nearby villages and they will be fed.

But Jesus wanted them to understand that the help could come from them. They, the apostles, the church, were the community of faith from which help can come! In the end, Jesus reached out to help the multitudes because of his compassion.

After the meal, Jesus sent the apostles across the Sea of Galilee in a boat, while he dismissed the crowds, and then Jesus went up on a mountaintop to pray. Remember that in the first place he had been seeking seclusion following the murder of John the Baptist. Now he has that time alone.

But a storm had risen, and the apostles were rightfully afraid. Even in our day with networks of safety, advanced weather prediction, and instant communication, storms can still catch recreational craft unaware, leading to capsizing, sinking, and death. However fearful the disciples were at their situation in the storm, they were even more afraid when they saw a figure walking toward them across the waters. Was it a ghost?

Jesus, however, spoke words of reassurance, and here is where Peter is to be commended. In response Peter said: "Lord, if it is you, command me to come to you on the water" (14:28).

Seriously? Is that what you or I would say? Might we not first call out to Jesus to save us before we'd suggest that we'd be willing to walk on water with him? The apostle Peter comes in for some criticism in the Gospels, and probably from many pulpits, for doubting Jesus and for denying Jesus after his arrest. Even though in a moment he will begin to sink and call out to Jesus, "Lord, save me!" (14:30) and will be lightly scolded for having little faith. I think he deserves all the credit in the world for volunteering to walk on stormy seas with this figure who has stepped across the waters toward him in the early morning half-light. Jesus said, "Come!" He came!

Really, he said the right things. Save me! That's Jesus' name, you know. Yeshua, Joshua, means "he delivers, he saves, he rescues." And I didn't see anyone else climb out of the boat with him to step toward Jesus.

Immediately following this, Jesus calmed the storm, causing even more amazement among the disciples. "Truly you are the Son of God" (14:33). And their joint declaration may be an important step for them, and for us.

In recognizing as a fellowship that Jesus reigns, we recognize our relationship to each other, and hopefully also come to understand that as the people of Christ Jesus we are to reach out to others on the stormy seas of life to save each other.

Call to mind how we began, talking about how communities that had networks, such as churches, had a higher percentage of survival during a natural disaster. Well, whether or not you agree about why there is climate change, many people are beginning to agree the climate is changing. We are seeing many natural disasters, areas that had formerly been safe are now endangered by storm and heat and cold.

As the people of faith we are responsible for each other, toward each other, and beyond, toward the folks who share our communities with us. Unlike Jesus we can't control the storm. But we can step forward in faith as Peter did. Peter had the faith to get started and recognized he could not do it on his own. In times of storm and struggle we need to reach out to each other and pull each other up!

Don't fail to reach out a hand to Jesus for help. And don't fail to reach out a hand to a sister or brother to help and to be helped! Creating and maintaining the networks of community is the way we save each other when the storms of life are raging. It's the way we are Christ. It's the way we demonstrate Jesus lives!

– Frank Ramirez

Hymns
Opening: I Sought the Lord
Sermon: When the Storms of Life Are Raging
Closing: Jesus Calls Us O'er the Tumult

August 17, 2014

10th Sunday after Pentecost (Proper 15)
RC/Pres/UCC: 20th Sunday in Ordinary Time

Lessons

Semi-continuous (SC)	Complementary (C)	Roman Catholic (RC)
Gen 45:1-15	Isa 56:1, 6-8	Isa 56:1, 6-7
Ps 133	Ps 67	Ps 67:2-3, 5-6, 8
Rom 11:1-2a, 29-32	Rom 11:1-2a, 29-32	Rom 11:13-15, 29-32
Mt 15:(10-20), 21-28	Mt 15:(10-20), 21-28	Mt 15:21-28

Speaker's Introduction for the Lessons
Lesson 1
Genesis 45:1-15 (SC)

An astonishing turn of events concludes the story of Joseph's family. As reconciliation takes place, Joseph understands that God was involved in it all along, through the dreams and the drama.

Isaiah 56:1, 6-8 (C); 56:1, 6-7 (RC)

In previous chapters of Isaiah, liberation and salvation were longed for. After the return from exile, these things are realized. Now, the task is to live righteously as God's people.

Lesson 2
Psalm 133 (SC)

A song of pilgrimage celebrates the gift of unity using metaphors of nature (oils used for anointing and the two chief mountains of northern and southern Israel, Hermon and Zion).

Psalm 67 (C); Psalm 67:2-3, 5-6, 8 (RC)

The psalm begins with the Aaronic benediction bestowed in Exodus upon Israel, and ends with such blessing beckoning all the earth and its people to praise.

Lesson 3

Romans 11:1-2a, 29-32 (SC/C); Romans 11:13-15, 29-32 (RC)
Struggling with issues about who is included in God's family – specifically, whether the Jews have been rejected or not – Paul affirms that the call to be God's people is irrevocable.

Gospel

Matthew 15:(10-20) 21-28 (SC/C); Matthew 15:21-28 (RC)
Questions abound in this story: Why does a foreign woman recognize Jesus' power and authority? Why does Jesus dismiss her? Why does she persist? Through it all, we gain a new understanding about Christian community.

Theme

Jesus holds up a mirror to our own attitudes and prejudices.

Thought for the Day

If you're uncomfortable with the way Jesus at first treated the Canaanite woman, look in the mirror and reflect on your reflection.

Sermon Summary

The notions of clean and unclean are turned upside down as an outsider, the Canaanite woman, proclaims the good news through her faith in the power of Jesus, his royal titles, and her persistence, a sure sign she takes God seriously.

Call to Worship

How very good and pleasant it is when we can come together in unity! It is as if we were gathered on someone's porch, enjoying the breeze, ignoring the summer's heat, and waving at each other as we pass by on the street. It is like the dew of the morning, cooling the day, like mountains on the horizon, reminding us of God's blessings, for God has come down to us from on high, and settled with us here, in our church home, to guide us in our worship, and strengthen us as a family.

Pastoral Prayer

Open our hearts not only toward each other, God of love and life, but help us to see your presence in every life we share, here in this community, and around the world. May we not need a reminder about the humanity of every soul that surrounds us. Instead, speak to us in our gathering today so that we may answer the needs of all, rather than a select few, recognizing your image in each precious person. Amen.

Prayer of Confession and Assurance

God of all, creator of all things larger than our imagining and small beyond our notice, we praise you that your image resides in each of us, and that everything bears your mark. Yet we confess that we have limited our perception of your unlimited grace. In this we hinder ourselves more than you. Hear us, heal us, deliver us from the boundaries we create, and set us free to serve you in the ministries you have called us to. This we pray in your mighty name. Amen.

Hear the words of Jesus: "Great is your faith! Let it be done for you as you wish."

Prayer of Dedication of Gifts and Self

From this very place, this point, this speck of earth where we have gathered in your name, may our gifts honor you, giver of all good things, inspiring us to give more, do more, be more of your presence in this suffering and struggling world. May our actions today say more about you than us. Magnify these gifts far beyond their material worth according to the spirit in which they are given. Bless us to your service in our giving and receiving. Amen.

Hymn of the Day
There's a Wideness in God's Mercy

Frederick William Faber, the author of this text, was a member of the Oxford movement who eventually converted to Roman Catholicism. The original text was 13 stanzas in length. In modern hymnals the number of stanzas has been reduced to four or possibly five. Faber was an evangelical who wrote this text to give praise to the grandeur of God's boundless love and the joy the singer finds in returning that love during worship and in

life. Depending upon the hymnal source, this wonderful text is sung to
WELLESLEY by Lizzie Tourjee; IN BABILONE, a Dutch melody; or GOTT
WILL's MACHEN, a strong tune by Swiss composer Johan Steiner. Each tune
emphasizes a different feeling of presentation and should be considered.

Children's Time: Looks Can Be Deceiving

*(Bring two dolls or stuffed animals, one that is new and in good condition,
another that is somewhat worn or tattered.Ask which of the two is better and
why? Allow time for the children to reply.)*
Things that look shiny, new, and perfect are usually thought to be much
nicer than old, scruffy things. But let's look again at this well-worn animal.
Part of the reason he is so tattered is because night after night, for many
years, this old toy was taken to bed and a little child hugged him tight.
The more frightened that child was, the tighter she hugged him. The old
teddy bear is really far more precious in so many ways, even though it
looks pretty sad on the outside.

Jesus wants his followers to learn that same thing about people. You
can't tell just by looking at someone whether they are faithful, or helpful,
or good. A person may look very different from others on the outside.
That person may look like he or she wouldn't love God at all. But when
we come to know and love that person, we may find something very wonderful – that he or she has a good, strong faith.

Jesus' disciples thought they could tell who the good people were and
who they were not. But once Jesus surprised them by telling them that a
woman who looked like a real outsider had a greater faith than all the disciples. They were surprised, no doubt, to learn that, but they should not
have been. All along, God has taught that friends of God come in many
shapes, sizes, and circumstances.

Let's pray: Dear God, thank you for helping us understand that faith
is on the inside, and we can't always know just by looking at someone how
much they love you. Amen.

The Sermon: Sometimes We're Not Ourselves
Scripture: Matthew 15:(10-20), 21-28

There's a document sometimes called Thomas Jefferson's Bible, which he created for his own devotional purposes and not for general distribution. Even so, at one time and for several decades all incoming US senators and congressional representatives received a copy.

What Jefferson did was cut out passages from the Gospels in four different languages and paste them side by side. He removed those portions involving miracles, which he didn't credit. Although most of us might deny ever being tempted to do any such thing ourselves, certainly for each of us there is a passage in the Bible that we could live without. But it is precisely those passages we are challenged to deal with, dialog with, confront, and talk back to. And this particular passage is one that makes us, with our 21st-century sensibilities, and our knowledge of the deep-seated animosities between peoples of the Middle East, just a little uncomfortable. Some, no doubt, would like to delete it, because Jesus comes off looking rude, insensitive, callous, even prejudiced. We don't like it when Jesus looks like us.

Prior to this story of the encounter between Jesus and the Canaanite woman with her sick daughter, Jesus has shown deep-seated compassion for the multitudes who came out to hear him. He healed their sick, spoke to their needs, and miraculously fed them with a few loaves and fishes. Now, having traveled to the gentile regions of Tyre and Sidon, Jesus is confronted by a Canaanite woman whose daughter is very, very ill. Her needs are as great as anyone in Galilee.

Jesus might well have been exhausted at this moment. After seeking a place to pray, he served the multitudes, crossed the Sea of Galilee, walking most of the way according to the Gospel, and then dealt with a very insulting dialog about issues of clean and unclean in which some suggested that Jesus and his disciples were not fit to minister because they didn't observe the rules of cleanliness.

These rules of cleanliness had little to do with actual antiseptic practice, of course. In every culture, in every area, there are ways we perform simple tasks that, if done properly, please everyone, and if not, give others the heebie-jeebies. Kind of like what some used to call cooties. Some cultures eat horses and dogs and are nauseated by cheese or corn, for instance. It doesn't always make sense, but it's very real.

Jesus sought to redefine clean and unclean, suggesting that the elaborate rituals developed among his people might not matter as much as what people say or do. But then, here is Jesus, responding to a Canaanite woman first with silence, not even acknowledging her existence, and when he does he uses a very insulting comment about dogs – for dogs were not considered the lovable pets as in our culture.

This is a little embarrassing. One is tempted to cringe. Perhaps Jesus was not expressing himself well. This conversation probably took place in Greek, not his native Aramaic, and most of us are not as comfortable or articulate in a second language.

Of course, maybe Jesus, very human as well as very divine, was responding out of his exhaustion. Perhaps you have seen the series of commercials in which an ordinary person becomes rude and verbally abusive, to the point of looking like a celebrity well known for such behavior, until a friend offers a candy bar and we are reminded, "You're not yourself when you're hungry." After the snack the person returns to normal. Perhaps Jesus was experiencing some sort of low blood sugar.

Now many of Jesus' listeners would have been themselves prejudiced against anyone identified with Canaan. The book of Joshua identified Canaanites as outsiders who were unclean.

But this Canaanite woman really challenges the notions of clean and unclean. The religious leaders had just challenged Jesus, his credentials and his credibility, while in contrast this outsider called Jesus "Lord" and "Son of David." And she was persistent. She did not accept first his silence, then his assertion that he had come to serve the children of Israel, and finally the statement by Jesus that it is not proper to give the food for children to the dogs. She kept pushing!

How many of us give up on prayer because we do not immediately receive a positive response? But this woman's passion for her daughter is not deterred by the standard prejudices of her day, prejudices shared in both directions by Canaanites and Judeans. She has faith in Jesus. Jesus says so himself. Having just told Peter, during the storm, that he had little faith, Jesus here applauds the great faith of this woman who is an outsider. And because of her persistence, her willingness to talk back to Jesus, to pester until she gets what she wants, she is rewarded and her daughter is healed. Yes as sometimes happens in scripture, the outsider demonstrates biblical faithfulness while insiders flounder. Talking back to God is expected. Abraham was not struck dead by lightning for arguing with God over the fate of Sodom and Gomorrah. Neither was Moses condemned for talking God out of destroying the people of Israel in the desert. Job railed against his inability to get justice from God. Jonah talked back, as did Habbakuk, as did the woman at the well with Jesus. The psalms and the book of Lamentations call God into question. Talking back to God means we take God seriously, as an authentic, personal being.

This story is addressed to us, and at our prejudices. If you think Jesus looked bad in this encounter, at least at first, think of how we seem to others when we rattle off prejudice that masquerades as conventional wisdom. And while Jesus may have had a theological reason for ministry to Israel first, then to the nations, a person with a desperate need is not in a position to hear such fine points of theology. We may be tempted in the face of the desperate needs of the world to offer perfectly correct theological explanations for why we are taking a certain course of action. But, like Jesus, we sometimes need to be reminded that unless we address suffering we cannot walk together with others on the road toward discipleship. Let us put away the scissors for now. This passage can stay in the Gospel. Especially when we treat it like a mirror and see ourselves as insiders who might make ourselves outsiders, while learning from outsiders who are really those proclaiming the truth of the good news of Jesus Christ.

– Frank Ramirez

Hymns
Opening: Called or Not Called
Sermon: How Good a Thing It Is
Closing: Will You Let Me Be Your Servant

August 24, 2014

11th Sunday after Pentecost (Proper 16)
RC/Pres/UCC: 21st Sunday in Ordinary Time

Lessons

Semi-continuous (SC)	Complementary (C)	Roman Catholic (RC)
Ex 1:8—2:10	Isa 51:1-6	Isa 22:15, 19-23
Ps 124	Ps 138	Ps 138:1-3, 6, 8
Rom 12:1-8	Rom 12:1-8	Rom 11:33-36
Mt 16:13-20	Mt 16:13-20	Mt 16:13-20

Speaker's Introduction for the Lessons
Lesson 1
Exodus 1:8—2:10 (SC)

Genesis concludes with Israel having gone down to Egypt. Exodus
narrates the fulfillment of God's promise to Abraham that his descendants would multiply and possess the land God gave them. Without
knowing Joseph or his leadership, Pharaoh sanctions Israel, setting the
stage for Moses, the future leader of Israel's return from exile.

Isaiah 51:1-6 (C)

Isaiah unpacks the full dimensions of God's judgment and salvation.
Chapter 51 is contained within a larger unit, chapters 49 through 57,
which narrates the ministry of the Suffering Servant and the restoration of Israel.

Isaiah 22:15, 19-23 (RC)

Isaiah unpacks the full dimensions of God's judgment and salvation.
This lesson is part of a larger unit, chapters 13 through 23, containing
a series of nine oracles against foreign nations. In the midst of this,
however, there remains promise concerning the house of David.

Lesson 2
Psalm 124 (SC)

The psalm celebrates God's deliverance of the community from some
unidentified but precipitous danger.

Psalm 138 (C); Psalm 138:1-3, 6, 8 (RC)
The psalmist offers thanks to God for interceding when the psalmist called out. The psalm underscores God's regard of the lowly, and God's presence in times and places of vulnerability.

Lesson 3
Romans 12:1-8 (SC/C)
Paul's letter to the church in Rome is a dense account of God's power for salvation for everyone. Here begins Paul's teaching on how the gospel should be lived out in everyday life and not as isolated individuals but as unity of believers with a single purpose.
Romans 11:33-36 (RC)
Paul has just narrated a difficult section on the hardening of Israel's heart against God. Still, he refuses to see this as anything less than God's inscrutable plan culminating in glorious praise across all the ages.

Gospel
Matthew 16:13-20 (SC/C/RC)
The disciples have been with Jesus for many, many months. Only now does Jesus ask the disciples about who he is. Peter answers "You are the Christ, the Son of the Living God." Thereupon follows a typical pattern of the patriarchal pattern of blessing, a new name, and an inheritance (that is, a future).

Theme
Resist the tide of this false age and be transformed by God's love.

Thought for the Day
If you're out of step with the world maybe you're in step with God's will.

Sermon Summary
Information cascade theory demonstrates that even if we know the right answer, if surrounded by wrong answers we'll go along! Paul exhorts us to resist the cascading tide of this age which dehumanizes us, and as transformed believers celebrate the unique gifts we bring to the body of Christ.

Call to Worship

One: If God had not been on our side, let the people now say,

All: If God had not been on our side, we would have been swallowed up alive by the storms of life all around us!

One: Like a flood, we would have been swept away, the torrent would have gone over us, the raging waters would have washed us away.

All: Blessed be God, who has made the heavens. Our help is in the name of God, who created the earth! Let us gather in worship! Let us, as one fellowship, praise God!

Pastoral Prayer

Praise, honor, glory, and thanksgiving, we praise today for the gift you have given in each heart, in each voice, through every hand, with every aim and aspiration, for you have crafted us individually, blessing us with different gifts which, when combined, make for the whole body of Christ. May we, transformed by your Spirit, cherish each other as we are, so we may cease to seek to be conformed to some nonexistent standard, but be set free to worship you as a blessed people of peace. Amen.

Prayer of Confession and Assurance

All: Hear our prayer, which we offer together, confessing individually how profoundly we are tempted to live by the ways of our society. You have called us, not to conform to the world around us, but to be transformed by the renewing of our minds in Christ Jesus. May we give more than lip service to the life of discipleship to which we are called. May we truly be blessed as peacemakers, as the humble, as those persecuted for righteousness sake, and may our lives, transformed by faith, shine as emblems of hope to those who walk, by choice, in darkness. Lead us, guide us, guard us. Amen.

One: By God's grace, through God's will, our sacrifice is good and acceptable and perfect!

Prayer of Dedication of Gifts and Self

We bring before you this day our gifts, emblems in themselves of the unique story you have told in each one of us as givers. Our lives represent different paths, different ways in which you have been made flesh to dwell among us, so we all offer individually and as your body, not only a portion of what we have, but the entirety of who we are. By your mercy, Giving God, we present ourselves as a living sacrifice, holy and acceptable to you. Receive our gifts, we pray, in your name. Amen.

Hymn of the Day
Built on a Rock

More often than not, finding the hymn that is just right for a particular occasion requires a fair amount of pondering, leafing through hymnals, and imagination. Such is the case with today's texts, which offer several directions for the musician. One intriguing possibility is Nikolai Grundtvig's "Built on a Rock," set to the tune KIRKEN DEN ER ET GAMMELT HUS by Ludvig Lindeman. Grundtvig's opening line echoes precisely Jesus' words to Peter in the Gospel lesson, while the remainder of the hymn reflects ideas presented in the Romans text.

Children's Time: Strength in Union

(Bring a picture of a team sport, preferably football, with players lined up and ready for action.)

How many of you like football *(or other sport pictured)*? This is a picture of a football team lined up for a play. Who can describe the action? *(Affirm all answers.)* The center is ready to hike the ball to the quarterback, and the quarterback will either pass to a receiver or hand off to a running back. Which team member do you think is the most important one on the team? *(Allow time for answers.)*

If some of you think the quarterback is the most important one on the team, answer this: What would happen if there were no center to hike the ball? And what would happen if there were no people to block the defenders? What if no one was there to run the ball? Surely every member of the team is as important as every other member. The team that plays best is usually the team whose members work in union with each other.

The church is like a team, and each of you is just as important to the strength of this team as every member of this church. Thank you for being a part of our team.

The Sermon: Conformation or Confirmation
Scripture: Romans 12:1-8

It's funny how one person can have a bad idea, and pretty soon others follow. We all think everyone ought to obey the law, but if you're in the middle of traffic and everyone's breaking the speed limit by ten miles per hour, the odds are you will too. If a lie, or a hurtful truth, about a celebrity or politician is spoken on television or at the coffee shop, others begin to repeat it. Perhaps you have too.

It's like something John Muir, the self-made naturalist, wrote in his diary the first summer he spent in the Yosemite wilderness while traveling with a shepherd and a great flock of sheep. While Muir had tremendous admiration for the wildlife he encountered, he noted wryly in *My First Summer in the Sierra*, "A sheep can hardly be called an animal: an entire flock is required to make one foolish individual" (p. 62).

Or like the comic playwright Menander once said (which was later quoted by Paul in 1 Corinthians 15:33), "Bad company ruins good morals." That's not only a pithy saying, it's also good science. There's a branch of mathematics known as information cascade theory, which simply states that in the company of folks making bad choices, people will do the same even when they know better. Bad choices are contagious. Cascade theory demonstrates mathematically that in bad company the odds are good that we'll be stampeded to share the opinion of fools.

One sees this in the hysteria that follows a national trauma. The real danger of World War II led Americans astray in the hysterical act of herding loyal Japanese Americans into detention centers. Americans traumatized (rightfully so) by 9/11 came to believe Iraq was not only the source of terror but also posed a nuclear threat. Sometimes the sky is really falling. Sometimes it's just Chicken Little.

The very long mathematical algorithm that undergirds the theory proves that the answer to your mother's plea, "If all your friends jumped off the bridge, will you jump too?" is "Yes!"

Writing to the Romans, and to all Christians, Paul pleads with us to answer "No!"

One of the reasons Paul wrote to the Romans was because of pressure to conform to different cultural values. Jewish Christians encouraged Gentile Christians to conform to their cultural practices. Roman society, which was strictly stratified with regard to self-segregation of slave and free, rich and poor, male and female, along with other categories, pressured Christians to separate along the same lines.

But the apostle has been encouraging the believers in this most cosmopolitan of cities to create one body of Christ by combining their God-given individuality, not negating it. So in this passage he invites all of us to take a good look at ourselves. On the one hand he asks us all "not to think of yourself more highly than you ought to think, but to think with sober judgment, each according to the measure of faith that God has assigned" (Rom 12:3).

His central theme, however, is a flat warning against giving into the cascade. "Do not be conformed," he writes, "to this age." Although sometimes translated "world," the word refers to the mindset of the times. Instead, he tells us all to be transformed, changed, metamorphosed "by the renewing of your minds," so that we might discern God's perfect will (12:2).

We are not to think of ourselves, Paul writes, "more highly than you ought." And what better example do we have of this than Jesus himself? In another letter, written to the Philippians, Paul tells us that Jesus did not consider equality with God as something to be taken advantage of, but humbled himself obediently to the cross.

Sometimes our society gives lip service to the idea of individuality, but the political sphere, the advertising circles, the peer pressure that seems ingrained in the structure of every age group, the covenants that set standards in housing developments, the community standards when it comes to something as simple as what colors you may paint your home, nn these and many other ways there is intense pressure to conform.

It can become very difficult to avoid conforming. When a style takes hold, whether it be the length of men's short pants or the style of women's blouses, it can be almost impossible to find something dissenting for sale. Perhaps we should expect this in society at large. But in our congregations there can be pressure to conform as well. The apostle Paul encouraged diversity in practice. He chose to practice his Jewish cultural customs, but insisted that Christians from the Roman world maintain their practices, and he encouraged the Celts of Galatia, who conformed neither to the Jewish or Roman standards, to remain the people they were when they first accepted the gospel. He expected that all would accept Jesus Christ as Lord, as Jesus has accepted us. But beyond that he spoke out against those, even apostles as respected as Peter, who succumbed to peer pressure to become cookie-cutter Christians.

So should we, in our congregations, demand that all Christians dress alike, eat the same foods, belong to the same political parties, speak the same language, enjoy the same music? On the contrary. In this passage from Romans, Paul points to the many gifts given to us, and then deliberately uses the word we translate as members, because that word, in the English language, refers not to interchangeable units, but the different parts of the body. Listing some of the gifts shared by people – prophecy, ministry, teaching, exhorting, giving, leading, and compassion – he insists all are necessary to our corporate well-being.

This grace of difference, granted to us, and granted by us to each other, is what Paul calls our "spiritual worship," and without it, we are not truly God's people.

We are all needed in the body of Christ. We are all welcome. In contrast to a world that attempts to make us conform to impossible standards of self-worth, we are loved and welcomed as we are, because that is how God made us. We bring our weaknesses and strengths and, most of all, our gifts to the work of Jesus Christ. We are transformed, so that we no longer look at God and each other, as the world does.

Rather than an information cascade theory, which drags us and draws us into false conclusions, we encounter a great, overwhelming tidal wave of love, which transforms us and the landscape of church to one of love, acceptance, salvation, and peace. Amen.

– Frank Ramirez

Hymns
Opening: Breathe upon Us, Holy Spirit
Sermon: *Una Espiga*/Sheaves of Summer
Closing: Heart and Mind, Possessions, Lord

August 31, 2014

12th Sunday after Pentecost (Proper 17)
RC/Pres/UCC: 22nd Sunday in Ordinary Time

Lessons

Semi-continuous (SC)	Complementary (C)	Roman Catholic (RC)
Ex 3:1-15	Jer 15:15-21	Jer 20:7-9
Ps 105:1-6, 23-26, 45c	Ps 26:1-8	Ps 63:2-6, 8-9
Rom 12:9-21	Rom 12:9-21	Rom 12:1-2
Mt 16:21-28	Mt 16:21-28	Mt 16:21-27

Speaker's Introduction for the Lessons

Lesson 1

Exodus 3:1-15 (SC)

Moses was reared in Pharaoh's household but fled to Midian after he murdered a Egyptian for beating a Hebrew slave. In the desert, Moses raises sheep, gets married, and starts a family. But, God still has a purpose for Moses, one that includes his returning to the scene of his crime.

Jeremiah 15:15-21 (C)

For Jeremiah, God was ultimate, the creator of all that exists and thus the all-powerful and everywhere-present Lord. This is the message he delivers over and over in a series of warnings and exhortations to Judah. Today's lesson, however, is the second of six personal laments Jeremiah makes before the Lord.

Jeremiah 20:7-9 (RC)

For Jeremiah, God was ultimate, the creator of all that exists and thus the all-powerful and everywhere-present Lord. This is the message he delivers over and over in a series of warnings and exhortations to Judah. Today's lesson, however, is the fifth of six personal laments Jeremiah makes before the Lord.

Lesson 2
Psalm 105:1-6, 23-26, 45c (SC)
This extended "salvation history" song focuses upon Israel's plight in Egypt and God's sending of Moses and Aaron for the Hebrews' deliverance.

Psalm 26:1-8 (C)
This psalm of lament cries to God for help against enemies before moving to praise of God as one who hears and helps and saves.

Psalm 63:2-6, 8-9 (RC)
A psalm of David when he was in the wilderness of Judah, this is a psalm of trust in a time of need.

Lesson 3
Romans 12:9-21 (SC/C)
Previously Paul articulated the concept of unity among believers, a unity in which all use their gifts for the good of the body. Now, he continues teaching on the importance of living out the gospel in everyday life by giving specific character traits that mark a true follower of Jesus Christ.

Romans 12:1-2 (RC)
Paul's letter to the church in Rome is a dense account of God's power for salvation for everyone. Here begins Paul's teaching on how the gospel should be lived out in everyday life, not as isolated individuals but as unity of believers with a single purpose.

Gospel
Matthew 16:21-28 (SC/C); Matthew 16:21-27 (RC)
Following upon the acknowledgment of Peter that Jesus is the long-awaited Messiah, Jesus explains to his disciples the specifics of what it means to be "the Christ" as well as what is required for those who follow him.

Theme
Love is stronger than hatred.

Thought for the Day

The best revenge is kindness. The best response is love.

Sermon Summary

In what we might call Paul's sermon on the mount, we are urged to take the mask off love and to be motivated by love in all things, and especially love in action, especially toward those who might be considered our enemies.

Call to Worship

> One: O give thanks to God, call on that name, make known God's
> deeds among the peoples.
>
> **All: Sing, sing praises to God; tell of all God's wonderful works.**
>
> One: Glory in that holy name; let the hearts of those who seek God
> rejoice.
>
> **All: Seek the presence of the creator continually. Remember
> God's wonderful works, the miracles, the judgments, all you
> people, all who share in the family of God.**

Pastoral Prayer

God of love, if it were easy to love we would not be praying to you this day. Yet we desire to love all, even when it is difficult. We need you to strengthen us so that our love is genuine, and not a mask that we conveniently put on and take off. Lead us to share each other's burdens, to know each other better, to care more deeply, and to live sincerely as one family in your name. Amen.

Prayer of Confession and Assurance

> **All: We confess, God of truth, that we have subscribed to the
> falsehoods that surround us. We have given our heart to the
> call for vengeance that rises up out of our culture in opposi-
> tion to peace and justice. We have repeated half-truths and
> outright lies about others and about other peoples. Yet you
> call us to return good for evil, to give food and drink to our
> enemies, to bless those who curse us. You challenge us to turn
> the world upside down by shining the bright light of love at**

the core of darkness that enshrouds so many. Forgive us for
having ignored you. Inspire us to listen and live your written
word, and your living word, Jesus. Amen.
One: Hear, people of God! God's steadfast love, enduring forever, is
our eternal covenant with the eternal!

Prayer of Dedication of Gifts and Self

Giving God, receiving God, our gifts today, given with ardor and zeal, are
meant to bring hope to the suffering, serve the needs of our fellow saints,
and extend your love to strangers, all those we do not yet know near at
hand and far away. Bless our gifts, suit them to your purposes, speed them
by your will, that your name might be known and your love may be felt
the world over. Strengthen us in our giving, that we may accomplish even
more in your name. Amen.

Hymn of the Day
Take up Your Cross, the Savior Said

Christianity's chief symbol is the cross – an assertion supported by its
frequent appearance in Christian hymnody. Merely count the number of
hymns whose titles contain the word *cross* to see how deeply it has inspired
hymn writers through the centuries. "Take Up Your Cross, the Savior
Said," by Charles Everest, has been set to a variety of tunes. BOURBON, a
strong melody in the minor mode attributed to Freeman Lewis, is particularly effective in underscoring the gravity of Jesus' words to those who
would follow him.

Children's Time: Share + Serve = Love

Let's start out today with a math equation. Who loves to do math homework? *(Affirm all answers.)*

Who can tell me the answer to this equation: share plus serve equals?
(Respond favorably when children suggest this is not math.)

In the lesson today from Romans we hear some directions for living a
life with God in it. Share your belongings with those who need things. Serve
the Lord. Love one another. *(Emphasize the words from the equation.)* Can
you hear what the Bible is telling us? Share, serve, love. That might help you
solve the math problem.

Who can help me solve it now? Share plus serve equals? *(Wait for the answer "love.")*

God want us to share with others and always serve God by showing love – even toward those people we might not call friends.

Let's pray together: Dear God, thank you for showing us in the Bible what you want us to do. If we share with others and serve you, we will share in your love. Amen.

The Sermon: Love without a Mask
Scripture: Romans 12:9-21

Some might consider the era of the first Queen Elizabeth of England to be a golden age for theater. One of the most popular plays of the time was *The Spanish Tragedy* by Thomas Kyd (1558-1594), written between 1582 and 1592. It was known as a revenge tragedy. The play included stabbings, hangings, betrayals, a man on the scaffold who believes he will be pardoned right up to the moment he is hanged, a ghost intent on revenge, the character of Revenge, and, of course, revenge. Plenty of it.

For the Elizabethans, revenge tragedies were like horror movies. The desire for revenge might seem very human to some, but the Elizabethans knew it was a terrible sin, one that condemned a soul to hell, because, after all, scripture told them that vengeance belonged to God! In today's passage from Romans the words of Paul in verse 19 ("Beloved, never avenge yourselves, but leave room for the wrath of God; for it is written, 'Vengeance is mine, I will repay, says the Lord'") and his advice about vengeance are the centerpiece in one of the most Jesus-like passages in his writings.

There are some who complain that Paul doesn't seem to know anything about Jesus, but truth be told Paul quotes him all the time (see the appendix "The Jesus Tradition Utilized by Paul," pp. 236-260, in *Irish Jesus Roman Jesus: The Formation of Early Irish Christianity*, by Graydon F. Snyder, Trinity Press International, 2002). In Paul's day, however, one did not put quotation marks around everything or use footnotes. And indeed, one could make the case that Romans 12:9-21 could be called Paul's sermon on the mount. This passage is filled with moral instruction that relies heavily on the teachings of Jesus, both his own words and the passages from the Hebrew Scriptures that Jesus quoted.

No doubt Paul is alluding to Deuteronomy 32:35 ("Vengeance is mine, and recompense…") and possibly to Proverbs 24:29 ("Do not say, 'I will do to others as they have done to me; I will pay them back for what they have done.'")

And he quotes outright in support of his thesis Proverbs 25:21-22: "If your enemies are hungry, give them bread to eat; and if they are thirsty, give them water to drink; for you will heap coals of fire on their heads, and the Lord will reward you."

This is a radical thought, both for the ancient sages who preserved the proverbs and for Paul who wrote a few centuries later. It was commonplace for enemy prisoners to be mistreated in the ancient world, but this wisdom suggests just the opposite. The way to truly get even is to kill your enemies with kindness.

This counterintuitive advice is a fairly sophisticated strategy. It actually proved successful when, following World War II, the Allies worked together to rebuild and rehabilitate their enemies in that bitter war. Programs like Heifer International, where "seagoing cowboys" delivered cows from American farmers to German families living in the ruins built bridges of peace. Leaving embittered survivors only plants the seeds for the next war. But long-term peace and stability can result from unexpectedly kind behavior.

The book *Amish Grace*, which is concerned with the horrific murder of the young girls at the Nickel Mines school in Pennsylvania, outlines the way that treating enemies with kindness is an automatic response on the part of the Amish people, not because it is easy, for it is not, but because it is expected. Among the Amish, the words of Jesus from the Lord's Prayer "forgive us our debts, as we forgive our debtors" are not a suggestion, but a command.

The same day the young girls were murdered by a man who ended up killing himself, representatives of the Amish community went to the murderer's family to express forgiveness, and some of the money that came streaming in from around the world in sympathy to the parents' pain was given to the murderer's family because they realized it might be hard for them to find jobs in the tight-knit community.

One biblical passage quoted by both Paul and Jesus is "You shall love your neighbor as yourself." But that's only a part of the verse. The first half of Leviticus 19:18 is concerned with revenge! "You shall not take vengeance or bear a grudge against any of your people, but you shall love your neighbor as yourself: I am the Lord."

Turning away from revenge, justified or not, and putting love first is why Paul writes the words often translated as "Let love be genuine." But to understand the true meaning of these words it is necessary to turn to the world of the theater once more.

The theaters of the ancient Greek world, which still existed in Paul's times, were large structures seating tens of thousands of people. Although they were acoustically perfect, the actors still might seem very small to those sitting far away. As a result, the actors wore tall masks with exaggerated features to make it clear what emotion they were expressing. These masks were called *hupokrites*, from which we get the word *hypocrites*.

Wearing a mask as an actor is one thing. Wearing a mask as sharers in the body of Christ is another. We expect an actor to display emotions appropriate to the character, whether or not she or he is actually feeling those emotions, but we ought to be suspicious of people who wear a mask, figurative, to hide what they are really feeling. We might translate Romans 12:9 as "Don't wear a mask; show real love!"

Genuine love is at the heart of everything else the apostle commands us to in the name of love: holding fast to the good, loving each other with mutual affection, rejoicing in hope, sharing patience in suffering, persevering in prayer, contributing to the needs of our fellow believers but also showing hospitality – a Greek word that literally means "love for foreigners" or strangers – all of this is summed up with the final words of Paul in this chapter: do not be overcome by evil, but overcome evil with good.

No doubt there are times when we have to put a good face on things, when we tell someone they're looking good even after they have endured difficult treatments for instance. But the challenge of Jesus, through these words of Paul, is to turn away from evil, turn away from vengeance, and to stop wearing a mask. We should be honest, open, generous, and thoughtful while we actively serve each other in real and unfeigned love in the name of Jesus. Amen.

– Frank Ramirez

Hymns

Opening: Breathe upon Us, Holy Spirit
Sermon: God of Eve and God of Mary
Closing: O Perfect Love

September 7, 2014

13th Sunday after Pentecost (Proper 18)
RC/Pres/UCC: 23rd Sunday in Ordinary Time

Lessons

Semi-continuous (SC)	Complementary (C)	Roman Catholic (RC)
Ex 12:1-14	Ez 33:7-11	Ez 33:7-9
Ps 149	Ps 119:33-40	Ps 95:1-2, 6-9
Rom 13:8-14	Rom 13:8-14	Rom 13:8-10
Mt 18:15-20	Mt 18:15-20	Mt 18:15-20

Speaker's Introduction for the Lessons
Lesson 1
Exodus 12:1-14 (SC)

In Exodus we find God fulfilling his promise to Abraham by both multiplying his descendants and leading them home again. These verses tell us how God wants the Israelites to remember the freedom he has given them.

Ezekiel 33:7-11 (C); Ezekiel 33:7-9 (RC)

Ezekiel was both a prophet and a priest. Exiled to Babylon in 597 BCE his messages of warning and judgment were to the exiles and those left in Judah. Here he identifies himself as a "watchman" for the house of Israel.

Lesson 2
Psalm 149 (SC)

The summons to sing praise to God is coupled with a curious call to bear arms so as to defeat Israel's foes.

Psalm 119:33-40 (C)

This portion of the Bible's longest acrostic (alphabetically structured) psalm on the keeping of God's law focuses on the seeking of understanding for the sake of Torah observance.

Psalm 95:1-2, 6-9 (RC)

> This is the first in a series of psalms devoted to worship and praise. An invitation to worship, the psalm has been a vital part of liturgies.

Lesson 3
Romans 13:8-14 (SC/C); Romans 13:8-10 (RC)

> "Love your neighbor as yourself" is the summation of all the other commandments in this call to be alert now to the day of salvation, putting aside all that stands in the way of living a life for Jesus Christ.

Gospel
Matthew 18:15-20 (SC/C/RC)

> Clearly understanding human nature, Jesus teaches how disagreeing believers should resolve their differences, and he promises his presence in the midst of even the smallest gathering number.

Theme

We are called to love each other, no matter what.

Thought for the Day

The simple test of all we do can be to ask ourselves: through this act am I loving my neighbor?

Sermon Summary

Often we look for things in life to be black and white, but it is not that way. Perhaps that's why Jesus pointed out that love for God and neighbor were paramount. St. Paul goes a step further and says that if we love our neighbor we are fulfilling the entire law.

Call to Worship

> One: Jesus said, "Where two or more are gathered in my name, I am
>   there among them."
> **All: And so we gather today in Christ's name.**
> One: We come to praise God, and to be renewed and strengthened in
>   our faith.
> **All: We come to remember God's simple truth for us: in all
>   things, may we love one another.**
> One: Come, let us worship God.

Pastoral Prayer

Loving God, your commands are simple. You ask that we love each other, and do no harm to each other. It might seem at first black and white, but ultimately our world is filled with gray. We want to do one thing, and yet, another causes us to have questions. Help us move away from making things too complex. Fill us with a simple passion for doing what you ask of each of us. We pray in Christ's name. Amen.

Prayer of Confession and Assurance

One: When we make things too complicated to make any sense,
All: Loving God, forgive us.
One: When we ignore others around us, or discredit their needs,
All: Loving God, forgive us.
One: When we do not stop to think how our actions affect others,
both good and bad,
All: Loving God, forgive us.
One: Fill us with your Spirit, and lavish us with your grace. Help us to live simple truths: to love each other, and do no harm to each other. Amen.

Prayer of Dedication of Gifts and Self

Gracious and giving God, we are grateful that you love us – always and without condition. We offer these gifts that, through our common mission and ministry, we may participate in acts that spread to others the love you have shared with us. Amen.

Hymn of the Day
Seek Ye First the Kingdom of God

This contemporary song is a wonderful connection to many Old Testament scriptures that, on their own and without explanation, may feel too graphic. Karen Lafferty reminds us that we must first seek God and then when in a proper relationship with God we should ask for our desires. Lafferty, a former nightclub entertainer, felt the power of God's call to a simpler, more spirit-centered life. This song is a result of that call and possibly the prime focal point in her movement to a more spiritual life. Often thought to be a youth chorus or camp song, "Seek Ye First," through its simple melody and direct text, has found its way into numerous denominational hymnals. Make sure you teach some of your higher voices, both female and male, the descant.

Children's Time: Random Acts of Kindness

(Start by sharing an experience you have had with a random act of kindness. For example, did someone allow you to take the last cookie? Did a neighbor shovel your sidewalk?)

When someone does something so nice for another person, they both feel good. I smile just thinking about that day. It makes me happy to surprise someone/be surprised by someone. You might have heard it called a random act of kindness.

Ask the children if they have received a random act of kindness. *(Affirm all answers.)*

To do something kind and loving for another person, not expecting anything in return, is to do what we are told in the Bible lesson from Romans for today. The Bible tells us to love our neighbors as we love ourselves.

This week I want you to remember that and try to surprise someone with a random act of kindness. Maybe you can help your teacher or let someone behind you in line move ahead or offer to read a book to your friend. See how much fun it is to be a friend.

Let's pray: Dear God, thank you for reminding us to love our neighbors. And thank you for reminding us to love ourselves! Help us surprise our friends and family, and even people we might not know, with kindness. Amen.

The Sermon: That's All. That's Everything
Scripture: Romans 13:8-14

At an ordination service within the United Methodist Church, the bishop was asking the ordinands a series of "historic questions" that John Wesley had first asked more than 200 years before. "Are you in debt so much as to embarrass you in your work?" The entire gathered assembly chuckled – politely, of course, but they chuckled.

Wesley first asked the question long before people began accumulating student loans. To someone who had just finished three years of seminary education on top of four years of undergraduate college the question seemed silly. But as someone pointed out, the key issue was "so much as to embarrass you." There really was or is no shame in having student loans.

Romans 13:8 also speaks of debt and challenges us not to be in debt to anyone. In this day of credit cards and mortgages (and student loans), it might seem a ludicrous commandment. But the real rub comes next: "except for the obligation to love each other" (Common English Bible).

The verse is not really speaking about debt the way we might understand it today, but rather about the entire focus of our daily living. We are called – challenged, commanded – to love one another. We have no "out."

Immediately one might say, "Well, that's silly. You can't command love. How do you make someone love someone else?" In terms of commanding one's emotions, you cannot do that. We cannot tell a person how to feel about someone else; well, you can, but you cannot enforce it.

But Paul isn't really talking about feelings here so much as about actions. *The Theological Dictionary of the New Testament* suggests that the verb *agapao* (love) used here speaks more about actions than feelings. The idea is that the command "love" might be better translated as "do loving things." Or, we might use verse 10 to define it: "love doesn't do anything wrong to a neighbor."

If we think of random acts of kindness we're on the right track. To do something kind and loving for another person, not expecting anything in return, is to fulfill this commandment – and to do that, according to Paul, is to fulfill the law in its entirety.

One has to wonder why this commandment does not appear on courthouse walls. Many folks seem driven to ensure that the Ten Commandments (which arguably are not even commandments, if one reads them in Hebrew rather than King James English) are proudly placed in courthouses, outside government buildings, and enshrined publicly around the country. It's a curious thing, however, that this verse is strangely absent.

"Love each other." That would cover it.

If we love each other, we do not want to hurt each other, want to cheat each other, or want each other's possessions to the point of being consumed by it. We would honor and care for our parents, and for others in need. We would want to make sure that the decisions we make as individuals and as a society would be of the most benefit to the most people.

And maybe that's the problem.

The Ten Commandments have a blunt, matter-of-factness to them. Or so we think. But do they really?

Does that one say "Thou shall not kill" or "You will not kill" or "You will not murder" (notice the difference)? There is a certain vagueness, or ambiguity, that leads us into conversation and occasional argument, based on details.

On the other hand, if we measured all our laws and regulations against the simple standards "Love each other, and do no harm to each other" from Romans 13:8 and 10, then we might find ourselves drawn into a richer conversation.

At the time of his trial in 2013, the media was overwhelmed with news about the acquittal of George Zimmerman in the death of Trayvon Martin, and in all of that the words "Thou shalt not kill" have been used by people on both sides of the argument. One wonders, though, what would happen if we tried to measure a case such as that on the basis of How would this fulfill loving one's neighbor? How would this prevent harm from happen to another?

The point of this sermon is *not* to take a stand on the right or wrong of the decision in that case, or of the actions of any individual involved in it, but simply to invite us to see it in this context: how does it fit with the command to love?

Is it straightforward?

No. But then life is almost never straightforward, no matter how we like to see it.

I cringe a little when I see a bumper sticker that says, "God said it. I believe it. That settles it."

My biggest concern is that it isn't true; indeed, I defy anyone to try and prove they are a biblical literalist – that they "believe" everything in scripture. There's enough contradiction within the Bible itself, let alone contradiction of aspects of reality (do you believe the world is flat, for example? the Bible indicates it is) that we simply cannot do it. We all are forced to choose some pieces of scripture over others. The bumper sticker suggests a black and white that, no matter how much we may wish for it, simply does not exist.

That may be why this verse is so important. It takes us out of any comfort zone we might try to create and reminds us that life is messy and confusing and ambiguous, and full of shades of gray. No book, no sermon, no statement is ever going to change that, no matter how much we might wish it to be so.

Indeed we are invited, called, challenged to measure life in an intriguing way. Rather than look for simple and blunt answers to complex issues, we are told instead to love each other.

Or, to put it another way, the only debt we should owe anyone is to be Christ to them. To seek to be loving to a fault.

That's all. That's everything.

– Donald Schmidt

Hymns

Opening: Joyful, Joyful We Adore You (Thee)
Sermon: Won't You Let Me Be Your Servant?
Closing: Sent Forth by God's Blessing

September 14, 2014

14th Sunday after Pentecost (Proper 19)
RC/Pres/UCC: 24th Sunday in Ordinary Time

Lessons

Semi-continuous (SC)	Complementary (C)	Roman Catholic (RC)
Ex 14:19-31	Gen 50:15-21	Numbers 21:4b-9
Ps 114 or Ex 15:1b-11, 20-21	Ps 103:(1-7) 8-13	Ps 78:1-2, 34-38
Rom 14:1-12	Rom 14:1-12	Phil 2:6-11
Mt 18:21-35	Mt 18:21-35	Jn 3:13-17

Speaker's Introduction for the Lessons
Lesson 1
Exodus 14:19-31 (SC)
> The first 15 chapters of Exodus are God leading the Israelites from slavery. God demands a great deal of obedience from Moses and demonstrates to the Israelites repeatedly just how powerful his authority is over nature.

Genesis 50:15-21 (C)
> This passage depicts the culmination of the long saga of Joseph and his brothers and challenges us to consider how forgiveness looks and feels from both perspectives.

Numbers 21:4b-9 (RC)
> When the people grumbled, the Lord sent snakes. Moses made a bronze snake and whoever looked at it would live.

Lesson 2
Psalm 114 (SC)
> The psalm celebrates God's deliverance of Israel from God, invoking the witness of natural elements involved in that story to witness to God's working.

Psalm 103:(1-7) 8-13 (C)

> The psalmist invokes a familiar blessing and benediction to rejoice in the gracious and forgiving character of God.

Psalm 78:1-2, 34-38 (RC)

> This is an instructive psalm providing the history of God's people of Israel until the time of David.

Lesson 3

Romans 14:1-12 (SC/C)

> Paul continues his exhortation on how to live together in peace. Today's reading focuses on respecting the differences of people and how they live out their faith day to day. We find comfort in the promise that whether we live or die we are the Lord's.

Philippians 2:6-11 (RC)

> Paul writes an early Christian hymn or confession of faith in this letter, which calls believers to live in the identity of who they are in Christ.

Gospel

Matthew 18:21-35 (SC/C)

> In Matthew we find extended discourses with Jesus and his followers. And, throughout his ministry, forgiveness is a major theme. But it becomes evident in today's reading how difficult it is to have a generous spirit.

John 3:13-17 (RC)

> Today we hear again the verse that brings the message of God's love for the world and God's promise of eternal life.

Theme

Forgiving is not always easy, but it is key to faithful living.

Thought for the Day

The difficulty of "forgiving and forgetting" does not let us off the hook; God calls us to seek ways to forgive others.

Sermon Summary

Sometimes, like the disciples, we think we "get" what Jesus was teaching. But sometimes his teachings are amazingly radical, like the call to forgive, no matter what. How can we find ways to do that? Perhaps remembering that making an honest effort is helpful.

Call to Worship

One: In ancient times, the people knew God was with them

All: Even when they were slaves in Egypt, the people knew God had not abandoned them.

One: God showed great power in bringing the people of Israel to new life through the exodus.

All: God's power delivers us from slavery and into freedom.

One: Come, let us worship the God of grace, forgiveness, and new beginnings.

Pastoral Prayer

God of grace and understanding, we seek to be your people. You have called us to new life, to a new way of being your community in the world. Part of that call is to be forgiving, to be loving, to open our hearts beyond our imagining. Help us to do that. Help us to see others as people whom you love, as people who are also called to serve you. Challenge us to find ways to get along one with another. We pray in the name of the forgiving Christ. Amen.

Prayer of Confession and Assurance

We come to this place keenly aware of the need of your grace and forgiveness, O God. We know the many times we have done things that are not in keeping with your will; the times we have hurt others – both intentionally and unintentionally – and damaged the fragile earth you have given as our home. Yet we know, too, the majestic power of your forgiveness and grace. Hear our prayer, remove our guilt, and set us free to be your people in the world. Amen.

Prayer of Dedication of Gifts and Self

We offer to you, loving God, all that we have and all that we are. Take and shape our gifts, and take and shape our lives, that we might be agents of justice and fairness in this hurting world. We pray in Christ's name. Amen.

Hymn of the Day

O God of Every Nation

This week marks the anniversary of the horrific felling of the World Trade Center in 2001. The Gospel lesson from Matthew finds Jesus teaching about one of Christianity's most central topics: forgiveness. The coinciding of this anniversary and this text could hardly be more spiritually charged. An excellent selection for this occasion is William Watkins Reid's "O God of Every Nation," a hymn found in many sources and set to a variety of tunes. "Keep bright in us the vision of days when war shall cease, when hatred and division give way to love and peace." Amen. Let it be so.

Children's Time: Forgive One Another

(Bring a teenage or adult guest to help and place the cap on your head.) This is my favorite cap. It was a birthday present. *(Have your guest remove the cap from your head and play "keep away" with it, tossing it to the other children.)* Would you please return my cap to me? *(Have your guest continue the game of "keep away.")* Now, I'm getting angry! Please return my cap. You know it's my favorite! *(Have your guest catch the cap and hand it to you while saying, "I'm sorry." Respond by saying, "I forgive you.")*

We all make mistakes and do wrong things. And people we know sometimes hurt our feelings and make us feel sad too, like when you played "keep away" with my cap. What can we say when we do something wrong? Yes, we can say, "I'm sorry." And when someone tells us "I'm sorry," what can we say in return? Yes, we can say, "I forgive you." In today's Bible story, Jesus told a story about how God forgives us and wants us to forgive each other.

Let's pray together. Dear God, please help us to be kind and forgiving to others. Amen.

The Sermon: Forgiving and Forgetting
Scripture: Matthew 18:21-35

A tale is told in the Jewish tradition of the Hebrew people being led to freedom from slavery in Egypt and of their desire to rejoice. But God scolded them and told them to be quiet. "Do you not know that some of my children have died? I am glad to give you freedom – but know that it does not come cheaply."

Perhaps the same can be said of forgiveness. It always seems to come at a price. Yet, the cost of not granting it can often be greater.

We are people forgiven by God, and we are, in turn, called to be forgiving of others. We may even be told quick and easy maxims, such as "forgive and forget." Yet perhaps we know that forgiveness can be difficult at best, and forgetting can at times seem impossible. Yet that is the challenge the scriptures place before us.

Jesus and the disciples are all familiar with Jewish law, and so it stands to reason that Peter knew the practice was to forgive someone three times, that is, to forgive them for three wrongs. Such a practice is alluded to in the book of Amos, where God proclaims several times "for three crimes, and for four," suggesting that the people were forgiven for wronging God three times, but they kept at it a fourth time and thus "earned" God's wrath.

Peter, however, has been hanging around with Jesus long enough to know that Jesus tends to stretch God's law, and so – probably in an effort to look like he was "getting" this compassion thing figured out – he suggests that perhaps he ought to forgive someone what, seven times?

"No," Jesus responds, "not seven. Seventy times seven." Even if you read a Bible that renders the number as 77 (an alternative reading), the point is not to wait for the 491st – or 78th – wrong and then stick it to them.

Jesus seems to be suggesting something radically different – that we break the cycle of wrongs and forgiveness.

Now, often when people hear biblical commands about forgiveness, they tend to go on the defensive. We might seek to apply this to criminal matters, and say, "Well, you can't forgive a mass murderer," or "How do you forgive someone who is going to repeat a crime that hurts others?"

It's hard to take biblical law and apply it to our modern, daily living. But maybe the clue lies in Jesus' parable.

Someone owed a massive debt, a debt so inconceivable it's beyond laughter. Jesus basically says, "A slave owed his master 500 trillion dollars." Let's face it, no one owes that kind of debt. But the slave tried everything to convince the master that he would try to repay it, and the master relents and forgives the debt. Nice story; but it's not over.

The slave bumps into someone who owes him a nickel, and he goes ballistic. Even when the second slave begs for mercy – it's only a few cents, after all – the first, forgiven slave won't hear of it, and throws the second slave into prison until he can pay the debt. (As an aside, one has to wonder how a person in jail will earn the money to pay off a debt.)

When the master hears of this, he is understandably furious with the slave for not extending the same mercy the master extended.

"And that," Jesus says, is how God will deal with us if we do not forgive.

Strong stuff.

One time I had taken my car into the shop to get the brakes done. I had misjudged the time and realized I was going to be horribly late for an appointment. I asked the clerk when the car would be done, and when she told me, I went into a rage. "This is ridiculous!" I screamed, all the while knowing it was my miscalculation of the time that was the real problem, not their work. "I'll never bring my car back here again! You people are irresponsible! This is appalling! The manager will hear about this!" Frankly, I don't remember all the things I said, but I know that I railed against the poor clerk, whose fault it most definitely was not.

They hurried up, and got my car done, and I paid – still spitting nails – and I got to my other appointment later.

And I felt lousy.

It was not the clerk's fault. Truth be told, it was not the repair shop's fault. It was mine, for mixing up my schedule. I thought I should probably just let it go, but I could not.

The next day I went back to the repair shop and faced the same clerk. She looked at me with a combination bewildered and terrified look, assuming – rightly so, I'll hasten to add – that I was going to fly off the handle again.

"I'm sorry," I said. "I'm really sorry. Yesterday I got my schedule wrong. It was entirely my fault, and I had no business taking it out on you."

I waited, assuming she would let me know what a jerk I had been.

"I've had days like that, too," she said with a smile. "It means so much to me that you apologized. Thank you."

We chatted a bit, and when I needed work done on my car again, I took it back to the same place. And she and I became friends – not terribly close, but I can tell you that any and all animosity between us went away.

I'll grant that not all situations are that simple. Yet I think Jesus is suggesting that if we look hard enough, we can find ways to move through patterns of wrong and forgiveness. We can break the proverbial cycles.

We can harbor grudges, and not want to be forgiving. Or we can have the courage to say, "Let's stop this. Let's find a way to get along."

In the biblical translation *The Message*, the familiar statement about forgiveness from John 20:23 (where Jesus says, "If you forgive someone's sins they're forgiven, and if you do not, they are not") is rendered, "If you don't forgive sins, what are you going to do with them?"

Maybe that's the key. We can let them fester and nag at us, or we can find a way to move beyond, to not let them stand in the way of a relationship.

Forget? Maybe not. Forgive? Perhaps.

— Donald Schmidt

Hymns
Opening: Come, Let Us Sing to the Lord Our Song
Sermon: Forgive Our Sins as We Forgive
Closing: Amazing Grace

September 21, 2014

15th Sunday after Pentecost (Proper 20)
RC/Pres/UCC: 25th Sunday in Ordinary Time

Lessons

Semi-continuous (SC)	Complementary (C)	Roman Catholic (RC)
Ex 16:2-15	Jonah 3:10—4:11	Isa 55:6-9
Ps 105:1-6, 37-45	Ps 145:1-8	Ps 145:2-3, 8-9, 17-18
Phil 1:21-30	Phil 1:21-30	Phil 1:20-24, 27
Mt 20:1-16	Mt 20:1-16	Mt 20:1-16

Speaker's Introduction for the Lessons
Lesson 1
Exodus 16:2-15 (SC)

In their flight from slavery in Egypt, God provided the ancient Israelites with daily sustenance. Their experience invites us to consider how to respond to God's faithfulness without hoarding, jealousy, or complaining.

Jonah 3:10—4:11 (C)

The book of Jonah is read aloud at Jewish Yom Kippur worship services as an expression of repentance. In learning of the wide inclusiveness of God's mercy, Jonah repents of his own narrow nationalism.

Isaiah 55:6-9 (RC)

The prophet Isaiah speaks to the real problems of people in exile. He brings a word of hope of return in this image of an invitation to a bountiful banquet, symbolic of God's faithful provision.

Lesson 2
Psalm 105:1-6, 37-45 (SC)

Praise of God's saving acts centers on God's leading Israel out of Egypt and through the wilderness, providing manna and water and bringing them into the land of promise.

Psalm 145:1-8 (C); Psalm 145:2-3, 8-9, 17-18 (RC)

A psalm to God as sovereign ruler invites succeeding generations to praise God's works and goodness that reveal God's gracious and just character.

67

Lesson 3
Philippians 1:21-30 (SC/C); Philippians 1:20-24, 27 (RC)

From prison, Paul encourages Christians facing persecution, as he did, in Philippi. Their friendship and trust enables Paul to be honest in sharing the difficulties of his experience and the strength of his witness.

Gospel
Matthew 20:1-16 (SC/C/RC)

Only Matthew records this parable of God's provision being offered according to a radically different standard. This story of workers' compensation invites trust that there will be enough in God's economy to meet everyone's needs.

Theme

None of us deserve God's grace; all of us receive it.

Thought for the Day

God has lavished grace on all of us; why is it, then, that some of us want to keep it all for ourselves?

Sermon Summary

It's hard to watch other people "get ahead." Even though we often know better, we often think someone who has been an active Christian all his or her life is somehow more deserving of God's love and care than someone who is new to the faith. But God has different ideas.

Call to Worship

One: I have some sad news:
All: What is it?
One: You can't earn God's love. But I have some good news:
All: What is that?
One: You can't earn God's love. Come, let us worship the God who loves us all no matter what.

Pastoral Prayer

Some days we can get overwhelmed, O God. We see escalating problems and believe we can do nothing; we might feel defeated by our work, by friendships gone awry, or by financial woes. Yet, in the midst of all this, when we pause and look at ourselves and the world in which we live, we recognize how much you love us. You care for each one of us as if we were your favorite, precious child. We may not understand your love, but we appreciate it, and pray you may lavish it always on us and others. Amen.

Prayer of Confession and Assurance

One: When we see others "getting ahead" of us in life,
All: Loving God, forgive us and make us new.
One: When we think we are more deserving than others,
All: Loving God, forgive us and make us new.
One: When we want to put others down because we don't think they
are as worthy of your love than we are,
All: Loving God, forgive us and make us new *(pause for reflection).*
One: Friends, know that God has love for each of us, no matter who
we are, where we have been, or what we have ever done.
All: Thanks be to God! Amen.

Prayer of Dedication of Gifts and Self

We give ourselves to you, O God, as the least we can do. You have unconditionally poured out your love on us, and called us into new relationship with you. May we – through our giving and our living – model your unconditional love for others. Amen.

Hymn of the Day
My Hope Is Built on Nothing Less

The Gospel reading for this Sunday shatters the illusion that God's grace works in any way akin to our earthly sense of justice. The idea of earning this or deserving that is washed away by Jesus' proclamation, "The last will be first, and the first will be last." It all depends on grace. A wonderful hymn for today is Edward Mote's "My Hope Is Built on Nothing Less." Many know it to the melody by William Bradbury, but consider John

Dykes's MELITA for its chromaticism. A sublime alternative is Frederick Faber's "There's a Wideness in God's Mercy," set to Calvin Hampton's ST. HELENA.

Children's Time: Better Late than Never
(Bring birthday party hats and goodie bags for all the children.)
Let's pretend we are at a birthday party. I brought along a few things to help us do so. Everybody needs a party hat. Does it feel like you're at a party? What sort of things would you do at a party? *(Affirm all answers, but comment in particular on the notion of giving gifts.)*

At a party there are two kinds of gifts. You bring a gift to the birthday boy or girl. And you might go home with a little goodie bag too. Imagine you were at a party where one girl came right when everyone was going home. She apologized for being late, but said she was glad to come by and wish her friend a happy birthday although she didn't have a present to bring. If you were the birthday boy or girl passing out the goodie bags at the door, what would you do? Would you give the latecomer who didn't have a present a goodie bag? I hope so.

Jesus taught us that God is so loving and caring that even if people start to love and follow Jesus late in life, God will show them just as much love as if they had grown up going to church from the first moment of their life. We don't need to be stingy with our goodness and love, because the gift of God's love is freely and fully given to all. Enjoy! *(Distribute goodie bags to the children as they return to their seats.)*

The Sermon: All In
Scripture: Matthew 20:1-16

Had it not been for Andrew Lloyd Webber and Tim Rice's musical *Evita*, I might never have heard of her. Eva Peron died of cancer in 1952, at the age of 33. She had held no elected office, was not formally educated, and while an actress, was never considered to be a very good one. She lived in Argentina – half a world away – long before I was born. Yet for a few brief years, she held all of Argentina – and much of the world – in the palm of her hand.

When Juan Peron became president of Argentina in 1946, his wife, Eva, became first lady. Having grown up an illegitimate child in the back of beyond, she had always dreamed of power and success in the big city. And now she seemed to have arrived.

Tradition dictated that the First Lady of Argentina would be elected chairperson of the Society of Beneficience, a sort of "lady's aid society" that handled virtually all charitable work throughout the country. But she was not. The upper crust women of the society could not tolerate the fact that Evita, albeit First Lady, came from such a dirty background, and was someone of such minor significance; the fact that she had been an actress was the last straw.

Eva Peron tossed off this snub and formed her own foundation, which ultimately became one of the most profound charities of all time and affected the lives of everyone in the nation, elevating Eva to virtual sainthood prior to her early death. Yet throughout her life, the society women despised her.

All this is a simple reminder that too often we do not like to see those "beneath" us get ahead of us. It's something about the human pecking order, perhaps, that leaves us feeling like we deserve certain things, a certain status perhaps, and we begrudge those who would challenge our view of it all.

In the midst of all this, we read this parable about the vineyard workers. The story is unique to the Gospel of Matthew, and is introduced in Matthew's typical style: "The reign of God is like…"

The Jesus Seminar, a group of scholars that gathers to try and sift through the Gospels and determine which passages Jesus might have spoken, and which may have been altered or even made up by the Gospel writers, give this a red rating, meaning that beyond any doubt they believe this to be the authentic words of Jesus. Part of their rationale is striking: because of its blatant confrontation with expectations of who is in and who is out.

Jesus told a simple story about a landowner going to hire transient workers. You may have seen the very kind of workers. They are often people we might view as being at the bottom of the social ladder, standing in the parking lot of the local home improvement store, hoping someone will need a laborer for a few hours or perhaps the whole day. It was common in Jesus' time; things don't change much over the years.

71

Throughout the day the landowner hires groups of workers, some as late as an hour before finishing time. There is nothing too surprising here, until it comes time to pay the workers. The ones hired last get paid first and, to everyone's surprise, they are given a full day's wage. We can only imagine those hired first thinking, "Hey, if they get a full day's pay, imagine how much more I'm going to get!" Thus, their sense of disappointment is totally understandable when they, who have worked for 12 hours, get the same as those who worked for one.

Except…

Except that's how things work in God's world, Jesus tells us. "The reign of God is like this."

There is something intriguing about this parable that so bluntly challenges the way in which our entire society seems to operate. Pull yourself up by the bootstraps; the Lord helps those who help themselves; the early bird catches the worm. Not in this parable.

Maybe that's Jesus' point. Maybe Jesus is trying, in a bold and radical fashion, to tell us that the way in which we operate may well not be in keeping with the way God operates, and we would do well to notice that. Yet we may never know for sure, for it seems Matthew has different ideas.

The Gospel of Matthew was written for a church that had a lot of issues with membership. Those who had been around for generations as devout Jews, who now eagerly embraced Jesus as the Messiah, couldn't quite get their heads around the influx of new converts, Gentiles, outsiders. "Them," in other words.

I cannot help thinking that it is clearly in this context that Matthew makes sure he includes this parable. Just at a time when people in the church were grumbling rather loudly about newcomers coming in and taking over, bam! Here comes a parable that seems to be saying, "It doesn't matter when you got here, God loves you, and God wants to give you what you need."

Maybe you've been here before. I think most of us have, at least occasionally. Someone who seems new, brash, different, an outsider, comes in and gets treated as well as (maybe even better than) someone who's been around for a long, long time. Or, "worse" still are those who have led wild and crazy lives, seemingly without a care in the world for others, and suddenly they come in and steal the thunder away from those hardworking saints who have been pious and proper for a century. It may not seem fair.

But to God is does.

God is in the grace business, if you will. God is in the business of setting right a world that's gone haywire in many directions. We readily can admit – often without much prodding – that we are not worthy of God's love, and yet God gives it to us, anyway. We do not earn it; we cannot earn it. But still our God lavishes it upon us day after day.

And God lavishes it on others, too, even the ones we may not like, or who we think are less deserving. Because in the final analysis, none of us deserves God's love. But all of us receive it.

– Donald Schmidt

Hymns
Opening: Glory, Glory, Hallelujah
Sermon: Wellspring of Wisdom
Closing: Sent Forth by God's Blessing

September 28, 2014

16th Sunday after Pentecost (Proper 21)
RC/Pres/UCC: 26th Sunday in Ordinary Time

Lessons

Semi-continuous (SC)	Complementary (C)	Roman Catholic (RC)
Ex 17:1-7	Ez 18:1-4, 25-32	Ez 18:25-28
Ps 78:1-4, 12-16	Ps 25:1-9	Ps 125:4-9
Phil 2:1-13	Phil 2:1-13	Phil 2:1-11 or 2:1-5
Mt 21:23-32	Mt 21:23-32	Mt 21:23-32

Speaker's Introduction for the Lessons

Lesson 1

Exodus 17:1-7 (SC)

The Israelites are moving forward in their difficult journey to the promised land. We hear Moses call to them – and to us – to recognize God's provision and come back to faithful, obedient living.

Ezekiel 18:1-4, 25-32 (C)

God corrects a longstanding misconception in Israel's thinking that the sins of parents are inherited, along with their punishment, by their children. God declares that each person is responsible for her or his own behavior and its consequences.

Ezekiel 18:25-28 (RC)

The image of wandering is picked up in the prophet Ezekiel's call to the people to trust in God, repent, and come back to living in God's way.

Lesson 2

Psalm 78:1-4, 12-16 (SC)

This psalm of instruction calls attention to the teaching that is about to occur and seeks to keep the people faithful.

Psalm 25:1-9 (C); Psalm 25:4-9 (RC)

The psalmist seeks to follow the path God desires and only through study can we discover those paths.

Lesson 3
Philippians 2:1-13 (SC/C); Philippians 2:1-11 or 1-5 (RC)

Paul incorporates an early Christian hymn into a call for unity among the Philippians. Christian unity can best be grounded in following the example of Christ, who took on a servant ministry.

Gospel
Matthew 21:23-32 (SC/C/RC)

Jesus' parable about the sons who did or did not fulfill the master's request surprises listeners with questions about the agreement of words and actions and the reversal of expectation.

Theme

When we commit to God, we have to mean it.

Thought for the Day

God wants us to place our hearts where our mouths are. When we say something we need to mean it. God's counting on us.

Sermon Summary

When some religious leaders hemmed and hawed and couldn't answer Jesus honestly, Jesus left them to play their own games. He then offered a parable that reminds us we are to be sincere when we are dealing with God. Sometimes we need to say and do what is right, no matter what the costs.

Call to Worship

One: Our God calls us to worship.
All: We are here, God, we are here.
One: We have made a choice to be here today.
All: We are here, God, we are here.
One: It is a joy to gather in sacred community, to sing our praises together.
All: We are here, God, we are here.
One: Come, let us worship God.

Pastoral Prayer

We live in a world of confusion, O God. People say one thing, and mean another, and do yet another. People try to stare each other down, each believing and proclaiming – often violently – that they are right. We hear you calling us to be honest, and to proclaim your simple truths in all we say and do. Equip and empower us to do that, we pray in Christ's name. Amen.

Prayer of Confession and Assurance

Loving God, we thank you for your patience with us. Yet we ask you to challenge us, too. When we become complacent, or when we are not sure what to say or do, give us the courage to speak out and stand up for what is right. When we want to turn away from being loving, just, and fair, bring us back to that. Shape us into your people: loved, forgiven, and called to do and say what is right. Amen.

Prayer of Dedication of Gifts and Self

Take our whole selves, O God, we offer ourselves to you. Take our gifts, the work of our hands and hearts, and use them to further your reign in our world. Amen.

Hymn of the Day
Come, Celebrate the Call of God

This hymn was originally written by Brian Wren for the service of ordination to ministry. However, with one text change (permission already given in all hymnals) this hymn becomes a call to ministry, in its broadest sense, for all. Change "her/him" to "our." Even the words "a chosen one today replies" in stanza 2 take on a new and personal meaning for all who wish to continue in the ministry of the church. There is a real sense of rededication, of making a statement for Christ. Hal Hopson's tune, ALIDA'S TUNE, is folklike in quality. It can be easily taught to a congregation. Lines 2 and 4 are identical and basically a repetition of line 1. Line 3 has some wonderful musical patterns that once pointed out will allow anyone to sing this delightful tune.

Children's Time: Looks Can Fool Us

(Bring two small boxes, one beautifully gift wrapped with a rock inside, and a second, corrugated and crushed with a valuable object inside, such as a ring or coin.)

I have two boxes today and both of them have something inside. Can you hear it? *(Rattle the boxes.)* Look how beautiful this one looks. The other one is not exactly beautiful, is it?

If I were to let you pick which one you'd like, which would you choose? *(Encourage the children to indicate not only which they'd choose, but also why.)*

We usually choose the things that look nice and fancy on the outside. But what about what's inside? That matters too. Let's see what we have. *(Ask a child to open the fancy box and point out the rock. Then ask a volunteer to open the plain box to disclose what's inside.)*

Jesus taught his followers not to be fooled by a person's outward appearance or actions. Someone who looks nice, acts nice, and seems to be better than others is not necessarily a person filled with love. Love of God and love for others comes from how we think or feel. How we dress, or whether we are wealthy or nice looking doesn't tell others about whether we are faithful in following Jesus.

It is easy to be fooled by how things look. These two boxes showed us that. Let's remember to think about ourselves and others as people loved by God, no matter how we appear to others.

The Sermon: Performance, Not Promise
Scripture: Matthew 21:23-32

Rather curiously, it seems the bulk of commentaries on the Gospel of Matthew 21 make a clear distinction between verses 27 and 28. That is, they readily separate this reading into two parts: Jesus' initial conversation with chief priests and elders about authority, and then the parable of the two children.

However, Bruce Malina and Richard Rohrbaugh, in their *Social-Science Commentary on the Synoptic Gospels*, put them together. They seem to recognize, as does the lectionary, that they do indeed belong together. The parable appears to illustrate the truth of the previous conversation. And it is stinging.

The first part, the conversation, brings to mind a *Peanuts* cartoon from many years ago. Violet offers Charlie Brown a candy. She has two different kinds, and asks him to choose. Lucy discreetly tells Charlie Brown to say he can't make up his mind so that Violet will give him one of each. However, when he gives that response Violet says, "Well if you can't make up your mind then I won't give you either," and walks away.
The chief priests and elders – the religious leadership – are stymied by Jesus. On the one hand, he seems to be doing some good things, but they don't quite get it. By whose authority is he doing all this? Or, to put it another way, "Who said you could say the things you say and do the things you do?"

Jesus' response is in the style of traditional rabbinic conversation: answer a good question with another good question, and so he asks them, "From whom did John (the Baptizer) get his authority?" And they're immediately in a pickle, because if they say he got it from God, Jesus will rightly ask them why they didn't pay John any mind, and if they say he didn't, then the crowds will be at their throats. They take the easy way out. "We don't know." And Jesus says, in essence, then I'm not going to play your game.

It's a bit like the time that Jesus told someone that their sins were forgiven (Mt 9:1-9). He was immediately challenged by the religious authorities, and so said, "Which is easier? To tell someone their sins are forgiven, or to tell them they're healed?" In other words, the result is the same. The person is restored to wholeness, and that's the point. What we call it is secondary.

A key in today's passage is the simple reality that Jesus is here doing the will of God. He is proclaiming a message of unconditional love to all people, and restoring many to wholeness of life. The wrappings, the explanations, the arguments really don't matter. They just get in the way. What may well be the rub for the authorities, however, is who is listening to Jesus and responding to him. Tax collectors and prostitutes, Jesus says, listened to John the Baptizer. And it's people like that who are listening to Jesus, who are responding with exuberant joy to his amazing message, and who are finding new life in the gospel he is proclaiming. The "old" religion offered rules, rules, and more rules. Jesus offers life. It's kind of a no-brainer.

Jesus then tells a parable to illustrate his point. A parent asked his two children to go and work in the vineyard. One child said yes, and then didn't follow through. The other said no, but changed his mind and did follow through. It seems rather straightforward. The first child pleases the parent, but then disappoints him. The second infuriates, even shames, the parent, but then ends up doing what is right.

How often do we do that? How often do we, when facing a question or a decision, ponder not what is right but what is expedient? When might we be more concerned with answering a question not with what we think is right but with what we think is safe?

Jesus here is calling us to a higher standard. God is not impressed with those who might say yes quickly because, well, it's what's expected, but then sneak off and do nothing to further the reign of God in our world. Let's face it, are we that impressed with that? If you ask someone for something, what you want is an honest answer that you can count on rather than someone quickly saying the "right" thing when they don't mean it.

The world is full of people who can say yes. What God wants, what God requires, what God demands are people who can live yes. Can we dare to live in God's way, seeking justice for all people, and not settling for anything less than that, even when it's not popular?

A woman attended a play at her child's school. It was a play that had been written a couple generations previously, and the language reflected that. Consequently, on the one hand it was not a huge surprise that a rather racist comment came up as part of the dialog. For this woman, the real problem was that everyone laughed. She tried to dismiss it, but it happened again.

She went home and tried to put it out of her mind. "They're just kids," she said, trying to ignore the nagging at the back of her head. "It was written a long time ago; no one really thinks like that anymore." But as she thought about it, she realized people did think like that, albeit innocently and without thinking, and that's what needed to be challenged. She spoke with the principal of the school, and the principal – instead of trying to discount the woman – not only apologized but worked with her to make this a "teachable moment." People learned how old and quaint ways of saying things do not excuse them if they're wrong. The woman initially wanted to say no to God, but found she could not. She had to say yes.

For all of us, this is all God demands. Not that we fix everything or that we change the world. Simply that we do what God wants. God is far more interested in our performance than our promise. Or, to put it another way, we are called to say yes to God and mean it.

– Donald Schmidt

Hymns
Opening: Come, O Fount of Every Blessing
Sermon: What Does the Lord Require of You?
Closing: I, the Lord of Sea and Sky (Here I Am, Lord)

October 5, 2014

17th Sunday after Pentecost (Proper 22)
RC/Pres/UCC: 27th Sunday in Ordinary Time

Lessons

Semi-continuous (SC)	Complementary (C)	Roman Catholic (RC)
Ex 20:1-4, 7-9, 12-20	Isa 5:1-7	Isa 5:1-7
Ps 19	Ps 80:7-15	Ps 80:9, 12-16, 19-20
Phil 3:4b-14	Phil 3:4b-14	Phil 4:6-9
Mt 21:33-46	Mt 21:33-46	Mt 21:33-43

Speaker's Introduction for the Lessons
Lesson 1
Exodus 20:1-4, 7-9, 12-20 (SC)
> Ancient Israel's understanding of how to relate to God and person to person if a community wished to become and remain free.

Isaiah 5:1-7 (C/RC)
> A metaphor for the stages in human-divine encounters, the life cycle of the vineyard illuminates the attraction, passion, hope, disappointments, and destruction inherent in a dream that is shattered by unfaithfulness.

Lesson 2
Psalm 19 (SC)
> This poem of David combines prayer and praise. Nature speaks to David just as the word of God does.

Psalm 80:7-15 (C); Psalm 80:9, 12-16, 19-20 (RC)
> This psalm is a lament in which the people call on God to rescue them. Its central theme is restore us that we may be saved.

Lesson 3
Philippians 3:4b-14 (SC/C)
> The apostle Paul pondered what really mattered to him.

Philippians 4:6-9 (RC)
> Paul cannot be outdone in adherence to Jewish law or in his alle-

81

giance to Christ. Yet he insists that none of it matters except union with Christ through faith, shared suffering, death, and ultimately resurrection.

Gospel
Matthew 21:33-46 (SC/C); Matthew 21:33-43 (RC)
One of the parables Jesus told, disturbing then and still.

Theme
There are many ways to follow God.

Thought for the Day
It doesn't matter how you serve God, just that you do it.

Sermon Summary
Paul sometimes is misunderstood. He does not condemn Judaism as being insufficient; he just thinks that following Christ is easier. He is proud of his Jewish heritage, but believes it counts for nothing compared to knowing Christ.

Call to Worship
One: The heavens declare the glory of God,
All: And the skies proclaim God's handiwork.
One: Day and night, while silent, proclaim louder than words the goodness of our God.
All: For God's law is perfect; it revives the soul.
One: God's law is sweeter than honey,
All: Sweeter than honeycomb.
One: Come, let us worship God.

Pastoral Prayer
Loving God, we can be intimidated by our understandings of you. We hear of your "law" and, clouded by our own perceptions, we cower in fear. Yet your word is a blessed thing, a gift to keep us on your path, sweeter than honey and more to be prized than the finest gold. Help us to take

your law, made flesh in Jesus, into our being, and live as people in covenant with you. Amen.

Prayer of Confession and Assurance

One: For times when we live in fear of your law,
All: O God, forgive us.
One: For times when we seek to get around your law,
All: O God, forgive us.
One: For times when we impose unfair laws on others,
All: O God, forgive us.
One: For times when we hide behind laws and rules, instead of sharing the love of Christ,
All: O God, forgive us. Amen.

One: Friends, know that the God who created us offers us a word of guidance and a word of hope. Our God seeks not our condemnation, but our deliverance and resurrection.
All: Thanks be to God! Amen.

Prayer of Dedication of Gifts and Self

You have given us so much, gracious God: deliverance from captivity, new life, guidance for our living, and Christ, our life. We offer you now just a small portion of all you have given us, praying with faith that you will take all we have and are, and use it for your work. Amen.

Hymn of the Day
This Is a Day of New Beginnings

The text for this hymn was written by Brian Wren for a New Year's Day service in Oxford, England. Wren acknowledges that New Year's is an arbitrary convention, a mark on the ever-running calendar. In the ongoing Christian story "a day or a month or an hour can become charged with promise, and be a springboard to a changed life." This text is a proclamation of the good news of the gospel and teachings of Christ. The tune, BEGINNINGS, was composed by Carlton Young for this text. Young was editor of *The United Methodist Hymnal* (1989). Sing it with energy and conviction. An alternate fourth stanza written for the Holy Communion is found in *The New Century Hymnal* (1995).

Children's Time: A Priceless Treasure

(Beforehand, use a white crayon to draw a big white cross on a piece of white paper. Color in firmly. Around the cross use a pencil to write or draw: a fancy car, a big house, jeans, a TV, a smartphone, and an iPad or other tablet. Bring a blue washable marker.

Ask, If you could have one treasure in the whole world, what would it be? Let the children offer answers. Point to each item on your paper and let the children talk about what would be their favorite treasure on the paper.)
In today's Bible passage, Paul writes in his letter to the church in Philippi: "I once thought things were valuable, but now I consider them worthless because of what Christ has done. Yes, everything else is worthless when compared with the infinite value of knowing Christ Jesus my Lord. For his sake I have discarded everything else, counting it all as garbage, so that I could gain Christ and become one with him" (Phil 3:7-9a).

Hold up your paper. If Paul lived today, would he think any of these things were treasures? This is what Paul would say his treasure is. *(Use the blue marker to color over and around the cross until it clearly appears.)* For Paul, the new life Jesus has given to all of us through his life, death, and resurrection is the greatest treasure of all!

(Close by making the sign of the cross together.)

The Sermon: Knowing God
Scripture: Philippians 3:4b-14

Our hang-ups can cause us problems sometimes. That's probably an extreme understatement, except for the fact that we do not always recognize our own hang-ups. Those of others, yes, but not always our own.

Today's reading from Philippians is no exception. Our hang-ups about sexuality and the body can always make it difficult to address Paul's near obsession with circumcision. Similarly, the church's tragic history of anti-Semitism, or at least blind indifference to the anti-Semitism of others, can make it difficult to address Paul's statements about Judaism. Yet confront these hang-ups we must, or we can never really deal justly with this powerful text.

Context is, of course, everything. Paul is writing from prison, to a new church in Philippi. He warns them (just prior to today's reading, in verse 2) to watch out for dogs, those who do evil, and "mutilators," which is Paul's not-so-subtle word for those who have been insisting that, in order to become a Christian, one must be circumcised.

Let's clear up one thing here: Paul really does not have an issue with circumcision per se, but rather with the notion that somehow God requires it. "Phooey!" is what he essentially says to that idea. "Utter nonsense."

And let's clear up another: Paul is not anti-Jewish. This is hardly surprising, if you think about it, because he is Jewish. However, 2000 years of Christian history have at times sought to find anti-Semitism in Paul's writings, and it can be found if we forget what he so boldly states here in his letter to the Philippians.

As N.T. Wright translates verses 4b-6 so beautifully: "If anyone has reason to trust in the flesh, I've got more. Circumcised? On the eighth day. Race? Israelite. Tribe? Benjamin. Descent? Hebrew through and through. Torah-observance? A Pharisee. Zealous? I persecuted the church! Official status under the law? Blameless." It's not that Paul wants to reject his Jewishness. Far from it. He simply doesn't think it counts for much compared to what Jesus Christ (another Jew, remember) offers him.

In a sense, we might see Paul here really wanting to contrast Jesus' version of Judaism with a more traditional one. And the beauty of Christ's, Paul hastens to point out, is that it is available to a wider community.

Flesh – that is, one's physical descent from Judaism – isn't worth much in Jesus' world. Circumcision, while there's nothing wrong with it, doesn't count for much either. Jesus has demonstrated, over and again, that pedigree counts for very little at all compared to the content of one's heart.

This is good news. Not because it rejects Judaism. Far from it. Rather, because it opens it up. As far as Paul is concerned, to be a follower of Jesus is to become a Jew. It's that simple, and that wonderful. Paul does not even "reject" a stricter, law-based Judaism for those who might want that sort of thing. He just doesn't really understand why anyone would want it.

Paul's primary concern seems far more with people coming to know God by coming to know Christ, and to be known by Christ. Paul has a sense of urgency in his writing and in his theology, and it comes through here. "Sure, you can memorize the law, get circumcised, study the Torah in the original languages (after all, Paul adds, I did). Or, you can get to know Jesus Christ." For Paul, it's a proverbial no-brainer. Why would you go to all that trouble and difficulty – not to mention physical pain for men – when you have the option of getting to know Jesus Christ, of learning his teachings, of sharing in the promise of resurrection and eternity?

Rudyard Kipling, who had a reputation as quite a British traditionalist, shared a wonderful story in his memoir *Something of Myself*:

> General Booth of the Salvation Army came on board. I saw him walking backward in the dusk over the uneven wharf, his cloak blown upwards, tulip-fashion, over his grey head, while he beat a tambourine in the face of the singing, weeping, praying crowd who had come to see him off ... I talked much with General Booth during that voyage. Like the young ass I was, I expressed my distaste at his appearance on Invercargill wharf. "Young feller," he replied, bending great brows at me, "if I thought I could win one more soul to the Lord by walking on my head and playing the tambourine with my toes, I'd – I'd learn how."

That seems rather to be Paul's sentiment. I often get the impression that Paul, left to his own devices, could have been a stick-in-the-mud. I think that, for much of his life, he rather liked the various ins and outs of the traditional Judaism with which he had grown up. It offered life, and a powerful relationship with God – our creator, to be sure, and also the one who called us to a higher living. Paul seems very aware of the fact that God expects of God's people (the Jews) a higher standard of living, which at the very least cares passionately for the widows, orphans, and other outcasts of society. The law makes it plain and clear to follow and – I'm guessing Paul would admit this, too – there are those for whom it works really well.

But there are also those for whom it does not work, and Paul wants to address them. He's not saying "you must not follow the Torah" but rather "you need not." Paul even goes so far at times (this is, after all, a theme that recurs for him a lot) to suggest that he doesn't really understand why anyone would want to follow the Torah, and be circumcised, and seek to follow kosher food laws, and so forth. To be frank, Paul considers it all to be a load of nonsense. But to each his own.

We must not turn this into anti-Semitism, but instead celebrate the truth that Paul offers. We can know God by knowing Jesus Christ, and we can serve God by seeking to follow Jesus Christ.

Paul is eager to say, "All that I had and all that I was is nothing, compared to all that I am through knowing Christ, which is everything." Paul did not abandon the law because it didn't work, but simply because following Christ superseded it.

May we, like Paul, find the same liberation that comes from knowing God in Christ.

– Donald Schmidt

Hymns
Opening: I Feel the Winds of God
Sermon: Your Hand, O God, Has Guided
Closing: I Heard My Mother Say (Give Me Jesus)

October 12, 2014

18th Sunday after Pentecost (Proper 23)
RC/Pres/UCC: 28th Sunday in Ordinary Time

Lessons

Semi-continuous (SC)	Complementary (C)	Roman Catholic (RC)
Ex 32:1-14	Isa 25:1-9	Isa 25:6-10
Ps 106:1-6, 19-23	Ps 23	Ps 23
Phil 4:1-9	Phil 4:1-9	Phil 4:12-14, 19-20
Mt 22:1-14	Mt 22:1-14	Mt 22:1-14 or 22:1-10

Speaker's Introduction for the Lessons

Lesson 1

Exodus 32:1-14 (SC)

Oh, how inclined we are – and ingenious too – at creating false gods when we are bored or distracted.

Isaiah 25:1-9 (C); Isaiah 25:6-10 (RC)

Verses 1-5 are a psalm of praise to God who destroys enemies and provides shelter and refuge for the threatened. Verses 6-9 describe the celebration in Jerusalem, a place from which God forever banishes grief and even death.

Lesson 2

Psalm 106:1-6, 19-23 (SC)

A confession of God's love unfolds into a confession of sin, highlighted in this portion by Israel's sin at Mount Horeb recounted in the Exodus passage for today.

Psalm 23 (C/RC)

This is a prime example of a psalm of serene trust in God, using the image of God as shepherd, who accompanies and provides for us on our journey.

Lesson 3
Philippians 4:1-9 (SC/C); Philippians 4:12-14, 19-20 (RC)
What in the world shall we do to settle a spat between two key congregational leaders that is now an open, negative conflict that is tearing the church apart?

Gospel
Matthew 22:1-14 (SC/C/RC); or Matthew 22:1-10 (RC)
God keeps inviting us to be honored guests at a banquet to celebrate fidelity and devotion within God's family, but we keep ignoring the personalized invitation. How rude! And how careless too! Suddenly, our seats at God's party have been taken by those we regarded as less important in God's family and in God's empire.

Theme
The peace of God can guard the hearts and minds of believers even when eschatological urgency and anxiety threaten to stress and divide the fellowship.

Thought for the Day
The peace of God, which surpasses all understanding, will guard your hearts and your minds in Christ Jesus (Phil 4:7).

Sermon Summary
"The Lord is near," Paul proclaims. So surely it's time to be on best behavior. Yet, there is difference and tension between two faithful leaders in the Philippian church. Euodia and Syntyche are women who struggled beside Paul in the work of the gospel. No stronger admonition from Paul about being ready for the Lord than "to be of the same mind in the Lord." Such accord is characterized by rejoicing, gentleness, hope, anticipation, and praying in all things with thanksgiving.

Call to Worship
One: The Lord is near!
All: Let us stand firm in the Lord.
One: The Lord is near!

All: Let us replace fear and worry with prayer and peace.
One: The Lord is near!
All: Let us rejoice with gentleness and gratitude.
One: The Lord is near!
All: Let us unite that we might love God with all our being and neighbors as ourselves.
One: The Lord is near!
All: And the God of peace will guard our hearts and minds in Christ Jesus.

Pastoral Prayer

O God who is always near us, grant us freedom from fretful worry and tension that we might draw near to you. In times that are stressed and that compress, build us up with confidence and joyful anticipation of your future. We deeply need your peace to guard our hearts and minds lest we become divided. With so many forces pulling at us, draw us into the same mind that was in Jesus. Help us to live in his self-emptying love that we might stand firm in the face of withering change and that by your persistent grace ever be formed into his likeness. With Christ as our helper we pray. Amen.

Prayer of Confession and Assurance

O God of peace, whose day draws near, we confess to you that we are usually not paying attention. We glibly assume that time stretches out eternally in our own self-image. We are either distracted by the things of the world or anxious about what we don't have. But when we do take account of ourselves, we often worry and become fearful. Because we trust too much in ourselves, the future is either too rosy or too dreadful. We want assurance but search for it in all the wrong places. In our fears and anxieties we sometimes turn on one another and become divided. We deeply need a peace that passes all understanding. Forgive us, we pray, and free us for joyful obedience. Amen.

Prayer of Dedication of Gifts and Self

Praise you, O God of joyful giving. Praise you for all that you have made and given, that we might have life and have it more abundantly. You did not guard your sovereignty but risked it in covenant with the world. You did not treasure your own self-sufficiency but emptied yourself in your Son that we might have eternal joy and peace. Help us now to be more like you and open ourselves to joyful gratitude and extravagant generosity. And magnify our gifts that they might bring our neighbors and us closer to you. Amen.

Hymn of the Day
Rejoice, Ye (You) Pure in Heart

Edward Plumptre wrote this text as a processional for a choral festival held at Peterborough Cathedral, England, in 1865. He was a well-known Anglican priest and professor of theology at Oxford University. The text was inspired by Psalm 33:1 and Philippians 4:4. It was on us to rejoice in God at all times. Originally ten stanzas in length, the text has been reduced to four or five in most contemporary hymnals. The tune, MARION, was composed by Henry Messiter in honor of his mother. It was conceived as a processional and is a joyful match to Plumptre's text. Use brass, or trumpet, and organ to make the singing more festive.

Children's Time: Don't Worry, God Cares

What are your favorite things to eat? Let's pretend to be some of these foods:

Popcorn – jump up and down

Pretzel – sit on the floor and cross legs

Pancake – lie on back

Ice cream cone – stand up slowly droop down as if melting

In Philippians 4:6-7a, Paul writes in his letter to the church in Philippi: Don't worry about anything; instead, pray about everything. Tell God what you need, and thank him for all he has done.

God shows care for us by giving us food. What are some other ways God cares for us? Paul tells us not to worry because God will take care of us. What does Paul tell us to do instead? To pray. Let's gather in a tight circle and pretend that we are a bunch of grapes. Now follow my actions as we pray together:

Thank you, God *(take one step back, raise hands high, and look up)*,

For delicious food *(rub tummy)*,

91

For homes to shelter us *(bring fingertips together over head)*,
For cozy clothes to wear *(snuggle self)*,
And all sorts of wonderful animals *(pat a dog)*.
Thank you, God *(raise hands high and look up)*,
For bright sunshine *(make a circle with arms)*,
Rain *(wiggle fingers, slowly lowering hands)*,
And for all the people who love us *(all join hands)*.
Amen *(raise joined hands high)*!

The Sermon: The Lord Is Near
Scripture: Philippians 4:1-9

Every church has them: nagging tensions, disagreements, and conflicted situations. For leaders, these tensions can be distracting, worrisome, and downright draining. They often prevent the congregation from doing its best in ministry and mission and moving forward with its vision.

The church at Philippi was no exception. Even for this his most beloved church, Paul knew that it was beset by conflict in a variety of ways. First, the church was hounded by outside pressures from the circumcision faction – those Christians who still believed male converts should be circumcised in keeping with true Mosaic covenant (Phil 1:15-17; 3:2-3). But then there was the familiar tension about how and when to be ready for the Lord's return. After all, Paul declares in this passage, "The Lord is near."

Paul had to deal with this tension in congregations from the beginning. There were those who believed that if the Lord was coming soon, there was no need to do much except focus on one's own spiritual readiness. Then there were those who believed that until Christ returned the believers were to evangelize as much as possible, disciple the converts, and serve the least.

Although the tension between Euodia and Syntyche is not specifically named, perhaps it is in relation to what the church should be doing if indeed "the Lord is near." It appears that Euodia and Syntyche were mature disciples who had struggled alongside Paul from the beginning. So they were seasoned believers and faithful members. But Paul is so concerned about the tension between the two leading women that he asks the loyal companions to "help these women."

Why was Paul so pointedly concerned about salving the tension between Euodia and Syntyche? Because for Paul the most crucial witness of the transforming power of the love and grace of Jesus Christ was God's power to reconcile people in their differences and to bring them together in a working harmony. Paul even believed God's power to reconcile could bring together Jew and Gentile, slave and free. This was the radical and revolutionary nature of the gospel of Jesus Christ for Paul. He got it! The point comes up over and over in the Philippian letter. Four times Paul appeals to the members to be of the same mind. "Make my joy complete," he says in the second chapter. "Be of the same mind, having the same love, being in full accord and of one mind" (2:2). In chapter 3: "Let those of us then who are mature be of the same mind; and if you think differently about anything, this too God will reveal to you" (3:15). And in our text for today, "I urge Euodia and I urge Syntyche to be of the same mind in the Lord" (4:2).

Is this not one of the core qualities of the church – the body of Christ – to be able practice tough love with one another that we can live, work, and minister together with the same mind in Christ? It is not that Paul expects the believers to always have the same views and opinions on important discernments. There is room for creative tension, debate, and mediation. But Paul believes the essence of the church is to be able to work at love patiently and persistently until the tension results in a new order of love. Loving and laboring together takes time and intention. Giving up on one another is not an option. Struggle together, listen together, and walk in one another's shoes.

Paul says it clearly, "Therefore, my beloved ... work out your own salvation with fear and trembling; for it is God who is at work in you, enabling you both to will and to work for his good pleasure" (2:12-13). So Paul appeals to the companions of the congregation, "Help these women." Would that we helped one another when we have differences and conflicts. Too often we pretend it's not there, sweep it under the rug, and let it fester. Too much church conflict lies under the surface, hampering the congregation from being about its ministry. I think Paul wanted the leaders of the church to go to Euodia and Syntyche, sit with them, pray with them, help them listen to one another, and for however long it takes, come to a better place of rejoicing in the Lord.

With Euodia and Syntyche on his mind, Paul breaks into the meat of his sermon: "Rejoice in the Lord always; again I will say, Rejoice. Let your gentleness be known to everyone. The Lord is near. Do not worry about anything, but in everything by prayer and supplication with thanksgiving let your requests be made known to God. And the peace of God, which surpasses all understanding, will guard your hearts and your minds in Christ Jesus" (4:4-7).

O how we need in the church today our hearts and minds guarded by God's working grace. All too often our congregations are weakened by petty conflict and dysfunctional behavior. Instead of earnestly struggling to feed hungry children in our neighborhood, we argue over the color of the new carpet in the sanctuary. We break into open conflict over why our older adult Sunday school class needs to move to a smaller room to give way to a growing young adult class. And we dare not talk about Republicans and Democrats, reducing the national deficit, or health-care reform, because we fear we could not contain the rancor.

Yet Jesus lived, died, and was raised from death for God to create the new humanity through redeeming grace. For Paul this new humanity should be capable of meeting and resolving the most wrenching and intractable challenges that face us. But only if we have the mind of Christ, "who, though he was in the form of God, did not regard equality with God as something to be exploited, but emptied himself, taking the form of a slave, being born in human likeness. And being found in human form, he humbled himself and became obedient to the point of death – even death on a cross" (2:6-8).

If we can even closely approximate Christ's self-emptying love and let our pettiness, pride, and narrow ambitions be crucified, then God can and will "exalt" us. "And the peace of God, which surpasses all understanding, will guard your hearts and your minds in Christ Jesus" (4:7).

– John Collett

Hymns
Opening: Standing on the Promises
Sermon: Love Divine, All Loves Excelling
Closing: Nearer, My God to Thee

October 19, 2014

19th Sunday after Pentecost (Proper 24)
RC/Pres/UCC: 29th Sunday in Ordinary Time

Lessons

Semi-continuous (SC)	Complementary (C)	Roman Catholic (RC)
Ex 33:12-23	Isa 45:1-7	Isa 45:1, 4-6
Ps 99	Ps 96:1-9, (10-13)	Ps 96:1, 3-5, 7-10
1 Thess 1:1-10	1 Thess 1:1-10	1 Thess 1:1-5
Mt 22:15-22	Mt 22:15-22	Mt 22:15-21

Speaker's Introduction for the Lessons
Lesson 1
Exodus 33:12-23 (SC)

> Moses wanted to see all of God he could in order to confirm that he wasn't imagining things. It's shocking and mind bending, but God said to Moses, "The only part of me you can see is my back side!"

Isaiah 45:1-7 (C); Isaiah 45:1, 4-6 (RC)

> The Persian king Cyrus claims he does not know God, yet in spite of that fact, he is called to liberate the Israelites from their Babylonian captivity. The God of Israel is the power behind the power with which Cyrus acts.

Lesson 2
Psalm 99 (SC)

> The psalmist celebrates Yahweh as king/sovereign over all, whose prophets and priests called upon God.

Psalm 96:1-9, (10-13) (C); Psalm 96:1, 3-5, 7-10 (RC)

> An enthronement psalm, perhaps used in coronation ceremonies, that witnesses to God as creator and judge of all families and nations.

Lesson 3
1 Thessalonians 1:1-10 (SC/C); 1 Thessalonians 1:1-5b (RC)

> Paul's thoughts on the importance of being "imitate-able" as Christians.

Gospel
Matthew 22:15-22 (SC/C); Matthew 22:15-21 (RC)
There are still those today who want the civic arena and the spiritual arena to be blended, unified, one. Listen to Jesus, of all people, saying, no to that notion.

Theme
Living the kingdom of God for Jesus meant understanding loyalties – earthly and heavenly – temporal and spiritual – and knowing how to prioritize and make the hard choices of ultimate loyalty to God.

Thought for the Day
Because we often live with confused and compromised loyalties, we lead duplicitous lives, not really knowing who and whose we are.

Sermon Summary
Jesus refused to be trapped in the politics of false choice. His was and is a kingdom that is implicit and imbedded in all human and worldly affairs but is not measured by the standards of the passing kingdoms. Jesus leaves us with a core question: What belongs to God? All things belong to God! How then do we live in that reality?

Call to Worship
One: Come, people of God, into the realm of God's reign unfolding as we speak.
All: We come with awe and wonderment.
One: Come, people of God, into the clash of empires, hopeful and fearful at the same time.
All: We come wanting to believe in an empire of tough love and an economy of costly grace.
One: Come, people of God into choices that only the eyes of faith can discern.
All: We come with hope that God will grant us spiritual wisdom and the courage of faith.

Pastoral Prayer

O Sovereign of all that is or ever will be, we come before you this day
daring to entertain what it means when your kingdom clashes with ours.
We need all the mercy, grace, and spiritual wisdom you can give us to have
a chance in this ordeal. You have given us the human standard in Jesus
Christ. We take amazing hope in the reality that he faced these choices,
lived his life fully, celebrated his humanity with others, and loved you and
them to the end. Give us hope and assurance that we too can live in this
tension, remain faithful, and aspire to the example of our Lord. Amen.

Prayer of Confession and Assurance

O God, who is creator of all and who reigns in love over all, we seek to be
transparent in this hour of worship. We confess to you that in the clash of
kingdoms – yours and ours – we too often choose the immediate security, the least threat, and the most pleasurable. We should be ashamed!
We know in a deep sense we are trapped. We are trapped in the world of
our own making. Ours is a world that is amazing in many ways but self-
defeating in others. In this tension, we usually shy away, cower, and run.
We give to the emperor of commerce what he has already claimed of us
without batting an eye. We rarely remind ourselves that all belongs to you.
Only your steadfast love, long-suffering mercy, and forgiveness can save
us. We beg of you to intervene in our entrapment. Amen.

Prayer of Dedication of Gifts and Self

We bring these gifts this day, O God, confessing that we do not give our
all. We hold back in our giving, deceiving ourselves into thinking that
most of what we have deservedly belongs to us. We beg your forgiveness
and patience. Open us to the freedom of living as though all things belong
to you. We ask you to help us let this act of giving be a fresh start in making available to you all that we are and all that we have. By your persistent grace may we become as self-emptying as did our Lord Jesus Christ.
Amen.

Hymn of the Day
O God Beyond All Praising

Michael Perry wrote a wonderful text giving many examples of why we give praise to God. Yet he also states that God is beyond all of this – God is beyond praise. It is a remarkable statement that gives honor and praise to God without the use of kingdom or martial language. Perry wrote this text for the tune THAXTED by Gustav Holst. An arrangement of Holst's "Jupiter" theme from his suite *The Planets*, it is a powerful and energetic tune that ideally suits the text. This hymn makes a wonderful response to the reading from Matthew. The use of orchestral instrumentation will greatly enhance the presentation of this hymn.

Children's Time: What Belongs to God?

(Bring a one-dollar bill, a quarter, and a penny. Begin by asking the children to identify each piece of money. Whose faces are on this money? Abraham Lincoln and George Washington were both presidents. We honor our leaders by placing pictures of them on our money. In Jesus' time, the Roman emperors ruled the land. Romans placed the pictures of the emperors on their coins.)

In today's story some officials tried to trick Jesus. They showed a Roman coin to Jesus and asked him a question about it. Jesus answered them, "Give to the emperor what belongs to the emperor and give to God what belongs to God."

What belongs to God? God created the world, so everything belongs to God. What are some of your favorite things that God created? What about this money? *(Hold up your money.)* Does money belong to God? During our worship service, when do we give money back to God? In our offering we collect money. We use the money to serve God in many ways. Some of these ways include paying our worship leaders, paying for our church building, and giving money to help people in need.

Let's close with an echo prayer:
Thank you, God, for
Sun and seas,
Birds and trees,
Toes and knees,
Pizza with cheese.
Thank you, God,
for everything!
Amen!

The Sermon: No Easy Answers
Scripture: Matthew 22:15-22

Jesus didn't give easy answers. He often turned a question into another question. Except harder. The Pharisees kept pressing questions to try to entrap Jesus in some violation of the pure religious law, thus discrediting him with the religious establishment, or trick him into an act of sedition – resisting the absolute power of the emperor and the Roman empire. Pharisees represented one religious faction of Jewish life in the first century, along with Sadducees, Essenes, and Zealots, just to name the most notable ones. Each sect had its answer to living in an occupied state with its military presence and oppressive taxes. Sadducees were the aristocratic class with strong attachment to temple bureaucracy and always advocating an easy peace with Rome. The Essenes decided to leaved it all behind and live in the desert, an ascetical and deeply spiritual life. And the Zealots were borderline revolutionaries, eager at any time to marshal an uprising against Roman presence. The prime motivation for the Pharisees seems to have been strict obedience to Mosaic law, with the hope that personal and social righteousness would either win God's mercy or tip history into the messianic age. Saul of Tarsus was an acknowledged Pharisee and did his part, you remember, to turn righteous fury against the Jesus people. From the view of the Pharisees, Jesus was a threat to strict holiness of life that the sect worked so hard to advance. Jesus was a threat because he preached the nearness of the kingdom of heaven while playing loose with much of the letter of the law.

The Pharisees hated Jesus because he didn't follow strict laws on Sabbath practice, he associated with sinners, he didn't fast often enough, he cast out demons, enacted signs of the messianic age, and practiced indiscriminate kindness to all people. It drove the Pharisees crazy that Jesus seemed to possess a mysterious power to make people's lives right and whole. And they didn't!

In the closing days of Jesus' ministry in Jerusalem the Pharisees turned up the heat. This time they enlisted a strange coalition with the Herodians. The Herodians represented the legacy of Herod the Great, whose bumbling sons tried to carry on a Roman proxy government with a Jewish veneer. But Jesus saw through it all.

The Pharisees played the patriotic card by trying to trap Jesus into a violation of either religious code or imperial loyalty. They even tried to psych out Jesus by complimenting his impartiality; exactly to whom was he impartial – God, people, or the emperor? They then posed an insidious dilemma, the dilemma between church and state. Surely they would catch him now. But Jesus saw through it all.

They thought they could catch him in mixing religious values with state values. "Is it lawful to pay taxes to the emperor, or not?" Lawful in this case refers to Jewish religious code. In fact almost all Jews believed in their heart of hearts that paying taxes to Rome was borderline blasphemous, but they swallowed strict code and paid them anyway. Not paying taxes to the emperor was obviously an act of sedition. So what is it, Jesus? They underestimated Jesus. They knew that Roman taxes were paid with Roman currency. They knew that offerings to God, if paid at the temple, could be paid only with kosher coins or with animal sacrifices prescribed by religious law. Purity of the offering was most important when offered to God.

Jesus in part simply pointed out the inevitable. In an imposed economy using an imposed currency, then pay the taxes to the imposing government using the imposed currency. But be sure you give to God out of your total proceeds.

So Jesus turned a question into another question. Holding a Roman denarius, Jesus asked, "Whose head is this, and whose title?" Obviously, the emperor's image. Making his point by implication, Jesus then went for the main thing: "Give to God the things that are God's." They knew Jesus had then entrapped them. They knew in their heart of hearts that all things belonged to God – even Roman taxes, albeit provisionally. Amazed, this band of Pharisees left him and went away.

Jesus presents us, however, with the dilemma we would rather not face. Does loyalty to God trump all other loyalties, even loyalty to nation and government? Could there be times when our faith demands that we not pay taxes toward government actions that we deem immoral? Could we ever really have to decide that there is a demarcation of values and ultimate loyalties between church and state? What happens when faith and patriotism become allies? And do we sometimes use one in the self-interest of the other? Hard questions, no easy answers. Sadly, we sidestep these important questions and would rather argue about the proper positioning of the American flag in the chancel!

Could it be that what Jesus taught at the core can help us here? He was clear that the main thing is to love God with all our heart, soul, mind, and strength and love our neighbors as ourselves (Mt 22:37-39). Loving God and neighbor go deeper than church-state, economy, and currency. More fundamental. For sure, one of the ways we love God and neighbor is through giving the money of our labors. But love all goes deeper than that. Paul declared in his immortal chapter on love – 1 Corinthians 13:3 – "If I give away all my possessions, and if I hand over my body so that I may boast, but do not have love, I gain nothing."

Jesus gets us all out of the trap by going through the hard choices, all the resistance and opposition, all the vile punishment inflicted upon him and remaining uncompromisingly committed to loving God and neighbor. Even more, he died for our sins. He died to free us from our own entrapment, our unsolvable dilemmas, our clash of kingdoms.

A lifestyle of loving God and neighbor goes deeper than the lesser loyalties that confuse and divide us. God has given us the way, the truth, and the life in Jesus. We can hope and trust in the reality that he faced these choices, lived his life fully, celebrated his humanity with others, and loved God and us to the end. We pray to God to give us assurance that we too can live in this tension, remain faithful, and aspire to the example of our Lord. Amen.

–John Collett

Hymns
Opening: Rejoice, the Lord Is King
Sermon: O Young and Fearless Prophet
Closing: Maker, in Whom We Live

October 26, 2014

20th Sunday after Pentecost (Proper 25)
RC/Pres/UCC: 30th Sunday in Ordinary Time

Lessons

Semi-continuous (SC)	Complementary (C)	Roman Catholic (RC)
Deut 34:1-12	Lev 19:1-2, 15-18	Ex 22:20-26
Ps 90:1-6, 13-17	Ps 1	Ps 18:2-4, 47, 51
1 Thess 2:1-8	1 Thess 2:1-8	1 Thess 1:5-10
Mt 22:34-46	Mt 22:34-46	Mt 22:34-40

Speaker's Introduction for the Lessons

Lesson 1

Deuteronomy 34:1-12 (SC)

Moses got to see a part of God, although not the part of God he wanted to see; he saw God's backside! When Moses died, however, he was remembered ironically as someone whom God knew face to face.

Leviticus 19:1-2, 15-18

The list of behaviors unacceptable to God's people provides guidelines on being holy. The question of not being partial to the poor seems to contradict laws in other parts of scripture.

Exodus 22:20-26 (RC)

God's people are charged to remember their times as aliens and to use that memory to serve those in need. The warnings for going against this direction are dire: death by the sword and more widows and orphans.

Lesson 2

Psalm 90:1-6, 13-17 (SC)

The only psalm attributed to Moses, this psalm confesses the timeless character of God's presence and refuge in our midst coupled with a concluding petition for God's turning and favor.

Psalm 1 (C)

The psalmist confesses an orderly world of cause and effect, where the righteous flourish and the wicked dissipate like chaff in the wind.

Psalm 18:2-4, 47, 51 (RC)

The psalm is a royal hymn of gratitude and praise.

Lesson 3

1 Thessalonians 2:1-8 (SC/C)

Are we doing church the way we do church to please others? Paul once justified his ministry by insisting that he and his missionary team speak not to please any mortals whatsoever, but to please God alone.

1 Thessalonians 1:5-10 (RC)

Paul is grateful for the courage with which the Thessalonians received God's word in the face of persecution. They live the word as positive and powerful examples of faithfulness to Christ.

Gospel

Matthew 22:34-46 (SC/C); Matthew 22:34-40 (RC)

Jesus is tested by the Pharisees who ask his opinion regarding the greatest commandment. In the end, Jesus turns the tables on the questioners and they are the ones put to the test.

Theme

Jesus embodied the full nature of the triune God. God who wills God's being to be in complete relationship with God's creation. What an amazing God – to join with God's creation in God's Son!

Thought for the Day

The triune God – Father, Son, and Holy Spirit – wills that all things have their being and fullness in God and that all things will ultimately be gathered to God (Eph 1:10).

Sermon Summary

The Pharisees persist in trying to trap Jesus in a religious legalism. But Jesus turns the trap on them by pressing their understanding of the Messiah. Whose son is he? The Pharisees could answer only within their predetermined paradigm: He is the son of David. Jesus, however, left them with a proposition they could not fathom: that Messiah is the Son of God and fully embodied before them.

Call to Worship

One: We come before the mystery that loving God and loving neighbor is somehow of one nature.

All: We come awed by the union of God and God's creation.

One: We come drawn by the mystery of being able to love God, neighbor, and self as one.

All: We come confessing that we are worlds apart from this divine-human union.

One: We come in the hope that Jesus – both human and divine – embodied this mystery.

All: May this time of worship infuse us with God's transforming power to unite all creation, even ourselves, into the union of God's love.

Pastoral Prayer

Immortal, invincible, God only wise, we praise you that you are the mystery of our being, both as transcendent beyond any of our imaging and at the same time with us, even in us. We are drawn to you because we cannot fully comprehend you. Yet we believe you became one of us in Jesus Christ. You have thus bonded yourself with us, yet you are not beholden to us. You have given yourself completely to the promise that as you have become like us we can become like you. Descend upon us afresh with the power of your Holy Spirit that we might see you in our neighbors, all our neighbors both familiar and strange. Empower all of us to grow together as you would have us. Amen.

Prayer of Confession and Assurance

O God, who knows our minds and hearts, we acknowledge that while we can recite the two great commandments with ease, we can barely live them. We like the convenience of thinking that an act of kindness to a stranger is an act of kindness to you. We shy away from the thought that as disciples of Jesus we are to embody Christ's presence to others. Forgive us for not grasping the awesomeness of your becoming flesh and living among us. May we take hope in your steadfast love and promise that as we love one another we are loving you and as we love you we are loving one another. Keep converting us that we might grow into the-Word-made-flesh.

Blessed be God, who hears and forgives. Amen.

Prayer of Dedication of Gifts and Self

Touch these gifts and our giving with your love, O God. Then, may the same spirit that was in Christ Jesus be served through them in our world, today, now. Amen.

Hymn of the Day

Jesus a New Commandment Has Given

This remarkable hymn (*Un mandamiento nuevo*) comes from Puerto Rico. Written by William Loperena for a Maundy Thursday service, it has received much use in that country. Like most hymns from Latin America, it is rhythmic yet easy to sing. It is probably best taught orally rather than looking at the music, as the rhythmic notation may cause some confusion at first. Teach your congregation the refrain first and let the choir or soloists sing the stanzas. Once the congregation learns this delightful piece they will want to sing the whole piece. The addition of percussion, especially hand drums and shakers, will give it an authentic and spirited presentation.

Children's Time: The Most Important Commandment
(Bring pipe cleaners, paper, and a brown marker.)
Ask the children to name the most important rule in their homes. At school? At church?

One day an expert in religious law asked Jesus, "Teacher, which is the most important rule?" Jesus answered them, "You must love the Lord your God with all your heart, all your soul, and all your mind." Then Jesus added, "A second is equally important: Love your neighbor as yourself."

Hold up a pipe cleaner. What number is this? It's a number one. I'm going to turn this number one into a symbol that shows that Jesus is first in my life. (Bend the wire in half to make a fish body and twist the two pieces together about 1-1/2" from the ends to make the tail. Distribute the pipe cleaners and have the children create their own fish.)

The fish was a secret greeting for early Christians. They would trace one arc in the sand like this (draw one arc). If the person they met was a Christian, he or she would draw a second arc to complete the fish shape (draw the second arc). Where can you see this symbol today? Lots of Christians have the fish on their car. Place your fish shape in a special place at home to show others that loving God and Jesus is the most important thing in your life.

Let's pray: Help us, loving God, to put you first in our lives. Fill us up with your love so that we can share your love with others. Amen.

The Sermon: The Body of Christ
Scripture: Matthew 22:34-46

If you and I could have experienced Jesus in person, would we have perceived and discerned that he was the Son of God, God in flesh? Would our spiritual sensibilities have been keen enough? Would our wisdom have been deep enough? Would our minds and hearts have been big enough? Probably not!

Nor were the spiritual sensibilities of the people of Jesus' time keen enough. The Pharisees represented an almost fanatical religious sect of Judaism that was convinced that if people would obey and practice strict religious code, then God would usher in the messianic age. The messianic age, they believed, was when all is at one with God.

Jesus presented a threat to the campaign of the Pharisees, because he played loose with strict religious code. He bent the rules of Sabbath idleness if someone was in need. He associated with vile sinners, unclean folk, and rabble-rousers. He befriended the traitorous tax collectors, Jews who did Rome's dirty work. He even touched unclean and diseased people.

The Pharisees, and lots of other religious special-interest groups, were also dumbfounded as to how Jesus seemed to have the power to heal the sick, forgive the guilty, and raise the dead. Worst of all for the Pharisees, Jesus was gaining a large following. They needed to put a stop to him. The Pharisees persisted in trying to trap Jesus in religious legalism. One of their lawyers – experts in Mosaic law – tested Jesus by asking him which law was the greatest. Most of the faithful in those days could have given the right answer: "'You shall love the Lord your God with all your heart, and with all your soul, and with all your mind.' This is the greatest and first commandment. And a second is like it: 'You shall love your neighbor as yourself.'" On these, Jesus declared, hangs all the law and prophets. Wow! Maybe this summation, in all its simplicity and yet profundity, was just too straightforward for these Pharisees.

But Jesus wants to go deeper with these adversaries. He turns the trap on them by pressing their understanding of the Messiah. "Whose son is he?" Jesus asked. The Pharisees could answer only within their predetermined paradigm: "The son of David." This was the correct answer within Jewish tradition. Jesus, however, left them with a proposition they could not fathom: that Messiah is the Son of God and fully embodied in him! It was an unfathomable mystery for the Pharisees and perhaps for us too that God could be embodied in a person who lived among us, who modeled the self-emptying love of God, who manifested God in everything he said and did, and who mediated God's redeeming power to save us!

Great indeed is the mystery of the gospel! The mystery is how God chooses to love, bond with, and save his creation as incarnate God, God-in-us-and-with-us, the triune God, God in three persons, God everywhere in every way, God who decides to be in and with every dimension of creation and who refuses to be elsewhere. Jesus embodies and discloses all of this – God's full and unconditional love and God's persistent and uncompromising resolve to save the world.

Over all the centuries since Jesus lived on earth, even we his followers have pondered and debated how he could be both human and divine. We have struggled to grasp the commingling of his human and divine natures without compromising either. Yet his redeeming power can be fathomed no other way. He cannot be contained in an either-or definition. The power of his humanity begs a divine dimension and his divinity cannot redeem the human condition without being truly one of us. When we hold in tension these dimensions of Jesus, they eventually give way to and fulfill the other. We can't have him any other way. Great indeed is the mystery of the gospel.

Jesus then is the quintessential sacrament of God. Jesus makes the fullness of God present to us. Paul proclaimed as much in the epistle to the Colossians: "For in him all the fullness of God was pleased to dwell, and through him God was pleased to reconcile to himself all things, whether on earth or in heaven, by making peace through the blood of his cross" (1:19-20).

The very name of Jesus, the stories of Jesus, the people gathered in his name, the bread of his body broken, the cup of his blood poured out, all mysteriously release a presence that is redeeming, forgiving, healing, reconciling, saving.

The Pharisees of Jesus' time, though well intended, trapped themselves in a narrow and shallow way of perceiving reality. Their worldview wouldn't let them perceive that Jesus could open them to the deeper mysteries of God. Could it be that too many of us are the same way? Could it be that even though we are professed Christians we don't allow Jesus to take us into the glorious and redeeming depths of God?

The redeeming mystery of Jesus as Son of God who emptied himself in love of God and neighbor, even to the point of death of a cross, is ever available to us and to everyone. But the mystery doesn't stop with our own salvation. In God's redemption of us in Jesus Christ we are also commissioned to be his representatives in the world. We are baptized into Christ, into a mystical union with him. We live in Christ, and Christ lives in us. We are then continuously nurtured in this union around the table of Jesus. Beginning in our baptism and continuing with his table fellowship, Christ is working his grace in us until we are perfected in love, either on this side of eternity or the other. But all this is preparation for being sent by Christ to join God's saving work in the world. We declare this spiritual reality in the eucharistic prayer: "Pour out your Holy Spirit on us ... that we may be for the world the body of Christ, redeemed by his blood. By your Spirit make us one with Christ, one with each other, and one in ministry to all the world."

When we go into our day-to-day lives as "the body of Christ" and faithfully minister to his redeeming presence, we release him to be in our relationships with all kinds of people. We do not do the redemptive work; Christ does. As Paul said of his ministry so it shall be for ours: "Think of us in this way, as servants of Christ and stewards of God's mysteries" (1 Cor 4:1). Amen.

– John Collett

Hymns
Opening: Immortal, Invincible, God Only Wise
Sermon: How Can We Name a Love?
Closing: *Camina, pueblo de Dios*/Walk On, O People of God

October 31, 2014

Reformation

Lessons
Jer 31:31-34   Ps 46   Rom 3:19-28   Jn 8:31-36

Speaker's Introduction for the Lessons
Lesson 1
Jeremiah 31:31-34
> Imagine relating to God strictly on the basis of the lure and movement of God's presence within you, with no reliance whatsoever on anything outside yourself.

Lesson 2
Psalm 46
> God's powerful and protective presence means we have nothing to fear.

Lesson 3
Romans 3:19-28
> Although humanity is broken by sin, faith becomes the path by which we can rest confidently in God's righteousness.

Gospel
John 8:31-36
> Jesus calls us out of slavery to sin into the freedom of discipleship.

Theme
Christ rescues us from the quicksand of pride and despair, placing us on God's solid ground.

Thought for the Day

I began to understand God's righteousness as something by which the righteous lives as by God's gift, that is, by faith.

> – Roy A. Harrisville [quoting Martin Luther], *Augsburg Commentary on the New Testament, Romans*

Sermon Summary

Wherever we find ourselves there is a word for us in Paul's letter to the Romans: God's gift of Jesus Christ puts us on new solid ground. He rescues us from the quicksand of sin. We live trusting in Christ so that neither despair nor pride overcome us.

Call to Worship

One: Come, let us worship the Lord!
All: God is our refuge and strength.
One: Come, behold the works of the Lord.
All: God brings peace to all nations and peoples.
One: When we are on shaky ground,
All: God rescues us in Jesus Christ.
One: When changes bring hardship and overwhelm us,
All: God holds us in Christ and will not let us go.
One: When pride rules in our hearts, blinding us,
All: God holds us in Christ and will not let us go.
One: Christ is our solid ground.
All: Thanks be to God, our refuge and strength!

Pastoral Prayer

God, we praise you for your many good gifts: creation, harvest, family, friends, home, and work. Especially we praise you for the gift of our Lord Jesus Christ. Thank you for sending him to live, die, and rise in order to claim us as your own forgiven and renewed people. On this Reformation Day make us ever mindful of the good news of Christ, which the reformers proclaimed so boldly. Like them give us insight, courage, and faith to trust only in Christ who rescues us from sin and places us on your solid ground of grace. Amen.

Prayer of Confession and Assurance

God of grace, we confess to you the sin of our pride. Too often our confidence is placed in ourselves and our accomplishments. Too often we take off in our own direction, leaving you, your word, and care of our neighbor behind. Give us confidence, God, but let it be grounded in your grace in our Lord Jesus Christ. O God, when pride does not overwhelm us, our own despair does. We confess to you those times of hopelessness and uncertainty. Steady us when we are afraid to trust in you and act according to your good purposes. Give us courage and faith grounded in your grace given to us in Jesus Christ. Above all assure us that, as the apostle Paul preached, you are faithful, passing over our sins and rescuing us with forgiveness through our Lord Jesus Christ. Amen.

Prayer of Dedication of Gifts and Self

We return to you, O God, what you have first given us: time, talents, resources, and life itself. You have lifted us out of ourselves and onto the solid ground of Christ. Help each of us to share this good news with others. Empower our congregation and the wider church to be communities of grace toward one another and toward the world. Open our eyes and hearts to all who struggle with pride or despair so we may share, in both words and deeds, your help, strength, forgiveness, hope, and love that are in Christ Jesus. Amen.

Hymn of the Day
All My Hope on God Is Founded

Written by Joachim Neander and translated by Robert Bridges, the text has gone through a number of reworkings, including a new translation by Fred Pratt Green, which is closer to the original German text. This translation was created at the request of composer and editor John Wilson. The original tune, NEANDER, was also written by the author and appears in a number of hymnals. A new tune, MICHAEL, was written by Herbert Howells specifically for the Green retranslation. Both tunes are meant to be sung with vigor and confidence. Regardless of the translation or the tune chosen, this is a hymn of faith and trust. It is an affirmation of our beliefs.

Children's Time: God Loves Us Anyway

(Ask the children if they have ever heard someone say, "I've got some good news and some bad news." Give them an example such as, "The good news is you don't have to brush your teeth after your snack today. The bad news is that you don't have to brush because you won't have a snack today.")
One of our Bible readings is kind of like that today, only it goes the other way around. It tells us some bad news, but then it tells us the good news. First of all, it says, "All have sinned and fallen short of God's glory." That means that nobody is perfect, everybody has done some things that make God sad. *(You might talk with the children about what some of those things might be.)*

The good news is that God loves us anyway. God wants us to be good, kind, loving people, and God is sad when we're not. But God still loves us and helps us do better next time.

Pray: Dear God, thank you for the good news that you love us all the time. With you there is no bad news. Amen.

The Sermon: On Solid Ground Because of Christ
Scripture: Romans 3:19-28

The apostle Paul was an exemplary Pharisee: scholar of the law and the scriptures and zealous protector of the Jewish faith. If anyone would have asked Paul, "How are things?" before his conversion, he would have answered that they were just fine. Paul, the Pharisee, knew where he stood and what he was about.

Some 1500 years after Paul, we have the German reformer Martin Luther. He too was a scholar of the Holy Scriptures and devoted to God. But especially as a young theologian he struggled in his understanding of God. God seemed distant and judgmental and left Luther feeling as if he stood on very shaky ground, never measuring up to all that God required him to be.

In Paul we have a confident, zealous person of faith. In Luther we have someone less confident and more troubled by the weight of his imperfection and sin. Both would come to find comfort in the same good news. Both would find freedom and hope in the righteousness of God through faith in Jesus Christ. Why? Because this good news put them in a new place – on new ground – the firm ground of the grace of God.

Paul and Luther lived hundreds of years ago. Can we truly relate to them? Hasn't a great deal changed since then? Of course, a great deal has changed due to great advances in all areas of life and learning. But we human beings still are concerned about our place in this world. Some of us still ponder the God who made us and wonder what God wants from us. For us. Others of us don't wonder at all. We feel we are quite well established and secure. We are on track and have certain and fixed goals ahead of us. Today we may feel most like the confident, secure Saul/Paul standing on the solid ground of his learning and commitment or most like the anxious Luther or somewhere in between. Wherever we find ourselves there is a word for us in Paul's letter to the Romans: God's gift of Jesus Christ puts us on new solid ground.

The apostle Paul understood well what it is to be so absolutely confident and certain in one's commitment and purpose and then have the rug pulled out from right under him. He went from zealous Saul to blinded Paul in just a few moments. Paul's world turned upside down when Jesus Christ found him on the road to Damascus and brought him to faith; brought him to confidence in Christ rather than in himself. It's a common human experience, having the rug pulled out from under you. Illness, a terminal diagnosis, the loss of a job, a forced retirement, the breakup of a marriage, or a financial crisis can quickly destroy our confidence and self-sufficiency.

A friend of mine had spent many years working in a high-powered law firm, putting in impossible hours, jumping through "hoops," only to finally be told there would be no partnership for her. She'd followed the rules, written and unwritten, but it wasn't enough for a few people at the top. Paul's words in verses 19-20 help capture what it is to find out that you can follow all the rules but it isn't enough. No one is "justified ... by deeds prescribed by the law." My friend, like Paul, had to discover some new ground on which to stand. Paul's words in verse 24 are at the heart of finding new ground. "They are now justified by his grace as a gift, through the redemption that is in Christ Jesus." Paul found new ground on which to stand and once more confidently took up a mission, but this time the mission was based on the grace of God and not his own abilities.

Perhaps, though, you never had the confidence of a Saul/Paul. Instead you have lived with the feeling and experience of often being on shaky ground. You know only too well that you are not in control of very much in your life or this world. There have been plenty of disappointments, hard knocks, and failures. Paul's letter to the Romans points to the solid ground that is ours through Jesus Christ. Paul proclaims that God has passed over (forgiven) sins previously committed (verse 25) and that God is righteous in the face of our struggle and failure. The righteousness of God is God's faithfulness to us in spite of our failure and sin. It is God's faithfulness to us that puts us on new solid ground. We know all too well our weakness and failure, but God doesn't come demanding perfection from us, giving us just one more chance. No, God comes in Christ and does something about our weak and sinful condition. God gives us Christ, crucified and risen, who pulls us out of the muck and calls us to cling to him.

Our passage closes in verse 28 with the good news that by the grace of God we stand on new ground, God's ground, that holds us forever. It is this good news that enabled Paul to channel his energy and commitment to proclaiming Christ as Lord. It is this good news that enabled Martin Luther to find confidence and courage to proclaim the grace of God in the face of opposition and threats.

Here's an illustration that might help us picture our situation. We are all like people who have found ourselves in quicksand. Quicksand undisturbed looks safe enough, but when a person steps off into it, it creates a liquefied soil that cannot support weight. The person begins to sink but can actually manage to keep the head above water and stay afloat for some time. But staying afloat only works for so long. Trapped in quicksand, a person is in danger of other threats such as sunlight, dehydration, predators, hypothermia, or tides. When the quicksand of sin traps us, we can stay afloat, but we cannot get out. God is faithful to us in our weakness and need. God sends Jesus, crucified and risen, to pull us from the quicksand and bring us to solid ground. The rescue to solid ground is a gift. With the apostle Paul, with Martin Luther, and all the reformers we cling to this great gift of grace and proclaim it to the world. Amen.

– Jeanette Strandjord

Hymns
Opening: That Priceless Grace
Sermon: My Hope Is Built on Nothing Less
Closing: Come to Be Our Hope, O Jesus/ *Vem, Jesus hossa esperanca*

November 1, 2014

All Saints' Day

Lessons

Semi-continuous (SC)	Complementary (C)	Roman Catholic (RC)
Rev 7:9-17	Rev 7:9-17	Rev 7:2-4, 9-14
Ps 34:1-10, 22	Ps 34:1-10, 22	Ps 24:1-6
1 Jn 3:1-3	1 Jn 3:1-3	1 Jn 3:1-3
Mt 5:1-12	Mt 5:1-12	Mt 5:1-12

Speaker's Introduction for the Lessons

Lesson 1

Revelation 7:9-17 (SC/C); 7:2-4, 9-14 (RC)

The martyrs glorified in heaven and the saints struggling here on earth are part of one great communion praising the Lord Jesus.

Lesson 2

Psalm 34:1-10, 22 (SC/C)

We can find hope in David's song of thanksgiving for deliverance by God from oppression.

Psalm 24:1-6 (RC)

This song emphasizes God as creator of all things, and we are blessed who worship God.

Lesson 3

1 John 3:1-3 (SC/C/RC)

Just as Jesus is both divine and human, so the church must be concerned with both the spiritual and the physical needs of its members and the world around it.

Gospel

Matthew 5:1-12 (SC/C/RC)

Jesus turns the world upside down with the rules for God's kingdom, which will be perfectly realized in the future but that he intends for his disciples to live now.

Theme

By God's grace in Jesus Christ we receive blessing and mercy.

Thought for the Day

The beatitudes usher the reader into a new world, and its inbreaking is marked by a royal distribution of gifts … by surprising and surpassing generosity.

> – Robert H. Smith,
> *Augsburg Commentary on the New Testament, Matthew*

Sermon Summary

When we read the beatitudes we get a new vision, God's vision for us and the world. God blesses us in our need, forgives sin, and showers us with mercy. We are called to share blessing and mercy, and we give thanks for those who did so before us.

Call to Worship

One: Let us bless the Lord at all times.
All: We boast in the grace of our Lord.
One: Let us praise the name of the Lord,
All: With heart and voice.
One: Listen to the Lord who delivers us;
All: Taste and see that the Lord is good.
One: Look to the Lord who hears our cries,
All: And deliver us from all our fears.
One: Happy and blessed are they who trust in the Lord.
All: Those who seek the Lord lack no good thing.
One: The Lord redeems the life of his servants.
All: Bless the Lord!

Pastoral Prayer

God of blessing and mercy, we praise you for your surprising and surpassing generosity to us and our world. Keep our hearts and minds fixed on our Lord and Savior Jesus Christ, the lamb who is our shepherd. Make us strong in the hope and promise that one day all will be made right around your throne. May your word that one day there will be no more hunger, thirst, tears, or suffering give us courage to live generous and merciful lives now. Bless us as we serve and keep our faith centered on you during times of struggle. Amen.

Prayer of Confession and Assurance

Most merciful God, we confess to you that many things in life tear us away from you. Too often our hearts are set on our own plans and desires, and we think we are self-sufficient. Too often we give in to pride and selfishness instead of walking humbly and faithfully with you. Too often we lack the courage and faith to endure hardship and even persecution for your sake and the sake of our neighbor. Forgive us, God, and create in us hearts that are centered in you and are ready to do your good will. Create in us hearts that show mercy to others whatever the cost. Remind us of the good news that none of those who take refuge in you will be condemned. Let your Spirit proclaim to us that the lamb is our shepherd and leads us to springs of the water of life. Amen.

Prayer of Dedication of Gifts and Self

Thank you, Lord, for those daily things we need and for the gift of your own dear Son, Jesus Christ. Give us thankful hearts that count your many blessings to us and your world. Give us a spirit of gratitude that opens us up to sharing blessings with others. Help each of us and your whole church to live in the humble spirit of mercy so that we may seek your will and care for our neighbors with generosity. Lead us to be about care, concern, and justice on behalf of others, even when it brings us struggle and conflict. Amen.

Hymn of the Day
O for a Thousand Tongues to Sing

What an outpouring of joy and praise! This text, by Charles Wesley, was written on the anniversary of his Aldersgate conversion. Originally this hymn was 18 stanzas in length; contemporary hymnals have reduced it to four or five. There are differences in stanza order and inclusion in many hymnals, but Wesley's passionate language is the same, nevertheless. This hymn is often referred to as the "anthem of Methodism," and is traditionally the first hymn in hymnals of that denomination. AZMON, the Hebrew word for fortress or strong defense, was arranged from a German melody by Lowell Mason. It is a strong tune that is a good match for the text. This hymn can be used throughout the liturgy; however, it makes an especially strong opening hymn or invitation to discipleship.

Children's Time: Surrounded by Saints

(Bring adhesive foam glow-in-the-dark stars.)
Hold up a star and ask, Who made the stars? How many stars did God make? When can we see the stars?

Today is All Saints' Day. On All Saints' Day we remember and celebrate all of the saints. Saints are all of the baptized people who have followed God before us and all of the people who follow God today. Were the early Christians saints? Are you saints? Of course you are! And in God's eyes you are special, you are stars, just as glamorous as movie stars and rock stars. How many people throughout history have followed God? Many, many people are saints, just like many, many stars are in the night sky.

Give each child a glow-in-the-dark star with instructions to stick the star in a place where they can see it from their bed. When they turn off the lights at night, the little star will glow. The glowing star can remind them that they are saints, God's special stars. And the next time they see the stars in the night sky, they can remember all the Christians who have followed God who are saints in heaven.

Pray: Dear God, thank you for sending all the Christians who have gone before us, who have lovingly shared your faith. Help us to continue to spread the good news of your love. Amen.

The Sermon: Saints by the Grace of God
Scripture: Matthew 5:1-12

What does it mean to celebrate All Saints' Day? When we celebrate All Saints' Day we do not have in mind a short, approved list of especially holy people (a list of the superstars of faith). Rather, as Martin Luther and other reformers held, we are speaking of all Christians being saints. All Christians are saints, not because they are perfect, but rather because they have been made holy by God. Luther points to this in his explanation to the Third Article of the Apostles' Creed in the Small Catechism. He writes

119

that it is the Holy Spirit who "made me holy and kept me in the true faith" and makes "holy the whole Christian church on earth." Holiness is a gift and God's Spirit gives it in many ways, including that daily this Holy Spirit "abundantly forgives all sins."

Today then is a day to remember and honor all those ordinary Christians, those saints, who have gone before us. It is also a day to include ourselves in this company of saints. There is precedent for this. The apostle Paul, when he wrote a letter, would call his readers saints. In his letter to the Ephesians Paul wrote, "To the saints who are in Ephesus ..." (Eph 1:1). Reading further in the letter, and between lines, it becomes clear that the community is less than perfect: there is disunity and practice of some gentile or pagan ways contrary to the Christian faith. Still they are saints by the grace of God in Jesus Christ, which brings forgiveness and new life.

It might surprise you that quarrelling Ephesians and arrogant Corinthians were classed as saints by Paul. It might surprise you that you are saints as well. But then, God is full of surprises. Take our Gospel reading of the beatitudes, for instance. Full of surprises. In this teaching sermon of Jesus, such unlikely people are listed as blessed or favored by God. In these nine beatitudes we have poor, humble, mournful, gentle, trusting, and persecuted people lifted up as blessed. How different from today. They would never have made it on any of the recent, popular "survivor" shows or TV reality competitions to be the best chef or interior designer. They are hardly models of worldly success and power, but the power of God is at work in them and their lives.

When we read the beatitudes we get a new vision. God's vision for this world and for us. Each of the beatitudes reveals God's power at work in our lives and our world. At the heart of each beatitude we find both righteousness and mercy. These are the things God desires for us and in us. And they are possible in our lives, by the grace of God, no matter what our vocation or work in life. An unemployed beggar is capable of righteousness and mercy, as is the CEO of a large corporation. A sixth-grade crossing guard and a police sergeant are equally capable of righteous and mercy. It's important for us saints to remember this, lest we think God is not at work in our daily lives.

What then is righteousness? It is to have a heart set on God and doing God's good will. Lest we turn this into a competition of who has the most

November 1, 2014
All Saints' Day

dedication or faith, notice that in the beatitudes it is the poor in spirit, those who mourn, the meek, and those who yearn for righteousness who will be blessed. What is it about these people? All of them know that they are not righteous within themselves. They all know that they need God. Those who have few spiritual strengths (v. 3), who grieve over suffering and sin (v. 4), those who persist in gentleness rather than competition and selfish ambition (v. 5), and finally those who yearn for God's will to be done (vv. 6, 8), are focused not on themselves but on God. They are not particularly successful people – certainly not by the world's standards – but still they matter to God.

Next, what is mercy? Mercy grows out of setting one's heart on God. It is forgiving as we have been forgiven in Christ (v. 7). It is the single-minded desire to live with affection and devotion to God's merciful purposes (v. 8). It is being willing to make peace with others by including, befriending, and loving instead of hating (v. 9). And finally, it is to live this way even when it means you pay a price for doing so (vv. 10-12). Mercy persists in the face of persecution, whether that is simply being excluded by others and thought to be too generous and "soft" or being physically wounded and beaten down by others.

Today we give thanks for those people of faith who have gone before us. We give thanks for the righteousness that we saw in their lives. Certainly not 100 percent of the time, but some of the time. Thanks be to God for the times when their heart set on God shone through their words or their actions. But thanks be to God for just the opposite: those times when they came up empty and were poor in spirit and grieving over the suffering and sin of this world. Then they could only point us to God's grace. I think of times when my parents had to bury their own parents or when family members faced serious illness or when someone lost their job. Thanks be to God for people of faith who could be honest about their grief and their limitations and seek to trust in God's help.

We also give thanks for the mercy we received through those who have gone before us. For family, friends, teachers, pastors, and neighbors who showed kindness and compassion even when we did not deserve it. But finally today, along with our prayers of thanks for those who have gone before us, we pray too that the Spirit of Christ and Christ's words may be at work in our lives. Whatever our vocation or work, we receive God's forgiveness and mercy. This grace frees us to set our hearts and minds on God and leads us to be compassionate and merciful people. Amen.

– Jeanette Strandjord

Hymns
Opening: *Soli Deo Gloria*
Sermon: Blest Are They
Closing: Lord Jesus, You Shall Be My Song

November 2, 2014

21st Sunday after Pentecost (Proper 26)
RC/Pres/UCC: 31st Sunday in Ordinary Time

Lessons

Semi-continuous (SC)	Complementary (C)	Roman Catholic (RC)
Josh 3:7-17	Micah 3:5-12	Wis 3:1-9
Ps 107:1-7, 33-37	Ps 43	Ps 23:1-6
1 Thess 2:9-13	1 Thess 2:9-13	Rom 5:5-11
Mt 23:1-12	Mt 23:1-12	Mt 5:1-12a

Speaker's Introduction for the Lessons
Lesson 1
Joshua 3:7-17 (SC)

> This passage occurs soon after the death of Moses. It confirms Joshua as God's newly appointed leader for Israel, the one who will lead the people into the promised land.

Micah 3:5-12 (C)

> Micah lived in Judah around the time of the Assyrian invasion of the Northern Kingdom of Samaria. His message is clear and simple: what happened to Samaria will also happen to Judah if its people do not repent.

Wisdom 3:1-9 (RC)

> We are assured that the souls of the righteous are in the hands of a gracious God.

Lesson 2
Psalm 107:1-7, 33-37 (S)

> We celebrate the goodness of God, who hears our cries and responds. God's steadfast love endures forever.

Psalm 43 (C)

> Even in times of struggle we can hope in God, our refuge.

Psalm 23:1-6 (RC)
The Lord is a great shepherd who tends the sheep and supplies our every need.

Lesson 3
1 Thessalonians 2:9-13 (SC/C)
First Thessalonians is believed to be the oldest book of the New Testament. Here Paul recounts his initial visit to Thessalonica as he encourages them to remain true to the word of God.
Romans 5:5-11 (RC)
Paul tells the Romans that God's love has been poured into our hearts through the Holy Spirit.

Gospel
Matthew 23:1-12 (SC/C)
This passage occurs late in the Gospel of Matthew in Jerusalem as Jesus is teaching inside the temple. His condemnation of the Pharisees should not be understood as a condemnation of modern-day Judaism.
Matthew 5:1-12a (RC)
Jesus, in the Sermon on the Mount, pronounces blessings on those who suffer in the world because of their allegiance to his kingdom.

Theme
Jesus, our Lord and teacher, is living and present with us now and we follow humbly.

Thought for the Day
The Gospel writer Matthew holds that teaching and teachers be evaluated "by the standard of the will of God, as taught by the one Teacher, Jesus (23:10)."

– Robert H. Smith,
Augsburg Commentary on the New Testament,
Matthew

Sermon Summary

No teacher or leader is above the word of God. Jesus is the true word, the teacher and "mind" of the church. We look to Jesus above all others because Jesus is the living, present Lord. We are all students of this one Lord we humbly follow.

Call to Worship

One: Gather us in, O God,
All: From east and west and north and south.
One: Bring us together in the light of your truth,
All: That we may be fed and restored in body and spirit.
One: Turn the deserts of our longing and despair
All: Into life-giving springs of forgiveness and hope.
One: Lead us to the feet of Jesus
All: That we may learn ways of humility and love.
One: Let us hear again of the steadfast love of God in Christ Jesus,
All: That we may rejoice and give thanks to the Lord our God.

Pastoral Prayer

Thanks and praise to you, O God, for your steadfast love shown to us in the gift of this beautiful creation, the gift of home, family, and community and especially the gift of Jesus Christ. Too often we experience life as a continual struggle to elevate ourselves and achieve great success and glory. Today place us at the feet of Jesus as we hear your word. Open our hearts and minds to Christ our teacher and savior, and help us to see one another as fellow students and servants of Christ. Amen.

Prayer of Confession and Assurance

God of grace, we confess to you that our deeds do not always match our words of our faith. Save us from our hypocrisy. Help us to have the mind of Christ; to live humbly seeking to do your loving will above all else. Help us to put aside our own hunger for power and glory and, instead, to hunger for the well-being and rights of others. Make us eager to share leadership especially in the church, treating all equally as brothers and sisters in Christ. As we sit at the feet of Jesus, give us ears to listen to his word above all others. Then may that word sink deep into our hearts and minds, giving us the strength to follow in humility and faith. Above all, O God, assure us that Christ lives and is present now to forgive and strengthen us. Amen.

Prayer of Dedication of Gifts and Self

Generous God we dedicate ourselves, our time, and our resources to you. Every good thing is on loan from you and our security is not in ourselves or our possessions. May we so trust in your care that we gladly give to help neighbors here and around the globe. Through Christ, open our eyes and hearts to the pressing needs of this hungry and hurting world. Make us more concerned for others than we are for ourselves. Give us the humility of Christ so that we may humbly walk with those who suffer and are in need. Amen.

Hymn of the Day
Tis the Gift to Be Simple

The tune, SIMPLE GIFTS, is the best known and most loved Shaker tune. Its simplicity and charm are a perfect match for the text. Aaron Copland used it in his ballet *Appalachian Spring*, and also set it for solo voice and piano. The origin of this remarkable little piece is not clear. It appears in more than 15 Shaker manuscripts and is also part of the oral tradition. Whatever its origin, the message is very clear. It is only when we "come down where we ought to be" that we find the freedom to be real, to be whole, to be one with God. Use this hymn as a sung response to the Matthew reading. It says it all in a simple, direct way.

Children's Time: An Upside Down Message

(Bring a children's picture book, a mug, and a pencil.)

I'm going to do three actions. The same thing is happening with each of them. *(Hold the picture book upside down and flip through the pages. Pretend to drink from the mug upside down and write with the eraser end of a pencil.)* What did I do with all three of these? *(Affirm all answers.)*

God sent Jesus to teach us about God's love. Many of Jesus' messages were upside down. This means they were surprising and unexpected. Today, our Bible passage is from the book of Matthew. In this upside down message Jesus told the people, "The greatest among you must be a servant."

During Jesus' time, great rich people had many servants. Servants prepared the food, washed clothes, played music. Now Jesus is telling the people that in God's eyes, if you want to be great, you must serve others. So money and power don't matter to God!

How can we be God's servants? Let's use the book, mug, and pencil for ideas. *(Ask for children's responses. Suggestions include reading Bible stories to others. The mug can remind us to share our food and drink with others. With a pencil we can write prayers for others, help others with homework, or give the pencil to someone who needs one.)*

Say, "Go in peace. Serve the Lord." Invite the response, "Thanks be to God."

The Sermon: We Are All Students of Jesus
Scripture: Matthew 23:1-12

Today we might say this: "He is so heavenly that he is no earthly good." Or we might issue the challenge: "You can talk the talk, but can you walk the walk?" Both relate to the concern that someone will put their words into deeds, into concrete actions consistent with what they say.

Words and deeds are Jesus' concern in our Gospel reading from Matthew 23. Jesus has been in the temple engaging in a contentious dialog with the scribes, Pharisees, and other authorities (Mt 21:23), but now he turns to the crowds and the disciples to address the hypocrisy of religious leaders. When he is finished he will have pronounced several woes upon these hypocritical leaders (ch 23). However, it is important to note that Jesus' main accusation against these religious leaders is not the word they speak but the actions they take.

Jesus respects the scribes and Pharisees. Look at verses 2 and 3 of our reading. Jesus bids the disciples and the crowd to listen to their teaching. Why? Because they sit on Moses' seat. This most likely was a real bench, perhaps of carved stone, that was reserved for the teacher in the synagogue. This seat carried authority, the authority of teaching the word of God. Jesus directs his hearers to listen to this word and the teaching of it. The problem arises when these teachers begin to think that their authority and importance are to be found in their own person. They have transferred the authority of God's word to themselves. When this happens everything gets "out of whack."

When the leaders focus on themselves and become greedy for special status and treatment, then all the problems Jesus lists in verses 3-12 occur. There is preaching without practicing what is preached (v. 3). There is a double standard, with leaders demanding far more from their listeners than they are willing to do themselves (v. 4). There is a public parading of piety and a hunger for flattery and prestige (vv. 5-7). It is this selfish and hypocritical behavior that Jesus condemns. The scribes, Pharisees, and other leaders can talk the talk, but they can't walk the walk.

We could say they have a king-of-the-hill mentality. King of the hill is a game kids play. My friend, his siblings, and his cousins used to play it on the sand dunes in northern Michigan. There can only be one king in this game who stands at the top of the dune. Everyone else must scramble up and try to knock him off. If someone is successful, then there is a new king and the whole struggle begins again. It is just a game, but any one of us who has played it with friends or siblings knows that it can become plenty rough, and it usually ends with some fight or injury with a parent intervening and ending the game.

Jesus ends the game. Following him is not about being a king of the hill. It is not about competition and dominance. This is Jesus' word to the religious leaders of his day, but it is also his word to his church. In verse 8 the wording changes to "you." Jesus drops the address to the scribes and Pharisees and speaks to his disciples and the crowds directly. The problem of selfish and power-hungry leaders exists everywhere, including among the disciples and in the early church. A glance at James 3:1 shows the early church's concern about the integrity of teachers. First Peter 5:1-6 gives wise instruction about the humility needed in the church community. Discipleship in the church is not about being a king of the hill. It is about humility.

True humility means setting yourself under the word of God, especially the word that is Jesus. Jesus says it plainly in verse 8, "You are all students." All are equal in the community. Of course, we each have our own function; some are called to be musicians, pastors, administrators, and so forth. But no one is greater than the other. Since we are all under the word of God, we are not to set up special groups or leaders (v. 9). As Jesus says, we have only one Father, God. But the temptation is to set up an earthly figure on whom to depend. We rely on this one leader to interpret almost everything for us, and we obey him or her blindly. Cults are an extreme example of this. Cliques and ruling groups in any congregation are a more moderate example. Whatever form, any time one person or a small elite group sets themselves up as the ruling authority in the Christian community, they are counter to Jesus' call for humility and obedience to God.

Why do we human beings seek to be the king of the hill? The autocrat? The final authority? Why do communities seek one leader or a small elite to tell them what to do? I suppose there are many answers: selfishness, insecurity, fear, greed, and so forth. But one very important answer is that we forget we have the true living Lord present with us now. Verse 10 of our scripture reading speaks of one instructor, "the Messiah." The word *instructor* here means the one guiding the mind. It is Jesus who is the mind of the new faith community. The early postresurrection community would see in the crucified and resurrected Lord Jesus the meaning and power of true humility. We look only to Christ to determine how we live and serve.

The apostle Paul said just this in Philippians 2:5 and following, "Let the same mind be in you that was in Christ Jesus." It is Jesus who emptied himself to save the world. It is Jesus whom God raised from the dead. Jesus Christ lives! Jesus Christ, by the power of the Spirit, continues to forgive, guide, empower, and save us. Why look to any other leader for the final word, the truth? Jesus is the one who has lived, suffered, and died for us and our world. He is the one God raised from the dead for us and our world. He is the one who lives eternally. Only Jesus, the Messiah, is the guiding mind, the instructor, and the savior of ourselves, the church, and the world.

No need for some sort of competitive faith Olympics. No need for a hierarchy of power in the church. No place for mindless cultish behavior. We are all students, and Jesus Christ is our living, present teacher and Lord. Amen.

– Jeanette Strandjord

Hymns
Opening: All Are Welcome
Sermon: Where True Charity and Love Abide
Closing: When We Are Living

November 9, 2014

22nd Sunday after Pentecost (Proper 27)
RC/Pres/UCC: 32nd Sunday in Ordinary Time

Lessons

Semi-continuous (SC)	Complementary (C)	Roman Catholic (RC)
Josh 24:1-3a, 14-25	Wis 6:12-16 or Amos 5:18-24	Wis 6:12-16
Ps 78:1-7	Wis 6:17-20 or Ps 70	Ps 63:2-8
1 Thess 4:13-18	1 Thess 4:13-18	1 Thess 4:13-18 or 4:13-14
Mt 25:1-13	Mt 25:1-13	Mt 25:1-13

Speaker's Introduction for the Lessons

Lesson 1

Joshua 24:1-3a, 14-25(SC)

> With the tribes of Israel newly established in the promised land, Joshua gives this final speech before his death, exhorting the tribes to "choose this day" to serve the Lord.

Wisdom of Solomon 6:12-16 (C/RC)

> Ascribing one's work to a great figure of the past was thought to be a way of honoring that person; thus the author of Wisdom has ascribed this book to King Solomon. In personifying Wisdom as a feminine figure, the author is drawing on a tradition also seen in Proverbs 8.

Amos 5:18-24 (C)

> The heart of Amos's message was that the indifference of Israel's wealthy to the plight of the poor rendered their worship unacceptable to God. The people of Israel believed that if they called upon the Lord, they would be saved from the Assyrian threat. Amos cautions them not to presume upon God's mercy.

Lesson 2

Psalm 78:1-7 (SC)

> The psalmist invites the people's hearing and then teaching of the wisdom God reveals and the law God decrees for their sake and that of coming generations.

Psalm 70 (C)
The psalm is an urgent plea ("make haste . . . do not delay!") for deliverance from enemies, and closely parallels Psalm 40:13-17.

Psalm 63:2-8 (RC)
This poem is a prayer of trust addressed to God.

Lesson 3
1 Thessalonians 4:13-18 (SC/C/RC); 4:13-14 (RC)
With dramatic celestial imagery, the writer offers assurance to those troubled by the deaths of their brothers and sisters in faith, that the dead shall be raised.

Gospel
Matthew 25:1-13 (SC/C/RC)
While sitting on the Mount of Olives, Jesus shares with his disciples this parable and many others to assure them that costly faithfulness sustained through times of persecution and despair will be rewarded.

Theme
We must be prepared not only to wait but to respond.

Thought for the Day
Staying awake is not a virtue, but staying alert is. Staying alert sometimes requires taking a refreshing nap while waiting for the bridegroom.

Sermon Summary
The best model for preparation is in how the wise virgins successfully prepared, not how the foolish ones failed. The wise ones were prepared to wait and to respond – and to celebrate in between. The same is true for us.

Call to Worship
One: God's decrees are established to teach our children
All: That the next generation might know them and rise up to tell their children.
One: So that they should set their hope in God

All: And forget not the works of God but keep the commandments.
One: Let us worship God.

Pastoral Prayer

Loving God, thank you for inviting us to the extravagant celebration of your kingdom. We are gathered here to receive your blessings and become a blessing to others. We are grateful for your presence with us and ask that through your Spirit we may be given a heart full of wisdom. Help us in the decisions we make for ourselves and for others. Watch over those who struggle with infirmities, loss of life, and loss of income; empower us to help. Guide us as we seek to follow you and bring us safely to your home. In Jesus' name. Amen.

Prayer of Confession and Assurance

O God, our choices are not always easy for us, especially when we wonder what Jesus would do. We confess that we weigh our wants and needs against the cost of sacrificing for others. We run short of love and mercy. We leave behind the very things we need for your kingdom's service. We pride ourselves more in keeping our resources than expending them for your work. Our lack of gratitude burns low in our lamps for welcoming you into our lives. Forgive us and renew a right spirit within us. Amen.

God has freely invited all of us for the kingdom celebration that Jesus proclaimed. We rejoice that God's Spirit is ever flowing and that forgiveness comes from the cross, not from our own doing. I declare unto you in the name of Jesus Christ, we are forgiven.

Prayer of Dedication of Gifts and Self

O Giver of all good things, we rejoice that you have called us as citizens of your kingdom. We commit ourselves to you before all other loyalties. We know that the world and everything in it is yours. Increase our joy as we celebrate by sharing the very gifts you entrusted to us. Open our hearts, our minds, and our hands so that the good news of our Savior's generosity and mercy may grow and prosper in this congregation and throughout the world. Amen.

Hymn of the Day
Keep Your Lamps Trimmed and Burning

This African American spiritual is a retelling of the intent of the reading from Matthew. In *The New Century Hymnal* there are four verses, however in the oral tradition of the African American people, a song leader would have called out substitutions to make up new verses. Try the verses written and also make up those that speak closest to the message you wish to give. This spiritual is also thought to be one of many used for the Underground Railroad. It was a signal to "be ready, your time is coming." The uses for this spiritual are numerous, from services of dedication to prayers of discipleship.

Children's Time: Be Ready!

(Practice having the children say, "Five" when you hold up five fingers and "Ten" when you hold up ten.)

This is the story Jesus told of (*ten*) bridesmaids who took their (*ten*) lamps and went to meet the bridegroom. It was night. The (*ten*) bridesmaids were waiting to lead the bridegroom by lamplight to the bride's house. The bridegroom was late. All (*ten*) bridesmaids fell asleep. At midnight someone shouted, "The bridegroom is coming!" The (*ten*) bridesmaids prepared their lamps. But (*five*) foolish bridesmaids forgot to bring extra oil. The (*five*) foolish bridesmaids asked the (five) wise bridesmaids for extra oil. But the (*five*) wise bridesmaids answered, "Go buy some for yourselves." While they were gone, the bridegroom came. The (*five*) wise bridesmaids led him to the home of the marriage feast, went inside with him, and the doors were locked. Later the (*five*) foolish bridesmaids knocked on the door and called out, "Lord! Lord! Open the door for us!" But he called back, "I don't know you."

In this story Jesus was telling us that we should be ready, like the (*five*) wise bridesmaids, by following God every day. One way we can be ready is by praying.

Dear God, thank you for weddings, feasts, and worship services where we can gather to celebrate your love. Help us to be ready. Amen.

The Sermon: Learning from the Wise Ones
Scripture: Matthew 25:1-13

So the foolish virgins didn't bring enough oil? Poor things. One poorly prepared event and they were on the outside looking in. Is that the way you see this passage? If so, I know how that feels. Not so long ago, I knew that I had a big wedding coming up for the mayor's daughter with several hundred people expected in attendance. I had the date on my calendar for the rehearsal and the day was set in my mind as "Friday." But three days before rehearsal, I took another look and discovered that it was not Friday but Thursday. Oh no! That was the day I was giving a midterm at Texas Christian University, and I could find no one else to take the class. The bride had already sent out 100 invitations to the rehearsal dinner, so I was sunk! My oil had run out, and there I was with the foolish virgins.

One snafu and the door is shut. Is that the message of this parable? Actually, it turned out pretty well for me. The wedding coordinator worked out the details for the wedding party and I made my class. Afterward, the bride and groom still welcomed me at the rehearsal dinner where there was laughter and forgiveness. They were very gracious. I doubt that God would be any less gracious. When I think of the prodigal and Jesus' teachings on forgiveness, "one snafu and you're out" doesn't hold water.

So what's the interpretation here? Maybe instead of looking at the foolish virgins, we should focus on the wise ones. They were wise because they were prepared. But prepared for what? What was all that extra oil about? I think the answer is that they were prepared to wait for the bridegroom. The problem comes in our actual practice.

Do we get on a bus and wait for Jesus on a mountaintop? Do we stay tense and alert like driving on the westbound in rush hour traffic? What is Christian waiting like? For the wise virgins, it was like a wedding, a joyous occasion. We read that their celebration was followed by a nap. It was not an uptight situation, because they were prepared.

For me, this parable is like celebrating on a Monday afternoon when my friends and I get in an old pickup truck and go fishing on Sally's ranch. (It's Texas, what illustration did you expect?) We are invited because Sally enjoys two things: the fish we fillet and the laughter we share together afterward. When our spouses join us, our pleasure doubles. It's a great time.

My friends and I are truly committed to fishing, but none of us likes fishing alone. It's not much fun catching a fish all by yourself and yelling "I got it! I got it!" Celebrating solo doesn't work very well. In fact, the kingdom celebrations described by Jesus are always with others. We also understand that the word is "fishing" not "catching." Some days we may not catch anything, but we keep our hooks in the water, because we know the fish are there. In a way, it's like faith, the substance of things not seen requiring patient waiting.

We persevere in our fishing; we don't give up until the sun goes down. (Like the wise virgins, we have to sleep sometime.) We have the right equipment just as God equips us in faith. We are prepared with our favorite rods and lures and we are prepared to wait. After a couple of hours with no bites, we may relax and sit down on a rock, but we're still ready for the big one. That's the way I see the wise virgins at the wedding – full of the enjoyment of life but ready for the big moment. The big moment, in which Jesus comes to us in the present or the future, is not passive but calls for active duty. And at times it's costly.

Philip Hallie, in his book *Let Innocent Blood Be Shed*, tells the story of Pastor Trocme who preached to his members in the little village of Le Chambon in the French Alps during World War II. The pastor told them in a repeated message that "one day Jesus will come into your life and ask you to do something just for him." When the Nazis came looking for Jews, the villagers were prepared and waiting in response to their pastor's message. At the risk of their own lives, they successfully hid their Jewish neighbors (Michael A. Turner, "Get Ready for God," *Pulpit Resource*, 36, no. 4). Preparation means that we are not just hearers of God's word but doers. We are not just waiting, but waiting to respond.

Of course, waiting for the Lord may not always be like a wedding or even doing something extraordinary. There are rough times and moments of discouragement in our personal lives, in our work, or even at church. But as a Christian community, we don't go fishing alone. We weep with those who mourn and rejoice with those who celebrate. We offer our prayers of needs and concerns and we praise God, giving thanks for all that is good. In life or death, we are still God's children. Sometimes it takes tears to restore our vision and perhaps realize that the Lord is waiting there for us even as we wait for him. As with the wise virgins, we are

prepared to wait in hope and service, whether Jesus comes to us or we go
to him. It is a hope that will never disappoint us.

– Charles Somervill

Hymns
Opening: Come, Christians, Join to Sing
Sermon: I'm Gonna Live So God Can Use Me
Closing: My Hope Is Built on Nothing Less

November 16, 2014

23rd Sunday after Pentecost (Proper 28)
RC/Pres/UCC: 33rd Sunday in Ordinary Time

Lessons

Semi-continuous (SC)	Complementary (C)	Roman Catholic (RC)
Judges 4:1-7	Zeph 1:7, 12-18	Prov 31:10-13, 19-20, 30-31
Ps 123	Ps 90:1-8, (9-11), 12	Ps 128:1-5
1 Thess 5:1-11	1 Thess 5:1-11	1 Thess 5:1-6
Mt 25:14-30	Mt 25:14-30	Mt 25:14-30 or 25:14-15, 19-20

Speaker's Introduction for the Lessons
Lesson 1
Judges 4:1-7 (SC)
> God's people again forgot their God, and once more God sends an unlikely deliverer.

Zephaniah 1:7, 12-18 (C)
> The prophet's message to all the churchgoers of his day is, don't be smug and sure about that great day of the Lord.

Proverbs 31:10-13, 19-20, 30-31 (RC)
> God expects that the stewards of the household will not only be wise managers but kind and charitable as well.

Lesson 2
Psalm 123 (SC)
> A terse, beautiful, and powerful supplication to God that blends trustful reliance with frank expression of having had one's fill with a contemptuous situation.

Psalm 90:1-8, (9-11), 12 (C)
> This portion of the psalm focuses upon the eternal nature of God, the fleeting nature of human mortality, and a concluding plea to thus be wise in the use of time given to us.

Psalm 128:1-5 (RC)

This is a statement that God will bless the reverent for generations to come.

Lesson 3

1 Thessalonians 5:1-11 (SC/C); 1 Thessalonians 5:1-6 (RC)

God has not revealed to anyone – anyone – the day of glory, so stay alert.

Gospel

Matthew 25:14-30 (SC/C); Matthew 25:14-30 or 25:14-15, 19-20 (RC)

Jesus doesn't seem to care much if you proclaim him Lord. He wants to know what you've done lately for the least of these.

Theme

God entrusts us with grace so that we might invest it in others.

Thought for the Day

Grace is not in short supply; it grows when we give it away.

Sermon Summary

The problem with the one-talent man was not based on how little he had – he had plenty – but in how little he trusted his master. (One talent = 6000 denarii, about 1 million dollars; see Luke 10:35.) God's grace is plentiful for us and for our investment in others.

Call to Worship

One: O God, you are my God, I seek you.
All: My soul thirsts for you.
One: Because your steadfast love is better than life,
All: My lips will praise you.
One: I will lift up my hands and call on your name.
All: For you have been my help, and in the shadow of your wings I sing for joy.

Pastoral Prayer

Thank you, God, for the kindness of those present and those absent from us today. We invest in your abundant grace so that the love shared with one another might be enriched. Make us faithful stewards in our benevolence to those in need – for those caught up in the despair of disasters and downturns, for those suffering physical or economic loss, or loss of hope. Help us not to hide our faces from the sorrow of others, but to join with them through our support and comfort. Hold us close to the Spirit of your Son, Jesus Christ. Amen.

Prayer of Confession and Assurance

O God, we confess that we bury our talents. We confine your grace to ourselves rather than passing it on to others. Regardless of what you have entrusted us, we often envy those who have more. At other times, we do not see possessions as an entrustment you have given us, but as that of our own doing and very little of yours. We prefer to invest in ourselves rather than in the life to which you have called us as disciples. Forgive us and restore our stewardship to us, through Jesus Christ. Amen.

If God should mark our iniquities and remember our sins, who of us would be left standing? But there is forgiveness with God that we may continue to worship and serve as participants in God's abundant grace. We have that promise of forgiveness in Christ's name.

Prayer of Dedication of Gifts and Self

Gracious God, you created us not as empty vessels to be tucked away from all good use. Instead, you chose to fill us with your Spirit and make us stewards of your creation. In gratitude, we give you praises and return a proportion of that which you gifted us. Open our hands and our hearts so that we may become conformed to the image of Christ and even more productive as your faithful servants. Amen.

Hymn of the Day
God of Love and God of Power

The New Testament parables provide a seemingly endless number of ways to envision and imagine God. In today's Gospel reading, God is like an investment banker who demands high returns on his investments and is more than willing to terminate an employee who plays it safe and doesn't deliver. Not surprisingly, there is a dearth of hymns inspired by this text. However, Gerald H. Kennedy's "God of Love and God of Power," set to the music of Joachim Neander, pairs well with it. "All our lives belong to thee, thou our final loyalty." Today both preacher and musician do their best and trust God for the rest.

Children's Time: Naming and Using Our Talents

(Bring something that shows what your own particular talent is.)
I brought something with me today I want you to see. (*Say whatever else you wish about it, such as "I made this" or "This is my favorite song," and show them the item.*) This tells you a little about me and shows you what interests me. We all have things we are interested in and because we work at it more than at some other things, we get better at it as time goes by. These things become our talents, the things we do best.

What are some of your talents? What are the things you do best? (*If you know the skills of some of the children, share what they are.*)

God is our creator. God made us, and it is God's plan that we be creative also with these talents we have, and a lot more that you are going to discover as you grow older. God has put us in this world, and while we are here we are to take one or more of our talents and use them. Maybe someday one of you will draw plans for buildings, another will be a singer, another a really good parent, or even president of the United States. Some of you will use your friendliness to visit sick people, your cooking ability to treat your friends or feed hungry people, or your interest in cars to invent a new safety device or to give older people rides to doctor appointments. (*You might also spin off the interests and talents they listed before and imagine where those traits might take them later in life.*)

Whatever our abilities are, God gives them to us to use in some way. Hopefully, we will use them to make the world a better, happier, more loving place.

Let's pray: Creator God, you are wonderful beyond all words, and you have put some of your wonder inside of us too. Help us to discover our talents and to use them to your glory. Amen.

The Sermon: Losing a Bundle on Jesus
Scripture: Matthew 25:14-30

The story is set in a little West Texas town 40 miles outside of nowhere. It begins with a chapter meeting of some 30 members – business people, oil ranchers, and me as their token preacher. The speaker is a financial manager from the big city (well, Lubbock).

The financial manager, aware of the presence of a preacher, prides herself on her knowledge of the Bible. She introduces her speech by reading from the parable of the talents in Matthew, noting that it is also in Luke. After that, she waves a bill that looks like money at her audience.

"Have you seen this bill?" the financial manager walks from the podium toward the audience. "It says one million dollars! Is it real? No, there is no such thing as a one million dollar bill. Now let's switch topics for a moment. I want to talk about the parable of the talents. We're not talking about skills and abilities. We're talking about real money; that's what a talent is."

One of audience members whispered to me, "Is that true? Talents are money?"

"Yes," I replied.

"And there's something else you might not know," the speaker continued, "a talent is worth a lot of money. But just like a million dollar bill, there's no such thing as a talent coin; it's a unit a measure, the largest in the time of Jesus. One talent is worth 6000 denarii and one denarius pays for a day's work. You do the math! That's over a million dollars!"

"Really? Is that right?" A friend in the audience, truly amazed, grabbed me by the shoulder. "I thought the one-talent man had very little."

"Basically, she's right, I said, "but it's too far back to know dollar for dollar."

"Wow! I didn't know that!"

"My friends," the speaker said. "One million dollars won't last long after retirement. Spread over 20 years, you won't be taking many cruises and you won't have that extra money for your grandkid going to college."

The financial manager made a dramatic pause and then walked out to me. She was coming in for the kill. "The preacher knows," she said. "He knows the problem. The one-talent man did not invest. He hid it under a mattress. Right, preacher?"

"Well, yeah," I reluctantly replied. "Of course, it's a metaphor."

"The preacher knows," she walked away in triumph. "The one-talent man had a million dollars and he didn't invest. The parable is about investment and for those who invest wisely, that means security. There is nothing greater than security, whether it be in heaven or on earth. It applies to all of us."

Aristotle had it right. You agree with the premises and you're dead in the water. I didn't have an opportunity to preach a countersermon on "Seek ye first . . ." The audience left with a favorable impression of the speaker's biblical and financial knowledge.

Billy Jo, one of the oil ranchers, was especially impressed. He felt that Jesus was calling him to invest, and he did – one million dollars. Unfortunately, the year was 2008. Billy Jo later told his friends, "I lost a bundle on Jesus."

In a sense, Jesus was talking about security. "Well done ... enter into the joy of your master" (v. 21) is something we all want to hear. The promise of an unending friendship with the master is a treasure beyond all treasures. But for our lives now, it's a peculiar kind of security. We save by losing. We gain by giving up, even as God gave up his Son. In fact, we are indeed asked to lose a bundle on Jesus, to push in all the chips!

So what's the risk factor here? Why not save it all like the millionaire one-talent man? I asked a study group to name one commandment that the one-talent man violated. They thought about it and shook their heads. Murder, theft, adultery? Nope. He seemed like a good neighbor to have, the type who says "live and let live," the type who shuts his doors to the worries of the world and keeps his dog from barking. He does no harm.

Do no harm. That sounds like a good motto. It's a long-standing principle of the Hippocratic oath for doctors. Of course, we want more than that from doctors; we want treatment. Imagine going to a fearful doctor who says, "I promise to do no harm, but I'm not going to treat you. Treatments carry a risk and I'm afraid of being sued. From what I've heard about you, you're the type who would sue."

Like the doctor afraid of being sued, the one-talent man was fearful of his master. He saw his master as harsh and unreasonable and didn't trust him. It's hard to like someone you don't trust, much less love them. The trust relationship in the parable was zero. There was no way he could obey the first commandment, to love God with all your heart and soul.

His fear of God was not one of worshipful respect, but a mean-spirited fear that drives out love. It was not based on how little he had – he had plenty – but on how little he trusted his master. He carried a picture of God that ruled out the relationship God wanted. When he looked in the mirror, he saw a fearful person because he believed in a God that was not *for* him, but out to get him. Trusting his life to a god like that was out of the question. So he dug a hole to save his life and lost it.

As with the talents, the decision on how we invest god's grace is ours. The parable suggests two things that we must do. First, to receive grace, we must trust in a gracious God who freely bestows grace on us. Then we must commit ourselves to a lifelong investment and lose a bundle by freely bestowing grace on others. It's the best investment we will ever make.

– Charles Somervill

Hymns
Opening: Be Thou My Vision
Sermon: I Love Thy Kingdom, Lord
Closing: Take My Life

November 23, 2014

Reign of Christ/Christ the King (Proper 29)

Lessons

Semi-Continuous (SC)	Complementary (C)	Roman Catholic (RC)
Ez 34:11-16, 20-24	Ez 34:11-16, 20-24	Ez 34:11-12, 15-17
Ps 100	Ps 95:1-7a	Ps 23
Eph 1:15-23	Eph 1:15-23	1 Cor 15:20-26, 28
Mt 25:31-46	Mt 25:31-46	Mt 25:31-46

Speaker's Introduction for the Lessons

Lesson 1
Ezekiel 34:11-16, 20-24 (SC/C); Ezekiel 34:11-12, 15-17 (RC)

Ezekiel was both a prophet and a priest. After condemning the faithless shepherds of Israel's people, the prophet envisions a time when God will become Israel's faithful shepherd, rescuing them from the places where they have been scattered, feeding them with good pasture, while binding up the injured and strengthening the weak.

Lesson 2
Psalm 100 (SC)

This simple but profound call to praise and worship anchors the image of God as shepherd with God as creator. We belong to God, not the other way around.

Psalm 95:1-7a (C)

This is a call to praise and thanksgiving that associates with God as shepherd of all God as creator of all.

Psalm 23 (RC)

A former shepherd, King David begins this psalm by putting himself as a sheep in the care of the Lord. From personal experience, the psalmist knows a shepherd needs, to lead the flock on rough terrain, but goodness and mercy are theirs all the days of their lives.

Lesson 3

Ephesians 1:15-23 (SC/C)

Paul writes in Ephesians about the breadth of God's eternal plans for humankind. In today's reading we find Paul blessing the church in Ephesus, expressing his pleasure in the way they are embracing God's eternal plan.

1 Corinthians 15:20-26, 28 (RC)

The Corinth church was floundering under the pressures of sexual immorality that was present in their culture. Paul calls for the church to be unified in its belief, reminding them of the foundational truths of their faith.

Gospel

Matthew 25:31-46 (SC/C/RC)

Jesus' criticism, "observe whatever they tell you, but not what they do," is leveled at the Pharisees' behavior, not their teaching. Service, not self-importance, is the path to greatness.

Theme

With the Spirit's leading and practice, ministering to others becomes second nature.

Thought for the Day

Shakespeare said it well, "The quality of mercy is not strained. It droppeth as the gentle rains from heaven."

Sermon Summary

What was the "shepherd" like? Maybe like that fourth grade teacher who changed your life but who doesn't remember doing so. She wasn't out for self-glorification; she just loved kids! Training and practice go into the teacher's kind treatment – and ours too.

Call to Worship

One: Make a joyful noise to the Lord, all the earth.
All: Worship the Lord with gladness.
One: Come into God's presence with singing.

All: For the Lord is good with steadfast love that endures forever.
One: God's faithfulness is to all generations.
All: We are God's people and the sheep of God's pasture.
One: Let us give God praise.

Pastoral Prayer

Creator of all worlds, we thank you for making us in your image. You gave us your Son in whom we fashion our lives and promise to follow. Fill us with your Spirit once again that we may see the desperate needs of those around us. Give us the courage to offer assistance to strangers who seem alone or troubled. Open our hearts so that your Spirit may flow out to those who are hurting or in despair. Thank you for the love of each other and keep us in the same mind as in Christ Jesus. Amen.

Prayer of Confession and Assurance

Lord, we may not remember seeing you sick or in need. But we do remember when we were sick or in trouble. We confess that we sometimes feel more of your absence than your presence. We give you faint praise when help does come. When life is difficult, we are surprised by the callousness of people who pass us by. And yet in our own busy world when a stranger is in need, we too often fail to render aid. Forgive us and remind us once again that we are the keepers and caretakers of one another. Amen.

Hear the good news. God sent Jesus not to condemn but to save and restore us. If we really want to try again, God is there to help us. Even as Christ told us to forgive seven times seventy, so great is God's mercy. In Christ, we are forgiven.

Prayer of Dedication of Gifts and Self

Out of your love, O God, you gave us your Son and all that we have. We return a portion of that which you have given us as expressions of our love for you. Stir your Spirit within us that we might become actively engaged in alleviating poverty, hunger, and injustice. Increase our vision not only for the suffering ones of our community but for the mission fields around the world. Share with us the joy of giving bountifully, even as Jesus gave to us. Amen.

Hymn of the Day
Lord of Glory, You Have Bought Us

There are two surprising ideas in the Gospel text. The first is how very simple were the deeds the righteous did: they gave food, drink, a welcome, clothing, caring, a visit. The second is Jesus' declaration, "Just as you did it to one of the least of these, you did it to me." In this hymn, Eliza Alderson captures well this bedrock Christian idea, an idea that obliterates, as Jesus himself did, the false dichotomy between material and spiritual, divine and human. "Wondrous honor you have given, to our humblest charity. In your own mysterious sentence, 'You have done it all to me.'" In such simplicity, in such mystery: Jesus bids us to faithful shepherding of the whole flock of God.

Children's Time: A Caring Shepherd

(Talk about how, in the land and times of the Bible, many people kept sheep. Everywhere you looked, there were sheep – even in the city streets and in people's houses you were likely to find sheep. Because of this, people in the Bible talked about sheep a lot, and they often talked about how God was like a shepherd, taking care of us as if we were a flock of sheep. A shepherd is kind of like a parent, a nurse, a teacher, and a playground attendant all rolled into one.) A good shepherd leads the sheep to places where they can find food. If one of the sheep gets lost, the shepherd would go looking for it. Sometimes the shepherd might have to take a pebble or a thorn out of a sheep's foot, kind of like a nurse taking out a sliver. And, if some of the sheep tried to act like bullies, pushing the little ones away from the food, the shepherd might have to step in and make sure they played fair.

Even if we don't see many sheep or shepherds around today, it's nice to think of God that way. God is caring for us, watching out for us, teaching us how to live.

The Sermon: Favorite Things
Scripture: Matthew 25:31-46

Now we come to the moment of glory mentioned in the Apostles' Creed. We are looking at a vision of the end times with Matthew. Jesus no longer walks the dusty roads with his disciples, suffering and despised by the authorities and hanging from a cross. Now he sits on a glorious throne with all the peoples gathered before him. It sounds like Matthew is summing up his Gospel writings. (Maybe it's like those Cliffs Notes that some students use as a shortcut for reading the rest of the book. But hey, we don't want to look like bad students, so we might also include the sermon on the mount and First Corinthians 13!)

Indeed, the passage doesn't seem like it takes much thought. At first glance, it might appear to the casual reader that the Christian is simply defined as a good humanitarian. We have a ready-made list to build on. All we have to do is maintain a log to keep track of our efforts. Be sure and include the dates and times of your good deeds. That way, we can use them as talking points for heavenly entrance.

Looking further, we find that there are two groups considering the same list with different perspectives. Looking at the outcome, we'll want the first one. The first group, perhaps wearing T-shirts with a sheep printed on the front, did the following: They provided food for the hungry, water for the thirsty, hospitality for the stranger, clothing for the naked, treatment for the sick, and visits for the prisoner. The other group – now write this down for quick reference – looked the other way when they saw someone hungry, thirsty, a stranger, naked, sick, or in prison. That's simple enough, isn't it? But then comes the twist.

Both groups were puzzled when Jesus said, "I was the one" you saw hungry and thirsty. I was the person that you saw in need of clothes, medical help, or friendship for the stranger and the prisoner. I was the one you aided or from whom you turned away.

What's going on here? Why weren't the sheep aware of doing good deeds for Jesus? Did they forget their WWJD bracelets? Couldn't they see the face of Jesus in the people they helped? Apparently not. Verses 37-39: "Lord, when was it that we saw you hungry and gave you food, or thirsty and gave you something to drink? And when was it that we saw you a stranger and welcomed you, or naked and gave you clothing. And when was it we saw you sick or in prison and visited you?" They sound clueless. Why?

I think it has to do with their enjoyment of a favorite thing. What's on your list? What are your favorite things? There are some people I know whose entire day is ruined if they don't get a fourth for bridge. "Hello, Bill, we need a fourth."

"I'm not that good," Bill says.

"We don't care if you lose. We can't play without a fourth. We want to play. Please come. We're waiting."

You see, winning isn't everything. Bridge is everything. They'll play win or lose for the love of bridge. The same heartfelt feeling is there for other favorite things – gardening, for example. I think of gardening as manual labor with very little reward for the effort. My spouse disagrees. In good weather, she is out there every morning digging, pruning, planting. She never misses a seminar or workshop on gardening. "It isn't work," she tells me, "I love doing it."

I'm sure you can think of things you do simply for the love of your favorite thing. Is that the way it is with these people helpers in Matthew's passage? Are they doing it for the love of God? Well, maybe not so much for the love of God as for the love of God in us. There's a difference here that this passage highlights. The helpers didn't say, "I am doing this for the love of Jesus." (Certainly, that's not the way the good Samaritan saw it.) They did it because they couldn't imagine not doing it. "Anyone would have done the same," they say. But that's not true; too many people look the other way.

It sounds like the sheep are just naturally good-hearted, but according to 1 John 1:8, doing what comes naturally has its problems: "If we say that we have no sin, we deceive ourselves, and the truth is not in us." We all have some "goat" in us for which we seek cleansing and forgiveness.

Our hearts, through Christ's Spirit, are shaped and taught with the help of other Christians. For that reason we teach our children. We don't just turn them out to pasture to learn on their own. Instead, we learn together that it is good and pleasant to be in God's house, and our purest enjoyment comes in walking in the light Christ offers. In that way, we become more conformed to Christ so that our actions develop more spontaneously and are a blessing to others.

The outcome is described in John 7:38: "Out of the believer's heart shall flow rivers of living water." The goats never found the flowing waters. Instead they dammed them up and became stagnant. The sheep go along with the flow of the Spirit; they respond to needs and love doing it.

So what do we do with this list? Maybe we can look on it as a list of Jesus' favorite things. With God's blessing, it will become ours too. When we have the heart for it, we find ourselves doing things almost without thinking. For example, you are in a doctor's office reading a year-old magazine. The door opens and a woman on crutches comes in out of the cold. When she sits down, you say, "I was just going to get a cup of coffee. Would you like one too?" Then you find yourself sitting down beside her as she talks about her troubles.

What! You didn't check off that good deed on your list? Maybe that's because it's Jesus' list and it's written on your heart. Now you know how it is with the sheep that seemed so unaware, so clueless in the outpouring of their Christian kindness.

– Charles Somervill

Hymns
Opening: There's a Sweet, Sweet Spirit
Sermon: Christ of the Upward Way
Closing: Open My Eyes That I May See

November 27, 2014

Thanksgiving Day (USA)

Lessons

Semi-continuous (SC)	Complementary (C)	Roman Catholic (RC)
Deut 8:7-18	Deut 8:7-18	Sir 50:22-24
Ps 65	Ps 65	Ps 67:2-3, 4, 7-8
2 Cor 9:6-15	2 Cor 9:6-15	1 Cor 1:3-9
Lk 17:11-19	Lk 17:11-19	Lk 17:11-19

Speaker's Introduction for the Lessons

Lesson 1

Deuteronomy 8:7-18 (SC/C)

Moses prepares the people to enter the promised land by reminding them they must never mistake their good fortune for the work of their own hands, but credit God for all good things.

Sirach 50:22-24 (RC)

A prayer of blessing and thanksgiving for all God has done should include a prayer for deliverance as well.

Lesson 2

Psalm 65 (SC/C)

This psalm of thanksgiving moves from God's forgiveness, power in creation, and graciousness in the creation's providential care. The closing five verses are an especially vivid image of creation riches and beauty.

Psalm 67:2-3, 4, 7-8 (RC)

This is a song of community thanksgiving that resounds with renewed confidence in God's saving power.

Lesson 3

2 Corinthians 9:6-15 (SC/C)

Paul gently reminds the rich Corinthians not only that they had promised an offering to the starving Christians in Jerusalem, but also that the impoverished Macedonians have outdone them in generosity. He awaits their response.

1 Corinthians 1:3-9 (RC)

On this day of thanksgiving the apostle Paul gives thanks for the steadfast way that God strengthens believers in faithfulness and discipleship.

Gospel
Luke 17:11-19 (SC/C/RC)

In this story about Jesus and healing, nine were cured, while one, the outsider, was not only cured but made well. Find out how.

Theme
Although gratitude may not fit our natural inclinations, thanksgiving connects us to God.

Thought for the Day
We need a recovery of gratitude, because on Thanksgiving Day all over America, families sit down to dinner at the same moment – halftime.

Sermon Summary
The sermon addresses a Lucan text regarding ten lepers. One exhibited particular gratitude to Jesus, and that thankful one was an outsider. Gratitude and thanksgiving are traits we teach through demonstration and modeling. We know that gratitude is a virtuous quality, yet we too commonly forget to voice it.

Call to Worship
One: Praise is due to you, O God, in Zion.
All: To you shall vows be performed.
One: O you who answer prayer! To you all flesh shall come.
All: Happy are those whom you choose and bring near to live in your courts.
One: You crown the year with your bounty.
All: The pastures of the wilderness overflow, the hills gird themselves with joy. They shout and sing together for joy.

Pastoral Prayer

O God, we too rarely reflect on our prosperity, and yet on this Thanksgiving Day we offer our humble gratitude for life, community, church, and especially our salvation. Jesus' grace saved us from the wrath to come and for the ministry divinely given us. Bless our church, and create thankful hearts among these guests of Jesus. May we cherish loved ones whom you have given us as the precious gifts that they are. Count us as you do the foreigner [the Samaritan, disciple] who returned to offer you thanks. Say to us as you said to this grateful and healed leper: "Your faith has made you well" (Lk 17:18-19). Thanks be to God. Amen.

Prayer of Confession and Assurance

Dear God, when we think about all of our great treasures that you have provided us, we like the psalmist must confess that "we were like those who dream" (Ps 126:1). Certainly each of us has our own cloaked litany of woes that we make all too public all too often. Yet in our honest moments of integrity, we must confess how good you are to us. In our moments of complaint we forget that you are not only good to us, but you are good to us in constant ways. Help us offer thanks to you for your great bounty and inspire us to share our abundance. We pray this in Jesus' name who taught us the joy of giving.

> One: In the name of Christ, you are forgiven.
> **All: In the name of Christ, you are forgiven. Thanks be to God. Amen.**

Prayer of Dedication of Gifts and Self

On this day of Thanksgiving make us a thankful and grateful people. We know that to give is divine, so help us embrace generosity not only of spirit but also of our resources. Help us remember, O God, that Jesus humbled himself and became obedient for our sake. Therefore, inspire in us an attitude of thankfulness so that we may obediently and generously pour out our gifts for others. And may we make Thanksgiving, like Easter, not just a day but a season. Amen.

Hymn of the Day
God of the Sparrow, God of the Whale

There are a number of hymns appropriate to Thanksgiving Day. Some favorites are Pierpoint's "For the Beauty of the Earth"; Alford's "Come, You Thankful People, Come"; Rinkhart's "Nun Danket Alle Gott." A newer alternative is Jaroslav Vajda's "God of the Sparrow, God of the Whale," set to a tune by Carl Schalk. Through the soft text and gentle melody, we are invited to consider a wide variety of things to be thankful for. The hymn mentions care of the natural world, which the 21st-century church must further encourage.

Children's Time: Giving Thanks

(Bring in a bag of popped popcorn and small paper cups.)
What do you like about popcorn? The way it sounds when it's popping? The smell? The taste? Does anyone know who first discovered how to make popcorn? *(Native Americans.)* *(Give each child a small cup of popcorn to eat.)*

On the first Thanksgiving in 1621 – hundreds of years ago – the Pilgrims enjoyed a treat of popcorn with maple syrup prepared by the Wampanoag Indians. The Pilgrims and the Indians gathered together to celebrate the gift of a good harvest. They feasted on turkey, squash, corn, berries, apples, beans, bread, and popcorn.

Today we celebrate Thanksgiving as a time to give thanks to God for the wonderful friends and foods God has given us. We gather with family and friends, just like the Pilgrims and Indians did hundreds of years ago.

How many of you eat popcorn on Thanksgiving? Who eats Thanksgiving dinner with you? What is your favorite Thanksgiving food? *(Accept answers and share yours.)*

Let's pray together: Dear God, thank you for blessing us with many kinds of loving people and all kinds of tasty foods. Amen.

The Sermon: We All Ought to Be More Thankful
Scripture: Luke 17:11-19

The annual community ecumenical worship service sermon began: "We all ought to be more thankful." The congregation responded with a shrug that seemed to say, "Yes, we should!" After that I don't remember much except "Sure, we ought to be more thankful," but after that affirmation – really, what more is there to say? Perhaps our culture needs to relearn how to be thankful. Thanksgiving is a sign of appreciation and gratitude. Many adults are quick to point out to the younger generation that people ought to be thankful, but honestly, thanksgiving is a difficult attitude to grow and cultivate. We know caring people who know how to say thank you, but gratitude is a difficult attitude to manufacture.

Luke relates a thanksgiving story, because Luke knows that thanksgiving is not inborn, but rather we teach gratitude. (Read Luke 17:11-19.) On the final leg of a journey from Galilee to Jerusalem, Jesus told the disciples how important genuine faith is. Polite society considered lepers outcasts. They were ritually unclean and believed to be contagious. Some thought malevolent spirits possessed lepers. All ten lepers acknowledge Jesus as "Master" and have faith. Lepers in those days needed certification from "the priests" that they were disease-free and thereby restored to worship.

While all ten lepers confess Jesus as Master, only a "Samaritan," a "foreigner," thanks Jesus. God heals all, but only one is wholly "made well" – for the Greek word for healing also bears a notion of rescue. Earlier, Jesus infuriated the synagogue worshipers by recalling the story of Naaman, the leprous foreigner whom Elisha healed. That day, God healed no Israelites; but God did heal a foreigner.

The geographical site of healing is key to understanding this incident. Going to Jerusalem, Jesus and the disciples pass between Samaria and Galilee. Peter recently declared Jesus as Messiah, but the Twelve little suspect Jesus' fate. Clearly, Jesus warned them that he would be killed and raised on the third day. But as the events unfold, even Peter cannot accept what dutifully following Jesus means. Who could have?

Jesus and the disciples came to a village. Then ten lepers call to Jesus from a distance – as towns required lepers to keep a distance so no one would come into contact with uncleanness. Lepers thus were isolated and required to beg for food, because they could not carry on a trade. As if the

155

ravages of the disease were not enough, lepers were in essence quarantined from their family and friends and normal life, unable to return home even for holidays.

A remarkable fact about this leprous assembly was that it included both Jews and Samaritans. Certainly misery loves company. Samaritans and Jews had nothing to do with one another (see: John 4:9). Yet this group, excluded from both sides of the border, roamed together as their disease united them.

Somehow these lepers sensed that Jesus was near. They knew that Jesus was a healer. Maybe they heard how Jesus healed other lepers. They hoped that Jesus could heal them too. If Jesus healed them, then "they got their lives back." So in unison they cried out, "Jesus, Master, have mercy on us."

When Jesus healed other lepers, he actually touched them (Mt 8:2; Mk 1:40), healing those on the spot. Here they didn't want to come too close, but perhaps expected healing then and there. Instead, Jesus told them to go to the temple for examination by the priests and then receive certification because they were healed.

Imagine what was going through their minds, but despite any doubts, they left for Jerusalem, going in the same direction as Jesus and the disciples. Picture their surprise when the healing happened. On their way to Jerusalem and all of a sudden, someone or something healed them. Some no doubt pinched themselves to see if they were dreaming. Perhaps they started running to Jerusalem so that the priests could declare them clean. Only then could the lepers return to their families and life.

But one leper returned to Jesus. It was the Samaritan. When Jesus saw this display of gratitude he asked, "Weren't there ten of you who were cleansed? But only one has returned. Where are the other nine?" Why did God's Jewish people not return and give thanks?

We modern people have good, common-sense reasons to give thanks. If we counted all our blessings we might surprise ourselves. As Americans we enjoy freedoms about which people in some parts of the world can only dream. We enjoy an abundance of material blessings.

Yet we have something else for which to be thankful. Like Samaritans, we were once separated from God's people, and like lepers, we too were unclean in our unrighteousness. But one day, as Jesus was on the way to die on the cross, Jesus stopped at a village on the border between God's people and outsiders. Jesus healed some lepers, and one day Jesus stood on the border that separates us from his glory. When we asked for mercy, Jesus showed it. Jesus healed us of our uncleanness and made us part of Christ's holy church. Only one of the ten lepers whom Jesus cleansed, amazingly enough, came back to give thanks. That thankful one was an outsider, not one of those who had been brought up worshiping the God of Israel.

Jesus paints a story that is all too true. We habitually fail to give credit where credit is due. We are not the authors of our salvation. We are not the creators of our blessings and wealth. Yet only one out of ten of us remembers to give thanks to God who gave us all these things. Often it is not a worshiper of God who gives thanks but an outsider. And Jesus asks, "Was no one found to give praise to God except this foreigner?"

Children can frequently teach us about generosity as a sign of thanksgiving. When I lived in a little town, I took my son to the local drugstore. We adults drank coffee and visited. My three-year-old son got a candy-bar treat, his desire at the time. When the proprietor sat down with us, my three-year-old broke his candy bar in two and offered half to the proprietor. All he could ask was, "Is this some kind of preacher's kid trick?" Yet at that moment my son reminded me that life is best when life is shared. And that includes our belongings and our thankfulness. Children and Jesus' grateful Samaritan leper are mentors for good giving.

– David N. Mosser

Hymns
Opening: For the Fruits of This Creation
Sermon: We Gather Together (to Ask the Lord's Blessing)
Closing: What Gift Can We Bring?

November 30, 2014

1st Sunday of Advent

Lessons

Revised Common Lectionary (RCL)	Roman Catholic (RC)
Isa 64:1-9	Isa 63:16b-17, 19b; 64:2-7
Ps 80:1-7, 17-19	Ps 80:2-3, 15-16, 18-19
1 Cor 1:3-9	1 Cor 1:3-9
Mk 13:24-37	Mk 13:33-37

Speaker's Introduction for the Lessons

Lesson 1

Isaiah 64:1-9 (RCL)

Have you ever longed for God to act to deliver you from misery? Speaking for God's people, the prophet Isaiah reveals that spirit of longing.

Isaiah 63:16b-17, 19b; 64:2-7 (RC)

These passages describe the anguish of feeling separated from God and unworthy of God's presence. It also hints at the desire for restoration, though the pathway home is far from clear.

Lesson 2

Psalm 80:1-7, 17-19 (RCL); Psalm 80:2-3, 15-16, 18-19 (RC)

In this sorrowful prayer, the faithful earnestly request that God grant them relief from their circumstances.

Lesson 3

1 Corinthians 1:3-9 (RCL/RC)

This is the introduction to Paul's letter to the church at Corinth, and Paul is speaking encouraging words to a church that is troubled. Listen for the encouragement.

Gospel
Mark 13:24-37 (RCL); Mark 13:33-37 (RC)

Advent prepares us to celebrate Jesus' coming to earth as an infant. Jesus' words from Mark's Gospel serve to prepare his disciples for his second coming. Whenever we await his coming, we prepare the same: "Keep awake!"

Theme
Keeping alert doesn't mean sitting around. Serve others. Serve Christ.

Thought for the Day
We don't know when the Master will return, so we ought to work hard to keep God's world in order.

Sermon Summary
Mark 13 is called the "Little Apocalypse" but there's nothing little about it. This isn't just earth-shaking. It's cosmic! Keeping alert doesn't mean doing nothing but wait for Jesus to come in glory. The parable of master and servants makes it clear that until he returns we've got work to do!

Call to Worship
Come, people of God! Wipe the slate clean. Advent begins! This is a time for praise and prayer! This is a time for song and celebration! Our long time of waiting is past – God's promises are renewed! As we anticipate the birth of the Christ child, let us prepare as well for the day when all shall recognize that Jesus reigns, and will reign forevermore!

Pastoral Prayer
God of all good things, in this season of harvest you have called us to manage this world for more than just our benefit. We give you thanks that you have trusted us with the responsibility to have a part in the renewal and restoration of your good earth. We accept our responsibility for every living creature with humility, gratitude, and thanksgiving. What comes from the earth belongs to all the people of the earth. We will share your bounty with all. We will treat our fellow creatures with respect. We will

recognize you in all our comings and our goings. Bless us, bless all of creation. Amen.

Prayer of Confession and Assurance

One: Hear us, O Gentle Shepherd, you who lead us like a flock. You who are enthroned among the angels, shine forth before all the tribes of humanity. Stir up your might, and come to save us!

All: Restore us, O God; let your face shine, that we may be saved. O God of hosts, how long will you be angry with our prayers? You have fed us with the bread of tears, and given them tears to drink in full measure.

One: But let your hand be upon us, then we will never turn back from you; give us life, call on our name.

All: Restore us, O God of hosts; let your face shine, that we may be saved.

One: Hear these words of assurance: The God of hosts will restore us. God's face shines upon us. We are saved.

Prayer of Dedication of Gifts and Self

Now at the turning of the season, here in this house of praise and prayer, with our sisters and our brothers, sharing with each other and the world, we come before you, grateful at this opportunity to give and receive, intent upon sharing all good things with the world, in your name, as your people, God of light and love. Bless us as we bless others. All glory and honor be yours. Amen.

Hymn of the Day
As a Fire Is Meant for Burning

The Isaiah passage is part of a longer prayer for help and mercy. In it we experience the historic belief of God being distant or removed from us. The text of this remarkable hymn put the relationship straight. It describes who we are and what our relationship is to God. We are intended to be on a mission – learning, teaching, and seeking oneness with each other and with God. It is a strong hymn of discipleship and witness. The most common tune paired to this text is BEACH SPRING, a wonderful, singable melody attributed to B. F. White. In *Voices United*, you will find the text paired to JOYOUS LIGHT by Marty Haugen. This tune gives a whole different support to the text. It is more energetic and aggressive, a total contrast to BEACH SPRING. Both tunes support the text, giving a choice of mood and message.

Children's Time: What Is Advent?

(Bring a large calendar, a red marker, and 10-inch lengths of blue yarn.)
Today is the last day of November. What month comes after November? *(Open your calendar to December and circle December 25.)* What do we celebrate on December 25? Yes, Christmas. But before Christmas comes, we have to get ready for Jesus' birthday. This time of getting ready is called Advent. Advent means coming. During Advent we get ready for Jesus' coming. How many Sundays, counting today, do we have before Christmas comes? We have four Sundays in Advent." *(Point these out on your calendar.)*

Today is the first Sunday in Advent. What changes do you see in the sanctuary? Invite the children to join you around the Advent wreath. "How many candles do you see? The four blue (purple, pink) candles in the wreath remind us of the four Sundays in Advent. How many candles are burning? This burning candle tells us that today is the first Sunday in Advent. How many candles will be burning next Sunday? When do you think we light the white candle in the center of the wreath? We light it on Christmas Day to show that Jesus' birthday has come.

Take the children to the altar and the pulpit to examine the paraments. What color are they? For all four Sundays in Advent, the church will be dressed in blue (purple). Give the children a piece of blue yarn to tie onto their backpacks as a reminder that Advent is a time to prepare for Jesus' birth.

The Sermon: Get Busy!
Scripture: Mark 13:24-37

Julian of Norwich (1342–1416) was probably the first woman to write a book in English. She lived in a little cell attached to the side of the church of St. Julian in the village of Norwich in England. There was a small window through which she watched and listened to church services. And on

May 8 in the year 1373 she became gravely ill. Certain she was going to die, she called on clergy to visit her.

When the cross was placed before her eyes, she had a series of vivid visions, which she wrote about after she survived her illness. Julian's book, *Revelations of Divine Love*, has become a classic of Christian spirituality.

During her years in isolation, Julian heard many scriptures read, including, no doubt, the words Jesus spoke in today's Gospel passage, where he warned his disciples to remain alert, because the day of the Lord "is like a man going on a journey, when he leaves home and puts his slaves in charge, each with his work, and commands the doorkeeper to be on the watch" (13:34).

Julian also saw a vision of Jesus as the master and his followers as servants. She wrote:

Mine understanding was lifted up into Heaven where I saw our Lord as a lord in his own house, which hath called all his dearworthy servants and friends to a stately feast. Then I saw the Lord take no place in His own house, but I saw Him royally reign in His house, fulfilling it with joy and mirth, Himself endlessly to gladden and to solace His dearworthy friends, full homely and full courteously, with marvelous melody of endless love, in His own fair blessed Countenance.

Julian understood Jesus to be the master who would return, but for her there was nothing fearsome, nothing to be dreaded about the Lord Jesus, whether met in scripture, vision, or face to face. One might feel awe, but here was a master who would do his best to treat his servants with love and gentleness.

In recent times, endless novels, movies, and biblical commentaries have appeared explaining just how, where, and when the events of the end time are to take place. This has bred not only fascination, but also a good deal of fear and trembling. Indeed, it seems the whole point to frighten believers and nonbelievers alike.

Maybe in our era of social media, 24/7 news chatter, and endless distractions, it takes a good deal of bells, whistles, and even a sense of threat to get our attention.

But for most suffering and struggling people through the centuries, the idea of God's re-entrance into history invited patience, hope, endurance, and joy. Whether here in Mark 13 or in Revelation, Daniel, Zechariah, or in the many popular works devoured by believers in the first few Christian centuries, the essential message of apocalyptic literature was a call to endurance. Hold on! Because, though great things are promised and great things will happen, we who are servants ought in the meantime to keep busy doing the work of master, Jesus, who set an example in leadership by serving.

Mark 13 is sometimes called the "Little Apocalypse," but there's nothing little about it. This isn't just earth-shaking. It's cosmic! Sun and moon darkened, stars falling from the sky, Jesus revealed in glory, angels sweeping across the earth to gather the faithful together. This is quite a picture that Jesus paints.

No wonder he tells the disciples to keep alert for these events. But keeping alert doesn't mean doing nothing but wait for Jesus to come in glory. And the best example we have for the quality of self-sacrificing service expected of servants comes from the Master. How do we see him act in the New Testament? Jesus desires to go off by himself to pray, but the sight of hungry people – hungry for God's word, hungry for daily bread – moves him to a deep compassion. When others try to "protect" him from people on the margins who threaten to waste his time – the blind, the suffering, women, the children – he speaks, heals, and gathers together. And at the final supper with his disciples he removes his outer garments, takes up a towel and a basin, and washes the feet of his disciples, a menial task reserved for slaves.

Nowhere is this idea of sacrificial service seen more clearly, of course, than in the cross. Nor was this some idea that came out of the blue and that people were totally unprepared for. The study of the literature, both in scripture and beyond, surrounding the era before Jesus makes it clearer that the coming Messiah would not be a conquering commander but a suffering servant.

Take, for instance, the stone tablet, about three feet tall, on which is written in Hebrew letters a passage now known as "Gabriel's Revelation." It is dated roughly around the time of Jesus. Intriguingly, despite many frustrating gaps, it seems to tell the story of a Messiah, Ephraim, the son of Joseph, who will redeem the people through suffering, death, and resurrection. As translated by Israel Knohl, professor of Bible at the Hebrew University of Jerusalem, Gabriel addresses the Messiah, who has died, with these words: "In three days, live, I Gabriel com[mand] yo[u]." (To read more about the Gabriel stone, see "The Messiah Son of Joseph: 'Gabriel's Revelation' and the Birth of a New Messianic Model," by Israel Knohl, *Biblical Archaeological Review*, September/October 2008, pp. 58-62.)

Seen in this light, we have a different picture of what it means to be the ruler, and what joy awaits those who might consider themselves the ruled. During this Advent season, as we wait once more for the coming of the newborn king who we celebrate with carols, gift giving, and family feasts, we might also consider ways we can follow the sacrificial example of that Christ for whom we wait. We might set aside time to visit nursing homes. We might redouble our efforts to support our local food pantry, do more hospital visiting, reaching out to the marginalized in our society.

Perhaps Julian of Norwich was on to something with her vision of what Jesus the ruler is like: Jesus is one who desires the well-being and joy of those who serve. So remain alert, as Jesus says, for those opportunities to serve in that holy name. The parable of master and servants makes it clear that until he returns we've got work to do!

– Frank Ramirez

Hymns
Opening: Let All Mortal Flesh Keep Silence (Liturgy of St. James)
Sermon: Will You Let Me Be Your Servant?
Closing: I See a New World Coming

December 7, 2014

2nd Sunday of Advent

Lessons

Revised Common Lectionary (RCL)	Roman Catholic (RC)
Isa 40:1-11	Isa 40:1-5, 9-11
Ps 85:1-2, 8-13	Ps 85:9-14
2 Pet 3:8-15a	2 Pet 3:8-14
Mk 1:1-8	Mk 1:1-8

Speaker's Introduction for the Lessons
Isaiah 40:1-11(RCL); Isaiah 40:1-5, 9-11 (RC)

Four voices—the Lord, two messengers, and the prophet—bring good news to God's people who have been living in captivity for too long.

Lesson 2
Psalm 85:1-2, 8-13 (RCL); Psalm 85:9-14 (RC)

The past saving actions of God become the basis upon which this lament anticipates God speaking (and acting) again in saving ways, here embodied in the images of a kiss and a fruitful land.

Lesson 3
2 Peter 3:8-15a (RCL); 2 Peter 3:8-14 (RC)

Peter's readers have been influenced by those who scoff at the Lord's return. He is defending God's patience and exhorting his flock to practice being patient themselves and to live moral lives.

Gospel
Mark 1:1-8 (RCL/RC)

All who prepare to find God's comfort in the manger, including you and me, must travel through the desert where John is preaching his message of repentance.

Theme

The time is up! Live the good news!

Thought for the Day

Brace yourself; there is far to go. Calm yourself; we're already there!

Sermon Summary

We are still growing in "the beginning of the good news." God's story is already underway and it is going to end well. Though the Season of Advent is demanding, take a deep breath, and continue to grow in the season's good news about Jesus.

Call to Worship (based on Isaiah 40:1-11 and Mark 1:2-3)

> One: Receive God's comfort, people of God! Speak tenderly to each other – remember, it is time for the good news of Jesus Christ to be made real in our lives.
>
> **All: Let's prepare a way for God through the wilderness of clutter, distractions, demands, and obligations, a straight way through the desert of buying and selling and guessing what will be good enough.**
>
> One: Let us prepare a heavenly highway for our God and for God's people!
>
> **All: One is coming who is wonderful and powerful and present and peaceful! Emmanuel, Jesus, Savior, Infant!**

Pastoral Prayer

All praise, glory, and honor is yours, God of this season, God of all seasons, Emmanuel, God with us. Yet in this harried time we find it hard to sense your presence in our midst, not because you are not there, but perhaps because we have allowed ourselves to be consumed by all we have done and all that remains to be done. Still our hearts, that we may hear you. Calm our spirits, so we may feel your presence. Bless us today in worship, so we may know you perfectly, and perfectly love you. Amen.

Prayer of Confession and Assurance

Patient and eternal God, to whom a day is like a thousand years, and a thousand years like unto a day, bear with us a little longer, receive our confession, and forgive us our sins. For you are not slow about your promises. Though all things are to be dissolved, you are ready to burst into your creation and restore all righteousness, revealing a new heaven and a new earth. Let us wait for your coming day with joy and anticipation, ever more ready to be about your work, feeding the hungry, healing the sick, visiting those who are abandoned by society, sharing the good news of Jesus. Let our best will and your perfect will unite in your service and love. Amen.

Words of Assurance

It is not God's will that any should perish. Be transformed, living lives of holiness and godliness.

Prayer of Dedication of Gifts and Self

Giver of all good things, source of all that is seen and unseen, everlasting God, receive our earnest gifts, given in love, as tokens of our desire to become your emissaries of peace and wholeness in this troubled world. May these gifts, magnified beyond their material measure, witness to your perfect will that all people and all creation be reconciled, so that truly your will shall be done on earth as it is in heaven. As we have received, so we give. Amen.

Hymn of the Day
People, Look East

This Advent text was written by Eleanor Farjeon, who also wrote the popular "Morning Has Broken." One of the subtitles for this text is "Carol for Advent" as it is often sung one stanza for each Sunday in Advent. We look forward, with eagerness, to the coming of Jesus. The concluding line of each stanza gives yet another name for him: Guest, Rose, Star, and Lord. Use this delightful carol as a response for lighting the Advent wreath or as a call to worship. The traditional French tune, BESCANÇON, supplies a joyous and moving partnership to the text. Sing with lightness and energy. Try singing this carol without accompaniment.

Children's Time: Decorating the Christmas Tree

(Bring a small, green artificial pine tree or a real potted pine and a string of Christmas lights. Bring a jingle bell with a loop of blue ribbon tied through the top for each child.)
How many candles are burning on the Advent wreath? Today is the second Sunday in Advent. And we're going to talk about ways we can get ready for Jesus' birthday.

What kind of tree is this? What is special about an evergreen's leaves? They stay green all year long. Many people decorate their homes and churches with evergreens to get ready for Jesus' birthday. *(If you have greens around your Advent wreath and other greenery decorating your sanctuary, ask the children to look for these.)* The green needles of the evergreen remind us that God loves us all of the time – in the winter and in the summer. Do you put up a Christmas tree in your home? Where do you put it? What kinds of decorations do you put on it? Let's decorate our tree with lights. *(Add the lights and plug them in.)* Don't they look beautiful? There's a story about a man named Martin Luther. He was walking home one cold winter evening. He looked through the branches of a tall pine tree and saw the stars twinkling. He wanted to capture those twinkling stars to put on his Christmas tree. Instead he placed tiny candles all over the tree. Today we decorate with little lights instead.

Give each child a jingle bell decoration to hang at home to decorate for Christmas. It's one way we can get ready for Jesus' birthday. Close by giving thanks for God's constant love.

The Sermon: The Beginning of the Good News
Scripture: Mark 1:1-8

In the late third century AD, when Christianity was still illegal, and sometimes actively persecuted, there lived a Christian named Sotas near an Egyptian town called Oxyrhynchus (oxy–RINK–us), the city of the sharp-nosed fish. We do not know as much about Sotas as we would like, except that he was considered a holy man, a church leader, and was highly respected.

Surviving the centuries has been a small number of letters to and from Sotas, written on papyrus, and preserved because the Egyptian desert can be very, very dry. One of these is a letter of recommendation written to a fellow Christian named Paul. Such a letter was necessary for travelers, to assure those who received them that they were true Christians, and not spies. Here is the letter:

Greetings in the Lord, beloved brother Paul. I, Sotas, greet you.

Our brothers and sisters Herona, Heriona, Philadelphos, Pekusin, and Naarous, catechumens of the gathered, and Leona, catechumen in "the beginning of the gospel," are to be welcomed as is fitting. They will greet your fellowship in the name of our fellowship.

I pray for your health in the Lord, beloved brother (tr. by the author).

The letter mentions catechumens, who were members of the community still learning about the Christian faith before they were baptized and became full members. Several of these people are called "catechumens of the gathered," which may mean they are learning the fundamentals of what it means to be a church. One woman, Leona, is a catechumen in "the beginning of the gospel," which you probably realize is a phrase taken right out of today's scripture lesson from the Gospel of Mark.

What does this mean? No one is sure, but perhaps Leona was doing what we all ought to do – learning about the good news of Jesus Christ from the beginning, especially during this time of Advent, when the church calendar is wiped clear and we start all over!

Mark does not tell us a story about the birth of Jesus like Matthew or Luke, or take us back to the deeps of time like John (In the beginning was the Word…). Instead the evangelist wrenches us loose from our moorings and drags us back and forth across the loom of time in the space of a few words!

Mark bursts into the gospel story with the main characters either onstage or ready to make their first entrance. "The beginning of the good news of Jesus Christ, the Son of God" (1:1). Before we can get our bearings, Mark rushes us backward hundreds of years to the time of the prophet Isaiah, who spoke the truth to kings while the kingdoms of the north and south were crumbling. He then rushes us decades forward, past the exile in Babylon, to the time when the children's children of those carted away witnessed God's promises coming true with the return of the exiles to the promised land! "In the wilderness prepare the way of the Lord, make straight in the desert a highway for our God" (Isa 40:3).

Whew! Are you out of breath? Well, hold on! Because now Mark rushes us back to his present and there is John the Baptist citing same words from Isaiah as they come true again: "Prepare the way of the Lord, make his paths straight" (Mk 1:2-3).

And don't get too comfortable, because John points us forward in time again – to the one who will enter in a few short verses – Jesus, the Savior, the good news come to life! What a huge canvas that Mark paints with his words, ancient prophet pointing to God's glorious plan, kingdoms falling and rising, exiles returning in joy, the centuries-old words remembered, and refilled with new meaning as another prophet who again points to God's glorious plan, this time coming to life in one person!

I wonder if Leona, 1700 years ago, was filled with the same breathless wonder that we ought to feel when confronted with this grand picture. But we are not supposed to simply gawk. We too ought to listen and learn! Hear John "proclaiming a baptism of repentance for the forgiveness of sins" (Mk 1:4), and proclaiming that one is coming after him that is even greater – who is, of course, Jesus.

I am reminded of a story from the American Civil War. In 1861, Wilmer McLean moved away from his Virginia farm after a Union cannonball tore through his summer kitchen during the first major conflict of the Civil War, the Battle of Bull Run. He moved to small town known as Appomattox Court House, where around four years later, in his living room, General Lee surrendered to General Grant. He could truly say, "The war began in my front yard and ended in my front parlor."

In the same way, this gospel moment contains the past, present, and future – our past, present, and future, because each one of us ought to draw a fat arrow on this canvas and write above it the words, "You Are Here!"

This is what time looks like. With the arrival of Jesus a new era has begun. It is one in which the real ruler is going to be revealed, whose realm at least partially apparent, but also on the way. God's realm is near physically, and it is also on the way. It is fully present, yet not fully realized. In Mark's Gospel, the realm of Jesus is not an either-or proposition. It's not a question of whether it exists now or in the future. The answer is both. We are citizens of that kingdom and live in it now. But it will become apparent to all, and the authority of Jesus will become unquestioned, in God's own time.

What does this mean? It means the same for us as it did for Leona all those centuries ago. We are living in the past, the present, and the future, and most of all, we are living the gospel. Leona was still learning her gospel, but she was part of the good news, traveling with other Christians, and trusted enough to be sent and to be received as an emissary. Though we are still growing in "the beginning of the good news," God's story is already underway and it is going to end well. Though the Season of Advent is demanding, let us all take a deep breath, and continue to grow in God's good news about Jesus.

– Frank Ramirez

(Want to know more? Read *Greetings in the Lord: Early Christians and the Oxyrhynchus Papyri*, by AnneMarie Luijendijk or "Scattered Leaves: Letters from Acculturated Christians," by Frank Ramirez, *Brethren Life and Thought* vol.43, nos. 1&2, 1998, pp. 59-112, esp. 96-97.)

Hymns
Opening: Comfort, Comfort, O My People
Sermon: Come, Thou Long Expected Jesus
Closing: On Jordan's Bank the Baptist's Cry

December 14, 2014

3rd Sunday of Advent

Lessons

Revised Common Lectionary (RCL)	Roman Catholic (RC)
Isa 61:1-4, 8-11	Isa 61:1-2a, 10-11
Ps 126 or Lk 1:47-55	Lk 1:46-50, 53-54
1 Thess 5:16-24	1 Thess 5:16-24
Jn 1:6-8, 19-28	Jn 1:6-8, 19-28

Speaker's Introduction for the Lessons

Lesson 1

Isaiah 61:1-4, 8-11 (RCL); Isaiah 61:1-2a, 10-11 (RC)

Today we open our Bibles to the same spot Jesus turned to in the Isaiah scroll when he spoke before his home congregation, and the question we answer is the same then as now. What does the Lord require of you?

Lesson 2

Psalm 126 (RCL)

Thanksgiving for restoration of dreams and hopes moves to prayer for the reversing of tears and weeping then toward joy and the sowing of new possibilities.

Luke 1:46-50, 53-54 (RC); Luke 1:47-55 (RCL)

This is the bold witness of Mary to the God who looks with favor upon her and brings stunning reversals to the conventional wisdom and ways of this world.

Lesson 3

1 Thessalonians 5:16-24 (RCL/RC)

Get your pencils out. The apostle Paul has a list of instructions more important than our holiday to-do lists. There will be no need for returns after Christmas on any of these items.

Gospel
John 1:6-8, 19-28 (RCL/RC)
Heed the words of John the Baptist, the one who brings us the good news of our coming Savior. Listen.

Theme
We are messengers, not the message.

Thought for the Day
Much can be gleaned by comparing the various Gospel accounts to one another and asking ourselves, "What is 'missing' from this one – and why?"

Sermon Summary
Despite its name, the Year of Mark draws most of its Gospel readings from elsewhere. What was so compelling about these other views to prompt such a decision? In the case of John the Baptist, perhaps it lies in the boldness with which he embraced his role.

Call to Worship
One: The Lord has done great things!
All: Our mouths are filled with laughter and praise!
One: The Lord has done great things!
All: That which is dry and parched is watered anew; that which is wasted and barren springs forth with new life!
One: The Lord has done great things!
All: Tears of sorrow are replaced by shouts of joy!
One: The Lord has done great things!
All: The Lord has done great things!

Pastoral Prayer
We pray to you, O holy and ever-loving God, thankful for your compassion and justice. You have spoken to all people through your prophets, you have made your promises known throughout time and space. Help

us to hear your words on this day and on those to come; help us to take your call to heart and live it out in our daily lives. Deepen our faith and empower us to be your disciples in a world aching for your word. Amen.

Prayer of Confession and Assurance

We live in a world that aches to know your peace, O God, a world that pits person against person and people against planet. All too often, selfish desire is lifted above the common good. In spite of our best efforts – or perhaps because of them – we need your gentle love and guidance. Help us to be the people we long to become, help us to live in kindness and grace. Despite our failings, we are still capable of being made to reflect your love: help us to do so. We pray this, trusting in your most holy and good name. Amen.

Prayer of Dedication of Gifts and Self

O Source of all, we give you thanks for the many gifts and blessings with which you have entrusted us. We give you thanks, Creator of Life, for the many ways in which you have strengthened us to be workers in the vineyard of your creation. We give you thanks, Bringer of Peace, for the order and balance you have brought to the universe. Grant us direction and purpose, that we may live lives dedicated to your way and your will. Amen.

Hymn of the Day
Come, Thou (O) Long-Expected Jesus

The most loved Advent hymn is a prayer for Christ to come and dwell within us. It is also the answer to the Isaiah prophecy of deliverance. The text by Charles Wesley first appeared in *Hymns for the Nativity of Our Lord* (1744). Originally intended as a Christmas hymn, it makes a very useful inclusion in a Festival of Lessons and Carols. There are two tunes associated with this text, STUTTGART from *Psalmodia Sacra* (1715) and HYFRYDOL by Rowland H. Prichard. The former allows for four stanzas of four lines each and is more energetic and slightly martial. The latter has two stanzas of eight lines each and it more gentle and lyrical in nature. Both are good matches, allowing for different nuances in the text to be brought forth.

Children's Time: Spreading Christmas Cheer

(Bring the Christmas tree and lights from December 7, religious Christmas cards, and small ornaments.)
How many lights are burning on the Advent wreath? This is the third Sunday in Advent. We only have one more Sunday left before it's Christmas. Do you have a Christmas tree in your home? Have you decorated it yet? *(Plug in the lights.)* Something is missing from our tree. What do we need? Let each child add a small ornament to the tree.

Give each child a Christmas card. Tell me what you see on your Christmas card. Accept the children's responses and use their responses to point out the holy family: Jesus, Jesus' mother, Mary, and Joseph, Jesus' father on earth who cared for him. Encourage each child to give a brief description of the card.

Does anyone have an angel? Angels had an important job to do. An angel first told Mary that she would have a very special baby, God's son, Jesus. It was an angel who visited Joseph in a dream, telling Joseph about this special baby that would be born to Mary. And angels announced Jesus' birth to the shepherds. We can get ready for Christmas is by retelling the Christmas story. And a fun way to do this is by giving Christmas cards to others, cards that tell others about the first Christmas.

Close by singing a favorite children's Christmas carol such as "Away in a Manger." Point out that this is another way to retell the joyful Christmas story.

The Sermon: The Morning Sonshine
Scripture: John 1:6-8, 19-28

Readings like today's Gospel seem odd to me: if we're in the Year of Mark, why are we spending time with John? We're only three weeks into the new liturgical calendar, yet we're already drifting from the year's namesake – and will do so again next week. Looking ahead is even more striking: not a single Year B Christmas reading involves Mark, and Epiphany will veer away on three of this year's nine readings.

The seasons that follow are similarly light on Mark – a quick inventory of the readings at lectionary.library.vanderbilt.edu indicates that 57 percent (!) of the Revised Common Lectionary's Gospel readings come from outside Mark this year. Why? Most of us pay these Gospel tangents

175

little notice: over the years, the pattern "just is," and there's little time spent asking the reasons for it. But it's a valid question: "Why? Why not stick with Mark if this is supposed to be the year we hear his voice?" Or, to ask it from the other perspective: "What is so important about the way John presents this story that we should use it this week – what is he telling us that Mark didn't?"

It's no great insight to point out that John's voice is unique amongst the canonical Gospels; his language, point of view, and general literary structure tell us the story of Jesus of Nazareth in a different way than his biblical peers. Perhaps this is why we have "years" only for Matthew, Mark, and Luke in the RCL in the first place: John's vision of the Christ event doesn't "fit" with the others in a convenient enough manner. Still, John shows up frequently across each of the three years of the lectionary – especially during feast days or similar festivals – so his voice is clearly still being heard. What about it needed to be heard today?

The Isaiah reference, which John the Baptist quotes, is common to all four accounts of his arrival. Clearly, the association between the two was considered worth remembering by the early church. That said, though, there is an element to its use that is unique to John. The Synoptics use the Isaiah quote – whatever form of it they employ – to introduce John the Baptist to the hearer/ or reader. From their context it is unlikely that the words are actually spoken by John the Baptist as opposed to being written about him. In John's account, though, John the Baptist clearly makes this scriptural connection himself when he says, "I am the voice of one crying out in the wilderness ..." More interestingly, he says this in response to the direct question: "Who are you?" It is, in effect, how he defines himself. Much has been written about the role of John the Baptist in the early Christian church: the deliberate need to remind people that he was not the Messiah, to remove all doubt as to the centrality of Jesus. Little would be served to rehash all of that here. But along those lines, note the specific way John the Baptist refers to himself in this usage: not as "one crying out in the wilderness" but "the voice" of one crying out in the wilderness." It's an interesting image, one that clearly fits with the message he brings to his hearers.

As "the voice," John the Baptist is merely an instrument, a tool to be used by another. One's voice may be useful in getting a message across, but it does not originate that message, it does not control it. And yet, at the same time, one's voice can be used to shape that message and affect how it is received by the hearer.

Recently, my wife and I purchased our first house in a suburb of Seattle. It's nothing fancy, but it suits our needs and those of our young family quite well. Like an increasing number of people, one of our neighbors down the road keeps a small roost of chickens. The fresh eggs and clucking of the hens are a delight to the kids in the neighborhood. Unlike many others, though, these neighbors also keep a rooster on their property. And I'm not a morning person.

At daybreak, without fail – and earlier than I would prefer – I hear the sounds of that bird as it heralds the coming of the sun. "Cock-a-doodle-doo!" he cries. "It's a new day. Rise and shine!" Try though I might, I cannot ignore him. So, like clockwork, I begrudgingly give in to the local timekeeper and drag myself out of bed.

In a strange sense, John the Baptist is like that rooster. The sun/Son is not his to command, the light is not his to bestow, but he is compelled by his very nature to point out its existence to the rest of the world. "It's here!" he calls. "You have to take a look at this yourself. Don't miss it!" Like the prophet, that silly bird "himself [is] not the light, but came to testify to the light." I can only imagine that to some in his audience, John the Baptist was every bit as unwelcomed an intrusion as that bird. Why else would people have been so keen to determine his origin except to decide whether or not he was worth listening to? And, again like that rooster, I can only imagine the thoughts some of his hearers had as to what should be done with him.

But here's the kicker: I am actually starting to like the ritual of the rooster's call. While I cannot claim to be any more of a morning person, there is something compelling about the passion with which he cries, "Look! Look! Something important is coming!" I find myself smiling at his voice and happy for the message he brings. Like John the Baptist, despite my best efforts, he's made me see the light – in more ways than one. Amen.

– Chris Ode

Hymns
Opening: Come All You People/*Uyaimose*
Sermon: Christ, Be Our Light
Closing: Hark! A Thrilling Voice Is Sounding!

177

December 21, 2014

4th Sunday of Advent

Lessons

Revised Common Lectionary (RCL)	Roman Catholic (RC)
2 Sam 7:1-11, 16	2 Sam 7:1-5, 8b-12, 14a, 16
Lk 1:47-55 or Ps 89:1-4, 19-26	Ps 89:2-5, 27, 29
Rom 16:25-27	Rom 16:25-27
Lk 1:26-38	Lk 1:26-38

Speaker's Introduction for the Lessons

Lesson 1

2 Samuel 7:1-11, 16 (RCL); 2 Samuel 7:1-5, 8b-12, 14a, 16 (RC)

Reading on this Sunday, God's promise to give David a dynasty, we immediately think of Jesus, born in "David's town" of Bethlehem. The image of David the shepherd king reminds us that Jesus, too, will redefine what it means to be a leader.

Lesson 2

Luke 1:47-55 (RCL)

The Magnificat of Mary follows the Gospel passage of annunciation. In her song of praise to her cousin Elizabeth, Mary celebrates the world-changing implications of Gabriel's message.

Psalm 89:2-5, 27, 29 (RC); Psalm 89:1-4, 19-26 (RCL)

This psalm celebrates the Davidic covenant. The declaration of God's steadfast love and faithfulness, along with the promises of an heir and eternal line, lift Messianic themes associated with this season.

Lesson 3

Romans 16:25-27 (RCL/RC)

These final verses from Paul's letter to the Romans offer a simple benediction and yet, woven within is a brief history of God's relationship with humankind, reminding us that the life of Jesus is a part of God's overall plan.

Gospel

Luke 1:26-38 (RCL/RC)

Mary is probably about the age of 12 or 13 when visited by an angel. Gabriel's announcement changes not only Mary's life, but also the whole world.

Theme

We are called to live a life of active faith.

Thought for the Day

There is joy and burden in being called by God, but it is always a blessing.

Sermon Summary

Traditional images of Mary are meaningful for many, but they frequently overlook how vulnerable she must have felt at the annunciation. We can learn a great deal from her example – not only in her willingness to follow God's call – but also in her likely fears and doubts.

Call to Worship

(inspired by Psalm 89)

One: I will sing of your steadfast love, O Lord, forever!
All: You have promised to bless the generations!
One: Let the heavens praise your wonders, O Lord!
All: You rule the world with strength and justice!
One: O Lord, none shall ever surpass you!
All: You guide us in your ways and teach us your law!
One: I will sing of your steadfast love, O Lord, forever!
All: Blessed be the Lord! Amen!

Pastoral Prayer

Most gracious, good, and loving God, we praise you for your gentle kindness and mercy. We thank you for your blessed Son, God made flesh among us. As you sent words of comfort and commission to Mary, may you do so to us: steadying us in our walk as your disciples on earth, empowering us to carry forth your message of peace and justice into the world. We pray this, trusting in your most holy name. Amen.

Prayer of Confession and Assurance

O God, help us to look to you for direction in our lives. Too often we chase after idols and distractions instead of holding to the example of our sister, Mary: service and devotion even in the face of uncertainty and fear. We long to entrust our lives to you, and yet we struggle to do so, falling short time and time again despite our best intentions. Help us to rise up when we stumble, trusting in your mercy and promise of redeeming love. We pray this thankfully, knowing that you hear and forgive us, and that we are blessedly cherished by you. Amen.

Prayer of Dedication of Gifts and Self

You are the source of all, most wondrous God, and to you belongs everything that we dare to claim as our own. All that we have is truly yours. We praise you for your generous blessings and the opportunity to use them toward the betterment of this world. Guide us in our daily lives as we strive to live in ways which honor the potential you have placed within us. We pray this, trusting in you and your desire to guide us in ways of compassion and generosity. Amen.

Hymn of the Day
Gloria, Gloria

This short response is one of the better known pieces from the community of Taizé. The text is traditional with music composed by Jacques Berthier. While it may be easiest to sing in English, encourage your congregation to sing the original Latin. It is a well-known Christmas text and sings with better word stress. It is a canon. Once you have taught it to the people, help them to sing it as a round. Placing members of your choir within the congregation will help this process. Sing it as a processional, a response to the reading, a response to prayer, or a concluding benediction. Sing it with energy and great conviction.

Children's Time: Giving Gifts

(Bring the decorated Christmas tree and lights from December 7 and 14. Bring several small, wrapped gifts to place under the tree. Bring a box that has lots of little Christmas cookies to share too. Wrap a crèche scene to be opened on Christmas.)
How many lights are burning on the Advent wreath? This is the fourth Sunday in Advent. Christmas will be here very soon. Do you notice anything new about our little Christmas tree? Yes, we have gifts under the tree. What do you want for Christmas? Do you have gifts for your family and friends? What will you give them? I have a gift for each one of you. *(Give each child a Christmas cookie.)* Making Christmas cookies is one way we can get ready for Christmas. Making Christmas cookies and giving them as gifts is another way to get ready for Christmas. Why do you think we give each other gifts? We give gifts on Christmas to remind us of God's greatest gift to the world – God's Son, Jesus.

Close by singing a favorite Christmas carol.

Let's pray together: Dear God, thank you for helping us wait for your son, Jesus, as a baby. Jesus is the best gift of all. Amen.

The Sermon: A Joyful Burden
Scripture: Luke 1:26-38

When I was a kid, Christmas seemed so much simpler. Every year the youth group would go out caroling – heading out to visit older members of the congregation and local nursing homes before returning to the church for cocoa and cookies. My mother, a church secretary, would jot down her gift plans on a notepad, then leave it out on the kitchen counter where we kids would inevitably find it (our seeming victory rendered moot by her judicious use of shorthand).

Christmas Eve would be the candlelight service and, if I was lucky, I would get to help turn out the lights. The bulk of my extended family is quite close – both emotionally and geographically – so we'd gather for Christmas dinner and the exchange of presents. There were songs to be sung – in Swedish as well as English – and mountains of various tasty treats. When I turned 18 it was time to try the lutefisk and pickled herring, both less offensive than I feared, but less enjoyable than I'd been promised.

But, as I grew into adulthood, Christmas morphed. While I generally do my best to avoid the high "holy" shopping days, I'll never forget the years spent working retail – especially when it was at a bookstore amidst Harry Potter and Lord of the Rings fever! And even now, as a pastor I cannot help but associate the season with preparations for extra services and all that that entails. Additionally, the secular world creeps in with its constant advertisements – which appear earlier every year – and general crass commercialism. There are financial pressures, personal commitments, worship responsibilities, travel demands, decorations to hang, a house to clean. Sometimes I find myself wishing the season would just be over before it has even begun!

But I think that that blending of Christmas joy and burden began well before I ever experienced it.

Imagine what it must have been like for Mary. Picture spring in ancient Israel. The wildflowers are beginning to bloom since the "rainy season" (with its scant four to five inches of precipitation) has come and gone. A pot bubbles over a cooking fire while a young woman goes about her evening chores, humming a song to herself as she ponders her recent engagement and the adventures to come. Without warning, a light appears. We always associate a light with the appearance of the divine, don't we? But what kind? A flash? A dull, sustained glow? The raw glory of the Almighty illuminating from an angelic messenger? What sounds would she have heard? The tinkling of bells? A dull hum? Choirs? Trumpets? Thunder? Utter stillness and complete silence?

Whatever it was like for Mary, Gabriel has arrived and he has pronounced to her that her earlier dreams are irrevocably changed. He pronounces there is no choice involved, no opportunity to weigh the importance of what has been foretold. I can't help but think that a more realistic interpretation of her words, "Here am I, the servant of the Lord; let it be with me according to your word," would not be delivered with an unshakable resolve and steely spine but something more like swallowed panic and uncertainty. Was it a voice trying its best not to break under the incredible strain it has just been put through?

What does she do when he leaves? What is she feeling? I don't actually believe that it's like the medieval paintings or popular images. I don't picture her calmly going about the rest of her evening content and serene. She is a pregnant, betrothed, teenage girl. Her mind must be racing with questions and fears! "How will I tell Joseph? Will he leave me? What will my family say? Will anyone believe me? What will happen to me? Will I be hurt? Killed? How do I raise a child? I am a child!"

Even if none of these thoughts is present, she is still carrying the Son of God in her womb. I picture her sitting in stunned silence, softly crying, desperately trying to put the pieces of her life back together.

Today's Gospel reading ended with Mary's words, "Let it be with me according to your word," but there's more to the story. At this point in Luke, Mary leaves her home to visit her cousin Elizabeth, pregnant with John the Baptist. It's tempting to think that this is some sort of "mission of mercy" on Mary's part, that she's gone to help her expectant kin. I don't buy that for a moment. She went to give herself time to process everything that had just happened.

When Mary arrived, Elizabeth was six months pregnant. We know this because Gabriel says so. Mary stays there for three months, then leaves right before the birth. Now, I've never been pregnant, but I've been by my wife's side through two deliveries. And while having people around before the birth was helpful, it was the folks who showed up after the birth that truly made the difference. And that's why I firmly believe Mary went to go see Elizabeth for Mary's own sake, not Elizabeth's. She doesn't do that unless Gabriel's announcement has thrown her off balance.

But again, the story doesn't end there. When Elizabeth pronounced that Mary was "blessed among women," something changed. Mary began to experience her role in a new way, to accept it as part of her. She came to realize that God didn't just appear to her, but that God was with her, both in her pregnancy and in her life to come. Her life had a meaning beyond her comprehension. The task for which she was chosen was more than just a burden to be weathered.

That's the miracle of Christmas. The incarnation, God made flesh for our sake and for our betterment. And, in addition to that, the miracle of Christmas is the reminder that God used a humble human being to make that reality possible, and that God continues to work through people – simple, everyday people. It is a joy to be a child of God, and it is a burden as well, but it is also always a blessing. Amen.

– Chris Ode

Hymns

Opening: Gather Us In
Sermon: Take My Life, That I May Be
Closing: Sent Forth by God's Blessing

December 24, 2013

Christmas Eve

Lessons

Revised Common Lectionary (RCL)	Roman Catholic (RC)
Isa 9:2-7	Isa 9:1-6
Ps 96	Ps 96:1-3, 11-13
Titus 2:11-14	Titus 2:11-14
Lk 2:1-14 (15-20)	Lk 2:1-14

Speaker's Introduction for the Lessons

Lesson 1
Isaiah 9:2-7 (RCL); Isaiah 9:1-6 (RC)

Specifically set in the historical context of strife between Israel and Judah and the coronation of a king, we hear these words pointing to Jesus, the Messiah.

Lesson 2
Psalm 96 (RCL); Psalm 96:1-3, 11-13 (RC)

Closely paralleling the psalm selected for Christmas Day (96), and quoted in 1 Chronicles 16:23 and following, this psalm invokes the singing of a new song to God as savior and judge and sovereign over all.

Lesson 3
Titus 2:11-14 (RCL/RC)

This is an illustration of the early church's reflection on the birth of Jesus. He is named herein as God, one of the few times in the New Testament. And hearing of Jesus, we are encouraged to live ethical lives.

Gospel
Luke 2:1-14 (15-20) (RCL); Luke 2:1-14 (RC)

Listen for the prophecy, the history, and the symbolism in the story. Note how Luke intertwines this sacred story with the secular account of a census. Note the common response of angels, shepherds, and Mary is to praise God!

Theme
We are called to live a life of active faith.

Thought for the Day
Our word choices say as much about us as they say about our topic of conversation.

Sermon Summary
Within the telling of Christ's birth we can find a message of hope and action. But it helps if we finish translating the story.

Call to Worship
> One: Sing to the Lord and bless God's holy name!
> **All: Praise to the one whose glory is known among nations!**
> One: Sing to the Lord and bless God's holy name!
> **All: Praise to the creator of the heavens!**
> One: Sing to the Lord and bless God's holy name!
> **All: Praise to the righteous judge of all!**
> One: Sing to the Lord and bless God's holy name!
> **All: Let the heavens be glad, let the earth rejoice: the God of love comes near!**

Pastoral Prayer
God of love and forgiveness, tonight we remember and celebrate the grace you showed us in the birth of your Son, Jesus Christ. We thank you for your compassion and mercy, for your humility and might. Help us to live lives worthy of the promises you have made, lives dedicated to your Word and to your ministry among people. Guide us forward, that we might reflect your love in all we say and do. We pray this trusting in you, O giver of all. Amen.

Prayer of Confession and Assurance

Despite your presence, O God, we live lives of brokenness: we turn inward instead of out, we lift up our own needs above those of others, we fail to act when it is difficult or uncomfortable. Help us to turn from our own selfishness, to look to you and your grace as both a balm for our sickness and an example for our behavior. Help us to live mindfully, remembering your promise of forgiveness, that we may recognize your light in all of creation and endeavor to honor you by helping that light to shine. We pray this thankfully, knowing that you hear and forgive us, and that we are blessedly cherished by you. Amen.

Prayer of Dedication of Gifts and Self

All that we have comes from you, O Holy One, and we thank you for your generosity. Your blessings are abundant and varied: help us recognize not only those that are obvious, but also those that are less so. Keep us mindful of our dependence upon you and of our call to live lives of purpose and meaning. We pray this, trusting in you and your desire to guide us in ways of compassion and generosity. Amen.

Hymn of the Day
'Twas in the Moon of Wintertime

Considered by many to be the first hymn written in the New World and certainly the earliest Canadian hymn, this well-loved carol was written by a Jesuit priest, Father Jean de Brébeuf. He was a missionary to the Huron nation near Georgian Bay on Lake Huron. The Huron text was translated into French more than 100 years later and finally into English in 1926 by Canadian historian and author Jesse Middleton. A teaching tool, the traditional Christmas story is retold using imagery familiar to the First Nations peoples. Its haunting melody and pictorial language make it a favorite with many people throughout North America. Sing it immediately following the Luke passage, showing how scripture can be enriched with a new "translation."

Children's Time: The Greatest Gift of All

(Bring a Nativity scene, Christmas tree, lights, ornaments, and gifts from previous weeks in Advent.)
It's Christmas Eve. It's time to retell the Christmas story. *(Note: You may wait until tomorrow to add baby Jesus to the scene.)* I have something in this gift to help me retell the story. What do you think is inside this gift? Here's a clue. *(Remove Mary.)* Do you know who this is? Yes, it's Mary, Jesus' mother. *(Remove Joseph.)* And who is this? Yes, it's Joseph, Jesus' father on earth. Over 2000 years ago, Mary and Joseph were on their way to Bethlehem to be counted in the king's census. It was a long and bumpy road. And Mary was soon going to have a baby. *(Bring out a donkey if you have one.)* Mary rode on a gentle donkey. She was too tired to walk. When they finally reached Bethlehem, the inns were full of people. Finally one innkeeper said they could stay in his stable. It was filled with fresh straw. *(Bring out the stable. Place Mary and Joseph in it.)* That night someone very special was born – someone who was a gift from God. Who was it? *(Add the Jesus figure in a manger.)* Baby Jesus was born. Shhh! Baby Jesus is sleeping. Let's whisper, happy birthday, Jesus.

The Sermon: A Rose by Any Other Name
Scripture: Luke 2:1-14 (15-20)

Words fascinate me. I've always enjoyed puns and wordplay, the myriad ways in which the flexibility of the English language allows for double meanings and subtle jokes. Every language can be used in this way to one degree or another, but I can't help but think that English is especially inclined to it. Much of this is due to its origins: awhile back I recall seeing an online meme which read, "English doesn't borrow from other languages. English follows other languages down dark alleys, knocks them over, and goes through their pockets for loose grammar." It's true: English is incredibly messy, a mishmash drawn liberally from most every other language on the planet – living or dead. Each of us uses countless "foreign" words daily without recognizing that they are grafted from a different linguistic tree. And, as prevalent as this is in our daily conversation, nowhere is it more apparent than in the names we give each other and our surroundings.

If I told you a story with characters named Hope, Joy, and Faith, you would probably ascribe certain characteristics to each of them until these assumptions were either confirmed or contradicted. This makes sense: the names carry meaning in English, so it's easy for us to make the connection. But how many people know that Sarah means princess? That Richard means powerful leader? That Carmen means garden? You wouldn't bat an eye at seeing those names in a book, but it's doubtful you'd stop to think about any connection between the meaning of those names and the characteristics exhibited by their owners.

Without intending any disrespect toward scripture, we consistently make the same mistake with the Bible. While those with backgrounds in Greek and Hebrew may catch many of the meanings, most of us are at the whim of whatever translation we are reading – and most of those choose to leave the bulk of their proper nouns untranslated.

So what would happen if we did the opposite for a change? What would happen if we took a familiar story from the Bible, something we all have heard countless times before and "know" to its depth, and reread it without those native words? It might sound something like this:

In those days a decree went out from Emperor Magnificent that all the world should be registered. This was the first registration and was taken while the Warrior was governor of the Glowing Land. All went to their own towns to be registered. God Increases and Blesses Us went from the town of Watchfulness in the Circular Region to the Territory of the Tribe Who Praises God, to the city of Beloved called the City of Bread, because he was descended from the house and family of Beloved. He went to be registered with Bitter, to whom he was engaged, and who was expecting a child. While they were there, the time came for her to deliver her child. And she gave birth to her firstborn son and wrapped him in bands of cloth, and laid him in a manger, because there was no place for him in the inn.

Does anything stand out to you? I'll tell you what I notice (besides the unfortunate translation of Mary's name and the raw ego of the emperor). In Hebrew, Bethlehem is "the city of bread," you might have even heard that tidbit before. There are many theories behind this name, each firmly grounded in the historical baking profession. But there's something else interesting about the city's name: in Arabic, Bethlehem means "the city of flesh."

Where is Christ's life headed? Even at this moment, at his birth? The cross. Crucifixion, death, and resurrection – new life and new hope that we remember every time we celebrate the Lord's supper. Right there, in the name of his birthplace, is bread and body, foreshadowing of his ministry. Right there, from the start, is testimony to God's love for us. I don't doubt that Joseph was truly meant to register in Bethlehem for practical reasons, but isn't that an amazing coincidence that the name of Christ's birthplace would reflect the gift of his death and resurrection?

And as awesome as that is, do you know what might be even better? Look back at Joseph's itinerary for his family: from Nazareth to Judea, from the town of Watchfulness to the Territory of the Tribe Who Praises God. From watchful inaction to active praise.

That's the point to church, that's what the community of faith is about: active praise. Active praise through song and prayer, yes, but also active praise through our engagement with the world. Active praise through our commitment to Christ's call to "feed my sheep" and "tend my flock," to offer care and support to those in need. In the 21st century there is often the question, what role does the church serve these days? Or harsher still, does it still have a role? I would answer this with a forceful yes: the church exists to empower people to engage in an active exploration of our faith, praising God through word and deed, and recognizing the importance of exploring our faith connectively.

It's Christmas Eve, one of those obligatory church days, the ones where even the most jaded still feel some sort of pull to experience the old stories and spend time hoping to glimpse the divine. I don't know what prompted you to come tonight: maybe the last time you were here was Sunday morning, maybe it was last year, maybe it was a decade ago. But my hope and my prayer for you is that you leave here understanding that something special is taking place in the world: that God can, will, and is still using his people, and that you are invited to come and be a part of that. Amen.

– Chris Ode

Hymns
Opening: Good Christian Friends, Rejoice
Sermon: Lo, How a Rose E'er Blooming
Closing: Go Tell It on the Mountain

December 25, 2014

Christmas Day

Lessons

Revised Common Lectionary (RCL)	Roman Catholic (RC)
Isa 52:7-10	Isa 52:7-10
Ps 98	Ps 98:1-6
Heb 1:1-4 (5-12)	Heb 1:1-6
Jn 1:1-14	Jn 1:1-18 or 1:1-5, 9-14

Speaker's Introduction for the Lessons

Lesson 1
Isaiah 52:7-10 (RCL/RC)

The prophet Isaiah announces a homecoming for God's people. They will return to the ruins of their former country. This announcement of comfort to come is a hint of the good news when Messiah will arrive.

Lesson 2
Psalm 98 (RCL); Psalm 98:1-6 (RC)

This psalm invites joyful praise in a new song to God as sovereign of the universe. Its chorus of joy lifted by all peoples and nature itself was paraphrased by Isaac Watts in "Joy to the World."

Lesson 3
Hebrews 1:1-4 (5-12) (RCL); Hebrews 1:1-6 (RC)

The letter's author recounts salvation history for his readers, and these introductory words bring God's past actions into clear focus. Listen carefully to the first two verses for the new thing God had done.

Gospel
John 1:1-14 (RCL); John 1:1-18 or 1:1-5, 9-14 (RC)

Each Gospel writer has his own version of Jesus' beginnings. Matthew describes the generations before Jesus. Mark writes of John the Baptist. Luke tells Jesus' birth story. John says "the Word became flesh."

Theme
Both Jesus' being and his acts confirm God's sovereignty and give strength for nonviolent witness.

Thought for the Day
First they ignore you, then they laugh at you, then they fight you, then you win.

– Mahatma Gandhi (attributed)

Sermon Summary
Hebrews paints a cosmic context using Jesus' being and acts to reignite the public witness of a community that has been persecuted in the past. Hebrews is not anti-Jewish. Privileging one's own way of being Jewish over everyone else's was a common rhetorical device in Second Temple Judaism.

Call to Worship
One: The Son through which the world was created has been born anew this day!

All: Balm of Gilead, Emmanuel, Deliverer,

One: You heal us from the past so we may remember;

All: You embrace us in the present so we may love;

One: You free us for the future so we may act.

All: May the ends of the earth see the salvation of our God!

Pastoral Prayer
God of steadfast love, you who come again and again and again into our world, we scarcely know how to give thanks for your love that will not let us go. You are our shelter, our healer, our guide and our friend. Faithful beyond measure, we stand amazed at your continued coming. Nothing frightens you or frustrates you, nothing dissuades you or disappoints you; you come. And the unconditioned fullness of your presence brings life, again and again and again. O holy child of Bethlehem, be born in us today. Amen.

Prayer of Confession and Assurance

This morning we open ourselves to you, loving God. At times our Christmas celebrations become a brittle veneer to hide our grief or anxiety. We ask you to abide in those places where we hide, sometimes even from the ones we love, sometimes even from ourselves. One who comes, we are searching this morning – for a job, for a relationship, for security, for direction, for health, for forgiveness, for the will to just keep going. And we confess we feel alone. But your angels' songs of "good news, glad tidings!" cause us to pause along this weary way, reminding us that you are with us. Help us, heal us, and guide us we pray. Amen.

By the tender mercy of our God, the dawn from on high will break upon us, to give light to those who sit in darkness … to guide our feet into the way of peace.

Prayer of Dedication of Gifts and Self

Spendthrift God, you have given of your very self that we might have life and have it abundantly. We now offer these gifts and ourselves in gratitude and hope, that we might bear your good news to the world. Amen.

Hymn of the Day
Of the Father's Love Begotten

A Spaniard, Aurelius Clemens Prudentius wrote the text in the fifth century. John Mason Neale translated it into English and it was published in 1851. It has been further altered in a number of denominational hymnals to make the male God language more inclusive. Regardless the language used, this is a joyous proclamation of the never-ending love of God. For some it is not strictly a Christmas hymn, however the theme of Alpha and Omega makes it a wonderful musical support to the reading from John. The tune, DIVNUM MYSTERIUM, is one of the best known plainsong melodies in the Christian church. It is best sung in unison without accompaniment or with minimal, simple, free-flowing chords supporting the melody.

Children's Time: Angel Messengers

(Bring the Christmas tree, lights, ornaments, and crèche scene from earlier Sundays in December. Bring halos made from 22-inch length of Christmas garland or gold ribbon stapled into rings.)
Merry Christmas! *(Have the children repeat.)* Jesus is born! *(Have the children repeat.)* An angel was the first one to announce to shepherds that Jesus was born. The shepherds were sleepily watching their sheep on a quiet night outside of Bethlehem when a very bright angel appeared. They were terrified and fell to the ground in fear. "Don't be afraid," the angel said. "I bring you good news that will bring great joy to all people. The Savior – yes, the Messiah, the Lord – has been born today in Bethlehem, the city of David! And you will recognize him by this sign: You will find a baby wrapped snugly in strips of cloth, lying in a manger." Suddenly the angel was joined by many others. *(At this point give each child a halo to wear.)* Let's pretend that you're part of this great crowd of angels. Stand up, stretch out your angel wings, and face the congregation. Let's see big smiles as we praise God together for the gift of baby Jesus. Let's close with the angels' words from Luke 2:10-14. You can repeat this Bible verse after me:

"Glory to God in highest heaven and peace on earth to those with whom God is pleased."

Merry Christmas to us all!

The Sermon: Wholly Undeterred
Scripture: Hebrews 1:1-4 (5-12)

Hebrews opens in epic fashion: "Long ago God spoke to our ancestors in many and various ways by the prophets, but in these last days he has spoken to us by a Son." Cue the trumpet voluntary from *Star Wars*! (For fun you could play the overture!) These inaugural lines captivate; they make us pause to consider the cosmic implications of pledging our loyalty to God. They situate believers in the grand sweep of God's action since the beginning of time, through myriad witnesses, up to the present moment. These lines raise the stakes and set the context.

And they form the salvo for what is a short, impassioned sermon designed to awaken a community that has become timid and unwilling to publicly hold fast to the practices and confessions that defined the early followers of Jesus. Likely written from Rome and before the destruction of the temple in 70 CE, the sermon urges the wavering community of Christ followers to not succumb to temptation (Heb 2:18) and renounce their commitment to Christ (Heb 12:16-17). While the writer acknowledges their past courage, which cost them their property and public abuse (Heb 10:32-36), in order to empower them, he resituates their past acts as one part of the historic witness of ancestors in the faith and within the cosmic history of the salvation of the world.

In the lines of this overture, the writer crafts a new ontology, a new understanding of being itself. For Jesus, the Son, is the "exact imprint" of God's own being and through the power of the Son's word the entire creation is sustained (Heb 1:3). This, the writer argues, is a new and powerful understanding of the Jewish faith, one that builds upon yet distinguishes itself from the tradition of the prophets.

It is important to be clear that this is not an anti-Jewish argument. Now, such texts have certainly been used to promote supercessionist understandings of Christianity that have led to discrimination against and, we must also confess, persecution of our Jewish brothers and sisters. And such wrongheaded interpretations sadly continue today. But such readings gravely misunderstand the way that ancient Jewish writers constructed arguments. Remember, there's no such thing as Christianity at this point in time. There are simply different Jewish traditions being followed, among them are those Jews who believed Jesus was Messiah. Biblical scholar A. Katherine Grieb explains,

> Hebrews is often called anti-Jewish because of its new covenant language and its use of negative examples from Israel's past. But Hebrews uses many positive historical examples (see Heb 11): the new covenant comes directly from Jeremiah, and privileging one's own way of being Jewish over everyone else's was common among Second Temple Judaisms, as the Dead Sea Scrolls attest. ("Catholic Epistles," in *The New Testament – Introducing the Way of Discipleship*, ed. Wes Howard-Brook and Sharon H. Ringe, 175-176.)

Grieb invites us to read Hebrews and to see ourselves in continuity with Judaism, as "that part of Israel that believes Jesus is the Messiah (Christ)" and to dialog with Jews about theological commonalities and differences even as we confess past sins in our own interpretation and action.

Soon after these opening lines, which we've read this morning, the writer reminds the ancient community that this Son, is not a far-off principle; he is the "representative human" who pioneered our salvation through his own suffering (Heb 2:10). God understands and Jesus has lived the challenges that the community of faith continues to face. And when the community aligns themselves not only in confession but also in deed with God's action, their witness becomes a part of a cosmic doxology. The writer then complements this huge backdrop of divine being and action by recounting the many acts of faithfulness demonstrated by holy ancestors (see Heb 11:32-40).

On this Christmas morning we scarcely expect such bravado. Something touching perhaps, but not this clarion call to recognize and respond to God's sovereignty even if it costs us our own lives. After worship, many of us will head off to visit friends and family. We'll sit down to Christmas dinner and when Aunt Beatrice leans over and asks, "So what did the pastor preach about?" while passing the green bean casserole, "Oh, about being sawn in two for the gospel" is not going to be the response expected by anyone!

But the Christmas story is just that dangerous and just that radical. For into this world was born a Savior whose divine power called into question every dominating power of this world. The Jesus of whom we sing "he is King of kings and Lord of lords" means that he comes challenging the reigning powers of our world that manufacture violence, stoke injustice, and rob people of their dignity. And these "masters of the universe" aren't going to take this sitting down. They have and will react again and again to God's coming. They will try, without success, to starve it, jail it, saw it in two, crucify it. But all this is to no avail if we continue to hold fast and live boldly, the writer of Hebrews reminds us.

The writer of Hebrews reminds the community in verse 40 that their witness is essential to the history of salvation. They have an indispensable role to play. They must bear witness courageously in their own time and their own place. And by extension, we who hear these words 2000 years later must also bring to birth in our own life together God's vision of a world just and whole.

The Christmas story has cosmic significance, Hebrews remind us, and we are a part of God's great story of salvation. We too are called on this day to recommit our loyalty to Christ in a world flush with greed, hatred, and violence. Jesus pioneered our salvation through his own suffering (Heb 2:9-11). And we are called to a daring faith that prizes loyalty to the loving reign of God over our own security and comfort. "Long ago God spoke to our ancestors in many and various ways by the prophets, but in these last days he has spoken to us by a Son." Toward what powerful witness of faith might this Son be calling us this morning?

– Noelle Damico

Hymns
Opening: On This Day Earth Shall Ring
Sermon: The God of Abraham Praise
Closing: O Little Town of Bethlehem

December 28, 2014

1st Sunday after Christmas

Lessons

Revised Common Lectionary (RCL)	Roman Catholic (RC)
Isa 61:10—62:3	Sir 3:3-7, 14-17a
Ps 148	Ps 128:1-5
Gal 4:4-7	Rev 21:1-6a
Lk 2:22-40	Mt 25:31-46

Speaker's Introduction for the Lessons

Lesson 1

Isaiah 61:10—62:3 (RCL)

> The prophet proclaims a joyful message in the vocabulary of weddings and gardens concerning the vindication of Zion. The reference to nations and kings recognizing Zion's glory points us to the coming season of Epiphany.

Sirach 3:3-7, 14-17a (RC)

> This reading is essentially an explication of the commandment "Honor your father and your mother."

Lesson 2

Psalm 148 (RCL)

> All creation is summoned to praise and thanksgiving in a cacophony of animals and elements, big shots and lowly ones, raising the psalmist's primal chorus of joy to – and by – the world!

Psalm 128:1-5 (RC)

> This short psalm is a hymn of praise to the Lord.

Lesson 3

Galatians 4:4-7 (RCL)

> This is a rare Pauline reference to Jesus' birth, an affirmation of the Jewishness of Jesus' heritage with the phrase "born under the law." He adds that Jesus came "to redeem those those who were under the law."

Revelation 21:1-6a (RC)
> This beautiful text concludes with a declaration of the Alpha and the Omega, the beginning and the end. The phrase reinforces the absolute power and sovereign nature of God.

Gospel
Luke 2:22-40 (RCL)
> Here is an image of the church as extended family. The old man Simeon has looked at Jesus, seen him as Messiah, and while holding the infant, Simeon sings his blessing.

Matthew 25:31-46 (RC)
> Time and again we read that the kingdom of God is not typical. And that is good news to all of those who are oppressed – the least of these.

Theme
In this short life that only lasts an hour / How much – how little – is within our power!

> –Emily Dickinson

Thought for the Day
No matter the circumstances, we can be bearers of God's promise of redemption. Will we take up this challenge?

Sermon Summary
Anna, who began her temple practice under Jewish self-rule, acknowledges Jesus as a sign of God's redemption and, more important, spreads word of the child to Jews actively resisting or creating alternatives to Roman domination. How might we bear God's promise of redemption today?

Call to Worship
> One: In the violence of domination, the anguish of desperation, the callousness of isolation,
> **All: God comes;**
> One: With us, despite us, and for us.
> **All: We tremble at such redemption.**

One:Hope; an infant voice against the cacophony of fear.
All: In joy, we add our voice.

Pastoral Prayer

Eternal God, we stand before you at the closing of one year and the dawn of the next; time that we've structured to count and administer, to judge and weigh. How small our world must seem to you, how bound by our own perceptions and expectations! God beyond time, your love exceeds all categories and constraints. Broaden our awareness of your cosmos and our contribution within it. Increase our forbearance toward one another. Strengthen justice in our life together. Now and always. Amen.

Prayer of Confession and Assurance

Author of salvation, we confess that too often we write the end of the story before giving you a chance to respond. We assume the narratives of the powerful grind on, their plot unchanging. Believing ourselves insignificant, we try and control what we can and carve a small space to survive. Forgive our shortsightedness and timidity. Free us from our desire to control. Awaken us to our true power. Attune us to your call to faithfulness. Embolden us to dream and act together in love, that we may find our part in your story of salvation. In Christ's name we pray. Amen.

We have known and believe the love that God has for us. God is love, and those who abide in love abide in God, and God abides in them. Thanks be to God.

Prayer of Dedication of Gifts and Self

We give these gifts in trust and gladness for the church's works of love. And we recommit ourselves to one another and to you, that together we might be signs of your justice, freedom, and hope in our world. Amen.

Hymn of the Day
Lord, Dismiss Us with Your Blessing

The text is attributed to John Fawcett, a Baptist who served as minister in Wainsgate, England. He yielded to his congregation's wishes and served there for 54 years. He wrote more than 150 hymns. The opening of the stanza is based upon Luke 2:29 and the remainder of the hymn broadens the thesis of Christ's blessing and unending love. The tune, Sicilian MARINERS, while said to be from Sicily, is not a well-known tune in that country. The dotted rhythms and running eighth notes in the melody give a sense of energy to the text. Use as a closing hymn or whenever a blessing is required.

Children's Time: A Candy Cane Blessing

(Bring the Christmas tree, lights, and ornaments from previous December Sundays. Bring little candy canes.)
Merry Christmas! We have 12 days of Christmas and we are still celebrating the wonderful gift of baby Jesus! It's been a busy time for baby Jesus. First, angels sang a beautiful song for him, announcing to shepherds that he was born. Then shepherds came to visit him. The shepherds ran through the town of Bethlehem announcing that God's son, Jesus, was born. Baby Jesus probably had lots of other visitors. When Jesus was eight days old, his father took him to the temple (the place where they worshiped God) for a naming ceremony. And he was named Jesus, the name given to him by God's angel messenger. Finally, when Jesus was almost six weeks old, Mary and Joseph took Jesus to Jerusalem to present him before God. A faithful man named Simeon was worshiping in the temple. When he saw Jesus, Simeon knew that this was the special baby he had been waiting for. Simeon held baby Jesus in his arms and said, "Jesus is a light to reveal God to the nations and he is the glory of your people Israel." Then he blessed Jesus.

At Christmastime we celebrate the joy of Jesus' birth. Here's a sweet candy cane to remind you of the shepherds who were the first to hear the Christmas message and the joy that Simeon felt as he held God's Son in his arms. As you eat this candy cane remember God's greatest blessing to you, the blessing of Jesus. Merry Christmas!

The Sermon: Anna – Living Memory, Savvy Action
Scripture: Luke 2:22-40

When Mary and Joseph bring Jesus to be dedicated at the temple they encounter an elderly prophet, Anna, who for 67 years has been worshiping there "with fasting and prayer night and day." She's in her 90s at this point and, we learn, she was married earlier in life for seven years. The text isn't clear about how vocal she's been in the past – whether people regularly came to seek her counsel, whether she made public pronouncements, or whether she led a sequestered life. While Anna's words have been lost to history (and perhaps patriarchy, as some scholars believe Simeon's words may have originally been Anna's), the author of Luke portrays her as doing two critical things. She "seconds" Simeon's blessing and she began "to speak about the child to all who were looking for the redemption of Jerusalem."

Our tradition has paid scant attention to Anna. I would be interested in knowing right now, by show of hands, who gathered here has ever, in your entire life, heard a sermon that focuses on this prophet. (Invite worshipers to raise their hands; you won't find many, if any.) And yet, Anna's role in Luke's narrative is critical. For unlike Simeon, she does not simply offer a blessing to the family, she begins speaking about the child "to all who were looking for the redemption of Jerusalem."

Let's look at this sentence closely. It's interesting for what it does not say as well as for what it says. It does not say that Anna told everyone about Jesus. A cursory reading might leave that impression. But it's wrong. Anna was not simply proclaiming Jesus to anyone. She was specific and strategic in speaking with "all who were looking for the redemption of Jerusalem."

To better understand who these people would have been and why they would be seeking "the redemption of Jerusalem," we need to take a look at the historical context in which the author of Luke situates this story. While many of us have not heard of Anna, we certainly remember the words we hear each year on Christmas Eve that come from the Gospel of Luke. "In those days a decree when out from Emperor Augustus that all the world should be registered" (2:1). During the two generations before Jesus' birth, Rome had expanded its empire into the eastern Mediterranean, brutally conquering, enslaving, and suppressing the Hebrew people. Unlike the other regions Rome conquered, the Judeans and Galileans resisted both the invasion and the occupation from its inception. Biblical scholar and historian Richard Horsley paints this horrifying picture for us:

> In conquest and reconquest, the Roman armies systematically pursued "scorched earth" and "search and destroy'"practices in order to terrorize the population and ferret out all pockets of resistance. The legions destroyed villages, slaughtered the inhabitants, or at least the

elderly, and took tens of thousands of the younger and able-bodied to sell as slaves back in Rome and the rest of Italy. A standard feature of the Roman terrorization was the crucifixion of hundreds or thousands on stakes or crosses along the roads, a grim reminder of what would happen to those who rebelled against Roman domination. Right around the time Jesus was born, in the area around Nazareth where he presumably grew up, the Romans had burned the houses and enslaved thousands of people in response to a widespread popular revolt in 4 BCE (Richard Horsley, "The New World Order," in Wes Howard-Brook and Sharon H. Ringe eds., *The New Testament – Introducing the Way of Discipleship*).

Rome had appointed Herod as "King of the Judeans" and shrewdly used the temple-state in Jerusalem to consolidate and manage the Roman occupation. Herod installed his own appointees in the temple to replace the former Jewish dynasty of high priests, the Hasmoneans. Herod even embarked on a temple restoration project that made it one of the most magnificent temples in the ancient world. The Jerusalem temple was a center for Jews worldwide to make pilgrimages, offering tribute to God and also Rome – literally. The temple was a collection point for Roman tribute owed to the empire by conquered peoples.

Meanwhile the Pharisees, who were not in the temple but lodged in communities across Palestine, endeavored to teach and practice traditional covenant ways of life in less than ideal circumstances. Upon Herod's death in 4 BCE popular revolts ensued in every area that had been under his control.

Now with that history, let's look again at this elderly prophet who has been practicing in the temple for 64 years. Why might the author of Luke note the specific length of time she has been there? Because it signals that Anna was present in the temple during the reign of the Hasmonean dynasty, the Jewish families whose rule was conquered by Rome in 66 BCE. Anna embodies the living memory of the Jewish people's freedom and self-rule.

When Anna "speaks about the child to all who were looking for the redemption of Jerusalem," she is carefully speaking to those Jews who were seeking to resist, create alternatives to, or overthrow Rome's occupation. And she is doing so from the temple, the site Herod had co-opted to solidify Roman rule in the region. She is organizing from "the belly of the beast"; from the temple, the symbolic and administrative heart of Rome's brutal occupation.

Both Anna and Simeon are the first in Luke's Gospel to see and understand that Jesus' coming points the Jewish people back toward covenant ways of life that had been disrupted and corrupted by Rome. But Anna is the only one who cleverly reaches out. Through these conversations she laid the groundwork for the adult Jesus' message to take root. To people who still shook with the terror of past invasion, to mothers who had lost their sons to enslavement, to all who were fed up with Rome's manipulation of their sacred commitments, Anna spread the word of God's redemption. And through her strategic action, she renewed hope that God's covenant way of life could not be swallowed whole by Rome.

In our own time and place, what are the challenges we face as we endeavor to live out God's covenant? Who are our Annas whose living memory and savvy action bring hope and fiery determination? How are we being called to spread the dangerous and hopeful news of God's promised redemption?

– Noelle Damico

Hymns
Opening: Hark! The Herald Angels Sing
Sermon: Mary and Joseph Came to the Temple
Closing: God of Grace and God of Glory

January 4, 2015

2nd Sunday after Christmas

Lessons

Revised Common Lectionary (RCL)	Roman Catholic (RC)
Jer 31:7-14 or Sir 24:1-12	(See lections for Epiphany,
Ps 147:12-20 or Wis 10:15-21	January 6, 2015 p. 212)
Eph 1:3-14	
Jn 1: (1-9) 10-18	

Speaker's Introduction for the Lessons

Jeremiah 31:7-14 (RCL)

The assurance of God for a people scattered and bereft. God names self Father and Shepherd of the people, and promises comfort and joy.

Lesson 2

Psalm 147:12-20 (RCL)

The psalmist proclaims God's intent to protect God's people, bless the children, grant peace, and fill the world with the finest wheat.

Wisdom 10:15-21(RCL)

Highlights Wisdom's special relationship with Israel, both as savior and guide.

Lesson 3

Ephesians 1:3-14 (RCL)

The mystery of God's will includes the redemption of humankind and the gathering of all things into God's own self. This was the plan from before the beginning and will be in the fullness of time.

Gospel

John 1: (1-9) 10-18 (RCL)

The preexistent Word, participant with God in creation, came to humankind to make known the glory, the grace, the truth, and the heart of God, and humankind has eyes that see, or don't.

Theme
John's "Christmas" story is about *our* nativity.

Thought for the Day
Most ambitious Star! an inquest wrought within me when I recognised thy light.

—William Wordsworth from
"It Is No Spirit Who from Heaven Hath Flown"

Sermon Summary
John's prologue arrests our certainty of what Christ's coming means. Jesus, the Logos, is not born; rather through him all things were made. Alienated from the source of its very life, the world rejects him. But those who do pledge their loyalty are promised power to become children of God.

Call to Worship
One: God's Word; gift and troublemaker.
All: Perhaps our adoration will keep you at a safe, heavenly distance?
One: God's Word; flesh among us
All: Causing us to reexamine and decide who we are and what we stand for.
One: God's Word, grace upon grace.
All: Inexhaustible love, beckoning us forward.
One: We, your children, take our first, uncertain steps all over again
All: In joy, in awe, in praise.

Pastoral Prayer
Ancient whisper, present roar, tender secret, loving word, we greet you this day and attune our ears to you. We know you are not only one who speaks but one who hears. We pray this morning for our world, struggling to recognize you and fearing to follow in your way of nonviolence and justice. We are a part of that wounded, confused, and fearful world. Help us! We long to see you, to hear your word and to follow you, that your reign of love might be known. Amen.

Prayer of Confession and Assurance

One: We pray for *all things*, for all things were created by and through divine love. May nations and peoples who so condition the well-being of all creatures and the earth itself,

All: Begin to understand the source of our very being in you.

One: May all who are grieving the loss of a loved one, the loss of a job, the loss of a relationship, the loss of hope

All: Find solace in knowing your very being understands such anguish.

One: May all who are ill, limited, isolated, or forgotten

All: Know you are closer than our very breath.

One: We confess our loss of imagination, of wonder and of confidence in you.

All: Forgive our limited vision and trust. Grant that we may sense and share about and in your vibrant life. Amen.

One: God's forgiveness is farther than the east is from the west. Alleluia!

All: Alleluia!

Prayer of Dedication of Gifts and Self

We offer our gifts back to you, knowing they and we have always belonged to you. In giving we intentionally affirm your good purpose for our world and all within it. By uniting with you, may this good word be known and heard. Amen.

Hymn of the Day
Before the World Began

This lovely and lilting setting of John 1 is from the Iona community, courtesy of John Bell and Graham Maule. Their artful paraphrase also draws in themes from the Wisdom and Psalm texts and could be sung as a call and response: "Life found in him its source ... Death found its end." Bell's INCARNATION complements the text, making is an ideal focus for today's worship.

Children's Time: The Holy Family

During Christmas we remember the holy family. Who are they? *(Mary, Joseph, and baby Jesus.)* Did you know that we are part of God's holy family too? Even before God made the world, God loved us and chose us in Christ to be holy. God decided in advance to adopt us into his own family by bringing us to himself through Jesus Christ. This is what God wanted to do, and it made God very happy.

One way that God's family celebrates together is by sharing God's peace. Invite the children to go out into the congregation and share God's peace with their church family. Let's say an echo prayer. I'll say a line and you can repeat it after me:

> You, me, he, and she, *(Point to different children.)*
> We're all God's family. *(Raise arms up high.)*
> Here's my brother, my sister too. *(Point to a boy and a girl.)*
> 'Cause this is what God planned to do! *(Point upward.)*
> Thanks, God! Amen!

The Sermon: Our Nativity
Scripture: John 1: (1-9) 10-18

On this Second Sunday after Christmas, the writer of the Gospel of John has sketched a cosmic nativity scene that reorders the world's own understanding of itself and pivots on our response. In this account, Jesus was not born in a manger, heralded by angels, or adored by shepherds and magi. Indeed Jesus, the Word (Logos), was not born at all! In a grand reversal, the entire creation, life itself, was born through him (1:1-5). The Gospel asserts that the Word is no stranger to the world; indeed the Word knows it intimately for "all things came into being through him, and without him not one thing came into being."

Unlike Luke and Matthew's accounts, the coming of Jesus was not joyfully celebrated by people of high and lowly status, accompanied by angelic hymns, illumined by an unmistakable star, or punctuated with grand gifts. John writes bluntly, "the world did not know him" (1:10b).

It is worth pausing here, because John's discordant note should shake us from our bucolic celebration of Christmas in which familiarity plays a central role. While following a star or heavenly hosts and animals at the crib-side may be a stretch, certainly we've all experienced joy upon the birth of a baby. Most every one of us has at one time or another held a newborn in our arms and marveled at the intricate beauty and wonder of this new life. Those of us who have borne children have experienced the fetus growing within us and the terror and wonder of giving birth. For parents and grandparents we see the next generation of "us" carrying forward our family's name and legacy. There's hope and a sense of possibility. Of course there's the baby shower and visits after the birth when the family is offered gifts and best wishes. This is something we recognize when we hear the stories from Matthew and Luke. We see ourselves even across the millennia, even across cultures. God has come to us as a child, fully human. This is a human story, and we know what it means to be human, because we know ourselves; we have our life experience.

But the opening of John's Gospel calls all this into question. It's not that Jesus was in some sort of disguise; no! The very stuff out of which the world and we were made comes from and through him. The issue for John is that it is difficult to recognize the Savior because we have become fundamentally alienated from the very source of the world's life and being – of our own being. Now all this can sound very heady. But these verses cause us to stop and question whether we really do "understand" God's coming, even when the Word takes flesh and lives among us.

There are (at least) two core implications of John's arresting Christmas story. One has to do with how we think. The second has to do with how we live.

In a foundational sense, John argues that the coming of the Word provides us another, more accurate way of seeing what is important in the world. Stories of origins are philosophical undertakings that grounded ancient societies' understanding of who they were. They were not scientific explanations but narratives that constructed, through their telling, how human beings should properly relate to one another. Various types of ancient legends prevailed in the first century, but one that was particularly prominent during the writing of the Gospel of John was that of the Stoics. In the Greco-Roman world their teaching provided guidance for understanding one's place in the imperial order. They "thought of the universe as one cosmic city-state *(kosmopolis)*, of which the constitution *(politeia)* was reason *(logos)* and in which those creatures who shared reason were citizens *(politeis)*" (Richard Horsley, "The New World Order," in *The New Testament – Introducing the Way of Discipleship*, Wes Howard-Brook and Sharon H. Ringe, eds.).

The Stoic philosophy was aligned with the Hellenistic empire's actions and influence. Logos was the principle of reason that grounded certain powerful members of society's participation in it. John is alluding to this worldview, retelling it here in the prologue in a surprising way. "All things" are created through Logos, but many creatures (we will see they are the powerful of society as we progress through the Gospel), though they were made through this Logos, are not citizens or children of God, or because it runs counter to their understanding of how the world should and does work and they therefore they have rejected the Logos.

John alerts hearers and readers of the gospel that "receiving" the Word is neither an obvious nor a simple task. Those who follow Logos think about the world in a very different and potentially disruptive way from the prevailing worldview.

And the stakes are high. "He came to what was his own, and his own people did not accept him" (1:11). John's prologue signals that this will have implications for how those who do receive Logos will live and what they can expect. Gospel hearers and readers are warned at the outset, that the word was rejected and the unspoken implication is that we may be similarly rejected. But John offers a promise: "To all who received him, who believed in his name, he gave power to become children of God, who were born, not of blood or of the will of the flesh or of the will of [hu]man[ity], but of God" (1:13).

Now when we use the word *believe* in the 21st century, we mean to have faith in, perhaps to place our trust in. It principally refers to an attitudinal state. But in the Roman imperial context, the Greek word *pistis*, must be translated not as "believing in" but as "loyalty to." *Pistis* (in Latin, *fides*) was what Roman rulers demanded of their subjects: loyalty. Loyalty is not only about attitude, it is also about the obedience that stems from such allegiance. John says that it is those who have to pledge their loyalty to Christ (not Rome) who are given the power to become children of God.

John's nativity story is really a nativity story about us, not Jesus. Reimagining the world through Logos, he challenges readers and hearers of the Gospel to pledge their loyalty to Jesus and become children not of this world but of God. The remainder of the Gospel will be about how the community that pledges itself to Logos becomes children of God.

The Gospel of John presents Jesus as an honest mirror who reflects back upon us our own commitments, calling us to question to what and whom we have pledged our loyalty. This Christmas, let us pause and celebrate our own nativity in the very Word of God, and allow the mystery, questions, and promises open us to the unexpected fullness of life God promises.

— Noelle Damico

Hymns
Opening: Let All Mortal Flesh Keep Silent
Sermon: Born in the Night Mary's Child
Closing: The Play of the Godhead

January 6, 2015

Epiphany

Lessons

Revised Common Lectionary (RCL)	Roman Catholic (RC)
Isa 60:1-6	Isa 60:1-6
Ps 72:1-7, 10-14	Ps 72:1-13
Eph 3:1-12	Eph 3:2-3, 5-6
Mt 2:1-12	Mt 2:1-12

Speaker's Introduction for the Lessons

Lesson 1
Isaiah 60:1-6 (RCL/RC)

The light shines in the darkness, and perhaps we comprehend enough to go looking for what it illuminates.

Lesson 2
Psalm 72:1-7, 10-14 (RCL); Psalm 72:1-13 (RC)

The psalmist prays for Israel's king to reflect the qualities of God's own rule. The tribute brought by foreign kings has been heard by the church as suggestive of the visit of the magi.

Lesson 3
Ephesians 3:1-12 (RCL); Ephesians 3:2-3a, 5-6 (RC)

In Jesus, we believe, we see and know God most clearly. We do Jesus and God no favors, though, to presume Jesus explains mystery instead of participating in it.

Gospel
Matthew 2:1-12 (RCL/RC)

Jesus came to make a difference in people's lives. It is worth considering, is it not, how people responded (and respond) to life being different?

Theme

On Epiphany we are reminded there is always more to see, more to be revealed.

Thought for the Day

He is the Way.
Follow Him through the Land of Unlikeness;
You will see rare beasts, and have unique adventures.
     – From "IV Chorus" of W.H. Auden's *Christmas Oratorio*

Sermon Summary

Epiphany reminds us that it is God, not the Herods of this world, who reveals what is of value, setting the conditions – and the freedom – for our lives. There is always more that God is revealing to those who remain alert and wondering.

Call to Worship

  One: We seek you like the magi,
  All: Gifts ready, destination murky.
  One: We ask the advice of the powerful,
  All: But they know not the way.
  One: Only by stars and dreams can we discern you;
  All: Vulnerable and poor, we kneel before you.
  One: Holy, Holy, Holy Lord.
  All: We rise reoriented, and chart a new course.

Pastoral Prayer

No matter how we prepare to meet you, God, we are never ready for your coming. For who can prepare for the unexpected one, who confounds preparations and defies expectations? And so we are here, divesting ourselves of gifts we might offer, for there is no need to appease or flatter you. Your surprising love cuts through all that. Instead we offer open hands and open hearts; abide with us we pray. Amen.

Prayer of Confession and Assurance

God who would lead us in new ways, we confess we like the way things are. Even if we're on the receiving end of trouble, we'd rather have you tell us to endure than to change ourselves or to change our world. Change is difficult, it requires practice, and we don't like to fail. And we know your way will present many opportunities to fail in the eyes of the world, but also, we fear, in your eyes as well. Free us this morning from slothful inaction and perfectionist reactions that we may arise in the strength of love, freely offered and freely received. Amen.

Jesus came that we might have life and have it abundantly! May we live into such abundant life as individuals, congregations, communities, and nations.

Prayer of Dedication of Gifts and Self

We join our gifts with those of your people around the world. Through your mercy, may they provide comfort to the distressed, hope to the despairing, food to the hungry, and determination for all who strive for your shalom. Amen.

Hymn of the Day

From a Distant Home/*De tierra lejana venimos*

This popular carol for Epiphany comes from Puerto Rico. It was translated by George Evans and musically arranged by Walter Ehret for *The International Book of Christmas Carols* (1963). This carol also appears in *New Century Hymnal* under the name "The Magi Who to Bethlehem Did Go." Its Hispanic origin demands a rhythmic and spirited presentation. While it can be played on piano, guitar would be more appropriate and ethnically correct. Use plenty of rhythm instruments, including hand drums, castanets, tambourines, and shakers. Once this lively song is well-known, it will make a wonderful and, hopefully, colorful processional; however, it can be used anywhere in a service of worship.

Children's Time: Follow That Star!

(Place a shiny gold star on the end of a dowel. Have a youth sit near the back of the congregation with the star out of sight. Have another youth nearby to shine a bright flashlight on the star. Dim the lights. Invite your assistants to stand and shine the light on the star.) Let's pretend that we lived over 2000 years ago. We're star studiers, called magi. Every night we look up into the sky to find constellations like the Big Dipper and the North Star. *(Look up high.)* One night we see a bright star, one we have never seen before. It is a new star. And a new bright star means only one thing: a king has been born. *(Invite the children to turn around and look at the star.)* We want to travel to meet this new king. What gifts should we bring? Let's bring gold, incense, and myrrh, all very precious and expensive. Now climb onto your camels and here we go. *(Slowly bob up and down as you walk toward the star. Have the star carrier slowly move around the congregation, ending up where the children's time began. Gather around the star and sit down.)*

Who do you think the magi find at the end of the star? Yes, they find Jesus. But Jesus is no longer a baby. It took the magi almost two years to find Jesus. He is living in a home with Mary and Joseph. Mary and Joseph are amazed when these important magi come to honor Jesus with their precious gifts of gold, incense, and myrrh. A king had been born – a king for all people all around the world.

Let's sing "Twinkle, Twinkle Little Star" as a reminder that King Jesus is always watching over the world.

The Sermon: Those Stars We Have Not Yet Seen
Scripture: Matthew 2:1-12

Have you ever had the opportunity to gaze up at the heavens from a dark, open space? For those of us who have grown up in cities or near suburban malls with their 24/7 blare of lights, the experience can be astounding. While we may have been able to pick out the North Star or a faint Big Dipper and Little Dipper, until that moment when we see an open sky, we can never understand the expression "the sky was blanketed with stars." Seeing the plethora of stars, large and small, winking and burning, so far away and yet traveling toward us from millions of light years before fills us with wonder even as it unsettles. We may have known intellectually that there were millions out there, but stepping into the wilderness in the quiet blackness shows us instantly we truly had no idea.

Here we've been, living our lives, commuting to work, playing Uno with friends, apportioning our SNAP benefits, helping our spouse get used to her walker, buying a house, voting in elections, comparing prices at the grocery store, falling madly in love, figuring out our major at college, playing the piano, choosing a coffin and marker for a loved one, charging down the soccer field, mowing the lawn, shaking our head as we pay the oil bill, hauling the bags of nonperishable donations to the food pantry, reading the latest Sue Grafton novel, learning to take our first steps, weighing whether we can afford to go to the dentist, losing our home to the bank, getting 100 percent on our spelling test, landing the deal at work, recovering from rape, advocating an end to fracking, going for chemo treatments, calling members to see if they'll serve on the church council, getting our book published, trying to adjust our immigration status, washing and folding mountains of laundry, repairing that crack in the basement wall, purchasing our monthly commuter rail pass, rocking our newborn to sleep, gathering for worship. And all the time, right above us, is this fathomless universe, awash in stars, causing us to wonder: if we have not seen this, what else have we been missing? And how might we see rightly?

Today is Epiphany, a day when God reveals, discloses, uncovers, presents to us that which was once unseen and unknown. Truth be told, Epiphany is not a well-celebrated holy day among many Christian traditions. Few people will be showing up today for worship in those few congregations that will hold worship at all. But it is a holy day worth recovering, because through it we are reminded that there is always more to see, more to be revealed. And what we see shapes our sense of how to act in the world.

The writer of Matthew chose to open his Gospel with this story of magi seeking the one born "King of the Jews." He was compiling and writing about three generations after Jesus' birth to a community that had never known any existence other than that under the Roman occupation. "Matthew's" narrative is revealing. He exposes the illegitimacy of Herod, the brutal, Jewish, client-ruler who had been appointed by Rome as "King of the Judeans" to pacify the population. And by extension, by exposing the illegitimacy of Herod, he exposes the illegitimacy of Rome itself. In his introduction of the magi, the writer of Matthew reveals that Jesus has come to the Jewish nation and to all nations. His narrative insists that God's salvation cannot be thwarted and that people who are ready to listen intently to dreams, to be open and alert for alternatives to what is given, and to be ready to depart upon a different way will be the ones to experience God's coming.

In the ancient world, stars were both natural bodies by which navigation was fixed as well as supernatural portents announcing judgment or bestowing blessing. In this story they function in both ways. The magi – not kings but ancient astrologers – would have been well-recognized court figures. Astrologers were used to read "the signs of the times" and provide advice and counsel to rulers. Powerful figures, they shaped meaning and purpose within ancient societies by indicating what or who was important and predicting outcomes whether natural, military, or political. These magi, according to "Matthew," have seen a star so auspicious that they have traveled from afar to pledge their own and their nations' loyalty to this newly born king.

The irony plays out as they come to the current (illegitimate) "King of the Jews," Herod, to ask where the (real) "King of the Jews" will be born. Herod pretends interest in similarly pledging loyalty to such a king and calls upon them to report back when they have found him. After the magi find the child, they learn of Herod's disingenuousness in a dream and depart for their homelands by another way. In this setup interaction, hearers and readers of the Gospel would be reminded to think twice about how Rome used the people's dedication to God for their own ends of control. Fresh after the temple's destruction in 70 CE, Matthew's audience would have been reassured that any violence, targeting, or dislocation they may be experiencing is not new, and that facing up to this in creative ways has always been a part of what it means to be faithful.

And we, millennia later, are reminded that our faithfulness to God requires being ready to see our world differently, to go beyond what is given, to wonder and imagine God's coming in our time. Who are our Herods presuming to tell us what is of value and setting the conditions for how we must live?

This Epiphany, let us expect God to reveal to our eyes, those stars we have not yet seen, and by that vision to guide us in the very depths and practicalities and loyalties of our daily lives, to look up and chart our course by the birth of this disruptive, holy child who causes us to see and to question and ask, shall we too depart by another way?

– Noelle Damico

Hymns
Opening: We Three Kings of Orient Are 66
Sermon: Gentle Mary Laid Her Child 27
Closing: ~~Love Has Come~~ Angls, from the Realms of Glory 22

January 11, 2015

1st Sunday after Epiphany
The Baptism of Our Lord

Lessons

Revised Common Lectionary (RCL)	Roman Catholic (RC)
Gen 1:1-5	Isa 42:1-4, 6-7
Ps 29	Ps 29:1-4, 9b-10
Acts 19:1-7	Acts 10:34-38
Mk 1:4-11	Mk 1:7-11

Speaker's Introduction for the Lessons

Lesson 1

Genesis 1:1-5 (RCL)

In the midst of chaos, God spoke, created order, and called it all good.

Isaiah 42:1-4, 6-7 (RC)

In the midst of the turmoil of the exilic period, God chose a servant to create order by bringing justice and light to all nations.

Lesson 2

Psalm 29 (RCL); Psalm 29:1-4, 9b-10 (RC)

A sevenfold "the voice of the Lord" underscores the power of God evidenced in the imagery of storm, connecting to both Genesis and Mark in that voice's association with waters.

Lesson 3

Acts 19:1-7 (RCL)

Amid the confusion of the beginning church, Paul taught disciples in Ephesus that there are different types of baptisms.

Acts 10:34-38 (RC)

As questions arose about which laws Gentile Christians needed to follow, Peter told the crowd what was acceptable to God as found in the message of Jesus Christ.

Gospel
Mark 1:4-11(RCL); Mark 1:7-11 (RC)

Jesus used an everyday event in the lives of his listeners and taught a spiritual truth about the kingdom of God.

Theme
Our baptismal water must connect and renew earth's desecrated waters.

Thought for the Day
There is a tendency at every important but difficult crossroad to pretend that it's not really there.

— Bill McKibben, *The End of Nature*

Sermon Summary
This Sunday provides an opportunity to reconnect baptismal waters with the waters of the world. Confessing that we have allowed our sacred water to become divorced from the destruction and pillaging of water resources, through baptismal renewal we are invited to repent and recommit ourselves to care for creation.

Call to Worship
One: The vast expanse of sky stretches in praise.
All: The waters and streams cry out in longing.
One: The earth now hardened, incubates life.
All: And we your people awaken.

Pastoral Prayer
For the coming of this new day and the opportunity to begin again,
For the chance to think anew and the invitation to revisit and amend,
For the ways we have found refuge and challenge within this congregation and the community of Christ around the world,
For our bodies through which we know and celebrate life,
For this glorious, complicated, interconnected world that is our home,
We give you thanks and praise. Amen.

Prayer of Confession and Assurance

Tender One who gave shape to creation and who appointed us stewards
of its care, we confess that in wild abandon and willful ignorance we have
run roughshod over the earth and our fellow creatures. Renew within us a
right measure of ourselves and our place in your world. Help us recalibrate
from gluttony to gratitude, from cavorting to celebration, from domination to dwelling that we may join in your great chorus of shalom. Amen.

The time is coming, says the prophet Isaiah, when "they will not
hurt or destroy on all my holy mountain; for the earth will be full of the
knowledge of the Lord as the waters cover the sea." We trust your promise,
merciful God, and seek to know you more.

Prayer of Dedication of Gifts and Self

Out of your abundant love you have given us more than we can possibly
imagine. We offer these gifts and pledge ourselves, trusting that abundance
so that we may build just and sustainable lives together, glorifying you and
giving life to the world. Amen.

Hymn of the Day
Hail to the Lord's Anointed

The last time we encountered this Gospel lesson (a mere month ago), worship leaders faced the dilemma of presenting this text as pointing to either
Jesus' birth or the beginning of his ministry. Happily, both liturgical date
and biblical context are in agreement here.

A fine choice for today is James Montgomery's "Hail to the Lord's
Anointed," one of more than 400 hymns the author composed. One
stanza speaks of the compassion of Jesus' ministry, while another declares
the universality of his kingship. "Kings shall bow down before him ... all
nations shall adore him ... his kingdom still increasing, a kingdom without end."

Children's Time: Jesus Is Baptized

(Bring a plant mister bottle filled with water. Be sure there is water in the font. Invite the children to gather by the font, and use the mister to lightly spray them.) What do you feel? All living things need water to live. What are some ways you use water? *(Drinking, bathing, swimming, watering plants, and cooking are some answers.)* How do we use water in a special way in church? *(Baptism.)*

In today's Bible story we hear about Jesus' baptism. Jesus was baptized in a river by John the Baptist. Jesus stepped into the middle of the river where John was waiting for him. John dunked Jesus under the water, and when Jesus came up, the heavens opened and the Holy Spirit came down on Jesus like a gentle dove. And God said, "You are my Son, the Beloved, with you I am well pleased."

When we are baptized, we are washed with water and God's words. Through baptism we become children of God, members of God's family, and God calls us beloved. *(Have everyone dip a finger in the water in the font and mark their foreheads with the sign of the cross.)*

Let's pray together: Loving God, thank you for washing us with water and your word so we can become your children. Amen.

The Sermon: Baptized in Water
Scripture: Mark 1:4-11

Today we celebrate the baptism of Jesus by John in the Jordan River. In Mark's Gospel we hear that as Jesus was coming up out of the water the heavens were torn apart, the Spirit descended upon him as a dove, and a voice from heaven said, "You are my Son, the Beloved; with you I am well pleased."

Through this theological narrative we learn that God desires a renewal of covenant life. John's baptism seems to be a type of *tvilah*, the Jewish practice of immersion in a ritual bath *(mikveh)* for the purpose of purification. Tvilah was practiced in various situations: following a woman's cycle of menstruation, as a part of conversion to Judiasm, and at other times. As John is calling for repentance (1:4), the immersion in the river would have followed the person's profession to change.

By tradition, mikveh requires "living" water – water fresh from or connected to rainwater or groundwater. And as the church began to practice baptism as a mark of both repentance and incorporation into the community of Christ followers, whether through immersion, sprinkling, or pouring, water has always been the "outward sign" of the invisible grace that is the sacrament. And central to our image is Jesus, emerging from the river, water streaming through his hair and body, as God announces, "You are my Son, the Beloved; with you I am well pleased."

But if Jesus presented himself at same spot by the Jordan River today, he would find that what little water remains is polluted with saline, sewage, and agricultural runoff; it's little more than a stagnant canal of effluent. Today, the only baptism available would be in sludge.

In the last 50 years, the countries lying in the basin that drains into the Jordan have dammed and diverted more than 90 percent of the river's historic flow. Israel diverts about half of the river's average annual flow, while Syria and Jordan take about a quarter each. Palestinians, denied access to the river, take almost nothing, according to Friends of the Earth Middle East:

> As the river has dried up, the Jordan Valley has suffered an ecological collapse. Half the valley's biodiversity has been lost. The Dead Sea, sustained only by inflowing water from the Jordan, is sinking by more than a meter every year. This is not just a tragedy for wildlife. Springs that irrigated farmland for thousands of years have started to falter and fail. Wells used for generations have run dry. Refused access to the river and denied a fair share of the water pumped from beneath the land, Palestinian communities have seen fields turn to dust, livelihoods lost, and families forced to migrate ("River Out of Eden," Friends of the Earth Middle East).

The idea of our Savior being baptized in sludge is enough to stop us in our tracks. It's a blasphemous image, is it not? Are we just as outraged at the destruction and depletion of water resources at the Jordan River and around the world because of greed, conflict, and carelessness?

Pollution, damming, fracking, and unsustainable agricultural irrigation has diverted and depleted water resources globally. Sometimes these practices are legitimized as acts of survival in defense against other nations. Other times they are attempts by communities, governments, or corporations to cultivate crops or raise livestock in environments in which they would not naturally flourish. At other times corporations have dumped refuse and toxins both with and without government sanction. And some corporations have purchased or are depleting water reserves, creating enormous profit for themselves while draining what once was a public, free resource. (For Coke and the impact on the supply of water for farmers in India, see *PBS Newshour*, www.pbs.org/newshour; and Business and Human Rights Resource Center, www.business-humanrights.org).

Baptism is central to our very identity as Christians. Through it, we are pledged to Christ and incorporated into the church. Through Baptism we die to sin and rise with Christ. We are "sealed by the Holy Spirit" for God's good purpose. We too are named as God's own. But if we have lost our connection to the earth in which we live and to our impact on it, as the United Nations' prayer "Now the Waters Are Poisoned" puts it, we have truly forgotten who we are.

We have forgotten who we are.
We have alienated ourselves from the unfolding of the cosmos.
We have become estranged from the movements of the earth.
We have turned our backs on the cycles of life.
We have forgotten who we are.

We have sought only our own security.
We have exploited simply for our own ends.
We have distorted our knowledge.
We have abused our power.
We have forgotten who we are.

Now the land is barren.
And the waters are poisoned.
And the air is polluted.
We have forgotten who we are.
Now the forests are dying,
And the creatures are disappearing,
And the humans are despairing.
We have forgotten who we are.

We ask for forgiveness.
We ask for the gift of remembering.

We ask for the strength to change.
We have forgotten who we are.

(UN Environmental Sabbath Program. Pastors may wish to incorporate this prayer, together with the prayer for healing that follows, as a part of the liturgy or as a response to the sermon. See www.earthministry.org/resources/worship-aids.)

On this Sunday, when we celebrate the Baptism of our Lord and remember our own baptisms, let us begin to remember our connection between the earth and ourselves and to take up our God-entrusted responsibility as stewards of creation. Let us confess how separated our liturgy and lives have become; how we have shortchanged the very material sign of water, through which we are initiated into new life with Christ, into a liturgical abstraction. We've not simply "set apart" water but our sacred water has become dangerously divorced from its source, masquerading as apolitical.

Our baptismal renewal in the name of the one who created, the one through whom our world was created, and the one who hovered over the watery face of the deep at creation's dawn, provides an opportunity for us to refashion a sensate liturgy – alive to the challenges of preserving and sharing this precious gift of life.

May our remembrance of Jesus' baptism and our own strengthen us for the long-haul ministry of social, spiritual, and environmental wholeness God's covenant requires, that emerging from these ritual waters, we too might hear a heavenly voice, awaken from our forgetfulness, and remember whose we are.

– Noelle Damico

Hymns
Opening: Here in This Place
Sermon: Baptized in Water
Closing: I, the Lord of Sea and Sky

January 18, 2015

2nd Sunday after Epiphany
RC/Pres/UCC: 2nd Sunday in Ordinary Time

Lessons

Revised Common Lectionary (RCL)	Roman Catholic (RC)
1 Sam 3:1-10 (11-20)	1 Sam 3:3b-10, 19
Ps 139:1-6, 13-18	Ps 40:2, 4, 7-10
1 Cor 6:12-20	1 Cor 6:13c-15a, 17-20
Jn 1:43-51	Jn 1:35-42

Speaker's Introduction for the Lessons
Lesson 1
1 Samuel 3:1-10 (11-20) (RCL); 3:3b-10, 19 (RC)

> Transitions in power often require justification. And what better justification is there than divine justification? Always beware, though, of taking God's name in vain.

Lesson 2
Psalm 139:1-6, 13-18 (RCL)

> The psalm affirms how we are intimately and inescapably known by God in ways that escape human understanding – and that evoke deep trust.

Psalm 40:2, 4, 7-10 (RC)

> In this psalm we learn of the depth and strength of God's goodness.

Lesson 3
1 Corinthians 6:12-20 (RCL); 6:13c-15a, 17-20 (RC)

> We are given the freedom to make choices. Sometimes, that freedom itself dominates our choosing. "I am free to choose, so I can choose anything" is not the gift of freedom, but the tyranny of freedom.

Gospel
John 1:43-51 (RCL); John 1:35-42 (RC)

> When God calls us, it is often our own perceptions, and our own

assumptions, about where good news can originate – from whom good news can come – that limit our hearing.

Theme
We have no excuse for failure to respond to God's call.

Thought for the Day
God doesn't call the qualified; God qualifies the called.

Sermon Summary
With Eli and Samuel as examples, we learn that God will call us and equip us to speak God's word to a yearning world.

Call to Worship
Loving God, your Spirit calls us together this day to worship your name, be filled with your word, and be equipped to serve you. Help us leave our cares and worries at your feet, that we might attend fully to your presence with us today. May our worship glorify you, and bring us closer to your loving Son, Jesus our Lord. Amen.

Pastoral Prayer
God of all creation, your works sing your praise, and we your people join the chorus. We beg for your healing touch to fill the cracks where we have damaged what you declared "very good." We ask your sustaining presence for those who are ill, troubled, and in grief. We ask for your peace where violence reigns. Please grant wisdom, love, and grace to this congregation that we may spread the gospel of Jesus' love and forgiveness wherever we go. We pray in his name. Amen.

Prayer of Confession and Assurance
One: Trusting in God whose mercy knows no bounds, let us reflect on our need for grace, making confession together.
All: **Loving God, we know your voice calls us, and we should go. But often we listen instead to many other voices: the ones that say "Stay quiet," the ones that urge "Me alone," the ones that mock "You are not worthy." Forgive us the times that we**

stray. **Give us ears to hear your voice above all others. Then
grant us the courage to respond to that call. Amen.**
One: When we stray, our Lord only wants for us to turn back to God,
so we can receive the forgiveness already obtained for us by Jesus
Christ. Because of what Jesus did, and for his sake, your sins are
forgiven that you may live an amended life, and have joy in hearing his voice.

Prayer of Dedication of Gifts and Self

Jesus, you reminded your followers that where our treasure is, our hearts
will turn. Grant that as we return to you a small portion of what you have
first given us, our hearts may follow all the way, finding their true home
in you. Then may these gifts, given in your name, minister to the needs
of those whom you love and further the gospel we are sent to proclaim.
Amen.

Hymn of the Day
Here I Am, Lord

Daniel L. Schutte wrote both the text and the tune for this popular contemporary hymn for a service of ordination in 1980. While the refrain is
based upon Isaiah 6:8, the overall meaning has great similarity to the story
of Samuel's call by God. In this hymn the verses are in the person of God
and were originally sung by a soloist or cantor. The refrain is the people's
part, the response to the call. In most hymnals and in most churches the
whole congregation sings the complete hymn. If this is the case, make sure
that they understand the shift from first to third person. Try it with a soloist singing God's words and the people responding.

Children's Time: Listening to God's Call

(Teach this action.) Whenever I do this *[cup your hand around your ear],*
you say "Samuel." *(Practice this action several times. As you tell the story, cup
your hand around your ear whenever the word* Samuel *appears and let the
children say the name.)*
Samuel was boy, about the same age as some of you are. Samuel lived
many years before Jesus was born. Samuel worked with a priest named
Eli. One night, when Samuel was sleeping peacefully, the Lord called out,

"Samuel!" Samuel got up and ran to Eli. "Here I am. Did you call me?" "I didn't call you," Eli said. "Go back to bed."

The Lord called out to Samuel two more times. Finally on the third time Eli said, "If someone calls you again, say, 'Speak, Lord, your servant is listening.'"

And the Lord came and called as before, "Samuel! Samuel!"

And Samuel replied, 'Speak, your servant is listening."

God called Samuel because God had a special job for him to do.

God calls you too. I want you to loudly say your name when I make this sign *(cup both hands around both ears.)* God calls *(cup both hands around both ears)* too. God has a special job for *(cup both hands around both ears)* to do. Go and tell the story of Jesus. Amen!

The Sermon: Could God Be Calling Me?
Scripture: 1 Samuel 3:1-10 (11-20)

Can anything good come out of our town? Local headlines can certainly lead us to believe there is no good news here at all. Good news doesn't always make the news. It often seems to be a well-kept secret. And I wonder if sometimes we begin to believe our own bad press, expecting more bad news to follow. And when we expect bad news, why listen at all? Why not just hunker down and get through the moment?

I wonder if that is what was going on with the Israelites in the day of Eli and Samuel, when the word of God was rare and visions weren't widespread. Was God really silent? Or was it that no one was listening? Had people become resigned? Had even the faithful given up hope of hearing a life-changing word from God? Eli's eyes had become dim; he could no longer see the light. Had all of God's people gone to sleep?

To help understand Eli's story, here is the quick back story. Eli and Samuel lived before King Saul and King David, before the temple. "Israel" was simply 12 tribes in a loose-knit federation, led by heads of family and by judges who sometimes exercised military, legal, and/or priestly functions. Eli was one such priestly judge.

The tribes' primary bond was their common covenant with the Lord. Because there was as yet no temple, the ark of the covenant, symbolizing God's presence with the people, resided in a tent-shrine in Shiloh. Eli served as priest at this shrine, which was a hereditary position, but his sons were corrupt, irreverent, and unfit priests.

This is where Samuel grew up. He served Eli, did the chores Eli's aged bones and eyes no longer allowed: sweeping, hauling water, lighting fires. The night Samuel heard God's voice, Samuel may have been sleeping in the tent that housed the Ark. There he was, a young adolescent, curled up on his goat-hair blanket, just about asleep and someone called his name. Note how Samuel did *not* respond: He didn't say, "Go away, let me sleep longer." He didn't assume a friend was playing a joke. He didn't brush it aside as a weird dream. He acted as if the summons were true. He got up and went, saying, "Here I am. What is my task?"

It takes three times for Eli to get it: God is talking to his foster son! What do you suppose is going through Eli's mind? Jealousy that God chose this young pup who doesn't even know who God is? Excitement that God's voice is being heard once more? Fear because God doesn't tend to speak up when things are good?

Whatever was in Eli's mind, his words to Samuel were courageous. "Go back. Hear what God has to say." And Samuel obeyed. He grew to become a trustworthy prophet of the Lord, never letting any of his words "fall to the ground," never shying away from what needed to be said. So what does all of that have to do with us? First, we are reminded we do well to ask ourselves: "Does God's word fall on my deaf ears? Do I listen, but refuse to obey?"

When we lose faithfulness, it can seem as if God has fallen into deep silence. We may complain in our troubles that God has abandoned us, that God never cared. But if we have not been open, watchful for the Lord's presence, treating God only as someone to bail us out of our troubles, or or if we have not made a habit of hearing God's word, only to go on our own merry way, we may discover we have become like Eli, blind to sin in our midst.

But there is some good news here, wonderful news, in fact:
1. God is stubborn! Because God has a vision of whom we can grow to be, God doesn't give up on us; so we need not give up on God.
2. God's work doesn't depend on our belief! Samuel "didn't know the Lord yet," but God came to him anyway. Samuel got to know God, because God came to him, not because Samuel sought out God. Not that it is bad to seek God, but God doesn't depend on that. God often unexpectedly breaks into human life, revealing himself to the world.
3. God does not discriminate. Eli was old, Samuel young. God used both: Eli was mentor, interpreter, guide, and encourager. Age was no excuse to

relinquish his duties. Samuel was young and inexperienced. But youth is no excuse to fail to listen. That means God can use us too!

So the next question is: Are we going to let God use us? Because the problem with the word of God is that it can be really hard to hear. There is grace, but there is judgment too. And the judgment almost always comes when there is refusal to change. God's word almost always insists on movement forward, growth and change. God's word demands that we not just sit where we are and keep doing what we are doing.

So, while there is a lot of good going on in our town, there is need here, too. Need for the word of God to be proclaimed. There are those who live in dim despair, yearning for God to be revealed to them in their darkness.

They live right next door to you, and around the corner. You meet them in the grocery store and the post office, and in line at the bank. Children at the school just across the street didn't sleep last night because of hunger or because mom and dad had another fight. Your senior neighbor has to choose between money for medicine or for groceries. Your best friend's child may be in jail, in the grip of addiction. Who will bring God's word of hope and love and light to them? Perhaps Samuel or Samantha is sitting in our midst right now, eager, ready to go, needing only Eli's encouragement.

Of course, maybe you feel more like Eli, a bit tired, more ready for eternity than the world at hand. But God wants to use you too! Not next month, not next week, not tomorrow, but now! Those who are despairing and hopeless may not have a month or a week, or even a day. But God is here now! We are here now! The light of love in Jesus Christ shines in a dim world. Even in our town! What shall we do about it? Whom shall God send? Amen.

–Mary Corning Sanders

Hymns
Opening: God Is Here
Sermon: Here I Am, Lord!
Closing: Listen, Listen, God Is Calling!

January 25, 2015

3rd Sunday after Epiphany
RC/Pres/UCC: 3rd Sunday in Ordinary Time

Lessons

Revised Common Lectionary (RCL)	Roman Catholic (RC)
Jonah 3:1-5, 10	Jonah 3:1-5, 10
Ps 62:5-12	Ps 25:4-9
1 Cor 7:29-31	1 Cor 7:29-31
Mk 1:14-20	Mk 1:14-20

Speaker's Introduction for the Lessons
Lesson 1
Jonah 3:1-5, 10 (RCL/RC)

The prophet Jonah, delivered from the great fish, has an unpleasant surprise waiting: God is merciful beyond all measure.

Lesson 2
Psalm 62:5-12 (RCL)

The psalmist testifies to quiet but tenacious trust in God that recognizes the illusory nature of things and people who claim to have power. But ultimate power, and thus hope, belongs to God alone.

Psalm 25:4-9 (RC)

The psalmist is making a heartfelt expression of trust in the Lord.

Lesson 3
1 Corinthians 7:29-31 (RCL/RC)

The apostle Paul instructs the Corinthian Christians to live according to the urgency of God's emerging kingdom.

Gospel
Mark 1:14-20 (RCL/RC)

Jesus proclaims that the time is up and the kingdom of God is near – both on the way and already present in our midst.

Theme

God's love compels us to make room for all in the kingdom!

Thought for the Day

God does not belong to us that we may hide divine love. We belong to God, and are called to share the good news.

Sermon Summary

Even when we ignore God's claim on our lives, love will pursue us, offering surprising second chances, not only for us, but for a grand diversity of people. It is not up to us to decide who gets to hear the word of God meant for all.

Call to Worship

One: For God alone my soul waits in silence, for my hope is from God.

All: God alone is my rock and my salvation. I shall not be shaken.

One: On God rests my deliverance and my honor; my mighty rock.

All: God alone is my rock and my salvation, I shall not be shaken.

One: Trust in him at all times, O people; pour out your heart before God, our refuge.

All: God alone is my rock and my salvation, I shall not be shaken.

Pastoral Prayer

Heavenly Father, your Spirit calls and gathers from the four corners of creation. We are blessed to be in this place to praise your name with song and prayer, with the message and with our gifts. Turn our hearts toward you. Fill us, equip us for your service in a hurting world. For Jesus' sake. Amen.

Prayer of Confession and Assurance

One: Knowing that whatever our intentions, our actions often cause God grief and bring harm to our neighbor, let us turn to the one who can make our hearts new (*silence for reflection*).

All: Loving God, we confess to you that we have been careless in our care of creation. We have been reluctant to speak your

words of grace to our neighbors. We have judged others,
rather than forgiven them. We have thought of ourselves,
ignoring needs around us. Forgive us. Give us eyes to see
through the love of Jesus on the cross. Teach us to turn our
hearts toward you, learning to live toward others in your
grace, mercy, and love. Amen.

One: God hears our prayers, and for Jesus' sake, forgives us where
we have missed the mark. May God grant us peace, cleanse our
hearts, and move us to live in love for others.

Prayer of Dedication of Gifts and Self

Generous God, your bounty is endless, and you provide everything we
need for life, and to do the ministry to which you call us. We praise your
abundance, which goes beyond whatever we could ask for. Grant that
these gifts, tokens of our gratitude for all our blessings, be used in the
healing of your world, as a witness to the love you bear for all peoples.
Amen.

Hymn of the Day
Forth in Your Name, O Lord

This Charles Wesley text is one of the few that directly talks about work;
daily work specifically, but also spiritual work that is ongoing. Just as
Jonah had a task to do when he went to the people of Nineveh and just as
the people had a task to do to turn back to God, so we have a task to do
– to seek the true way of life as set out by our creator. There are numerous
tunes used for this text, the two most common being ROCKINGHAM and
CANONBURY. This is a song of commitment and of ministry. It makes an
excellent choice for a closing hymn.

Children's Time: God's Messengers

*(Invite your church organist, choir members, church receptionist, choir direc-
tor, Sunday school, and volunteers to join you in front and sit among the
children.)*

Long before Jesus was born, God chose messengers to tell the people about
God's love. One of these messengers was named Jonah. How many of you
have heard Jonah's story? He spent three days inside of a big fish because
he didn't want to be God's messenger. (*I'll bet it didn't smell very good inside*

the fish's stomach!) In today's part of the story, the Lord spoke to Jonah a second time. This time Jonah obeyed the Lord. He went to the city of Nineveh to tell the people about God.

Does God send messengers to us today? Of course. Let's meet some of the messengers who work at our church. (*Introduce all of the staff members and volunteers who have joined you and let them briefly describe how they share God's message. Be sure to say, "Thank you!"*)

Your moms and dads, grandmas and grandpas, aunts and uncles, and sisters and brothers are all God's messengers. Guess what? You're God's messengers too. Whenever we share the story of Jesus and share Jesus' love, we are God's messengers.

Let's pray: Dear God, thank you for surrounding us with messengers of your love. Help us to be your good and faithful messengers too. Amen.

The Sermon: Time Out!
Scripture: Jonah 3:1-5, 10

When my kids were little and were repeatedly defiant, I would give them a time-out. It might last 10 to 30 minutes depending on their age and their infraction. And while it didn't always change their attitude, it sometimes encouraged corrected behavior. Now, I see my oldest daughter practice the same measure with her five-year-old, with effective results.

Well, Jonah sure got a time-out that no child would envy in the (stinky?) belly of a big fish for three days! And when he had been released from it, he got another chance to follow through on the marching orders God had given. Which he did, rather grudgingly.

But this little snippet of the book of Jonah doesn't really tell us much at all. We need the whole story, which is only 48 verses long, but is packed with riches to be mined. To begin, we need to remember why Jonah was on time-out in the first place. The story starts: "Now the word of the Lord came to Jonah son of Amittai, saying, 'Go at once to Nineveh, that great city, and cry out against it; for their wickedness has come up before me.'" (Jon 1:1-2). God says, "Go at once." Right now. Right away. Immediately! And Jonah went, alright – as far as he could go in the other direction.

Then, the adventure ensues – a storm at sea; being pitched overboard by pagan sailors more willing to do the will of Jonah's God than was Jonah; being swallowed by a big fish, but not consumed, just stuck there to think about what he "coulda, shoulda" done. After being spit out on dry land and given his second chance, Jonah finally does what God requires of him (today's text). The Ninevites respond by repenting in a rather grand fashion, and God relents from punishing.

Now, if I were writing this story, this would be a great place to end it. God, through the prophet says, "Your wicked ways bring destruction on you all!" The people "get it." They make amends. God withholds disaster. A great moral lesson, with a bit of good news. God hates when you sin, will forgive when you turn over a new leaf. What more do we need to hear?

Well, apparently, Jonah still needed more, and perhaps we do too. Just in case, we'll recap what came next. Jonah got really, really annoyed with God for forgiving such a degenerate community. "I knew it! Your forgiving nature is exactly why I didn't want to come here. These people, even in repentance, don't deserve your forgiveness and should be wiped off the face of the earth. So I am going to just sit here, pout, and hope to die. So there!"

At this point, God, rather than doing to Jonah what Jonah had hoped would happen to Nineveh, provides shade for Jonah, then allows the comforting vine to die. Then, God engages the prophet in a conversation about what real grace might look like. The story ends rather abruptly, without any indication that Jonah has come around to God's way of thinking. Which, while perhaps unsatisfying to our need to have things neatly wrapped up, does offer us an opportunity to consider how the story might flow if we put ourselves in it as one of the characters. We might learn something about ourselves. Even more important, we might experience God in a deeper, more meaningful way.

While putting on Jonah's mantle might be the obvious way of entering this story, we'll leave him for a bit and consider the possibility that we are represented in these events by the pagans. Perhaps we are the fisherfolk or the Ninevites. Perhaps, even without ill intent, we have spent our lives worshiping other gods, living in ways that bring harm rather than healing. Then we hear that God of Israel is not provincial and restrictive, but that this God cares about a relationship with us as well. How might we react? Might we rejoice in a God whose love knows no ethnic boundaries, who reaches out to those on the margins? If so, would we turn our hearts toward that God, repent of our past, live amended lives? Perhaps you know the answer to this clearly, because you were once outside the fold and have been drawn by the Spirit's tether to follow God who loves, forgives, and transforms hearts and lives.

But what if we are more like Jonah – raised in the faith, around people who look and act just like us, and believe that God can only love such as we? What if we insist that we only take the message of God's love to those we deem "worthy" of it? What if we long for God, not to forgive but to punish all those who have harmed us, who think differently than we do, whose lives are such an anathema to us that we cringe in their company? What if we declare, "God welcomes all...*but* when you get here, you need to become more like us."

Who are our Ninevites? People of different ethnicity or language? Persons of dramatically different politics? Someone whose gender orientation is different than ours? Alcoholics and drug addicts? Prostitutes, politicians? Corporate CEOs? Do we even want God to change their hearts? Or would we rather be vindicated in our own self-righteousness? It is appropriate to search our hearts in these matters. And it would be better if we didn't need to end up in the belly of a big fish to do so.

But the good news is that whether we are like the pagans in this story, or like the prophet of the Lord, God's love and mercy are the same. God sent Jesus, not for some but for all. Forgiveness, reconciliation, transformation – not just for those who "deserve" it, but for those who know they don't deserve grace and could never hope to earn it. The good news is that God gives second chances. And when we say, as did Jonah, "Hell no, we won't go!" when we refuse to follow God, well, God's love will follow us all the way to hell and back, not to punish but to save us from ourselves and from the evil one, for the sake of bringing us to our true home in God. Ultimately, God invites all to the heavenly banquet. And far from being bouncers and gatekeepers, we are privileged to carry the invitations. Let us do so with joy and gladness! Amen.

–Mary Corning Sanders

Hymns
Opening: We Are Called
Sermon: Will You Come and Follow Me?
Closing: On Our Way Rejoicing

February 1, 2015

4th Sunday after Epiphany
RC/Pres/UCC: 4th Sunday in Ordinary Time

Lessons

Revised Common Lectionary (RCL)	Roman Catholic (RC)
Deut 18:15-20	Deut 18:15-20
Ps 111	Ps 95:1-2, 6-9
1 Cor 8:1-13	1 Cor 7:32-35
Mk 1:21-28	Mk 1:21-28

Speaker's Introduction for the Lessons

Lesson 1
Deuteronomy 18:15-20 (RCL/RC)

Moses is about to die. The Israelites ask for a prophet to help them remain faithful. God promises to provide one from among their own kin. This prophet will speak on God's behalf. The people must listen.

Lesson 2
Psalm 111 (RCL)

This psalm of praise for God's works and wisdom is structured as a memory aid for teaching. It is an acrostic poem that employs successive letters of the Hebrew alphabet to start each half line.

Psalm 95:1-2, 6-9 (RC)

This familiar psalm invites us to sing joyfully to the Lord.

Lesson 3
1 Corinthians 8:1-13 (RCL)

What is to be done with meat sacrificed to idols: eat it, or not? Some arrogantly say, "I know it means nothing at all if I eat it." But they offend weaker believers by eating. God doesn't want our freedom to inhibit another person's devotion.

1 Corinthians 7:32-35 (RC)

Our lives should be as free from complications as possible. Take marriage, for example. It's not wrong to be married, but it is distracting to a complete focus on the Lord. Our relationship with God should be priority number one.

Gospel
Mark 1:21-28 (RCL/RC)

Jesus teaches in Capernaum with uncommon authority. Suddenly a man possessed by a demon recognizes Jesus and cries out, asking if Jesus has come to destroy all demons. Jesus rebukes him and commands the demon to come out of the man. The people are amazed and, as a result, Jesus' reputation spreads.

Theme
God's authority rests in Jesus Christ and is above all things.

Thought for the Day
Because Jesus asserts authority belongs to God alone, we can trust that Jesus is God incarnate.

Sermon Summary
Written in the first person from the point of view of a woman worshiper at the synagogue, the sermon could be adapted to be told by a man, or put in skit form, proclaiming the message that Jesus has power over any demon that would try to claim our life.

Call to Worship
One: Let us praise the Lord. Let us give thanks to the Lord with all our hearts in the congregation.

All: Honor and majesty are God's work, and God's righteousness endures forever.

One: The works of God's hands are faithful and just. God sent redemption to the people.

All: God's praise endures forever!

Pastoral Prayer

Loving and gracious God, we give you thanks that you have made yourself known to us in the person of your Son, Jesus. Grant that our worship today both honors his name and, through his mercy, feeds our spirits with what they long for most: an awareness of your presence with us in every aspect of our lives, to guide us, keep us, and protect us in our life's journey. We ask humbly in Jesus' name. Amen.

Prayer of Confession and Assurance

One: Let us come together before God, confessing our sin and seeking God's grace in amending our lives.

All: Gracious and merciful God, we confess to you that we have often bowed to every authority but your own. We have listened to the voices that call us to worship idols of money, power, prestige, revenge and hate. We have tried to be our own authority and have failed to seek guidance from you, the source of our being. Forgive us. Turn us from false authorities, which often promise easy answers. Turn us toward you, the one who offers us the truth in love. For Jesus' sake. Amen.

One: Sisters and brothers, because of Jesus' life among us, his death on the cross, and his resurrection, we have been forgiven and called to be new creations in his name. Rejoice! Lift up your hearts! You belong to Christ forever!

Prayer of Dedication of Gifts and Self

Dear Lord, from your generous hands, we receive all that we need, and more than we dare ask. In gratitude, we return to you a mere token of your gifts to us. Grant that these gifts, and we ourselves, may be used in service toward all whom you love, that your graciousness may be known by all. In Jesus' name. Amen.

Hymn of the Day
Silence, Frenzied, Unclean Spirit!

An epiphany had already dawned upon the small band of disciples whom Jesus called; as a result they left all to follow him. Today we begin to hear how Jesus revealed himself in word and deed to the larger community. Mark reports many were "astounded" and "amazed" by Jesus, especially at his power to exorcise demons. While not for every congregation, this is the ideal Sunday to use the striking hymn by Thomas Troeger and Carol Doran, "Silence, Frenzied, Unclean Spirit!" Though the harmonies will be jarring to many, if introduced well and used sparingly, this can be a hymn that people will grow to appreciate.

Children's Time: Jesus, a Different Kind of Teacher

(Bring in a small chalkboard and chalk or a white board and marker.) *(Write "2 + 2 =" on the board.)* Can you tell me, what's the answer to this problem? *(Write "3 + 1 =.")* How about this one? *(Write "C A T.")* Now can you tell me what this spells? Good. Look at all that you have learned! How did you learn how to do math and how to read? *(From a teacher, from parents.)* Teachers help students learn many kinds of things. Who are some of your teachers? *(Accept names.)*

Jesus was a teacher, too. What did Jesus teach? *(He taught about God's love.)* Jesus taught by telling stories and telling people how to live in God's love.

But Jesus also taught in other ways that were pretty amazing. He did things that other teachers could not do. Jesus could change water into wine. He could walk on water. Jesus could heal people who were sick. Jesus could do these things because he was God's Son. Through his actions, Jesus taught the people that God's love is stronger than evil things in the world.

Let's pray: Dear Jesus, thank you for coming to earth to teach us about God's love. Amen.

The Sermon: Demon Slayer?
Scripture: Mark 1:21-28

Esther, Reuben, you should have been at Sabbath service last night! I know your kids were sick and you couldn't come, but it was worship like you've never seen before! I certainly hadn't. I expected the usual routine: the synagogue leader would invite one of the older, respected elders or rabbis to read from the Torah. You know, the ones who always sit at the benches along the side reserved for the dignitaries. Instead, the leader asked that new guy in town, Jesus, to read and speak. You remember him, he recently moved here from Nazareth? Anyway, I knew from the minute he took the scroll to read that last night's worship would be different. The way he unrolled it, as if he knew beforehand what it would say, which scroll he had been given. And after he unrolled it, he looked around at those gathered. He truly saw each person. Why, he even looked up to the women's balcony where I sat with the others behind the screen looking down on worship. I could swear that he looked right at me! His gaze was gentle, but seemed to penetrate to my very heart. I felt for a moment that he knew the deepest desire of my soul. But then, his attention turned back to the Word; he began to chant the psalm, "I will praise the Lord in the congregation! In the assembly of the people!" When he sang, Jesus brought to life the journey of our ancestors from Egypt to the promised land; he made it so real that it was as if I myself had trudged through the desert, eaten the manna provided by God. As he sang, the Word washed over me, and I knew in the deepest part of me, what I had not really known before: That God truly is faithful and just and merciful and generous and trustworthy.

It was as if Jesus were singing only to me.

And then – that awful man wandered in again! You know, poor Jacob and Ruth's oldest son. He never goes home anymore. He sleeps on the edges of the fields outside of town, snatches food from the garbage heaps, and scares the children with his mutterings and growling. I know if I should feel sorry for him but he just disgusts and frightens me. Last night, he started in again with this voice that didn't even sound human. "Jesus of Nazareth! What have you to do with us? Have you come to destroy us?"

You could have heard a pin drop! But Jesus looked right at him – he wasn't afraid at all. He just said in a ringing voice: Be silent. Come out of him!

And he was silent…at first. Time stood still. Then, the poor man twisted and convulsed and fell to the ground. And then, a miracle: he began to breathe deeply, his eyes became focused, and the son of Jacob and Ruth looked at this man Jesus as if Jesus had pulled him from the edge of hell.

At first, we were all stunned into silence. But then you could hear everyone mumbling and babbling at once. No one had ever seen anything like it – not even the eldest among us. The men's voices drifted up to the women's balcony in snippets:

"Maybe Jesus was possessed!"

"No, no, it couldn't be. He must be a powerful man of God, a prophet."

"Maybe, but whatever he is, we should keep any eye on him. I'm suspicious. This Jesus could be a dangerous man."

Those are the kinds of things I heard others saying. But this is what happened for me: I tell you chains fell from my own heart. A tiny light broke into my darkness. And I dared to hope! If Jesus could do this thing for the son of Jacob and Ruth, could it happen for me?

I know, you think I am an ordinary, pious woman, dutifully raising my children, respectful of my parents, obedient to my husband. You think I am happy. But I have never told a soul about the demons that live in my heart. I try to hide them even from myself, but their voices keep me awake at night. The voices of rage and despair, of jealousy and resentment. The voices of doubt and immobilizing fear. Maybe no one else can hear them, but at times, I feel them drowning out all other voices. They empty my heart and make me yearn for something that, before today, I could not name.

I see you looking at each other, Reuben and Esther. Maybe you are among those who don't believe in demons. Maybe you think my tale is crafted of stardust? But you yourselves have seen the work of demons. How else can you explain children hurt by those who should love them best? How else do you explain the invisibility of the homeless? How else do you explain the powerlessness good people feel when confronted with oppression that crushes an entire population?

But I know what I saw! I know what I heard! At Sabbath last night I experienced God's word broken open and made alive in a way I have never seen happen before. It didn't just go into my ears and head, but into my heart. I experienced hope that is totally new. This man of God wielded power, not to maim, but to make whole. In my brokenness, I heard a promise that I know in my heart I can trust: that somehow, there is purpose in my living; that somewhere, there is meaning, not just in my joys and triumphs, but in the pain and the questions, even in the defeat.

I have hope that maybe Jesus can do for me what he did for Ruth and Jacob's son. Maybe Jesus can imprison the demons that have imprisoned me. But after all I saw, after all I heard, I still hesitate. What if the demons inside me are "who I am"? If Jesus sends them away, will there be any of "me" left? And what would she look like? Who would she be? Would I still be Miriam? Dare I ask? Dare I follow?

I am not sure of much except this: I want to know more! How about you? I hear he will be at worship next week, too! Are you going to be there? I certainly will!

– Mary Corning Sanders

Hymns
Opening: Gather Us In
Sermon: All Glory, Laud, and Honor
Closing: We Are Marching in the Light of God

February 8, 2015

5th Sunday after Epiphany
RC/Pres/UCC: 5th Sunday in Ordinary Time

Lessons

Revised Common Lectionary (RCL)	Roman Catholic (RC)
Isa 40:21-31	Job 7:1-4, 6-7
Ps 147:1-11, 20c	Ps 147:1-6
1 Cor 9:16-23	1 Cor 9:16-19, 22-23
Mk 1:29-39	Mk 1:29-39

Speaker's Introduction for the Lessons
Lesson 1
Isaiah 40:21-31 (RCL)

Israel complains that God has abandoned them, but it isn't true. Isaiah tells them to look at creation and see God's presence. God created everything and still rules over all people and earthly authorities.

Job 7:1-4, 6-7 (RC)

Job complains to God that his life is nothing. Pain and suffering are Job's companions day and night.

Lesson 2
Psalm 147:1-11, 20c (RCL); Psalm 147:1-6 (RC)

This psalm's praise of God blends gratitude for the rebuilding of Jerusalem and gathering of outcasts (exiles from Babylon?) with God's care and providence seen in creation's cycle of life.

Lesson 3
1 Corinthians 9:16-23 (RCL); 1 Corinthians 9:16-19, 22-23 (RC)

Paul submits himself to the different lifestyles of people he's trying to reach with the gospel. In this sense he makes himself weak, a slave of sorts. Paul's desire is to share with them in the blessings associated with the gospel.

Gospel
Mark 1:29-39 (RCL/RC)
One day Jesus heals Peter's mother-in-law, along with other sick people. The next morning, while Jesus is praying alone, the disciples search him out to report that everyone is looking for him. Jesus then decides to leave for other villages where he can pursue his mission of preaching.

Theme
God lifts us up that we might be of service to others.

Thought for the Day
God's strength is often manifest in our struggles, and helps us grow through them, that in doing so, we bear witness to Jesus' transforming love.

Sermon Summary
When Jesus healed Peter's mother-in-law and she began to serve them, we are given an example of how we are given new purpose when we have been restored by God. As a contemporary example, the true story is told of a cancer survivor who learned blessing in serving.

Call to Worship
One: Praise the Lord!

All: How good it is to sing praises to our God; for he is gracious, and a song of praise is fitting.

One: The Lord builds up Jerusalem; God gathers the outcasts of Israel.

All: God heals the brokenhearted, and binds up their wounds.

One: The Lord lifts up the downtrodden; God opposes the oppressors.

All: Sing to the Lord! With thanksgiving make melody to our God on the lyre. Praise the Lord!

Pastoral Prayer

Dearest Lord Jesus, we give you thanks that your Spirit has gathered us here today, to attend to your word, sing your praises, and be nourished by your presence. Help us set aside the cares and worries of the day. Teach us to turn our hearts to you, that we may leave this place refreshed, renewed, and restored, ready to serve you with joy. Amen.

Prayer of Confession and Assurance

One: Trusting together in God's steadfast mercy, let us search our hearts, coming before God's throne to confess our sins (silence for reflection).

All: We confess, gracious God, that we have not lived as you have longed for us to live. We have failed to love you above all else, we have been blind to our neighbor's needs, we have spoken when silence would have been golden, and failed to speak on behalf of the voiceless. We have trusted everything but you to lift us from the darkness. Forgive us, dear Lord. Cleanse our hearts, make them more like yours, teach us to live like Jesus. Amen.

One: Our God is indeed, gracious and merciful, slow to anger, abounding in steadfast love and forgiveness. For Jesus' sake, your sins are forgiven. Go in peace to lift up those who are down, as you have been lifted up in Christ.

Prayer of Dedication of Gifts and Self

Blessed are you, O Lord our God, creator of the universe. From your hands we receive all that we need, often before we even know to ask. Along with our thanks, we return to you a portion of these gifts. Let them be used in Jesus' name to serve those in need, that whatever good works these gifts accomplish might glorify our Father in heaven. Amen.

Hymn of the Day
In Solitude

Seen as a whole, the Epiphany season is a crescendo to Transfiguration Sunday, when we hear the voice from heaven confirm that Jesus is, indeed, God's beloved son. Perhaps as a contrast, today could be a time to go with

247

Jesus to that quiet place in the heart where, in prayer, we speak to God and God speaks to us. Ruth Duck's "In Solitude," set to the tune LAND OF REST is a wonderful choice for such a journey. The sincere text and gentle tune meld seamlessly together, resulting in a beautiful invitation to and reflection upon prayer. Another great choice is Jay Beech's "Everybody Needs."

Children's Time: A Healing Touch

(Bring in a cotton ball, piece of satin, soft stuffed animal, and other soft materials.)
(Pass around the soft items you brought.) How are all of these items the same? *(They are soft.)* Can we tell they are soft by looking at them? Smelling, tasting, or listening to them? How can we tell whether or not something is soft? *(By touching it.)* We can use our sense of touch to tell if something is soft or rough. What are other ways we use our sense of touch?

Jesus was a wonderful teacher. People listened to his stories for hours. They followed Jesus wherever he went because they wanted to learn more about God's love. Jesus had another very special way of teaching. Jesus used the sense of touch. In today's Bible story, a woman was sick with a high fever. Jesus gently held her hand, and her fever was gone. Jesus used his touch to heal people. When people heard about Jesus' healing touch, people came from the whole city, bringing their sick loved ones to be healed. Through his healing touch, Jesus taught people about the power of God's love.

Let's pray: Dear Jesus, help us to share your love through our words and our actions. Amen.

The Sermon: Lifted to Serve
Scripture: Mark 1:29-39

The awesome thing about scripture is that when we read our ancestors' stories, we find our own there as well. Hundreds of years before Jesus, God's people had forsaken the path upon which God had placed them. As a result, God had allowed the leaders of Judah to be conquered by the Babylonians and carried off into exile. Because exile meant that not only were they far from their homeland, the Israelites were even more

importantly far from the temple. Thus, when they were torn from the promised land, they felt they had also been torn away from God. Yes, they had sinned despite prophets' warnings. But now they were contrite. Yet it seemed no matter how loud they cried, there was no God to hear. They were far from home, alone, suffering, feeling abandoned by God.
Haven't many of us have felt that way at times too? No matter who we are, there are periods during which we slog through grief, fear, anxiety. We wrestle with health issues, power struggles, poor economy, shattered relationships, and tattered dreams. We have experienced disappointment with ourselves, our circumstances, even with God. Sometimes, it has been due to our own sin; sometimes the sins of others; sometimes simply that we live in a broken and weary world. If we can pray at all, ours are prayers of despair: At such times, it might be tempting to choose not to believe in God at all, rather than in a God who seems not to care.

But Isaiah proclaimed to our ancestors, and to us, that into this darkness comes a light. The light is a word from the Lord. Not just any word, but a promise: "Wait on the Lord, he will lift you up." If you have ever been stuck in the "down position" and needed a helping hand, you know what it is like to have no other hope, except in the promise that when we can't even crawl, God will come lift us up, just as the prophet proclaims.
I wonder if Peter's mother-in-law had come to that point of resigned waiting. Had she given up on the possibility of ever being well again? Did she feel God had given up on her? Had she given up on God? Frustratingly, Mark leaves out all those details. We are simply told that Jesus came in, took her by the hand, lifted her up, and the fever left her.

Then, what comes next? "She began to serve them." Some today might react: "Really!? Is there no rest for the weary? We might worry about rigid, archaic gender roles. But such a knee jerk reaction to the story could cause us to miss the deeper promise here.

The promise is illustrated by the story of my friend Connie, who permits me to share it. Several years ago her husband and I were planning her funeral. She had a rare, virulent form of non-Hodgkin's lymphoma. The treatments were so brutal, they risked killing her before cancer did. Her goal was to live long enough to see her daughter graduate from junior high The ordeal was so intense at one point, her whole life became fogged in. She has since described it this way: "I lost about six weeks of my life where I don't remember anything but a few scattered moments. What would I have done without y'all praying for me and my family? I certainly couldn't pray for myself and had to depend on others to do it for me."

But prayer was all we had. We couldn't cure her, we couldn't lift her up. But with the help of her marvelous medical team, God did lift her up. Gradually, PET scans showed signs of retreating cancer. Eventually, she not only saw her daughter graduate junior high, but high school, and college! Connie wasn't lifted up as quickly as was Peter's mother-in-law, but healing happened nonetheless.

Connie related an important turning point in her recovery. Before her illness, as a professional woman, she never described herself as a domestic diva. Her very least favorite chore was laundry. While she was ill, her teenage daughter managed it, but clean clothes ended up not in closets and drawers but big, green garbage bags.

At first, when Connie was home from the hospital, she was so weak that the journey from bed to sofa took all energy she had. Eventually, though, a need to "do something" manifested and she began to fold the laundry. She marveled that this mundane chore, once a burden, felt like a privilege, a blessing, and even a joy. Rather than a sense of drudgery, folding sheets and matching socks became an occasion for gratitude.

This was more than "mere" physical healing. Connie experienced a soul healing also. She received restoration of purpose as well as a return to participation in family activities. Thus, her family began to heal as well. This is because healing of an individual is not an isolated event. We each play a role in the fabric of life, wherein, if one part is torn, the whole suffers. Thus, when Jesus lifts up one, all around that one also experience restoration. When we are healed, we are blessed to be a blessing.

The same God who raised Jesus from the grave, turning death itself into new life, uses our healed wounds as means of healing for others. Henri Nouwen called those who have been restored and serve others "wounded healers." Restored, we try to encourage others in their struggles so they may come to recognize that God has not abandoned them. Then, as others also experience healing, we make room for them to work alongside of us in also blessing others.

As if that weren't enough, we often experience that sweet paradox: that in attempting to pass on Jesus' blessing, we ourselves heal even more deeply. I don't know how it works. But I have seen it. Connie experienced it. I bet Peter's mother-in-law did, too.

So, remember these things: First, if you are so far down that "low" seems "up," God's promise is for you. God has not abandoned you. The God who turned death into life wants only wholeness and healing for you and will be your strength. Next, if you have experienced God's healing in any way, you were healed with a purpose: to reflect the light of Christ in such a way that others can trust God's promise is also for them. May we ever grow in trust of the one who loves us and longs to lift us up to serve with joy! Amen.

– Mary Corning Sanders

Hymns
Opening Hymn: On Eagles' Wings
Sermon Hymn: Healer of Our Every Ill
Closing Hymn: Go, My Children, with My Blessing

February 15, 2015

Last Sunday after Epiphany/Transfiguration
RC/Pres/UCC: 6th Sunday in Ordinary Time

Lessons

Revised Common Lectionary (RCL)	Roman Catholic (RC)
2 Kings 2:1-12	Lev 13:1-2, 44-46
Ps 50:1-6	Ps 32:1-2, 5, 11
2 Cor 4:3-6	1 Cor 10:31—11:1
Mk 9:2-9	Mk 1:40-45

Speaker's Introduction for the Lessons
Lesson 1
2 Kings 2:1–12 (RCL)

Elijah is taken away from Elisha by a chariot of fire. Elisha asks for a double measure of Elijah's spirit.

Leviticus 13:1-2, 44-46 (RC)

There was a direct connection between physical and spiritual health at the writing of Leviticus. Lepers were identified as outcasts and separated from others, just as Jesus would be.

Lesson 2
Psalm 50:1-6 (RCL)

The psalmist confesses a God who comes and enters into covenant relationship, summoning all creation to the one who "shines" forth on the mount of Zion.

Psalm 32:1-2, 5, 11 (RC)

The psalmist describes the blessings received when forgiveness is given.

Lesson 3
2 Corinthians 4:3-6 (RCL)

God has shown light in our hearts so that we may see the face of Jesus Christ. The truth is not veiled to us.

1 Corinthians 10:31—11:1 (RC)
Everything you do, may it be for the glory of God not of idols.

Gospel
Mark 9:2–9 (RCL)
Jesus takes Peter, James, and John to a mountain, and is transfigured before them. They hear a voice say, "This is my Son, the Beloved; listen to him!"

Theme
Transfiguration has to do with human transformation in God's imagination.

Thought for the Day
We think and then plan, but as Napoleon Hill suggests, "the beginning, as you will observe, is in your imagination."

Sermon Summary
Naturally, this sermon tries to shed light on the transfiguration of Jesus. The disciples lack perspective and Jesus supplies this when he takes Peter and James and John with him up the mountain to witness his meeting with Elijah and Moses. In the best way, this experience helps the disciples better cope later with Jesus' passion.

Call to Worship
One: The mighty one, God the Lord, speaks and summons the earth.
All: From the rising of the sun to its setting.
One: Out of Zion, the perfection of beauty, God shines forth.
All: Our God comes and does not keep silence.
One: Before him is a devouring fire
All: And a mighty tempest all around him. He calls to the heavens above and to the earth, that he may judge his people.
One: The heavens declare his righteousness, for God himself is judge.
All: Amen.

Pastoral Prayer

God of grace, as we witness the beauty of mountains may we remember as well that in the biblical narrative these fateful and marvelous terrestrial monuments of your creation serve also a revealing purpose in our faith story. On Calvary Jesus was crucified and from Bethany Jesus ascended. When you gave the books of Law to Moses, you, O Lord, did so on Sinai, and it was upon Mount Ararat that Noah's ark was lodged. When we read in our scripture about your holy mountains you remind us that something mysterious is at work – and so help us pay attention. As we begin our Lenten journey this coming week, give us the insight and discernment to once again see your truth revealed to us in Jesus, and we pray this in his name. Amen.

Prayer of Confession and Assurance

O Lord our God, king of the universe, we confess that as we approach Jesus' mount of transfiguration, that it is often difficult for us to recognize the deep things you want to convey to your people. Bestow on us your divine knowledge to encourage us to seek the truth that you offer us on this mountain of transfiguration. We also confess our need for the bountiful life that Peter, James, and John saw revealed in Jesus' meeting on this mountain with Moses and Elijah. Let us come down from the mountain to take up our cross and follow Jesus today, tomorrow, and forever. We pray this and everything in Jesus' holy name. Amen.

> One: Christ loves you and gathers you in as Christ is our savior.
> **All: Thanks be to God! May we all be forgiven in the name of Christ. Amen.**

Prayer of Dedication of Gifts and Self

Out of our great need, O Gracious Provider, we come not only to hear the word that will fulfill our heart's proper desire, but also to give of ourselves. Help us live in contentment and make us generous people. We desire to be able to be so strong of faith that, like those disciples who came down the mountain, we can truly follow Jesus as we give our lives away to those in need. In Jesus' sacred and holy name, we pray. Amen.

Hymn of the Day
Jesus, Take Us to the Mountain

Transfiguration Sunday is a liturgical mountaintop, capping off Epiphany like a jewel and giving us a glimpse of Jesus in his splendor. But though a high peak, it is not the highest; that honor belongs to Easter alone. Before then we sojourn the valley of Lent. "Jesus, Take Us to the Mountain" is a splendid hymn for Transfiguration Sunday by Jaroslav Vajda and Carl Schalk. The first verses have us on the mount of transfiguration; the fourth verse whisks us to that sadder mount, Golgotha; the final verse leads us beyond to the point of telling Jesus' story, just as Jesus instructs his disciples to do.

Children's Time: A New View

(Bring a pair of sunglasses.)
(Put on the sunglasses.) Do I need to wear sunglasses in here? *(No.)* When do people usually wear sunglasses? *(Outside on a sunny day.)* Why? *(The sun is very bright and it bothers our eyes.)* We wear sunglasses to protect our eyes from too much bright sunlight.

In our Bible story today, three of Jesus' disciples would have appreciated having some sunglasses! Jesus led Peter, James, and John to the top of a mountain. When they reached the top, Jesus changed right in front of them. His clothes became dazzling white and his face shown like the sun. The disciples shielded their eyes from the bright light like this *(shield your eyes with your hand)*. The disciples were terrified! That means they were very, very scared. Then a cloud softly floated down and covered the mountaintop. From the cloud came a voice saying, "This is my Beloved Son. Listen to him." God was giving the disciples a special message: Jesus was God's Son!

Let's pray: Dear Lord, on bright, sunny days remind us that your love surrounds us like the sunshine. Amen.

The Sermon: Follow Jesus to Transformation
Scripture: Mark 9:2-9

On Ash Wednesday – only four day from now – our congregation will join other churches around the world in a Christian Lenten observance. Some will ask their Lenten question: "What will I give up for Lent?" Perhaps, this is not a bad question. We can say that giving up something can put us in closer touch with God. But sometimes "the giving up something for Lent" mocks an otherwise good spiritual practice, as in "I am giving up chocolate for Lent" or "I am giving up texting while driving for Lent." Perhaps this last Sunday in Epiphany we can use our text to genuinely prepare for Jesus' suffering, death, and resurrection as individuals and as a community of faith. Rather than giving up something – even if we can – may we at least attend to the biblical story. (Read: Mark 9:2-9.)

How do we prepare for Lent? Maybe the disciples can offer us a path. Mark tells us the disciples have been with Jesus some time now. Right before their ascent of the mountain of transfiguration, two events had set the context of our transfiguration story. First, Peter answers Jesus' question about Jesus own identity: "You are the Messiah" (Mk 8:29).

Second, Jesus summarizes what it really means to be "messiah." The Messiah will suffer, be rejected by the religious authorities, and be killed. Yet, Jesus' final word is one of hope: "After three days I will rise again." The hope Jesus offers, however, seems lost on Peter, who immediately re-bukes Jesus to his face. But Jesus rebukes Peter right back, telling him that he is setting his mind on human things and not divine things. Is this any way to set the mood for the revelation of Christ's glory in transfiguration? The disciples must have been seriously questioning why Jesus would be so gloomy about being Israel's promised Messiah.

Clearly, however, Mark tells the Gospel readers that the disciples were not yet ready to understand who Jesus was or why he had come. Perhaps, later, they would understand, but not until after the resurrection. So, for the disciples to proclaim Jesus' messiah-ship, at this point in Mark's story, reminds us of Yahweh's words to Job: "Who is this that darkens counsel by words without knowledge? Gird up your loins like a man [adult], I will question you, and you shall declare to me" (Job 38:1-3).

The point, of course, in Job and with respect to the disciples was that neither understood the ways of God nor what was happening on the bigger, cosmic stage. The view from the mountain was a view to give perspective. Before Jesus' mountaintop revelation the disciples had been both perplexed and afraid. But all people need perspective – even disciples – maybe especially disciples! By perspective, I simply mean gaining an insight into separating what is truly important from things that only seem important. John Dewey in *A Common Faith* considered the religious as "whatever introduces genuine perspective . . . into the piecemeal and shifting episodes of existence" (*Reinhold Niebuhr and John Dewey: An American Odyssey*, by Daniel F. Rice).

The truth is unless we are looking for the right things with a proper perspective, then we will never see what it is we need to see to be God's people. My former district superintendent was in a local grocery store some years ago trying to find the items on his spouse's grocery list. One item stumped him: "a 19-inch graham cracker pie crust tin." He found the pie crust section, but no 19-inch graham cracker pie crusts. The manager said they were out of them, but would have some on Monday. But he said his spouse needed the pie crust tin now, so the search continued. After about ten employees and some other random customers looked high and low – a covered-dish dinner was at stake, after all – a woman said, "Let me see that list."

Then she said, "Could your wife have meant "one 9-inch pie crust tin" instead of a "19-inch-graham cracker pie crust tin?" Mystery solved, but my former district superintendent bought two to add up to 18 inches just in case. If we search for the wrong item, then we will never find what we need to give a properly divine perspective on life.

The life of prayer offers this perspective and is why we speak about prayer more at Lent than at most other times of our church year. Prayer is not simply needed at times when we know things are out of our control, as for example in the hospital's emergency room. Prayer helps us keep the perspective that, for those who follow Christ, the life God has given us is always out of our control. This is the rub for those who profess faith in the God of Jesus: We are not our own, we have been bought with a price (1 Cor 6:19-20). The transfiguration was a piece of pure experience for the disciples. This experience showed them in a mysterious way that Jesus was who he claimed to be. Seeing who Jesus really is in fact is a way that God transforms us.

A sign of a healthy spiritual person is one who takes Paul's guidance to heart. "Do not be conformed to this world, but be transformed by the renewing of your minds, so that you may discern what is the will of God" (Rom. 12:2). Transformation is a quest for life's meaning and allows God to change you into what God created you to be. God takes the stuff of brain and heart and shapes a unique creature. You.

Clearly the task of a church is to transform people, values, and meaning from something less than fully human into something fully faithful.

In fact, we could measure any church as successful by its ability to change people's lives. We might even measure our church's success by the measure of transforming people into something bearing marks of a new creation. The disciples as they were on the mountain of transfiguration no doubt received a new perspective! Amen.

– David Neil Mosser

Hymns
Opening: Christ, Whose Glory Fills the Skies
Sermon: O Wondrous Sight! O Vision Fair
Closing: Christ, upon the Mountain Peak

February 18, 2015

Ash Wednesday

Lessons

Revised Common Lectionary (RCL)	Roman Catholic (RC)
Joel 2:1-2, 12-17 or Isa 58:1-12	Joel 2:12-18
Ps 51:1-17	Ps 51:3-4, 5-6, 12-13, 14, 17
2 Cor 5:20b—6:10	2 Cor 5:20—6:2
Mt 6:1-6, 16-21	Mt 6:1-6, 16-18

Speaker's Introduction for the Lessons

Lesson 1

Joel 2:1–2, 12–17 (RCL); Joel 2:12–18 (RC)

> The prophet says the day of the Lord is coming, full of darkness and gloom. Even so, there is always time to return to the Lord, who is gracious and merciful.

Lesson 2

Psalm 51:1-17 (RCL); Psalm 51:3-4, 5-6, 12-13, 14, 17 (RC)

> This penitential psalm, traditionally attributed to David after Nathan has denounced his sin against Uriah, pleads for healing and restoration that leads to a clean heart and right spirit.

Lesson 3

2 Corinthians 5:20b—6:10 (RCL); 2 Corinthians 5:20—6:2 (RC)

> Paul describes the truth of his work as an ambassador of Christ and urges repentance upon the Corinthians. Christ has done the work of reconciliation; the reader is entreated to respond.

Gospel

Matthew 6:1-6, 16-21 (RCL); Matthew 6:1-6, 16-18 (RC)

> Before and after the verses that give us the Lord's Prayer (vv. 9–13), Jesus gives other instructions about how to pray. He warns especially against being like hypocrites who look sad in order to show their

repentance. Instead, the faithful, even while fasting, should be joyful before others.

Theme
Ash Wednesday concerns our coming to an honest assessment about who we are before God.

Thought for the Day
"The worst sin – perhaps the only sin – passion can commit, is to be joy-less."

–Dorothy L. Sayers, Gaudy Night

Sermon Summary
On Ash Wednesday, given the text Psalm 51, the sermon focuses on the idea of confession and restoration in God's continuing care for us. Modeled on David's prayer of confession, this sermon helps us confront our own need to confess.

Call to Worship
God of ash and dust, you molded us from the dust of the earth, and to dust we shall return. May the ashes placed upon our foreheads this day remind us of who we are, and whose we are. Pull us back to you, O God, for you are gracious and merciful, slow to anger, and abounding in steadfast love. Heal the hardness of our hearts, that we may be faithful disciples of the one who makes all things new, Jesus the Christ. Amen.

Pastoral Prayer
O God, we've allowed ourselves to be distracted and busy with many deceptive things we see as desirable. We've craved success and material bits and pieces. We've hurt one another. We've each participated in devastating your earth's resources. We have waged wars with your other children, O God, and now we ask you to forgive us. As the celebrants place ashes on our foreheads, we remember that we are nothing without you and that to ashes we will return. Make us people ready and willing to witness with our lives and words the truth that Jesus came to save sinners and redeem the

world. Create in us a clean heart, O God, that we might see you, love you, and serve you. Amen.

Prayer of Confession and Assurance

Gracious God, we confess that we have not loved you with our whole hearts, and we have not loved our neighbors as we love ourselves. Forgive us, we pray. Open our hearts wide to you, that you might renew our faith and strengthen us for obedient service. On this day, when the prophet speaks of the trumpet blast, Joel issues a warning to the people. May the trumpet for this Ash Wednesday beckon us to the dangers of our world and summon us to return to you, O God; may it help us lament the bitterness of our souls, and embrace our part of the sorry circumstances of our world. We pray all this in Jesus' name. Amen.

Hear the words of the prophet Joel: "Yet even now, says the Lord, return to me with all your heart, with fasting, with weeping, and with mourning; rend your hearts and not your clothing. Return to the Lord, your God, for [God] is gracious and merciful, slow to anger, and abounding in steadfast love, and relents from punishing."

Prayer of Dedication of Gifts and Self

At times we forget, O God, that it is in the act of being generous to others that we give you the occasion to bless us as your people. Enrich us with possibilities of reaching out and assisting those in need. Help us understand that in giving to others we too are getting the gift of a generous heart – all in the name of Christ. Amen.

Hymn of the Day
Ashes

Ash Wednesday is intended to be a time of penetrating self-reflection that lays the heart bare before God. Both the texts we hear and the rituals we use encourage this, yet we need to hear the promise of grace to truly go to such a vulnerable place. Tom Conroy's "Ashes" brings such a perspective to Ash Wednesday. He uses ashes as a metaphor for the repentance we show – the amends we make to our lives – that we then offer to God, not for the purpose of appeasing God; but in order to please God. Michael Joncas's accompaniment fills out Conroy's tune beautifully.

Children's Time: Ash + Wednesday

(*Bring ash mixture – ashes plus water or olive oil – a palm branch, a sheet of paper, and a marker.*)

(*Hold up the palm branch.*) Do you know what kind of tree this branch is from? (A palm.) Palm trees grew where Jesus lived. If I burned this palm branch, what would be left? (*Ashes.*) These are ashes from a palm branch. (*Dip a fingertip in the ashes and hold it up for the children to see.*)

What day of the week is it today? (*Wednesday.* Write *Ash + Wednesday* on the paper.) Today is Ash Wednesday. On Ash Wednesday we remember that God made us and we belong to God. We mark each person's forehead with a cross of ashes as we say, "Remember that you are dust and to dust you shall return." The ash cross tells us that the church season of Lent is beginning. It lasts six weeks. During Lent we hear stories about Jesus' life. When Lent is through, it will be Easter.

(*Mark each child's forehead with an ash cross as you say the words from the previous paragraph. Or mark them with the ash cross when the whole congregation comes forward.*)

Let's pray together: Dear God, thank you for making us and loving us. It's good to know that we belong to you. Amen.

The Sermon: Blotting Out . . . Washing Thoroughly
Scripture: Psalm 51:1-17

The substance of Psalm 51 is a plea for God's mercy. This remorseful one who prays this prayer admits sin and confesses to God that these trespasses are ever before the sinner. This contrite pray-er acknowledges to God that "against you, you alone, have I sinned." This prayer of confession asks God to offer the pray-er a new start and a way out of his sinful, transgressing, iniquitous ways. At last – and importantly – the penitential pray-er seeks both the joy of God's salvation and the gift of a willing spirit. As painful as the circumstance is from which this prayer comes, few of us do not recognize the situations in which we ourselves could pray this prayer.

On a day/evening like today we might ask, "What is Ash Wednesday?" We begin the Lenten season with this day designated as Ash Wednesday. As many Roman Catholics make a great deal of the day, too often Protestants let Ash Wednesday go more or less unobserved. Thus if we can preserve the day, then we make a better start in observing the Season of Lent. In some respects it is easy to see why people would avoid Ash Wednesday, because it is a day that is all about sin. Here is a contemporary situation posed by John Killinger in his sermon titled "Some Notes on Sin in the Modern World." Killinger writes:

It was one of those afternoon talk shows. I happened to be flipping channels and caught it for a moment. Several young people were sitting on the stage, with an audience out front. They were discussing lifestyles. Somebody accused a young woman, who apparently had just confessed to something she was doing, of being a sinner. There was laughter and applause from the audience.

It didn't flap the young woman. She appeared in high gear. "Does anybody really sin anymore?" she asked. "I mean, here we are living among all these rapists and serial killers and mass-murderers, the shadow of the Holocaust and all those assassinations and terrorists bombings, and everybody's doing whatever he or she wants to. Does what I do really matter?"

Nobody said anything. It was a big question, and they weren't sure of the answer. Does it matter what we do anymore in the kind of world we live in? (*Pulpit Digest*, March/April 1998, Logos Productions, Inver Grove Heights, MN, p. 35.)

Truly, John Killinger hit upon one of the chief questions of our time – a question that Ash Wednesday addresses in no uncertain terms. The church suggests that our psalm under consideration on Ash Wednesday cuts to the bone of that question. Psalm 51 says plainly: "Have mercy on me, O God, according to your steadfast love; according to your abundant mercy blot out my transgressions. Wash me thoroughly from my iniquity, and cleanse me from my sin. For I know my transgressions, and my sin is ever before me."

Even if the young woman on television did not know whether she was a sinner, no less a religious and leader-luminary than King David – one of our Bible's towering figures knows that he is – and he pleads for God's forgiveness. But more than that, King David calls for restoration. And like every age, this period of time too is an age where the need for restoration is palpable and intense.

The whole idea of human sin is a difficult one, no doubt, for us moderns. One of my seminary professors, Albert Outler told us a story about understanding sin that later appeared in his book *Theology in the Wesleyan Spirit.* He wrote:

> I still remember a lanky West Texas Pelagian [denies original sin] in one of my first classes here who came by the office to complain that I sounded as if human sinning were something deeper and more mysterious than a failure of free will or a moral lapse. Such a strange idea intrigued him and he asked for suggestions for further reading. At the time, John Whale's *Christian Doctrine* was newly published, so I mentioned that. To his credit, he went off and found Whales, but was back a fortnight later still more baffled – since Whales as some of you know, was a good deal more of a "classical Protestant" on this point than I have ever been. We talked about it a while and finally he gave vent to a real outcry from his heart: "Well," he said, "if we don't have the power to decide to sin or decide not to sin, all I've got to say is, 'God help us!' " This, of course, was an obvious cue for pointing out that he had unwittingly betrayed himself into involuntary orthodoxy! (Albert Outler, *Discipleship Resources.*)

What Outler's story reminds us is that without God people are frail with respect to action. It is God who continues to pull us and invite us into being the people God created us to be. King David prays: "Restore to me the joy of your salvation, and sustain in me a willing spirit." Joy is the purpose or target or aim or goal of the Christian life; we don't produce joy or manufacture it. Only God can do that! No one in this sanctuary – or any sanctuary – for an imposition of ashes worship service has that joy within us – unless given by God. We humans seek joy through entertainment and amusement, which offers fleeting joy – a kind of synthetic ecstasy.

Show business is a shrine to our culture's decline of joy. Many people need constant comedy – an endless parade of situation comedies to keep us lubricated with pleasure of mindless television. In spending time in this way – day in and day out – we display the dearth of any self-generated meaning in relationships in the house or in the neighborhood. Entertainment is not wrong and Jesus through his parables certainly demonstrated his well-tuned sense of humor. But it's foolish to believe we will ever find authentic joy from the American entertainment industry. Joy is not an artifact; it can't be purchased. We don't need a distraction from our nervous lives; we need a remedy. The only antidote comes from a vibrant connection with Jesus. Our need for joy is sincere, but how we get that need satisfied often is not reliable.

As we step into the spiritual desert of Lent, may we come out on the other side with a sense of joy. We find this joy in the confession of our sin and the hope of God's restoration of us in Christ.

– David Neil Mosser

Hymns
Opening: Lord, Who throughout These Forty Days
Sermon: Out of the Depth I Cry unto Thee
Closing: *Saranam, Saranam*

February 22, 2015

1st Sunday in Lent

Lessons

Revised Common Lectionary (RCL)	Roman Catholic (RC)
Gen 9:8-17	Gen 9:8-15
Ps 25:1-10	Ps 25:4-9
1 Pet 3:18-22	1 Pet 3:18-22
Mk 1:9-15	Mk 1:12-15

Speaker's Introduction for the Lessons

Lesson 1
Genesis 9:8-17 (RCL); Genesis 9:8-15 (RC)

> After the great flood, God establishes a covenant with Noah that never again will the earth and its inhabitants be destroyed by water. As a sign of the covenant, God places the rainbow in the clouds so that humankind may see it and know.

Lesson 2
Psalm 25:1-10 (RCL); Psalm 25:4-9 (RC)

> This psalm is a prayer for deliverance. Attributed to David, its acrostic form contains many elements of a psalm of lament and complaint to God.

Lesson 3
1 Peter 3:18-22 (RCL/RC)

> Christ, the righteous, suffered for the unrighteous. The writer refers to the days of Noah and the building of the ark when eight people were saved through the waters, prefiguring the waters of our baptism.

Gospel
Mark 1:9-15 (RCL); Mark 1:12-15 (RC)
Jesus is baptized in the Jordan River by John. Just as he is coming up out of the water, the heavens open and the Spirit like a dove descends, accompanied by a voice from heaven. Then Jesus went into the wilderness where he was tempted for 40 days.

Theme
The importance of building and rebuilding trust.

Thought for the Day
With whom do you need to rebuild trust?

Sermon Summary
In his book *The Five Dysfunctions of a Team*, Patrick Lencioni describes the five building blocks needed for any team or relationship to work. As we consider our relationship with God, we begin by looking at the way God rebuilds trust after the flood through the use of a covenant.

Call to Worship
One: To you, O Lord, I lift up my soul. O my God, in you I trust.
All: Make us to know your ways, O Lord; teach us your paths.
One: Lead us in your truth, and teach us, for you are the God of our salvation.
All: Good and upright is the Lord; he leads the humble in what is right.
One: All the paths of the Lord are steadfast love and faithfulness, for those who keep his covenant and his decrees.
All: Come, let us worship the Lord!

Pastoral Prayer
Creator God, we come thanking you for the ways you continually reach out to us in love, even when we do not deserve it. As you guided Noah and his family through the flood to safety and dry land, so we ask for your guidance today. Lead those who are feeling overwhelmed as they feel the flood waters surrounding them: problems in their relationships, in their

finances, with their health, and with their jobs. Remind us again and again to look for your rainbow amid the clouds of life and to follow as you lead us to safety. Amen.

Prayer of Confession and Assurance

Faithful God, the psalmists wrote how your paths are steadfast love and faithfulness for those who keep your covenant, and yet that is exactly what we have trouble doing, keeping your covenant. From the moment Adam and Eve bit that forbidden fruit, we have had trouble following you. Forgive us when we go our own way and forget your law of love. Help us to be open to the voice of your Holy Spirit within us as it directs our steps in love. As you are willing again and again to call us back to the way of love, and rebuild the trust in our relationship, help us to be willing to take the beginning steps of rebuilding trust in relationships that will glorify and honor you.

Words of Assurance

Look to God's covenant sealed with a rainbow and know that God forgives you and loves you! Amen.

Prayer of Dedication of Gifts and Self

God, as Noah trusted you and brought his family and the animals into the ark you directed him to build, we bring our gifts, our talents, and our very lives to you this morning asking you to bless them to be used in places where new life is needed. Amen.

Hymn of the Day
O Lord, throughout These Forty Days

Again we encounter Mark's account of Jesus' baptism, only this time the context of the pericope is tailored to place Jesus' temptation front and center. But if the day's question is temptation, then God's good news in Jesus is the answer. Claudia Hernamen's "O Lord, throughout These Forty Days," found altered in various ways and set to different tunes, both highlights the theme of temptation and serves as an introduction to the season of Lent. A bolder, more assuring choice is John Rippon's "How Firm a Foundation," set to FOUNDATION.

Children's Time: Purple People

(To prepare, identify all of the purple in your sanctuary: altar cloths, banners, in stained-glass windows, and so on. Wear a purple stole.) What's your favorite color? *(Accept responses.)* What color is the church wearing today? *(Purple.)* Let's go on a purple hunt. First of all, can you find someone wearing purple? *(Encourage the children to go out into the congregation and find people wearing purple, ask the purple people to stand briefly, then ask the children to return to you.)* Now let's find purple in our church. *(Lead the children to the purple altar cloth, point out purple banners, visit stained-glass windows with purple in them and other purple items in your worship space.)*

During Lent, the name of this season of the church year, the church dresses in purple, the color of royalty. It's a time to learn more about our king, Jesus. During Lent, we are purple people, people who love and worship Jesus Christ, God's Son, our king.

Let's pray: Dear God, today we give you special thanks for purple, the color of royalty. Thank you for our king, Jesus. Amen.

The Sermon: The Trust Issue
Scripture: Genesis 9:8-17

This Sunday begins the season of Lent, so I'm curious if you celebrated Mardi Gras or Shrove (Fat) Tuesday this past week? Did you eat your donuts or *fasnachts*, pig out on pancakes, clean your house, get rid of all your yeast from last year, and decide what you're giving up for Lent?
Are you doing anything special for the Season of Lent and if so, why? Is it so you will lose some of those extra pounds you put on during the winter? Or so you will have some extra money to give to missions? Or so you will take time to consider who God is to you?

The word *lent* is an old English word meaning "to lengthen" and refers to the lengthening of days that begins in spring. Our ancestors in faith used it as a reminder, for as we experience the new life of spring breaking forth from the cold deathly grasp of winter, we also should consider our own life, death, eternal life, and relationship to the Creator of it all.
Our ancestors in faith put together for us a series of readings each Sunday we have come to call the lectionary. The lectionary was first put together during a time when people could not read, so they created a systematic

269

way for people to hear the story of the Bible.

This season of Lent we are going to use an extra biblical source to help us understand what God might be trying to teach us through the lectionary texts. It is based on a book written by Patrick Lencioni, who has written numerous books about helping organizations and the people within them get healthier and hence more successful.

He wrote a book entitled *The Five Dysfunctions of a Team*. What he teaches are simple ideas and facts, most of which we already know, but need to choose to do and implement every day. The first and biggest dysfunctions that happen in teams and in our relationships with each other and God, is the lack of trust.

Our first lectionary lesson is from the first book of the Bible, Genesis. Genesis begins with the creation story and how God created humans with the ability to choose to do that which is right and just and good, or to choose not to.

Much like when a parent tells a two-year-old not to touch a stove because the two-year-old is not ready to use the stove without hurting him or herself, the book of Genesis teaches us the story of the first humans who were put into the Garden of Eden but were not ready to eat of the fruit of the knowledge of good and evil. With some coaxing, the snake talks Eve who talks Adam into eating the fruit, for what does the Creator of all things know? Why would God want to keep this fruit from them? Is God trying to hide something?

What happens in your life when you begin to mistrust someone? What is it you feel they are hiding from you? What is it that makes you begin to question their motives? Patrick Lencioni subtitles this first problem of relationships as the state of being "invulnerable." We are not willing to be vulnerable with that person. We are not willing to trust them, so we begin to take matters into our own hands; that is what Adam and Eve did when they ate the fruit of the forbidden tree.

With that one act they allowed mistrust to enter their relationship with God. God tries to warn their firstborn in Genesis 4 that sin is crouching at the door of his heart, but he also does not trust God or ask God for help as he takes matters into his own hands and kills his brother Abel, the first murder in the Bible. So by the fourth chapter humans are already killing each other. By the sixth chapter of Genesis, sin and evil have so overtaken the earth, God knew something needed be done. God chose Noah and taught Noah how to build an ark for his family and the animals. After the flood was over, God made a covenant with Noah and all living things on the earth.

A covenant is what we in today's language might call a contractual agreement between two parties. There are stipulations in this agreement, which come in the first eight verses of Genesis 9.

God restates the very first commandment he gave humans in Genesis 1: "Be fruitful and multiply, and fill the earth." Next God tells them that all the animals on the ground, in the air, and in the sea will now dread and fear humans, for now animals as well as green plants will be a food source for humans; only they are to not to eat the blood of animals. And maybe the most important part of the agreement, God will require a reckoning for any animal or human who takes the lifeblood of another human being.

God signs what we have come to call the Noahic covenant with his bow in the sky. The rainbow is the sign that God will never again destroy the whole earth with a flood. God begins to rebuild the trust between God and humans through this covenantal tool, this contract.

How do we rebuild trust in our lives? With God? With each other? When there is an absence of trust the beginning of rebuilding trust always begins with someone willing to take the first step, to be vulnerable in the relationship. God begins that process with Noah. In a way God starts all over again, "Noah, the earth and all that is in it is still yours, be fruitful and multiply and fill the earth. But also know that if anyone takes a life, kills a human who has been made in the image of God, there will be a reckoning."

With whom do you need to rebuild trust? What are the boundaries, the covenant, the agreement you need to put in place on which to begin to rebuild that trust? Like Jesus, are you ready to follow God's calling no matter where it leads? Are you willing to be vulnerable with God? Are you willing to invite God into your life and listen for where God leads you? Amen.

– Deborah J. Winters

Hymns
Opening: Trust and Obey
Sermon: I Will Trust in the Lord
Closing: *De Colores*/Sing of Colors

March 1, 2015

2nd Sunday in Lent

Lessons

Revised Common Lectionary (RCL)	Roman Catholic (RC)
Gen 17:1-7, 15-16	Gen 22:1-2, 9a, 10-13, 15-18
Ps 22:23-31	Ps 116:10, 15-19
Rom 4:13-25	Rom 8:31b-34
Mk 8:31-38 or Mk 9:2-9	Mk 9:2-10

Speaker's Introduction for the Lessons

Lesson 1

Genesis 17:1-7, 15-16 (RCL)

The passage reflects God's covenant renewal to Abram and Sarai, promising that they will become the parents of a son, even in their old age. Included in this passage are their name changes to Abraham and Sarah.

Genesis 22:1-2, 9, 10-13, 15-18 (RC)

The call to Abraham to sacrifice his son Isaac is the focus of these passages. About to kill Isaac, Abraham spots a ram in the bushes as the angel of the Lord instructs him not to kill his firstborn son.

Lesson 2

Psalm 22:23-31 (RCL)

While the opening verse of this psalm provides the cry of God-forsakenness by Jesus from the cross, this portion moves to extraordinary thanksgiving and a promise to bear witness to the God who delivers.

Psalm 116:10, 15-19 (RC)

David is giving thanks for God has loosed his bonds, and David offers praise and sacrifices.

Lesson 3

Romans 4:13-25 (RCL)

Paul reminds us that even the promise to Abraham did not come from Abraham's ability to fulfill the law. Rather he states that Abraham received God's covenant promise because of his faith.

Romans 8:31b-34 (RC)

Paul is certain that because of God's gift of grace, nothing will be able to separate us from the power of God's love through Jesus Christ our Lord.

Gospel
Mark 8:31-38 (RCL)

Jesus predicts his suffering and death. As he does, he not only rebukes Peter for his inability to accept the prediction, but he also invites his disciples to take their crosses and follow him.

Mark 9:2-10 (RCL)

Jesus' transfiguration is the central focus of this passage. Not only does Jesus receive God's approval, when the experience has ended, the disciples see Jesus only.

Theme

Honesty with God about who you are and what you believe is always the best policy.

Thought for the Day

Where in your life do you have "artificial harmony" and why do you allow it?

Sermon Summary

As Abram is willing to confront God on the promises of their covenantal agreement, God takes their relationship to the next level.

Call to Worship

One: From the four corners of the earth people are coming to their
   senses, are running back to God.
All: Long-lost families are falling on their faces before him.
One: All the power mongers are before him – worshiping!
All: All the poor and powerless, too – worshiping!
One: Along with those who never got it together – worshiping!
All: As the word is passed along from parent to child

One: Babies not yet conceived will hear the good news that God does what God says!
All: Come, let us worship God!
> — Based on Psalm 22:27-31 from *The Message*

Pastoral Prayer

God of all life, we come to you and praise you for the way you keep your word. You are a God who can be trusted and who loves us enough to allow us to bring our doubts and our fears to you, even when they are about you! Lord, hear our fears about rocky relationships, plummeting finances, ill health, and dreams that are dying. Hear our doubts about whether you really do hear and answer our prayers. May we have the faith of Abraham who brought his doubts to you, and yet believed you would hear and answer. Amen.

Prayer of Confession and Assurance

God, forgive us when we do not trust you. Forgive us when we are not honest about what we believe and what we doubt. Help us to be willing to trust that our relationship with you is important enough and strong enough that we can be honest with our feelings, our frustrations, our doubts and fears. Help us not to just walk away, but to find a way to share and to grow with you and in all our relationships.

God has never left you, God is always with you, and God will listen and guide you to abundant and eternal life!

Prayer of Dedication of Gifts and Self

God we bring ourselves to you, just as we are. We bring our gifts and our talents to you, asking for you to bless them and help them to grow that they might be food to the hungry, resources to the needy, and love to the unloved. Amen.

Hymn of the Day
What Wondrous Love Is This

As the story of Jesus' ministry approaches its mighty climax, his words to the disciples regarding his suffering and death, along with those about cross bearing, grow ominous. A hymn that captures the purple hues of this passage is the American hymn "What Wondrous Love Is This." Set to the haunting tune of the same name, the text profoundly captures our response to Jesus' prediction and assures us of the happy outcome of Jesus' self-giving – "And through eternity I'll sing on."

Children's Time: God Told Abraham to Go
(Ask the children who they respond to, and who gives them orders. Accept all answers, including mom and dad, teachers, or pastor.)
When people tell me to do something, or ask me to do something and I want to do it, I do it without thinking. But if they ask me or tell me to do something I do not want to do, I sometimes do not follow their directions.

When an order is given, a request is made. It is important that the one who is asked to respond knows that the one asking is making a reasonable request. If I asked you to jump up and down on one foot, most of you would try to do it. It would be fun. If I asked you to jump down from the balcony or the choir loft or off the roof of the church, you would not be eager to do that because you know you would be injured.

In the first book of the Bible, we meet a man named Abraham. He listened to God like you and I listen to our parents. One day, God told Abraham, "Go." He told Abraham to leave his home and go to a new land. And because Abraham believed that God would not ask him to do anything that would harm him, Abraham went. Children, we come here together to listen for God to tell us what to do.

Let's pray together: Dear God, help us to remember to obey our parents and to do what God wants us to do – love each other every day. Amen.

The Sermon: Honesty or Artificial Harmony?
Scripture: Genesis 17:1-7, 15-16

Last Sunday we began framing our Lenten journey this year through the eyes of the Hebrew Scriptures lectionary Lenten texts and Patrick Lencioni's book *The Five Dysfunctions of a Team.*

We looked at the first dysfunction of a team, the lack of trust. Trust is the foundational building block of every team and every relationship, for if trust is not there and you cannot be vulnerable with each other, the relationship or team will not grow.

From the beginning of the creation story, humans chose not to trust God when they ate of the forbidden fruit. Cain chose not to trust God when the first murder in the Bible occurs and Cain kills his brother Abel. Evil so overtook the earth that according to the biblical text, God sent a flood and in a sense began again through Noah and his family. Last week we considered the covenantal agreement God made with Noah and all living flesh, animals and humans, after the flood as God began to rebuild trust. God signed the covenant with his bow in the sky and promised the whole earth would never be destroyed by water. This week we see God taking the next step.

In Genesis 12, God chose Abram and Sarai and promised that if they were willing to trust God, leave their homeland in Ur, and follow God, God would give them land, make of them a great nation with so many descendants they will be like the dust of the earth, and God would use them to bless the whole world. They would be blessed to be a blessing.

In Genesis 15, when God reminds Abram he has nothing to fear because God is his shield and Abram's reward will be great, instead of thanking God, Abram confronts God about the promises God made to Abram and asks God point blank, "I have no children, where are the heirs you promised me?" Abram is not afraid to be honest with God about the questions he has. He is willing to confront God with his doubts and fears. Abram trusted God enough to be honest about who he was and what he was expecting out of his relationship with God, and in his willingness to confront God, God begins to take their relationship to the next level. Patrick Lencioni outlines the second dysfunction of a team and of a relationship as the fear of conflict. Because there is no trust, people are not willing to be honest about what they believe and think, and so they create what he calls "artificial harmony." They pretend to be someone they are not, and you can only keep up that façade for so long. When people trust each other and are honest about what they think, they are willing to engage in healthy conflict. They are willing to put on the table what they believe and begin to talk about it and share ideas. It is then and only then a team, a relationship, really begins to grow!

Because Abram was willing to be honest with God, God assured Abram that he would have a child of his own and descendants more than the stars in the sky if Abram can count them all. Both Abram and Sarai take on a new identity as their names are changed to Abraham and Sarah, and within the year Sarah is pregnant with their son, their heir to the promises of God, and God's relationship with humankind continues to grow. Abraham has grown to trust God and so he is willing to be honest with his questions, his doubts, and his fears.

Where in your life do you have "artificial harmony"? Where in your life are you afraid of conflict; of saying the wrong thing? Where are you afraid of "rocking the boat," or "putting your foot in your mouth"? Why are you unwilling to trust that that relationship will be able to go the next level as you share honestly about what you are feeling? Why have you put up a boundary in that relationship so it cannot grow to the next level? Is there a reason you are afraid to see if the relationship will grow? If you are afraid of being honest in that relationship, is it a relationship you should be in at all?

Is there a boundary in your relationship with God, or are you honest about your dreams, your fears, your desires, your expectations, your disappointments, and your love with God? Willingness to be honest about who you are and the willingness to begin to work with our differences is the beginning of growth in every relationship, in every team, in every church committee and ministry. The Hebrew Scriptures text we read today is God confirming the covenant Abram was willing to question and fight for, even with God. God rewards Abraham and Sarah with a new level of relationship as heard in the new names they will now be called and in the child they will now be blessed with.

What is interesting is that Abraham becomes known for his faith in God. Part of that faith is seen in Abraham's being willing to be honest with God; to ask about the things he does not understand and to push God on the promises God has made. Faith is not the absence of questions; rather it is the willingness to be honest about who we are and what we believe and to be open to where God will lead us.

Who is it you need to be honest with today? Amen.

– Deborah J. Winters

Hymns
Opening: *Yigdal Elohim Chai*/The God of Abraham Praise
Sermon: Cares Chorus
Closing: What a Friend We Have in Jesus

March 8, 2015

3rd Sunday in Lent

Lessons

Revised Common Lectionary (RCL)	Roman Catholic (RC)
Ex 20:1-17	Ex 20:1-17 or Ex 20:1-3, 7-8, 12-17
Ps 19	Ps 19:8-11
1 Cor 1:18-25	1 Cor 1:22-25
Jn 2:13-22	Jn 2:13-25

Speaker's Introduction for the Lessons

Lesson 1
Exodus 20:1-17 (RCL/RC)
> On the holy mountain, God gives to Israel the Ten Commandments that shall guide Israel in all righteousness.

Lesson 2
Psalm 19 (RCL); Psalm 19:8-11 (RC)
> This majestic psalm blends praise of God's revealing in creation with reverence for God's word in Torah.

Lesson 3
1 Corinthians 1:18-25 (RCL); 1 Corinthians 1:22-25 (RC)
> Paul tells the Corinthians that the message of the cross is foolishness when regarded from the standpoint of the world's "wisdom," but to those of us who are being saved in Christ, it is a sign of the great wisdom of God.

Gospel
John 2:13-22 (SC); John 2:13-25 (RC)
> Jesus, entering Jerusalem, drives the money changers from the temple, demanding that they "stop making my Father's house a marketplace."

Theme
Being willing to commit to follow God's lead in all our relationships.

Thought for the Day
Commitment is an act, not a word.

– Jean-Paul Sartre

Sermon Summary
After 400 years of living as slaves, through Moses God gives the Israelites the Ten Commandments to teach them how to live with God and each other. These ten become the basic building blocks of relationships, if we are willing to commit to them.

Call to Worship
(based on Psalm 19)
> One: The heavens are telling the glory of God; and the firmament proclaims God's handiwork.
> **All: The law of the Lord is perfect, reviving the soul;**
> One: The decrees of the Lord are sure, making wise the simple;
> **All: The precepts of the Lord are right, rejoicing the heart;**
> One: The commandment of the Lord is clear, enlightening the eyes;
> **All: More to be desired are they than gold, sweeter also than honey.**
> One: Let the words of our mouths and the meditation of our hearts
> **All: Be acceptable to you, O Lord, our rock and our redeemer.**

Pastoral Prayer
Creator of the universe, we praise your name for the coming and going of each season and the ebb and flow of each tide. We thank you for the Ten Commandments perfected through the love of Jesus the Christ. In love we ask your healing hands to be with those who are in need in our family, in our community, and in our world. Help us to reach out in love to those in need. Help us to live your law of love in every part of our life. Amen.

Prayer of Confession and Assurance

Dear God, you have only to listen to the news to know that we humans have a hard time living together. We have forgotten the basic Ten Commandments that begin to teach us what love looks like. We have made idols out of people and things in our lives, we have not always honored our parents, and we have coveted and wished we had what our neighbor had or been more like them than who you have made us to be. Forgive us. Help us to begin again to reach out in love to you, to others, and to ourselves.

Hear the good news: Through Jesus we are saved and able to begin again. In the power of the Holy Spirit we are able to live the law of love, we need only trust and follow God.

Prayer of Dedication of Gifts and Self

God of the universe, thank you for the abundance of resources you have given us. Forgive us when we use those resources only for our own good. Open our eyes to see the need of those around us. Help us to trust that you are the God of abundant life, and the resources you have blessed us with are to be shared so all may experience the abundance of your love. Bless these resources we give back to you now that the world might know of your love. Amen.

Hymn of the Day
O God, How We Have Wandered

The tumultuous scene of Jesus driving people out of the temple is superseded by what must have sounded like the most outrageous of claims: if the great temple in Jerusalem were destroyed, Jesus would raise it up again in three days. According to John, only after Jesus' death and resurrection was some sense of these words able to be made. A selection in line with this pericope and its Lenten context is set to the great Passion Chorale from Bach's *St. Matthew Passion*, Kevin Nichols's "O God, How We Have Wandered." It is a stark admission of our estrangement from God and a plea that God meet us with grace.

Children's Time: God's Rule Book

(Bring a rule book for a board game.)

I have a rule book here for a game called ____. Have any of you ever played this game? If you've never played it before, you probably need to read the rule book. You might even have to keep the rule book close by while you are playing, so you can check it. Sometimes when you are just learning a game, it's hard to enjoy it because you have to keep checking to be sure you are following the rules.

What if you had to stop every time you had a decision to make and find out what a rule book said? Sometimes people think of the Bible as a rule book. And they are partly right. The Bible has some rules in it; you may have heard about the Ten Commandments God gave to Moses. But the Bible is more of a story than a rule book. It's the story about how God's love can change our hearts and lives.

The good news that the Bible teaches us is that when Jesus is a part of our lives, we begin to treat each other in loving ways, even without checking the rule book. It says that God promises to put the law in our hearts. That means that the more we know how God loves us and how Jesus lived, the more we will know what God wants us to do in our lives. And we won't always be running to the rule book to find out what is fair, or right, or loving. We will just do it automatically.

Don't ever throw away the rule books to your games. Sometimes we forget the rules and have to go back and read them again to be reminded. But isn't it great when everyone knows the game so well that you don't need to be worried about the rules? Wouldn't it be great if everyone in the world knew Jesus, and had God's law written on their hearts? Then maybe we would all treat each other fairly without needing rules.

Let us pray: Thank you God for the rules you give us to live by and to love by. We need you to guide us in our lives. Amen.

The Sermon: To Commit or Not to Commit, That Is the Question
Scripture: Exodus 20:1-17

Imagine if you can that you have been a slave your entire life. In fact your whole family and extended family are slaves. Although you started out as a free people, even chosen by God some would tell you, all you know of your daily existence is what it means to live as a slave; to have no freedoms whatsoever; to not have the right to even think for yourself. Everything you do is based on the needs of your master or mistress: what he or she tells you to do, when to do them, how to do them. You simply say yes sir or yes ma'am and do them without question, no matter how inconvenient it is to you or even how much it may physically hurt you.

Your job is to clean the house all day or make sure the meals are prepared throughout the day whenever your mistress or master is hungry. You are to care for their children all day. Or take care of the fields all day, or move stone all day to build the next pyramid.

Now imagine you are suddenly given freedom. After 400 years your family is free to go and make a life for themselves. After your initial euphoria, what exactly do you do? How do you make a living? How do you begin to make decisions for yourself when you never had to before? How do you live as a free person? How do you behave and how are you supposed to behave?

If you can in anyway put yourself into this context, then you can begin to understand the depth of the responsibility Moses had leading the children of Israel out of 400 years of slavery in Egypt. Moses is the only person in a sense who had lived as a "free" man from the moment he was adopted by Pharaoh's daughter, and then escaped through the wilderness to Midian to live there and marry and raise a family.

It is God who called Moses back to Egypt to face his past and to lead God's people, Moses' family of origin, to freedom. After the series of plagues that encouraged Pharaoh to let God's people go, and the final escape through the Reed or Red Sea, Moses took the children of Israel to the foot of the mountain where he went up as their representative to receive what we have come to call the Ten Commandments.

These commandments have become the basis of our own legal system and are the foundation of beginning to understand how we are to live together, how we are to treat each other. One only needs to read the newspaper or hear the headline news to wonder if we all could use a refresher course on the basics of how to treat each other.

These commandments are the basics God gave Moses to begin to teach these ex-slaves how to live as free people, as people of God. The Ten Commandments are divided into two sections: The first set of commandments deals with how we are to be in relationship with God. We are to have no other gods but God. We are not to make an image of God that we worship or make anything else a god in our lives but God. We are not to misuse God's name and being. We are to make sure we spend time with God and take our sabbath rest.

The second section teaches us the basics of how to relate to one another, and almost all of the commandments are placed in the negative. It is almost as if God is teaching the ex-slaves as little children, and the word little children often learn first is "no." It is usually for their own protection, but "no" is what comes out first, the things they are not to do. We are not to take someone else's life, not to take their spouse, not to take anything they own, not to take their reputation, and as soon as you feel like you want anything that is your neighbor's, you are to stop yourself before you act upon it.

The only commandment worded positively in this section is that you are to honor, to respect, to make sure your parents are provided for. These commandments were given to ex-slaves so they could begin to learn how to live together as a society. By the time Jesus walks this earth he uses two scripture texts to sum up these two sections of the Ten Commandments and he put it not in a negative, but in a positive as to what they should do. "'You shall love the Lord your God with all your heart, and with all your soul, and with all your mind.' This is the greatest and first commandment. And a second is like it: 'You shall love your neighbor as yourself'" (Mt 22:37-39).

Throughout this Lenten series we have been comparing these covenantal texts with Patrick Lencioni's book *The Five Dysfunctions of a Team*. We've learned we need to trust God, we need to be honest about what we are feeling and experiencing, and we need to be willing to tell God our feelings as we face our conflicts.

Lencioni's third dysfunction of a team is their lack of commitment. Their ambiguity as to what they are doing and why. The team needs to commit to a plan of action and live it out. When a team trusts each other and they are willing to share honestly what they believe and begin to work their differences out, they are then willing to commit to their plan of action.

God gave the ex-slaves these ten basics as a plan of action on how to live together. Are we willing to commit to these basic ten in the relationships in our lives? Are we willing to make these basics the foundations of our willingness to learn to love, and are you willing to commit to follow God's covenant of love in all you do? Amen.

– Deborah J. Winters

Hymns
Opening: Called as Partners in Christ's Service
Sermon: O Jesus, I Have Promised
Closing: O Savior, Let Me Walk with You

March 15, 2015

4th Sunday in Lent

Lessons

Revised Common Lectionary (RCL)	Roman Catholic (RC)
Num 21:4-9	2 Chr 36:14-16, 19-23
Ps 107:1-3, 17-22	Ps 137:1-6
Eph 2:1-10	Eph 2:4-10
Jn 3:14-21	Jn 3:14-21

Speaker's Introduction for the Lessons

Lesson 1

Numbers 21:4-9 (RCL)

> Poisonous snakes attack the children of Israel while they are in the wilderness. Moses makes a snake out of bronze, places it on a stick, and lifts it up. When a person is bitten, he or she touches the bronze snake and is healed.

2 Chronicles 36:14-16, 19-23 (RC)

> In this final chapter of the book of the Chronicler, the writer describes the destruction of the temple in Jerusalem, and reports that those who are left in Jerusalem are carried into exile.

Lesson 2

Psalm 107:1-3, 17-22 (RCL)

> This psalm in thanks for God's deliverance focuses in verses 17-22 on gratitude for healing from near-fatal conditions attributed by the psalmist to sin.

Psalm 137:1-6 (RC)

> In this song from the captivity in Babylon, the psalmist reflects on the suffering endured.

Lesson 3

Ephesians 2:1-10 (RCL); Ephesians 2:4-10 (RC)

> This passage contrasts the Christian's former life of sin and death with the new life that is given by God. Included here is the traditional

verse that says we are saved by grace through faith, not by what we have done, but by what God has done for us.

Gospel
John 3:14-21 (RCL/RC)
John refers to the wilderness event in the first lesson and connects it to the lifting up of the son of man in reference to Jesus' crucifixion. This reference is followed by the familiar John 3:16, which often has been called the gospel in miniature.

Theme
We are accountable for the consequences of our actions or inactions.

Thought for the Day
It is wrong and immoral to seek to escape the consequences of one's acts.
                                                            —Mahatma Gandhi

Sermon Summary
During the exodus experience the Israelites once again complain about God and Moses and the situation they are in. God sends them poisonous snakes and a means to be healed if the people are willing to take responsibility for their actions and look to the bronzed serpent.

Call to Worship
One: O give thanks to the Lord, for he is good; for his steadfast love endures forever.

All: God satisfies the thirsty, and the hungry he fills with good things.

One: God shatters the doors of prisons, and cuts in two the bars of iron.

All: We give thanks to the Lord for his steadfast love, for his wonderful works to humankind.

One: God sent forth God's word to heal us, and deliver us from destruction.

All: Let us offer thanksgiving sacrifices, and tell of God's deeds with songs of joy.

Pastoral Prayer

Dear God, we come today to give you thanks, for you are good and your love endures forever. As the psalmist wrote, you heal the sick, shatter the doors of prisons, and set your people free. Be with those who need your healing touch today. Shatter the doors of those who are in prisons of addiction, financial ruin, abusive relationships, and depression. Remind us to constantly look up to you for our salvation. Thank you, Lord, for your steadfast love and your wonderful works for us! In the name of Jesus we pray. Amen.

Prayer of Confession and Assurance

God forgive us for the times we have not trusted you. Forgive us for the times rather than take responsibility for our actions or inactions, we instead blame anyone else, including you, for the mess we have made. Remind us Lord that no matter how rough life becomes or how bad we have made things, you are still there for us.

Just as Moses lifted up the serpent in the wilderness, so must the son of man be lifted up, that whoever believes in him may have eternal life. For God so loved the world that God gave his only Son, so that everyone who believes in him may not perish but may have eternal life. Indeed, God did not send the Son into the world to condemn the world, but in order that the world might be saved through him.

Prayer of Dedication of Gifts and Self

Help of the helpless, we turn to you this morning and give you praise for the way you have provided for us. For the air we breathe, the food we eat, the talents and skills you gave us to develop that enable us to help provide for ourselves and others. We give back to you now the offerings we have been able to earn that they may provide sustenance and growth for our church, the church universal and those in need. Amen.

Hymn of the Day
My Song Is Love Unknown

With words reflecting back to the prologue of this Gospel, today's lesson from John reiterates the reason for Jesus' coming: God's love for the world. And with Good Friday approaching, the great cost to God to express this love looms ever larger. Samuel Crossman's "My Song Is Love Unknown" is a good choice for today. Narrative-like in its retelling of the passion story, Crossman's hymn emphasizes God's love. The music, composed especially for this hymn by John Ireland, splendidly carries the text to its heartfelt conclusion: "This is my Friend in whose sweet praise I all my days could gladly spend."

Children's Time: Trust and Obey

Let's talk a little while about two words. The first word is "obey." What does it mean to obey someone? *(Accept all answers.)* When we obey someone we do what they tell us to do. The other word is "trust." What does it mean to trust someone? *(Accept all answers.)* To trust someone can mean we know they will be good to us and will not harm us in any way.

Who are some people you know you can trust? *(Possible answers: parents, teachers, minister, police officer, relatives, friends.)* If one of these people asked you to do something, would you do it? *(Likely, yes.)* It is easier to obey the people we trust. Trusting and obeying work together. When we trust someone we are more likely to do what they ask.

In one of our Bible stories today, Moses is leading his people, but they don't always do what God asks them to do. They complain and don't obey. You could say they do a lot of whining to Moses about God. They don't trust that God is taking care of them.

So God sends snakes that bite the people. And the people have a change of heart and tell Moses they will trust God, and they beg him to pray to God to protect them from the snakes. God does not remove the snakes, but God does teach the people a lesson about trust. God told Moses to make a bronze snake, and if the people get bit by a real snake, they can look at the bronze snake and the bite won't hurt them. The people have to obey God's directions to look at the bronze snake and trust that God will really protect them.

This Bible story teaches a lot about trusting and obeying. We can believe that God will always be with us, just as God was with Moses the Israelites.

Let's pray: Thank you, God, for always being here for us. Thank you for teaching us to trust and obey you and those we love. Amen.

The Sermon: The Blame Game
Scripture: Numbers 21:4-9

In our Lenten journey this year we have been using Patrick Lencioni's rubric found in his book *Five Dysfunctions of a Team* and placing it against Hebrew Scriptures from the Lenten lectionary texts to see how God has dealt with building relationships with humankind, with our ancestors in faith, with us.

The first level of any relationship – whether it is a team, a family, a marriage, or a friendship – is trust. We began with the Noahic covenant, as God promised Noah and all living things that God would not destroy the whole earth with water and God and humans began to rebuild their trust relationship with each other.

After trust is built in a team, the willingness to be vulnerable, to share one's feelings and thoughts and risk conflict and disagreement is the next building block of any relationship. We saw that as Abram was willing to approach God about God's promise of children and the Abrahamic covenant was made.

After trust has been established in a relationship and each party is willing to be vulnerable with each other in sharing their thoughts and working through conflict, there then needs to be a willingness to commit to the agreed-upon decisions and actions of the team. Through Moses God gave the freed slaves ten basic commandments to commit to as they grew together, as they learned to live together.

Once those commitments have been made, the team needs to be held accountable for delivering on those plans. It is living out that plan that the Israelites begin to have problems with in our text today.

As a dysfunction this is known as lack of accountability or low standards. If there is one thing God has constantly tried to do with us humans, it is to help us realize the consequences of our actions. From the very beginning of the biblical text in the Garden of Eden, after Adam and Eve had eaten the forbidden fruit and God confronted them and asked Adam if he had eaten of the forbidden fruit, Adam first blamed Eve and then God for what happened: "The woman who you gave me ..." God has tried to help us be accountable ever since.

God freed the slaves from Egypt, led them through the Red or Reed Sea, and gave them water from the rock, bread from heaven, and quails for meat to fulfill their basic needs. God gave them the basic guidelines on how to be in relationship with God and each other.

As the ex-slaves have traveled together in the wilderness they became impatient with God and with their leader, Moses, questioning their very reason for being in relationship, "Why have you brought us up out of Egypt to die in this wilderness?" Instead of delivering on their commitment, they once again try to get out of their responsibility for the situation they are in by trying to shift the blame to Moses and, in a way, to God. In the biblical text God sent poisonous serpents into the camp and anyone who was bit by a snake died. It is interesting that the snakes made the people realize that they had played a role in all that had happened as they realized they had not kept relationship with God and each other. They went to Moses, admitted their sin, and asked Moses to pray to God for them as they were still not ready to be in relationship with God themselves; they still worked through Moses.

Moses took the people's request to God in prayer, and what is interesting is that God did not remove the snakes, but instead God gave those who have been bitten a means to be healed. God instructed Moses to make a poisonous serpent out of bronze, put it on a pole, and whenever anyone was bit, if they looked at the bronze snake, they would live. It is God who provides the healing, but it is the people who need to begin to take responsibility, to take a step in faith in order to receive the healing. Rightly or wrongly, in our own lives we blame many things on God: our marriage falling apart, our bodies growing older, our finances shrinking, our waistline growing, the job we lost, the promotion we didn't get, the latest tornado or hurricane or earthquake or blizzard.

No matter what you are living through now, the questions are: Do you believe God is there with you? Do you believe God has a way out, a way that can bring healing to everyone involved? Jesus refers to this incident as a foreshadowing of his own death on the cross and the ability that all people have of looking to Jesus for their healing, for their salvation, for their eternal life.

If you have committed to a life of following Jesus as Lord and Savior, are you willing to live that commitment out and trust God no matter what is happening in your life that God will lead you through? There is a sense in which this is a circular process. We need to take the step in faith and trust God with our lives. As we take that step in faith, we make a commitment to follow God and seek to do God's will in our lives no matter what conflict arises. As we live a life of love and as the poisonous snakes of our world seek to do us in, it is once again in faith that we look to God to heal us and lead us through.

What poisonous snakes are you dealing with today? Are you willing to be committed enough to Jesus to trust God will bring you through? Amen.

– Deborah J. Winters

Hymns
Opening: God Loved the World
Sermon: I Would Be True
Closing: O God, How We Have Wandered

March 22, 2015

5th Sunday in Lent

Revised Common Lectionary (RCL)
Jer 31:31-34
Ps 51:1-12 or Ps 119:9-16
Heb 5:5-10
Jn 12:20-33

Roman Catholic (RC)
Jer 31:31-34
Ps 51:3-4, 12-15
Heb 5:7-9
Jn 12:20-33

Speaker's Introduction for the Lessons
Lesson 1
Jeremiah 31:31-34 (RCL/RC)

Jeremiah predicts a time when God's covenant with Israel and Judah will be renewed. The difference between this new covenant and the covenant given to Moses is that this covenant will be written on people's hearts.

Lesson 2
Psalm 51:1-12 (RCL); Psalm 51:3-4, 12-15 (RC)

This psalm is one of a (small) collection called "penitential" psalms. Its confession of sin moves to the liturgically familiar plea for the creation of a new heart and right spirit in hopes of restoration.

Lesson 3
Hebrews 5:5-10 (RCL); Hebrews 5:7-9 (RC)

The writer of Hebrews talks about Christ as the high priest. As he describes Christ's role, he says that Christ does not glorify himself, but as an obedient servant, he is similar to the ancient king of Salem, Melechizedek.

Gospel
John 12:20-33 (RCL/RC)

In Jerusalem, Jesus offers the parable of the grain of wheat as a prelude to the call to follow, which is the announcement that his hour, God's hour of glorification, has come.

Theme

The importance of evaluating and learning from our failures and our successes.

Thought for the Day

Insanity: doing the same thing over and over again and expecting different results.

Sermon Summary

Jeremiah writes to the Israelites who are now captive in Babylon, because they did not follow God's laws. God has evaluated the results of the previous covenants and is ready to take it the next step; God is going to put the law of love within our hearts.

Call to Worship (based on Jeremiah 31:31-34)

One: The days are surely coming, says the Lord, when I will make a new covenant.
All: It will not be like the covenant that they broke.
One: I will put my law within them, and I will write it on their hearts;
All: And I will be their God, and they shall be my people.
One: No longer shall they say to each other, "Know the Lord,"
All: For they shall all know me, from the least of them to the greatest, says the Lord.

Pastoral Prayer

Thank you, God, for the way you have always loved us. You led our ancestors in faith from slavery into freedom. You taught them through your laws and now you teach us through your Holy Spirit, who lives within us guiding us day by day. Teach us to listen to your voice. Teach us to follow your law of love. As you teach us, help us to teach others. As you heal us, help us to heal others. As you guide us, help us to guide others so that all may live forever in your love. Amen.

Prayer of Confession and Assurance

One: Have mercy on me, O God, according to your steadfast love; according to your abundant mercy blot out my transgressions.

All: Wash me thoroughly from my iniquity, and cleanse me from my sin.

One: Hide your face from my sins, and blot out all my iniquities.

All: Create in me a clean heart, O God, and put a new and right spirit within me.

One: Do not cast me away from your presence, and do not take your holy spirit from me.

All: Restore to me the joy of your salvation, and sustain in me a willing spirit.

One: For God so loved the world that God gave his only Son, so that everyone who believes in him may not perish but may have eternal life. We are forgiven, praise be to God!

Prayer of Dedication of Gifts and Self

Dear God, we dedicate to you all that we have and all that we are. Use these gifts to further your mission throughout the world. May all we have, all we do, all we say bring glory and honor to you. Amen.

Hymn of the Day
When I Survey the Wondrous Cross

The long shadow of the cross now colors all Jesus' words and deeds. Though there are many themes to key off of in today's Gospel lesson, it is the idea of glorification that attracts attention. In his signature hymn, "When I Survey the Wondrous Cross," Isaac Watts uses phrases such as "the Prince of Glory," "so rich a crown" that point squarely to glorification, while the hymn's closing idea reiterates Jesus' words about losing and serving: "demands my soul, my life, my all."

Children's Time: Written on Our Hearts

Who has ever seen the *Peanuts* cartoon with Charlie Brown? *(Accept all answers.)* Who is the little girl who always picks on Charlie Brown? *(Lucy.)* Do you know what happens when Lucy tells Charlie Brown to kick a football? *(She always pulls it away.)*

No matter how many times Lucy promises to hold the football, and no matter how many times Charlie Brown tries to believe Lucy will hold the football, she always pulls it away just when Charlie Brown runs up to kick it. And what happens to him? *(He falls on the ground.)*

Today we hear about another of God's promises. It is completely the opposite of what Lucy does in the Charlie Brown comic. While she always promises one thing and does another, God always makes promises and always follows through on those promises. But by not following God's rules, the people always end up on their backs – sort of like Charlie Brown. In the Bible lesson from Jeremiah, we learn that God wants to teach the people a lesson, and God is going to try a new way of making the lesson stick in the minds and hearts of the people.

Let's pray together: Dear God, thank you for giving us rules to live by and for always being the one thing we can trust, no matter what. We can always count on you, God, and for that we are thankful. Amen.

The Sermon: Are We All Insane?
Scripture: Jeremiah 31:31-34

There is a saying in our culture, "Fool me once, shame on you; fool me twice, shame on me." It is like the old *Peanuts* cartoon where Lucy tells Charlie Brown that she will hold the football for him so he can kick it. But every time, just as he runs up to kick it, Lucy pulls the ball away and Charlie Brown lands flat on his back. There is a sense in which Charlie Brown, as trusting as some might want to argue he is, does not learn from his mistakes and constantly misreads his relationship with Lucy and her behavioral patterns. So, he constantly ends up flat on his back never knowing what it feels like to kick a football while someone is holding it for you.

Not learning from our mistakes and successes is what Patrick Lencioni in his book *The Five Dysfunctions of a Team* entitles the fifth dysfunction: inattention to results. After a team has begun to trust, is willing to be vulnerable and confront conflict, commits to what they need to be about and hold each other accountable for what needs to be done, the last dysfunction is one of the hardest to confront. It is inattention to results. It is where egos, status, and pride can get in the way of evaluating whether what the team has committed to is actually working.

In some ways, it is what many people credit to Einstein as the definition of insanity: doing the same thing over and over again and expecting different results. We need to pay attention to what we or others do or don't do and what the results are. Our scripture lesson today teaches us that God is very attentive to the details, to results, and is constantly trying to teach us and help us grow. We have seen this perpetual fine tuning throughout this Lenten season.

In the biblical story after the initial creation of Adam and Eve and the introduction of disobedience and sin, God began anew in Noah with the Noahic covenant. God fine-tuned this by choosing one family to bless the world through the Abrahamic covenant. God through Moses gave us the Ten Commandments as the basic building blocks of how we should relate to God and to one another. In the wilderness God introduced the idea that people can begin to take part in their own salvation, for once they are bitten by a poisonous snake, they need only look to the bronze snake God provided through Moses and they will be healed; what many see as a foreshadowing of Jesus on the cross.

And in today's lesson from the Hebrew Scriptures, Jeremiah writes to the children of Abraham, who are now captive in Babylon because they did not follow the Ten Commandments and trust God for their salvation, that God is going to try something new. God has evaluated the results of the previous covenants and is ready to take it the next step; God is going to put the law within people's hearts, the law of love.

No longer will we have to hold a yardstick over someone else and say, "Know the Lord." We will learn to love God and each other, and God will forgive all the mistakes that brought us to this place and time. God will create a clean heart within us and put the Holy Spirit within us. This new covenant is made in the obedient love of Jesus. As the Greeks came looking for Jesus in the Gospel of John, Jesus knew his time on earth was drawing to a close. He had come to preach to the children of Abraham, the followers of Moses. It is his disciples who would take this message of love to the Greeks, the Gentiles.

Like a seed that is planted in the ground and bears fruit, so Jesus' death and resurrection bore the fruit of this new covenant. For all who look upon him and believe receive the gift of the Holy Spirit, who comes and lives within us, cleansing our heart and leading us in the law of love. It is a result we can measure every day and fine-tune: how well did you love today? Did you love God with all your heart, soul, strength, and mind? Did you love your neighbor as yourself?

This Lenten season we have been looking at our relationship with God through the lens of Patrick Lencioni's five dysfunctions of the team. We've used each dysfunction to learn how God has been teaching us through covenants and building relationship with us.

It is now our turn to take a step in faith and be honest about where we are in our relationship with God. Do we trust God? Are we willing to be vulnerable and open to God with our lives? Are we willing to commit to follow God and allow the law of love to be written in our hearts? Are we able to hold ourselves and others accountable to living out that law of love? Are we willing to evaluate and fine-tune how we love in the name of Jesus?

These questions can be asked of any and all relationships in our lives. Historically in the season of Lent we ask these questions of our relationship with God. As we continue the journey toward Holy Week we are reminded again how much God loves us through Jesus. Are you ready to move forward in your journey of learning to love God, yourself, and others?

Let us pray: Dear God, we thank you for your attention to the details of our lives and of the ways you constantly try to teach us and help us to grow. Help us in our dysfunctions to still find you. Help us to trust you, to be willing to bring our lives to you, the good, the bad, the ugly. Help us to be willing to be honest with you about what we are feeling and thinking and to be willing to commit to follow you with our whole lives, no matter where you lead. Help us to take the bold step of beginning to hold ourselves and others accountable to live out the law of love and to constantly evaluate how we are doing and how we need to change. Help us to hear your voice, follow, and love during this Lenten season and always. Amen.

– Deborah J. Winters

Hymns
Opening: Take My Life, God, Let It Be
Sermon: How Like a Gentle Spirit
Closing: Lift High the Cross

March 29, 2015

Passion/Palm Sunday

Lessons

Liturgy of Palms (RCL)
Ps 118:1-2, 19-29
Mk 11:1-11 or Jn 12:12-16

Liturgy of Palms (RC)
Mark 11:1-10 or Jn 12:12-16

Liturgy of the Passion

Revised Common Lectionary (RCL)	Roman Catholic (RC)
Isa 50:4-9a	Isa 50:4-7
Ps 31:9-16	Ps 22:8-9, 17-20, 23-24
Phil 2:5-11	Phil 2:6-11
Mk 14:1—15:47 or 15:1-39(40-47)	Mk 14:1—15:47 or 15:1-39

Speaker's Introduction for the Lessons

Lesson 1

Isaiah 50:4-9a (RCL); Isaiah 50:4-7 (RC)

One of Isaiah's Servant Songs, this reading emphasizes God's saving grace, even in the midst of pain and suffering, that asserts confidence in God's redemptive activity in the world for all peoples.

Lesson 2

Psalm 31:9-16 (RCL)

The psalmist prays for deliverance in the midst of excruciating circumstances. Yet in the midst of such suffering, the psalmist trusts utterly in God: "My times are in your hands."

Psalm 22:8-9, 17-20, 23-24 (RC)

This psalm of David begins in sadness, with David crying out in pain, but the psalmist is able to bring praise and glorify the Lord.

Psalm 118:1-2, 19-29 (RCL Liturgy of Palms)

This psalm of thanksgiving presents the familiar image of the stone rejected by builders now serving as the cornerstone.

Lesson 3
Philippians 2:5-11 (RCL); Philippians 2:6-11 (RC)
This ancient hymn invokes remembrance and imitation of Christ's reversal of the norms of conventional wisdom of power: in majesty, Jesus chose servanthood; in humility, Jesus was exalted.

Gospel
Mark 14:1—15:47 (RCL/RC)
The reading begins two days before the Passover and includes the story of the woman with the alabaster jar of ointment. It concludes with the placing of Jesus' body in the tomb.
Mark 11:1-11 (RCL Liturgy of Palms)
This is the moment in Jesus' ministry when God reveals Jesus as the Messiah.
John 12:12-16 (RCL/RC Liturgy of Palms)
John recounts the triumphal entry into Jerusalem, weaving in words of the phrophets.

Theme
Palm Sunday reminds us what time it is.

Thought for the Day
Half our life is spent trying to find something to do with the time we have rushed through life trying to save.

– Will Rogers

Sermon Summary
There is "calendar time" and there is the "right time." Our text from Mark 11:1-11 helps us recognize that Jesus' palm parade comes at just the right time. It is the moment of Jesus' ministry when God chooses to reveal Jesus' identity as Messiah.

Call to Worship

As a testimony to your faithfulness to us, O King of the Universe, you send Jesus on the back of a donkey. Remind us on this glorious day of entry that the same people who shouted, "Hosanna in the highest heaven" are also those who at the end of the week shouted "Crucify him!" May we beware as we stand before friends and foes to not betray or deny our Lord as did his closest friends. In Jesus' name we pray. Amen.

Pastoral Prayer

O God, forgive us for cheering so loudly at the parade when we thought Jesus was going to win one for us. Also forgive us for fleeing quickly when our high hopes collapsed. Deliver us from the worship of false values, and save us from selling the highest and best we know for a few pieces of silver. Strengthen us for the betrayals and disappointments we will face when we refuse to give in to the temptations that come to all who follow Jesus. We pray for health for those are ill in whatever way illness may come in life. In the name of Jesus we pray as a people of God. Amen.

Prayer of Confession and Assurance

Gracious God, you know our every grief, our every need. Hear us as we recall the periods of time when our strength failed, when our sorrow led us onto paths of hopelessness and despair. Forgive us when we betray you, when we deny you, and when we scorn you. Wake in us a new steadfastness to your call and presence. Help us stay awake, even when the days are hard and the nights are long. Strengthen us to walk with you in trust, even on a path to the cross. Let your face shine upon us, that we may know your steadfast love and trust in your resurrection promises. In Christ's name, we pray. Amen.

Know that the Lord is God, and that Christ's face shines upon us even when we turn away from God's brightness. Walk in the light, dear friends. Gaze upon the Son and know that in the name of Christ, God forgives us!

Prayer of Dedication of Gifts and Self

Our Heavenly Parent, we know that we are the great beneficiaries of your grace, forgiveness, and mercy. Grant that we too might offer others the tokens of kindness that have nourished us through our years. Help us remember that as we pass on the things that you have entrusted to us, then we become stewards of the divine things. May our gifts bless us as well as others. Amen.

Hymn of the Day
O Sacred Head, Now Wounded

The passion account lies at the heart of the Christian message and is capable of bringing the strongest and most callous among us to tears. Only a handful of hymns are both worthy and capable of being programmed alongside this text. Foremost among these is Paul Gerhardt's immortal "O Sacred Head, Now Wounded," set to Hans Leo Hassler's PASSION CHORALE, a melody the composer originally wrote for a love song and J. S. Bach later harmonized. The best contemporary choice I know is Marty Haugen's "Tree of Life," though it embodies a theology quite different from Gerhardt's.

Children's Time: A Royal Welcome

(Preparation: Bring palm branches and three-foot lengths of colorful gift-wrap ribbon for each child in the congregation. Ask a member of your congregation to portray Jesus in biblical costume.)

Today we're going to pretend we lived when Jesus walked on earth. These are the colorful cloaks you wore. *(Drape a ribbon around each child's neck.)* And we need palm trees. *(Ask people sitting along the aisle to hold and wave the palm branches you give them.)* One more thing: We have to learn a special word to welcome Jesus: Hosanna! Let's say it together. Now we're ready to begin the story.

Many people in Jesus' time hoped that Jesus would be king. Oh, look! Here comes Jesus now, riding on a donkey. *(Jesus stands in the back of the sanctuary, pretending to be riding a donkey.)* Let's welcome him as our king. *(Jesus pauses to let children prepare.)* Lay down your cloaks to make a beautiful path for Jesus to follow to Jerusalem. Quickly, pick a branch from a palm tree. (*Have the children line the aisle.*) Here comes Jesus! Wave your palm branch up high. Let's all say "hosanna" together. *(Have Jesus come up the aisle and then exit the sanctuary.)* This is the Sunday that we remember how people in Jerusalem waved palm branches to welcome Jesus as their king. Take home your palm branch and streamer as a reminder that Jesus will always love us and care for us.

Let's pray: Dear God, thank you for sending Jesus to love us. Amen.

The Sermon: Jesus Goes to a Parade
Scripture: Mark 11:1-11

Mark's lesson outlines a procession celebrated on Palm Sunday. The parade endorses our faith in Jesus the Messiah and trumpets God's triumph. Jesus rides into Jerusalem and into our lives as a conquering Lamb, "for he is Lord of lords and King of kings, and those with him are called and chosen and faithful" (Rev 17:14). And, no doubt, for a moment at the beginning of the palm parade we do feel called and chosen and faithful. But the there is a deep shadow cast by this parade, and similar to another parade that took place November 25, 1963. The John F. Kennedy funeral parade came up Pennsylvania Avenue in Washington DC It was one of the most gripping images of the 20th century. It was a parade that symbolized the broken heart of a nation. We now all know that for all the pageantry of parades, our palm parade has an ominous side.

Between Palm Sunday and Good Friday Jesus ritually cleanses the temple, teaches about taxes and resurrection, shares his few parables in Mark's Gospel, celebrates his last Passover, and prays in Gethsemane. Betrayed, Jesus surrenders to the religious authorities. After Peter's denial, Jesus comes before Pilate. Although we could explore Pilate's character from John's Gospel viewpoint, instead we now turn to Mark and his point of view with respect to the gospel story.

Jesus seemed to pick an odd time for a parade. In my experience people throw parades when the hometown ball team has won the state championship. People throw parades when a new president is inaugurated or when a nation crowns a new monarch. We throw parades, for goodness sake, when our astronauts return from a stroll on the moon. Have you ever wondered when would be a good time to throw a parade? Jesus' parade must have to do with what is going to happen rather than what has already happened.

As far as parades go, I suppose, timing would be everything. We wouldn't want to throw a parade too early, but at the same time, we wouldn't want to schedule a parade too late. Yes, throwing a parade must have to do with timing.

Let us also note that there are two ways to mark time, and parade planning must acknowledge these two kinds of time. One understanding of time is called *chronos* time, and from this word comes our word *chronological*. Chronology is the "science of measuring time in fixed intervals." A chronicle is "a story about a certain period of time." A pageant that had to do with chronos time might be like some town's "Christmas stroll." It is tied directly to the calendar and would make little sense to have such a parade on the 16th of April. It is unlikely that Jesus planned his Palm Sunday parade because he looked at the calendar and decided the chronological time was right to schedule such a thing.

There is, however, another sense of time, and that in Greek we call *kairos* time. This characterization of time means the time for something to happen is when it is time for it to happen. In bygone days it was pretty challenging to schedule a baby's birth – and sometimes even today it is difficult, if not surprising. That is kairos time. When a farmer looks out over a golden field of wheat he does not say, "Well, I guess I will harvest this 42 acres on August 23." No. The farmer drives the combine into his field when the field is ripe for harvest. That is kairos time. I suspect that when Jesus said to two of his disciples, "Go into the village ahead of you, and immediately as you enter it, you will find tied there a colt that has never been ridden; untie it and bring it," then the time had come for Jesus' parade. That is kairos time. If you read Mark carefully, then you think it is about time.

Over and over again in Mark's Gospel we know that Jesus silences any admission about who he is and why he has come. The "messianic secret" is the name given to an explanation about Jesus' command to both his audience and the disciples not to reveal who Jesus is after several messianic revelations. From the beginning, Mark's Gospel conceals Jesus' true identity as the Christ. Although we can find ample evidence of the messianic secret in Matthew (8:3-4; 9:29-31; 12:15-16; 17:9) and in Luke (4:41; 8:56; 9:21), Mark uses the mysterious unveiling of Jesus as Messiah as one of his artistic and interpretive motifs.

For example, do you remember what Jesus said to the leper he healed at the beginning of his ministry? He said, "See that you say nothing to anyone" (Mk 1:44). Or perhaps you remember when Jesus healed a deaf man Mark tells us, "Then Jesus ordered them [those who had seen the miracle] to tell no one; but the more he ordered them, the more zealously they proclaimed it" (Mk 7:36). Naturally, we all remember when Jesus had just been transfigured before Peter, James, and John that "as they were coming down the mountain, he ordered them to tell no one about what they had seen, until after the Son of Man had risen from the dead" (Mk 9:9). Up to this point in Mark's Gospel Jesus had commanded silence, but now he seemed ready to proclaim what God has sent him to do and be – the Messiah of God. For Mark, Palm Sunday is the signal that the time is right and the time is ripe for the announcement about who Jesus is and why he has come.

Whether our Passover parades or our Palm Sunday planned activities go as scripted we can say at least this much: when Jesus rode into Jerusalem on a colt or a donkey, this parade announced that God said the time was right and the time was ripe. We might ask: Ripe for what? The answer is earnestly for the fulfillment of the kingdom or realm of God on earth. Today our only question is, will we shout with our lives "Hosanna, Hosanna, Hosanna!" or will we live lives that shout "Crucify him! Crucify him!" How can we gauge the time for the beginning of our parade of discipleship? Do we look at a calendar? Or rather, do we look elsewhere – like into our hearts. Amen.

– David Neil Mosser

Hymns
Opening: Rejoice, Ye Pure in Heart
Sermon: Mantos y Palmos
Closing: Hosanna, Loud Hosanna

April 2, 2015

Maundy Thursday

Lessons

Revised Common Lectionary (RCL)	Roman Catholic (RC)
Ex 12:1-4 (5-10) 11-14	Ex 12:1-8, 11-14
Ps 116:1-2, 12-19	Ps 116:12-13, 15-18
1 Cor 11:23-26	1 Cor 11:23-26
Jn 13:1-17, 31b-35	Jn 13:1-15

Speaker's Introduction for the Lessons

Lesson 1
Exodus 12:1-4 (5-10) 11-14 (RCL); Exodus 12:1-8, 11-14 (RC)

God's instructions to Moses and Aaron concern preparations for the Passover. The connection between the blood of the lamb smeared on the doorposts of the Hebrews and the blood of the Lamb shed for us on the cross is one replete with meaning.

Lesson 2
Psalm 116:1-2, 12-19 (RCL); Psalm 116:12-13, 15-18 (RC)

The psalm is an individual thanksgiving for the gift of healing. In the selected verses, the imagery of lifting "the cup of salvation" blends into narrative of tonight's meal and its cup of salvation.

Lesson 3
1 Corinthians 11:23-26 (RCL/RC)

Here Paul instructs the church in Corinth in the celebrating of the Lord's supper. The words are the age-old words, calling the church to remembrance and to covenant.

Gospel
John 13:1-17, 31b-35 (RCL); John 13:1-15 (RC)

Unlike the Synoptic accounts, John does not describe the institution of the common meal in his rendition of the last supper, but tells of

Jesus washing the feet of his disciples. The community is invited to ground itself in this example of service and humility.

Theme
Observing is more than "regarding from a safe distance"; it is "participating in."

Thought for the Day
Wherever you are, be there. If you can be fully present now, you'll know what it means to live.

– Steve Goodier

Sermon Summary
The faithful experience of the Triduum is not intended to be merely an emotional or spiritual recollection of past events, however important. Instead, we are invited to remember through action that discipleship is our immediate, direct witness in and with the world.

Call to Worship
One: We are called to give thanks
Many: For bitter herbs softening our hearts to the bitter lives of our sisters.
One: We are called to give thanks
Many: For unleavened bread reminding us of brothers who live as refugees.
One: We are called to give thanks
Many: For water and basin, miracles to millions who have no access to clean water.
One: We are called to give thanks
Many: For eating in haste, for eating at all.
All: We are called to give thanks, and thanks again, for all things, in all places, at all times: Thanks.

Pastoral Prayer

Pillar of fire and cloud, you go out with us and you come in with us. Your presence goes before us and follows behind, companions us to the right and to the left. In every breath, you are there. Therefore, grant us the confidence to live boldly, to trust deeply, to journey beyond everything we have known into the new creation that is your realm of peace and justice without fear and without looking back. May it be so.

Prayer of Confession and Assurance

Creator God, we confess that we do not always welcome your gift of freedom with attention and gratitude. We confess that we spend most of our allotted hours in slavery to our own agendas, to the world's expectations, to accumulating material possessions, to tasks that are not ours, to wants that are not needs, to our fears, and to the many addictions we deny in ourselves. We know this is not your hope for us, nor is it your presence in us.

Creator God, lend us the courage to receive a new awareness of the preciousness of each moment, that we may become the people we have it in us to be: free, loving, joyful, grace-filled, merciful, hopeful, and compassionate. In your name we ask, trusting your promise that when we do, you will respond.

Prayer of Dedication of Gifts and Self

Beloved God of abundant life, receive not only the portion of our possessions that we return to your work of justice and mercy, but also receive our lives – offered sometimes with generosity and sometimes begrudgingly, sometimes with joyful abandon and sometimes in carefully measured increments. Bless all that we are and all that we bring to be lifeblood for a world that often chooses death. Amen.

Hymn of the Day
An Upper Room Did Our Lord Prepare

Written by Fred Green, and set to the English folk melody O WALY WALY, this hymn is an excellent telling of the story of the last supper and the washing of the feet. It could be used to introduce or conclude the service.

Children's Time: Meals That Remember

(Talk with the children about communion and about how it is celebrated in your congregation. Show them the elements, as appropriate.)
There are lots of reasons why we celebrate communion. One of them is to remember this night, the night that Jesus had what we call the last supper with his friends, the disciples.

Because Jesus and his friends were Jewish, they celebrated a very important festival called Passover. Jewish families all around the world are celebrating Passover this week. At Passover, we remember how God brought the people of Israel out of slavery in Egypt. It was a festival to remember that God hears us when we cry and that God saves people.

When Jesus was gathered with his disciples in Jerusalem long ago, they were scared about things that were happening. Some people didn't like the things Jesus said and did, and they wanted to kill him. Jesus took bread and broke it, and gave it to his disciples. And he took a cup of wine and gave it to them to drink. And he said, "When you eat this bread and drink from this cup, remember that I am with you."

Ever since that night long ago, Christians have celebrated communion, and remembered that Jesus is always with us.

Let's pray together: Dear God, thank you for sending your son, Jesus, to save the world. Help us remember that you are always with us. Amen.

The Sermon: Blood on the Doorposts
Scripture: Exodus 12:1-4 (5-10) 11-14

"This month shall mark for you the beginning of months."
This day, this night, we stand on a threshold between what has been and what will be. It is a new beginning, a new time, a new creation. We are surrounded by the simplest and most ordinary of things: food to share, wine and bread, basin and water. We stand in the midst of the familiar, but we stand here with a resounding call in our ears and the deep, ancestral knowledge that by this time tomorrow, by the next breath, by the next heartbeat, we will be in liminal space where nothing will be familiar at all.

Tonight is not about familiar, about comfortable, about remembering a transforming event that happened three millennia ago. Tonight is about risk, and danger, and the transformation of our own personal, precious, conventional, settled selves right here, right now. We are in the most profound denial if we think we can pass through this place and this time unchanged. "This month shall mark for [us] the beginning of months." Tonight we are starting all over – as new people, newly attuned to God's presence in, with, and between us.

And so, my friends, it is not enough merely to sit here and wait for the ritual to unfold so we can go home and do the same-old, same-old all over again tomorrow. We need to wake up. We need to take a deep breath and be all the way here: focused, centered, intentional, and attentive. We need to pay attention because the angel of the Lord is about to pass over this here-and-now and if we don't have blood on the doorposts, we are going to die. From the very beginning of beginnings, God has shown us through God's own actions that the gift of life comes at the cost of having skin in the game – literally. So there needs to be blood on the doorposts, and it needs to be our blood, our commitment of our whole lives to the unfolding of creation. It's no good thinking that beginnings happen any other way.

We do not live, and humanity cannot continue, and the universe is not replenished without our willingness to mark every threshold with life-blood. We cannot pass through the world in an antiseptic, unblemished, self-contained bubble; that is what we call a coffin. Living, living fully, living abundantly, living generously and justly, living so that we know we are actually alive requires skin in the game.

You remember, of course, that even God has skin in this particular game. That is what Advent and Christmas and Epiphany are about. It is what this week is about. That is what the birth of every creature, each created in God's own image, is about. It is what our discipleship is about: choosing to risk our own skin (and blood and bone and time and atten-tion and money) for those who most need our help, our compassion, our justice, our love, our generosity, our hope, our mercy.

And you remember, of course, that God always marks thresholds – es-pecially and most particularly the threshold between life and death – with blood. God's own blood.

And since we (you and I) are among those creatures created in God's image, we are imprinted and commissioned to do what God does. It's the only way to be born and born anew and born again and again and again. And, equally if not more important, it's the only way for God's common-wealth of shalom to be born again and again and again, in one life after another after another – because this is where Jesus told us God's "kin-dom" exists: in this life here, right here.

We mark the thresholds to say: Here we stood and here we stepped across into the wilderness to journey through another transformation toward another threshold. Here we cared enough to open our hearts – and shed our blood – for what matters, for what matters ultimately. Here we were broken open by sorrow and pain and injustice and inhumanity and fear, and here we left behind our mark of defiance in the face of death and our mark of hope in the promise of abundant life. We left part of ourselves because that is all we have to give: ourselves, our whole and holy selves.

This month, this day, this hour, shall mark for you the beginning of months.

Tonight we come together to eat with our loins girded, our sandals on our feet, our staff in our hand. Tonight we come to eat hurriedly because there is so much being to be and we have only this moment in which to be all that and more. Tonight we do not come to listen to the music, to let the words of scripture ripple past our ears, to sit awhile in mindless quiet. Tonight we come to eat bread and drink wine in the utmost gratitude that bread and wine exist. Tonight we come to wash one another's feet, or hands, or faces. Or bodies for burial.

And tonight we come to mark the doorposts with the symbol that proclaims that we are people of life, always and everywhere. We come to offer our whole selves: soul and sinew, heart and holiness, bone and blood. We come to reveal fully the image in which we are created. We come with our loins girded, our sandals on our feet, our staff in our hand; with gratitude for all that has brought us to this time, and with confidence for all that will be if we dare to live into it.

Tonight we come to proclaim the new beginning of time.

May it be so.

– Andrea La Sonde Anastos

Hymns
Opening: The Church of Christ in Every Age
Sermon: All Who Hunger
Closing: *Dayenu*

April 3, 2015

Good Friday

Lessons

Revised Common Lectionary (RCL)	Roman Catholic (RC)
Isa 52:13—53:12	Isa 52:13—53:12
Ps 22	Ps 31:2, 6, 12-13, 15-17, 25
Heb 10:16-25 or Heb 4:14-16; 5:7-9	Heb 4:14-16; 5:7-9
Jn 18:1—19:42	Jn 18:1—19:42

Speaker's Introduction for the Lessons

Lesson 1
Isaiah 52:13—53:12 (RCL/RC)

The fourth Servant Song from Isaiah invites us to see the Servant in a new way: not majestic, but marred; not one who graciously stoops from divine perfection to participate in human existence, but one already wounded by life.

Lesson 2
Psalm 22 (RCL)

Jesus' cry of God-forsakenness from the cross quotes the first line of this psalm. To comprehend the trust that emerges in the psalm's closing, it is well this Friday to linger in the psalm's opening laments.

Psalm 31:2, 6, 12-13, 15-17, 25 (RC)

David cries for help in this psalm; God provides help. And once again, David prays for help, and God sends help.

Lesson 3
Hebrews 10:16-25 (RCL)

This passage is a proclamation of the difference between the sacrifices of the old and the new covenants. It reminds the community that the sacrifice offered for us was "once and for all." We are invited to be in God's presence, and also invited to be changed by the sacrifice Jesus has made.

Hebrews 4:14-16; 5:7-9 (RCL/RC)

The key to this passage is not in the authority in the image of high priest, but in the obedience. Here is an unequivocal declaration of the full humanity of Jesus, which draws us into his very real pain and suffering.

Gospel
John 18:1—19:42 (RCL/RC)

This is the story of the arrest, trials, crucifixion, and death of Jesus from John's perspective.

Theme
In the spirit of Isaiah's Servant Songs, we are God's servant people.

Thought for the Day
One act of beneficence, one act of real usefulness, is worth all the abstract sentiment in the world.

–Ann Radcliffe, *The Mysteries of Udolpho*

Sermon Summary
The Servant is the one in all times and places who stands in solidarity with the powerless, the vulnerable, the marginalized, the abused. It is not only Jesus who can be a servant. We are called to that witness too.

Call to Worship
One: When we dare to feel the pain of our sisters,
Many: We are one with all faithful servants of God.
One: When we dare to share the hunger of our brothers,
Many: We are one with all faithful servants of God.
One: When we work to heal the broken places of the earth,
Many: We are one with all faithful servants of God.
All: We come not to be served, but to serve, not to be loved, but to love, not to be comforted, but to comfort. Give us the strength and grace to be a faithful servant people.

Pastoral Prayer

Living, loving God, you have bound us so closely together that we cannot fully live when any of our sisters or brothers are dying in wars, in domestic violence, in prison, in refugee camps, in hunger, of disease. Awaken us to your power in us, your blood and bone, your strength and sinew, your grace and health and hope.

Living, loving God, open us to be conduits of your promise, allowing our holiest instincts to inspire us to give not merely from our own store- house, but from the limitless abundance that is you in us. Amen.

Prayer of Confession and Assurance

God of the covenant, you promised that you would write your wisdom and compassion in our hearts. We confess that we ignore them when lis- tening would be inconvenient. We confess that we resist them when they challenge us to change. We confess that we forget them when something else seems more interesting or amusing or pleasurable.

God of the covenant, you also promised that you would forgive our sins and our refusal to follow your ways. Soften our hearts that we can want forgiveness; break them open so that we can receive forgiveness; shape them anew so that we can live as forgiven, forgiving people. We ask this in the name of the one who, even on the cross, asked forgiveness for those who hung him there.

Prayer of Dedication of Gifts and Self

We have been blessed with abundance. We have been drenched in joy. We have been entrusted with common wealth. We have been invited to share with prodigal abandon. Teach us to trust that there is more than enough life for all. Inspire us to pour out everything we have been given, knowing that when we all do this, there will be no more hunger or thirst or loneli- ness or violence. May we be wholehearted instruments of your promise. Amen.

Hymn of the Day
When Jesus Wept

It is customary this night to pare the music down to the most sacred of all instruments: the human voice. No organ. No piano. Nothing to detract from the story we have come to hear with trembling hearts. An oft-over-looked gem lying dormant at the back of most hymnals is "When Jesus Wept" by William Billings, a simple round for four voices. "When Jesus wept, the falling tear in mercy flowed beyond all bound . . ." The gently falling minor melody portrays not only Jesus' tears, but also the utter anguish of this night.

Children's Time: A Sad Day

(Set out a processional cross or other large cross with room for the children to gather around it. Bring in several roses with thorns, and rose petals.)
(Invite the children to sit at the foot of the cross.) This day is called Good Friday, when we remember the day that Jesus died on the cross. Jesus suffered greatly on that day. Some Roman soldiers made a crown of thorns and placed it on his head. The thorns were sharp, like these thorns. (*Hold out the rose stems and invite the children to touch the tips of the thorns.*) Jesus' mother, friends, and followers cried and cried on this day when Jesus died.

Roses have thorns, but they are beautiful too. We know that Jesus' sad story has a beautiful Easter ending. But on Good Friday, we remember the sad part of Jesus' story. Here's a rose petal. (*Give each child a petal.*) Smell the petal. It smells so good. Gently rub the petal across your cheek. How does it feel? (*Smooth, soft.*) Think of someone you love. Then whisper a thank-you prayer for that person while you place your rose petal at the bottom of the cross. *(You may need to help the children begin.)*

(Pray in a whisper): Thank you, God, for sending your only Son, Jesus, for our sake, who died so that we could always live with you. Amen.

The Sermon: The Iniquity of Us All
Scripture: Isaiah 52:13—53:12

We are gathered here to remember one of our defining moments, one of the transitional events that form the parameters of what it means to be Christian rather than Jewish or Hindu or Buddhist or Zoroastrian or Muslim. The temptation is always to lean into the gospel and forget that when these events happened, there was no written gospel. Jesus and the women and the other disciples experienced this moment in the context of their Judaic practice and hope. I would like to invite you to join me in contemplating God's Friday from something approaching that perspective. I would like to invite you to be with the prophet Isaiah and the marred, misshapen, bruised Servant of the final Servant Song.

I would also like to invite you to let the Servant be the Servant and not rush to Christianize him. Because I am quite sure Jesus didn't. I strongly doubt that when he heard these passages in the temple, he thought, "Ah, yes. That would be me." Let us join him in that place of quiet listening.

Scholars agree that the Servant is a metaphor, a symbolic, mythic being rather than a specific person. The exact meaning of the metaphor is impossible to pin down because sometimes the Servant seems to be an individual, sometimes a collective (the whole people of God). Sometimes there is a messianic tone; sometimes a confessional one. Yet there is a consistent thread throughout: the Servant's life and choices are radically at odds with the world's agenda and values. And what the Servant does and who the Servant is, is preferential in God's eyes, a witness to the alternative commonwealth of justice and peace that is God's tender promise and deepest wish for creation.

This passage is filled with material for a dozen sermons or more. There is so much we could contemplate in this liturgical time, but there is perhaps one aspect of the lesson that stands out with painful clarity in this early part of the 21st century as individualism trumps relational community nine times out of ten.

We see this aspect first in the description of the physical appearance of the Servant. (And, although I will refer to the Servant as "he" since that is the translated pronoun, let's try to sit lightly regarding gender.) He is almost inhuman to look on, so battered and bruised and wounded and marred that "his form is beyond human semblance." And the reason that is offered for his devastatingly broken body and face is that he has taken on our transgressions, our iniquities, our dis-ease. Verse 6 says, "The Lord has laid on him the iniquity of us all."

Do we believe that? Do we believe God is willing to punish one scapegoat for the good of all other creatures? Do we? Certainly the majority of us no longer look on diseases like leprosy or AIDS or cancer as divine judgment. But what about human judgment?

What about the radiation sickness and genetic mutations that followed Hiroshima and Nagasaki? What about the horrific health effects that plague children and adults living next to toxic waste sites or drinking contaminated water from upstream dumping? How about black lung? What about AIDS used as a weapon of war in Rwanda? Medical experiments performed in the concentration camps of World War II? The effects of toxic gases and waste spills from Concentrated Animal Feeding Operations in the United States?

Our participation in these, our chosen ignorance, our denial of consequence, our worship of capitalism are all transgressions. We transgress when we continue to use products or make choices we know are dangerous to the earth and its inhabitants. Radiation sickness and cancer clusters are not God's judgment on us; they are our judgment from positions of power on others who are our enemies, or who are strangers, or who have no value in our immediate circle. Yet these are the very people the Servant stands beside in all his mutilated condition, reflecting and incarnating in his hideous presence our iniquities and dis-ease and sin.

The Servant Jesus asked us to stop hiding our faces or turning away. On this Good Friday, might we commit – each and every one of us – to heeding his plea here and now? Might we commit to not closing our eyes as if we are still toddlers who believe that if we don't see it, it doesn't exist?

And then might we commit to the actual purpose of this passage of scripture?

It isn't in the canon, after all, to tell us about some other people in some other time and geographical location. Scripture is always, always, always about us and our relationship with God. There is not a word of it that is not about us, our human failings and our human triumphs. We are not offered this passage on the Servant so that we can listen to some archaic poetry and ponder metaphors. We are being offered an invitation – yet again – to take up our divine task.

Jesus, you may recall, never once said, "Don't worry folks. I am going to witness to God's hope on behalf of the poor and the outcast so that you can continue to live your self-referenced lives without any concern for each other. I know you are all busy getting ahead in the world, so I'll do it for you."

Jesus said, "Do you see what I have done? I have set you an example. If you are true to God's love in you, you will do this and even greater things."

Jesus reminded us that we are God's servant people. We are God's servants. Yes, Jesus was one, but only one. Albert Schweitzer was one; Mother Teresa was one; Oscar Romero was one, and Edith Cavell. And, dear sisters and brothers, each of you is one too. I am one too. There are Buddhists and Hindus and Muslims and Jews who are God's servants too, in ways that may not look the same as ours. But if we are baptized Christians, we do not have a choice. It is not optional for us. This is the service to which we are called until it is no longer needed.

On this day when we commemorate the death of one of God's greatest servants, may we take up God's word, his work, our work with commitment and dedication. May we honor Jesus of Nazareth not by telling his story, but by living with his spirit.

May we do this in God's name.

– Andrea La Sonde Anastos

Hymns
Opening: We Are Pilgrims
Sermon: From Heaven You Came
Closing: God Make Us Servants

April 5, 2015

Easter Sunday

Lessons

Revised Common Lectionary (RCL)	Roman Catholic (RC)
Acts 10:34-43 or Isa 25:6-9	Acts 10:34a, 37-43
Ps 118:1-2, 14-24	Ps 118:1-2, 16-17, 22-23
1 Cor 15:1-11 or Acts 10:34-43	Col 3:1-4 or 1 Cor 5:6b-8
Jn 20:1-18 or Mk 16:1-8	Jn 20:1-9

Speaker's Introduction for the Lessons

Lesson 1

Acts 10:34-43 (RCL); Acts 10:34a, 37-43 (RC)

These verses are part of the glorious Easter proclamation, which will be repeated throughout this season. Peter preaches to a group in Caesarea, witnessing to the risen Christ and Christ's continued presence among his people.

Isaiah 25:6-9

Isaiah describes the apocalyptic hope in which we still exist.

Lesson 2

Psalm 118:1-2, 14-24 (RCL); Psalm 118:1-2, 16-17, 22-23 (RC)

This psalm of thanksgiving couples gratitude for deliverance with how God's deliverance deems acceptable what (who) had been judged rejected, using the image of a stone rejected by builders now serving as a cornerstone.

Lesson 3

1 Corinthians 15:1-11 (RCL)

Christ is the one through whom all things are made alive. Christ's death and resurrection becomes the promise that death will not be the final word, for Christ's raising is God's ultimate word for all.

Colossians 3:1-4 (RC)
Here is the declaration of our resurrection life ("hidden with Christ in God"). Through Christ, we are already raised and will be revealed when Christ is revealed in his glory.

Gospel
John 20:1-18 (RCL); John 20:1-9 (RC)
Alone at the tomb, Mary is called by name by a seeming stranger. The speaking of her name brings remembrance and recognition: the voice of Jesus lifts her out of mourning into joy and witness.
Mark 16:1-8 (RCL)
Women are surprised at the tomb, finding it open. They tell no one what they have seen, because they are afraid.

Theme
We believe the good news, but we still live in a "not yet" world.

Thought for the Day
When I dare to be powerful – to use my strength in the service of my vision, then it becomes less and less important whether I am afraid.
– Audre Lorde

Sermon Summary
The passage from Isaiah describes the apocalyptic hope in which we still exist in this world at this time. It provides an antidote to the disconnect between what the gospel implies and what we experience so that we can respond fruitfully here and now to our mandate as people of God.

Call to Worship
One: God shows no partiality, none at all.
All: God's good news is for all times, all places, all creatures, all creation.
One: God's good news is for our friends, our family, our enemies, and ourselves.
All: God's good news is for those who are safe, those who are in danger, those who are free and those in prison.

One: God's good news heals what has been, reconciles what is, and
gives birth for what is to come.
All: God shows no partiality, none at all.

Pastoral Prayer

You are the good news you proclaim, Gospel God. You are the healing you
offer. You are the reconciliation between enemies. You are the freedom
from every imprisonment. You are the comfort of the grieving. You are the
companionship of the lonely. But you have chosen not to do it all alone.
So stir us to do our part. Nudge us to be witnessing disciples who not only
receive, but give. Impel us to be the transforming change you desire for
this time and this place. Amen.

Prayer of Confession and Assurance

Eternally Loving God, when you became incarnate among us, you showed
us how to reveal the divine within our own souls. Risking your life for us
and dying with the work unfinished, you entrust us with your ongoing
witness of truth, of hope, of love. You dare to leave your reputation in our
hands. You commission us to be your presence in a desperate and needy
world.

We confess that we have not always lived in ways worthy of your image within us. We have not always revealed the holiness that you imprinted in us.

Now bend us toward grace and compassion, toward the feast you
have prepared for all creation, toward being life-bringers today and always.
Amen. Amen.

Prayer of Dedication of Gifts and Self

Generous God, you show us how to give when you give everything. You
show us what it means to be your people when you become a servant-pres-
ence day after day, in soul after soul. We know what you invite us to do.
Grant us the courage and the faithfulness to do it.

Receive what we have brought, knowing it is only part of what is
needed. Receive our lives, knowing that we continue to withhold the
better part. And make us impatient and discontent with our halfhearted
selves. In Jesus' name we ask. Amen.

Hymn of the Day
The Strife Is O'er

This Latin hymn dates to at least the 17th century and has existed in a number of English translations, the one by Francis Pott being the most familiar. The words speak of the battle between life and death, and how Christ has triumphed over death on our behalf. Each stanza consists of three short lines, followed by an ascending alleluia. A refrain of three alleluias is traditionally sung at the beginning and the end. The hymn is most commonly sung to VICTORY, by William Henry Monk. However, a vibrant and exciting tune entitled THE STRIFE IS O'ER by Australian Anglican priest James Minchin appeared in the 1977 edition of the *Australian Hymn Book*.

Children's Time: Called by Name

(Talk with the children about friends. How many friends do they have? What do they like to do with their friends? What kinds of things do they do to show that they care for one another?)

One way we can know if people are our friends is if they call us by name. Sometimes good friends even have nicknames for each other. (*You might share a nickname your friends call you, or talk with the children about nicknames they have.*)

Calling someone by name is a very special thing. It's a lot nicer than just pointing or saying, "Hey, you!"

One of the parts of the Easter story is about Mary Magdalene; she was one of Jesus' closest friends. When she went to the tomb that first Easter morning, she saw the stone was rolled away, and she thought that someone had stolen Jesus' body. She felt terrible. She was crying.

Of course, Jesus was alive, but she didn't know that. She heard someone talking to her and she thought it was the gardener. And then the person called her by name, and she realized it was Jesus. Can you imagine how happy she must have felt?

Jesus knows each of us by name too. Jesus loves us, and calls us all his friends. On this most wonderful day of the year, we celebrate that Jesus came back to life long ago and is still with us today. Alleluia!

Let's pray: Dear Jesus, thank you for knowing each of us by name. You make each of us feel special. Amen.

The Sermon: It Will Be Said
Scripture: Isaiah 25:6-9

And so we come to Easter Day and to the very center of our faith. We come to our belief (or more appropriately to our *faith-ing*, since "belief" is a verb for Christians), we come to our faithing that death is not the last word, but that life will emerge renewed, reborn, transformed from every ending. Please note that we don't get to remain the same on the other side of death. All the early stories tell us that Jesus didn't. His disciples did not recognize him in his resurrected manifestation. If we are going to believe at all, we might as well believe the whole of it: resurrected life is not what we normally mean when we speak of eternal life and imagine that our lives will pick up on the other side of death with no disjunction between "now" and "then."

So today we come to our central and definitive faithing ... and yet ... and yet ... And yet the resurrection of Jesus almost two millennia ago has not, in fact, catapulted us into the new creation in which death will be swallowed up, the shroud that is cast over all peoples will be destroyed, tears and sorrow will be wiped away, and peace will reign. So most of us either pretend that we are there and live in a psychological disconnect, or we notice we are not there and discard most of the good news.

Which is why the text, the apocalyptic text, from Isaiah is so important today. We actually live in a between time. We don't need to deny it – and the gospel to which we witness is not yet fully revealed or fully experienced. Those we love still die; we still die. So, apocalyptic literature is our literature in the most real, and most profound way.

Let me put in a good word for apocalyptic writing here, because it is generally treated with a certain amount of scorn or trepidation by mainline churchgoers. We tend to believe that the books of Daniel and Revelation and a few other scripture passages scattered here and there belong to "them": fundamentalists, millennialists, and people who read the Left Behind books by Tim LaHaye. And, frankly, most of us prefer it that way. But we are missing a huge component of our hope and of God's promise when we let apocalypse be appropriated in simplistic or inaccurate ways by people who, among other things, do not appear to fully comprehend metaphor and myth.

So let me remind you that prophecy in ancient Hebrew Scripture falls into two basic categories. There is the prophecy that is offered by a classical prophet, usually in a court or temple setting, which calls the people to repentance and seeks to change the social order here and now. Not only does it seek to change the status quo, it has every expectation that it will change it. This type of prophecy is filled with the confident proclamation that God is active in this instant and with the warning that the people better pay attention or suffer the consequences. Micah, Amos, Jeremiah. and much of the book of Isaiah are excellent examples of classical prophecy. Jesus, even preaching outside the centers of power, was a classical prophet in this sense of the term.

And then there are the apocalyptic prophets (including the person who wrote the three chapters in Isaiah from which this morning's text comes). For these women and men, there is less confidence in God's desire to be active in the present moment. The fulfillment of God's realm of peace and justice will happen, but it is unlikely that it will happen today or tomorrow. It may not occur as a simple (simple!) uncovering of what Jesus (in his classical prophet mode) claims is already present among us; instead, it will emerge from the birth pangs of the universe groaning in labor. The metaphor (please note it is a metaphor, not a literal descriptor) speaks of cosmic upheaval, unmeasured turmoil, the sun and moon turning to blood. Apocalyptic prophets proclaim that we are still on the journey and the end is not yet in sight.

Apocalyptic writers may sound pessimistic – or "pie in the sky" depending on your point of view and the metaphor-vision they use – but they are incredibly courageous and realistic folks. They cling to their faith even in the midst of a world that seems to offer nothing to affirm that faith. They hold to the promise as they suffer exile, persecution, scorn, despair, war, poverty, alienation, and violent death. They will not let go of their stubborn faithing even as they walk an apparently limitless wilderness. They are not people who think that they can control any outcomes at all, no matter how skilled or powerful or sincere they are. And I would remind you that some of the classical prophets were enormously powerful, both socially and politically. They are not professional victims; they are just aware of their ordinary place in the scheme of things.

Apocalyptic prophets are, in other words, the very role models we most need on this particular day in the liturgical year. They are people who have learned stamina; they are the people who plant acorns knowing that they will not live to see the full grown oak; they are the super-marathoners who just keep breathing and moving ahead; they inspire and comfort the folks like Nelson Mandela and Aung San Suu Kyi during the years in prison or under house arrest. They are the leaders and preachers and hope-givers who strongly suspect that they will die (Jesus was among this group, too) and their children and grandchildren and great-grandchildren, but that some day in the far distant future, death will be no more.

And so they do what they can do: they live this moment in the promise. They plant the tree, they comfort the child, they put a dollar and a blessing in the cup of the panhandler, they work to change unjust laws, they plant gardens, they watch their energy consumption, their vacation week is used for a Habitat build, they thank the trash collectors, they lie down in front of trains carrying nuclear warheads, they treat their enemy with dignity. They keep on keeping on: refusing to let death or injustice or greed or fear or ignorance define them.

Jesus went to the cross to show his solidarity with them. He rose in surrender to God's unending love for them and for us. This is the day we are invited to recommit ourselves to being among them. May we do so in joy and in confidence.

– Andrea La Sonde Anastos

Hymns
Opening: Because You Live, O Christ
Sermon: Christ Is Alive
Closing: Come, Labor On

April 12, 2015

2nd Sunday of Easter

Lessons

Revised Common Lectionary (RCL)	Roman Catholic (RC)
Acts 4:32-35	Acts 4:32-35
Ps 133	Ps 118:2-4, 13-15, 22-24
1 Jn 1:1—2:2	1 Jn 5:1-6
Jn 20:19-31	Jn 20:19-31

Speaker's Introduction for the Lessons

Lesson 1

Acts 4:32-35 (RCL/RC)

Convincing evidence of Jesus' resurrection came from the amazing unity that characterized the community of those who believed in Jesus. The resurrection inspired personal compassion that found social expression in a depth of unselfish sharing.

Lesson 2

Psalm 133 (RCL)

A song of pilgrimage uses tangible elements from nature to celebrate in metaphors the gift of unity (oils used for anointing, and the two chief mountains of northern and southern Israel, Hermon and Zion).

Psalm 118:2-4, 13-15, 22-24 (RC)

Read in the context of the resurrection, this psalm underscores Israel's joyfulness in God's steadfast love and offers a metaphor for Jesus as the stone that the builders rejected.

Lesson 3

1 John 1:1—2:2 (RCL)

The writer of 1 John opens the epistle with a description of the epistle's message: Jesus provides all people with a way out of sin and an opportunity to live in forgiveness and truth.

1 John 5:1-6 (RC)

Children of God love God and love Jesus. The presence of this love is self-evident in a person's obedience to God's commandments and in a person's faith.

Gospel
John 20:19-31 (RCL/RC)
The risen Christ engaged in many acts, which are recorded in the scriptures, to help people believe in him and share in his life. He commissioned the disciples to continue his ministry.

Theme
Personal ownership is an illusion; we hold everything in trust from God.

Thought for the Day
We can tell our values by looking at our checkbook stubs.

– Gloria Steinem

Sermon Summary
Holding all things in common is not a utopian ideal, it is a reflection of who we understand God to be and how we live to reflect that image. We cannot keep ignoring this teaching of Jesus and continue to consider ourselves Christian. We need to commit to moving toward this radical choice.

Call to Worship
One: Jesus taught us to be of one mind and heart.
Many: Jesus taught us to hold everything in common.
One: Jesus taught us to hold justice in common, standing with the voiceless and the powerless sharing their oppression until we are all free.
Many: Jesus taught us to hold peace in common, refusing to do violence to our neighbor or our enemy until we are all released from fear.
One: Jesus taught us to hold all possessions in common, sharing everything we call our own until there is no more need, no more hunger, no more homelessness.
Many: Jesus taught us to do this. Here. Today.

Pastoral Prayer

Trusting and Empowering One, we praise you for inviting us to be more than we think we can be. We praise you for your trust that we will do what is needed and not only what is most convenient. We praise you for showing us that abundance surrounds us on every side, waiting to be given, received, and given again. May our praise become not words and feelings only, but acts of compassion, mercy, love, justice, and generosity. Amen.

Prayer of Confession and Assurance

Hopeful God, we confess that we are wholehearted when we receive the blessings of this life, but halfhearted when it comes time to share them. We confess we wholeheartedly welcome your love for us, but halfheartedly incarnate that love for others. We confess we enthusiastically and whole-heartedly accept all the benefits that come to us by virtue of our race or social class, our level of education, our gender, our health, but we be-grudgingly and halfheartedly work to insure those benefits to every sister and every brother, to friend, to stranger, to enemy.

Bless us with the prayer we need to pray: that our whole hearts will belong to one another and that we will hold nothing back from the common good. Let it be so today.

Prayer of Dedication of Gifts and Self

Generous God, we come today telling ourselves that we, too, are gener-ous; that we are giving so much; that we cannot do more. Wrap us in dissatisfaction. Enfold us in a vision of what will be when we believe that we really can do so much more. Bless us not only with hearts that want to share, but also with hands that do share. Amen.

Hymn of the Day
We Walk by Faith, and Not by Sight

Brimming with preaching and musical themes, it is the portrait of Thomas drawn by the Gospel writer John that is so memorable and inspirational here, because it puts a human face on doubt. We must also wonder what sort of doubts were faced by the infant church as it struggled to find its way. Henry Alford's "We Walk by Faith, and Not by Sight" is an ideal selection for this Sunday. His hymn is pure eloquence: "We may not touch his hands and side, nor follow where he trod; but in his promise we rejoice; and cry, 'My Lord and God.'" Gordon Slater's St. Botolph complements the silkiness of Alford's writing.

Children's Time: Peace Be with You

(Ask your church musician to play a peaceful, soothing piece as children come forward.)
Greet the children by saying: "Christ is risen!" Encourage them to respond, "Christ is risen indeed!" Listen to this music playing right now. How does this music make you feel? *(Accept responses.)* It makes me feel peaceful. What does peace mean? *(Sense of calm, safety, and quiet are possible responses.)*

On the night after Easter night, Jesus' followers had gathered in a house in Jerusalem. They locked the doors. They were afraid. They were afraid that they would be arrested and killed because they loved and followed Jesus. Suddenly Jesus appeared inside their house. He didn't walk through the door. He didn't climb through a window. He just appeared. The disciples thought they were seeing a ghost. They were even more afraid. Jesus knew they were afraid, so he said to them, "Peace be with you." Jesus showed his friends the nail holes through his wrists and ankles. How do you think Jesus' followers felt after Jesus appeared to them? *(Happy, joyful.)* Jesus was alive! They were amazed. Jesus had died, but now here he was, standing with them, sharing the peace that new life can bring.

When we share the peace during worship, we are celebrating the peace that Jesus brings to us, too.

Let's pray: Dear Jesus, thank you for bringing your peace into our lives every day. Amen.

The Sermon: In Common
Scripture: Acts 4:32-35

First, the bad news. There is no way to preach today's text as if it can be made to conform to the standards and practices of Western capitalism; it can't. The good news is that this is true of every passage of scripture: not one of them conforms to the current status quo. For Christians – whether we like it or not – scripture is the radical expectation by which the status quo is always measured. Any status quo that is out of alignment with scripture needs to be transformed to fit the Word, not vice versa. And today's lesson describes a massive transformation for most of us.

My text is the last phrase of Acts 4:32, "Everything they owned was held in common."

It seems communities that live in the power and faith of the resurrection have fundamentally different values than does the world. To the degree that we buy into the values of the world, we will find this proclamation from Acts uncomfortable. If it is any consolation at all, I am betting that every single person out there in the pews is finding it at least as uncomfortable as you are. And I can assure you that I preach this passage today because (as always) I preach the cutting edge of my own faith, the challenges that keep me awake at night (or should keep me awake), my slow process of maturing in discipleship.

"Everything they owned was held in common."

Since our ability to focus on things we don't want to hear is very limited, let's cut to the chase. First, let's not pretend that these words only apply to folks who expect the Parousia tomorrow, so having personal possessions doesn't matter to them. Luke wrote Acts around 70-85 CE (or 35 to 50 years postcrucifixion). People were no longer expecting the world to end that day. This community was living in "between time" just as we are. They were following the teachings of Jesus exactly as we are, using the stories that were collected and passed down to them to try to live each day a little more faithfully. They were not blessed with any spiritual grace that we are not, nor were they genetically immune to wanting worldly success. All you need to do is read the five verses that follow this lesson to know that these folks were wrestling with the same issues we are.

Second, let's not dismiss this passage as some kind of "ideal" that no one really took seriously. Followers expected to live this way because this is exactly how Jesus told us to live. More than once, in fact. And sources contemporary with the early church comment more than once on the fact that there were no destitute members of the community because they held all things in common and distributed what was necessary to those in need.

Now the whole group of those who believed were of one heart and soul, and no one claimed private ownership of any possessions, but everything they owned was held in common.

We may not like this teaching. We may not find it convenient. We may not practice it. But there is no question whatsoever that it was (and is) the expectation among Jesus' followers and is (even now) the practice in some Christian communities.

But that's not really the point, is it? It doesn't really matter whether some folks at some other time and place did this as an expression of their discipleship. Discipleship is not something that can be appropriated vicariously. It is only something that can be incarnate by any given disciple in real time, usually with real struggle. The point is not what someone else chose, but who we believe God to be and how we intend to live in order to reflect that image with integrity and beauty. If, that is, we intend to reflect that image in any way at all.

It should come as no surprise when I tell you that God is not the Great Capitalist. The universe is not a capitalist system. Nor is not based on zero-sum economics. Look around. The sun does not shine only when we pay the Sun-Ignitor for it to do so. And, conversely, if the sun were to go out, no amount of money would suffice to turn it back on. And, the sun shining on you does not leave less sunlight for me. Every gift and blessing that matters is free and prodigal and universally available: from the air we breathe to the water table that undergirds our food supply to the love that embraces us to laughter to starry skies to gravity.

The community of Jesus' followers understood that private ownership is therefore an illusion. Everything in some way, shape, or form originates with God and has been created for the common good. I can stop the free and generous cycle of resources by hoarding them for myself, but that is not what God does because that is not who God is. And in a community of resurrection people, we are practicing what it means to trust that life is so abundant nothing can stop it, not even death.

Is it easy? No. Our cultural training is very strong – the training that says scarcity is the final word. But, my friends, the resurrection is the proof that scarcity is not the final word. Which means that we truly can live in the same trust as these early disciples. We just need to start. Here. Now.

If it is too scary to sell everything, you could start by selling your third car, or the jet-ski, or maybe the bicycle you never ride. You could cut out the middleman and just give it away to someone who needs transportation. Or you could offer your sweater to the street person on the corner who is shivering. Okay, how about just your gloves and hat? You could increase your giving to the needy to an honest 10 percent of your annual income. Can you imagine the ripples in this city if every one of us here today did just one of these things regularly? Can you imagine what will happen to our hearts when we learn what Anne Frank noticed: "No one has ever become poor by giving"?

Private ownership is an illusion that our financial markets use to keep us enslaved. Break free, dear sisters and brothers, and dance with joy through your days as God intended and Jesus taught: in the confidence that unmeasured abundance is the essence of God's being and that God has created you to manifest God's true image in the world. Amen and amen.

– Andrea La Sonde Anastos

Hymns
Opening: O Sons and Daughters, Let Us Sing
Sermon: You Tell Me That the Lord Is Risen
Closing: As Those of Old Their First Fruits Brought

April 19, 2015

3rd Sunday of Easter

Lessons

Revised Common Lectionary (RCL)	Roman Catholic (RC)
Acts 3:12-19	Acts 3:13-15, 17-19
Ps 4	Ps 4:2, 4, 7-9
1 Jn 3:1-7	1 Jn 2:1-5a
Lk 24:36b-48	Lk 24:35-48

Speaker's Introduction for the Lessons

Lesson 1
Acts 3:12-19 (RCL); Acts 3:13-15, 17-19 (RC)

In a public sermon delivered before a large crowd at the temple's Solomon's Portico, Peter reviewed the key components of salvation history. He ended the sermon with a call to repentance.

Lesson 2
Psalm 4 (RCL); Psalm 4:2, 4, 7-9 (RC)

The psalmist calls on God to be heard, questions and advises the people, and closes with an assurance of God's peace in a psalm deceptively complex in its multiple purposes.

Lesson 3
1 John 3:1-7 (RCL)

The love of God is known most clearly through Christians' identity as "children of God." That identity is not dependent upon recognition by the world, but is a consequence of the revelation of God.

1 John 2:1-5a (RC)

The author of 1 John encourages the children of God to know the joy, forgiveness, and fellowship available in Christ. Children of God obey the commandments of God and walk as Jesus walked.

Gospel
Luke 24:36b-48 (RCL); Luke 24:35-48 (RC)

Jesus appears to the disciples, even as the two who traveled with Jesus on the road to Emmaus were telling the others of their experience. His greeting of "peace" is followed by further teaching.

Theme

There is more joy in heaven and earth than we bother to notice.

Thought for the Day

There are only two ways to live your life. One is as though nothing is a miracle. The other is as though everything is a miracle.

– Albert Einstein

Sermon Summary

Living into the resurrection is not about learning more rules and regulations intended to limit us. It is not about imposing limits on others to make them "better people." It is about learning to live in the miracles that surround us with gratitude, wonder, surprise, and joy.

Call to Worship

One: We have been invited to repent and turn to God.

Many: We have been invited to turn over our stressed lives and our endless lists of tasks.

One: We have been invited to turn away from our prejudice, our judgmental behavior, our self-righteousness.

Many: We have been invited to turn away from fear and toward love.

One: We have been invited to turn toward laughter and delight, toward wonder and joy, toward amazement and surprise.

Many: We have been invited to repent and turn to God.

Pastoral Prayer

Love, all lovely, love us into the joy that sees beauty in every creature. Love us into the generosity that offers forgiveness to those who are burdened by

333

guilt or fear or prejudice. Love us into the hope that sweeps away despair. Love us into the curiosity that resists apathy. Love us into the love that cares for the stranger, the powerless, the lonely, and the one we once called enemy. Love through us into a world that is hungry for love. May it be so. Amen.

Prayer of Confession and Assurance

Divine Joy, we confess that we are people motivated more by fear than love, and we don't know why. We know how to build walls and make rules and set boundaries. We know how to feel guilty. We are good at trying to make ourselves (and everyone else) conform to some ideal we have decided you want.

We confess we don't know what to do with your unconditional love. We don't know how to respond to your joyful surprises. We are afraid to stand under the flood of your miracle and wonder and goodness and healing.

Fold us in your comforting presence and bless us into courage so that we can join the dance at your side. Drench us in trust in the name of the one who trusted you even on the cross.

Prayer of Dedication of Gifts and Self

Beloved God, you continue to give with a generous hand even when we rent bigger and bigger storage lockers to house what we hoard. You love us with an expansive love even when we are busy measuring portions of abundance and wondering how little we can get away with.

Release our fear of scarcity and lift the burden of our possessions so that we may know the blessing of giving not only what feels safe, but also what feels wonderful. In hope we ask. Amen.

Hymn of the Day
Thine Is the Glory

In Luke's accounts of the risen Jesus and his disciples, it's as if Jesus is intentionally teaching them that he is always with them, even when he is not with them bodily. This is the same risen Christ who empowers Jesus' followers as they transition from being disciples (followers) to apostles (sent ones). Edmond Budry's "Thine Is the Glory" is a fine choice for today. The second verse, in particular, is perfect: "Lo, Jesus meets thee, risen from the tomb! Lovingly he greets thee, scatters fear and gloom." Handel's tune, JUDAS MACCABEAUS, composed in 1746 for his oratorio of the same name, fits the text splendidly.

Children's Time: Shout the Good News!
(Bring an inflatable globe or beach ball.)
(Whisper "Jesus is alive" to only two or three children. Say to the others): How do you feel when someone keeps a secret from you? *(Left out, sad, mad.)* How do you feel when you are keeping a secret? *(Important.)* I'm going to whisper something important to all of you. Jesus is alive! Let's whisper it softly all together. Now let's say it in a soft voice. *(Repeat "Jesus is alive!")* Now a little bit louder.

Did Jesus want his followers to keep his new life a secret? *(No.)* Jesus told them to tell everyone about his new life. This good news isn't a secret. It isn't only for a special group of people. Jesus' good news is for all of the people in the world. Is this happy news or sad news? *(Happy news.)* Let's share our Easter happiness.

(Throw the earth ball to a child while saying "Jesus is alive!" Explain that the child who catches the ball throws it to another, repeating the message. Repeat until all the children, and maybe some of the adults, have had an opportunity to do so.)

Let's pray: Dear Jesus, your happy Easter news is not a secret. Your Easter news is for all people. Help me to tell someone about you every day. Amen.

The Sermon: Turn to God
Scripture: Acts 3:12-19

It is important that we understand to whom Peter is speaking in his sermon: he is speaking to us. In historical context, he was speaking to a crowd of people who had come to see the folks (Peter and John) who had just healed a lame man in the name of Jesus. However, as we know from previous sermons, scripture is always addressed to us and the topic is always our relationship with God. So let's not waste any time talking about how "they" responded to Jesus – or Peter and John, for that matter – two millennia ago. It really doesn't matter what "they" did. All that matters is what we do right here and right now.

Let me paraphrase the opening of Peter's sermon a little so that we can hear it in slightly more contemporary vernacular. "The healing you just witnessed was not magic, dependent on our skill or sleight of hand. You witnessed a miracle: God's healing power at work right before your eyes. Nothing that human beings can do even comes close to God's power unleashed for good, so don't dismiss what you saw, or deny it, or misname it. Don't try to make it smaller or control it. Allow yourself to be changed by seeing it clearly for what it is. It is a miracle."

So, let me ask, how many miracles did you see on your way to church today? How many did you see yesterday? How many do you expect to see tomorrow? How many did you tell your spouse or partner, or colleagues at work, or children, or friends about?

My guess is that the vast majority of us are not aware that we saw any miracles. And that, my sisters and brothers, is exactly the point Peter is making. To the extent that we don't see the miracles that are happening every single nanosecond from the moment we draw our first breath until the moment we draw our last, we are living in death. We are living disconnected from God. In Peter's language, we are killing the author of life. Over and over. We are – you and I. Today.

Friends, we are a resurrection people. We have just reaffirmed the centrality of the resurrection in our lives. That means something. It means that we do not need to live any longer in the fear that death is the final word. We can trust ourselves to the Always Surprising Author of Life and to the unpredictable delight of miracles swirling around us on all sides 24/7/365. We can notice them and name them.

It means we can give up the illusion of control.

We can cut loose and live in this moment. This one right here, right now. And notice that we are breathing, gravity is working, there is grass, there is sunlight, there is food to eat, there are birds, and someone who loves us is nearby. In fact, we can lean joyfully and wholeheartedly into a love affair with the divine.

Instead of furrowing our brow and pursing our lips and taking colors and sounds and smells and laughter and babies and tears and digestion for granted, we can crack open our hearts and say, "Wow." We can say

"Thanks." Instead of plodding, we can dance. Instead of sniping or complaining, we can sing.

Now if you want to see life as a grind, no one is going to stop you. I would just like to point out (since this is my job, the vocation to which God called me and you appointed me) that this is a pretty mingy way to eke out existence. And I would like to observe that it makes for a lot of really stressed lives, and really cranky people, and really unhealthy experiences. Peter is telling us that we can expect more of life than that. We just need to repent, which only means to turn around and see things from a different perspective and align ourselves with joy rather than rigid control and narrow focus.

As it turns out, cultivating joy has significant health benefits, and friendship benefits, and career benefits. Trying to control the entire universe by our own power (or piety or ritual or rules or accumulation of retirement savings), on the other hand, is a sure path to despair, depression, and misery. And the harder we work at it, the less we notice that we are standing knee-deep in miracles. Certainly, a modicum of planning ahead for college tuition or retirement or an unexpected car repair can make most lives smoother. But Peter is telling us that rejecting God's infinite blessings in the conviction that you can do better under your own steam is to choose death.

As a minister, it has been my privilege to walk with people through the end of this life. I know from experience that not every human condition can be fixed medically. My mother's cancer couldn't. But I also know that the condition doesn't need to define the person or the journey. The folks who see the miraculous in what the rest of us see as the perfectly mundane, those women and men and children live until the moment of their last breath. They are not defeated by a worn-out body; their spirits and minds continue to soar. They know surprise and delight even in great weakness and indignity. They laugh and spread happiness and charm the hospice nurses. Then they step across the threshold with an eager expectation that something amazing awaits on the other side.

There are other people who sit in my office with tight lips and white knuckles if the third hymn on Sunday was too loud. They have no eager expectations of anything and rarely experience joy. I suspect they wouldn't see a miracle if it sat on their lap and purred. They may be in perfect health, but everything about them screams "death." They're life-rejecters. And the life they reject day after day after day is their own.

Peter is speaking to all of us who reject life, whether consistently or occasionally. He is reminding us that we have a choice. He says, "Oh stop with the control, already. Repent. Let go. Turn to the one who is Holy Wonder. Walk away from everything that separates you from the healing love, the abounding joy, the amazing surprise, the refreshing peace that is God's infinite shower of miracles. Live!"

We have that choice. You and I have that choice. Will you join me in choosing life? Today?

–Andrea La Sonde Anastos

Hymns
Opening: I Greet You, Sure Redeemer
Sermon: Because You Live, O Christ
Closing: Lord of the Dance

April 26, 2015

4th Sunday of Easter

Lessons

Revised Common Lectionary (RCL)	Roman Catholic (RC)
Acts 4:5-12	Acts 4:8-12
Ps 23	Ps 118:1, 8-9, 21-23, 26, 29
1 Jn 3:16-24	1 Jn 3:1-2
Jn 10:11-18	Jn 10:11-18

Speaker's Introduction for the Lessons

Lesson 1

Acts 4:5-12 (RCL); Acts 4:8-12 (RC)

When political and religious leaders in Jerusalem asked Peter and John by what authority they spoke and acted, Peter explained that their good work was being done in the name of Jesus Christ and called the leaders to recognize the unique identity of Jesus.

Lesson 2

Psalm 23 (RCL)

This is a prime example of a psalm of serene trust in God, using the image of God as shepherd, who accompanies and provides for us on our journey with loving care.

Psalm 118:1, 8-9, 21-23, 26, 29 (RC)

The stone that the builders rejected became the cornerstone, and this is the Lord's doing.

Lesson 3

1 John 3:16-24 (RCL)

Real love finds expression in action. We know that we abide in Christ when we obey his commandments to believe in him and to show love toward one another.

1 John 3:1-2 (RC)

The love of God is known most clearly through Christians' identity as "children of God." The reality of that identity is not dependent upon recognition by the world, but is a consequence of the revelation of God.

Gospel
John 10:11-18 (RCL/RC)
Jesus identifies himself as the good shepherd, who lays down his life on behalf of his sheep. Followers of Jesus know the voice of Jesus the shepherd and obey. God is pleased with Jesus the good shepherd.

Theme
God, our good shepherd, always guides us with tender care.

Thought for the Day
Whenever you feel lost and alone, remember that you have a good shepherd.

Sermon Summary
The metaphor of God as our shepherd is powerful and comforting. God watches over us with tender compassion. God protects us, provides for us, and keeps us safe. We can rest assured that Christ, our good shepherd, will enfold us with his love forever.

Call to Worship
One: You who are thirsty, come to the waters of life.
All: O God, your goodness and mercy follow us all the days of our lives.
One: You who are hungry, come to God's banquet of love.
All: O God, your goodness and mercy follow us all the days of our lives.
One: You who are yearning for wholeness, come to God's pasture of peace and unity.
All: O God, your goodness and mercy follow us all the days of our lives.

Pastoral Prayer
O God our shepherd, we praise you for your love that holds us in your tender care. Watch over all those who are in any trouble. Bring comfort to those who walk through the dark valleys of illness, grief, and loss. Help us to recognize all the quiet ways that you lead us to the safety of your mercy.

Give us the strength and courage to continue in the path of discipleship, all the days of our lives. In the name of Christ we pray, Amen.

Prayer of Confession and Assurance

O God our good shepherd, we confess that we have strayed from your will, wandering off to pursue our own ways. We have failed to listen to your voice and follow in your path. We have ignored the needs of our neighbors. We have resisted your gentle guidance. We have sought to stay in when you have tried to lead us out, and we have to stay out on our own when you have sought to lead us in to your love. We have viewed those who differ from us with suspicion and fear. In your mercy, forgive us. Lead us in your ways of mercy, love, and peace. Help us to know the assurance of your pardon and to accept the comfort of your shepherding care.

Prayer of Dedication of Gifts and Self

Good and Gracious God, all that we have comes to us through your abundance, which flows from your generosity and love. You have set a banquet before us. Our lives overflow with your goodness. We dedicate our lives and these gifts to your service. May we be signs of your goodness and mercy. Use us and all that we offer to further your purpose and make known your love for the world, through Jesus Christ, our good shepherd. Amen.

Hymn of the Day
The King of Love My Shepherd Is

Among the loveliest of biblical passages is Psalm 23, a reading often paired with today's Gospel lesson. Both describe a shepherd: the psalmist, one who leads the sheep safely home; John, one who cares so much for the flock that he lays down his life for them. Henry Williams Baker's paraphrase of Psalm 23, "The King of Love My Shepherd Is," is a fine choice for today. The language is such that the hymn doesn't seem a repetition of the psalm; indeed, Baker's rendering is as exquisite as the psalm itself. The gentle Irish melody St. Columbia is first choice for melody.

Children's Time: The Good Shepherd

(Bring name tags and markers. Encourage everyone to wear name tags today so you all can call each other by name.)
Good morning! My name is *(your name)*. What are your names? *(Let children say their names.)* When I call out each one of your names, I want you to stand up and sit down quickly. *(Call out each child's name.)* Why do we have names? *(Affirm responses.)* Who gave us our names? *(Parents, people who love us.)* Who calls you by your name? *(Parents, friends, family members, teachers.)*

During Jesus' time there were lots of shepherds. Shepherds took care of sheep. They often named each one of their sheep. The sheep recognized their own shepherd's voice. In the evening, the shepherd would call the sheep by name, gathering them into a large pen to keep them safe from wolves and thieves.

Jesus says that he is our shepherd. Jesus knows each one of us by name. Jesus cares for us like a good shepherd cares for his sheep. Jesus is watching over us in the daytime and the nighttime. We all belong to Jesus' flock. Jesus sends people to call us by name, to share his love and care. Let's pray: Dear Jesus, thank you for watching over us like a good shepherd cares for his sheep. We love you. Amen.

The Sermon: God Is Our Shepherd
Scripture: Psalm 23

Psalm 23 is both familiar and beloved. Together with the Lord's Prayer, Psalm 23 is a scripture passage that is so treasured that countless generations of Christians have learned it by heart. It has been recited at bedsides and gravesides, taught in Sunday school classrooms, and inspired hymnwriters and artists, especially when paired with John's Gospel and Jesus' words "I am the good shepherd." From hymns like "The King of Love My Shepherd Is" to pictures of Christ standing beside a flowing stream among a herd of sheep, holding a wooden shepherd's staff with one hand and cradling a tiny lamb in the other, the imagery of God as our shepherd tugs at our heartstrings. The psalm evokes comforting images of pastoral landscapes and pastoral care.

This psalm invites us to meditate and reflect on the goodness of God and God's unwavering love for us. The psalmist captures our imagination with the metaphor of God as our shepherd: leading us beside still waters, making us lie down in green pastures, comforting us with God's rod and staff, guiding us through the valley of the shadow of death. The psalmist fills us with hope of divine goodness and mercy, overflowing with abundance in a feast of love set before us, following us all the days of our lives, and with the promise of dwelling in the house of the Lord forever.

While the imagery can be so familiar for us, so woven into the fabric of Christian language that we barely notice it anymore, it remains powerful and deep. It is language of close connection and trust. The language of shepherd and sheep provides rich imagery about God's relationship with us. Shepherds in the ancient world lived with their sheep. They remained with them night and day, watching over them and protecting them from human thieves and wild predators. Shepherds protect, lead, and guide their sheep. God watches over us and cares for us, as a shepherd watches the sheep. God gathers us into relationship with God and with one another. God invites us to follow in loyalty and trust. God walks ahead of us to lead the way. God walks alongside us to encourage us and to keep us from straying from our path. God walks behind us to prevent us from lagging behind and to pick up and carry those who are too weak or tired to continue.

The words of the 23rd psalm also give voice to the full reality of our human experience, with all of its blessings and challenges. While we may know the joy of green pastures and still waters, the pleasure of full plates and overflowing cups, and the contentment that comes from resting until we feel fully restored and rejuvenated, we also walk through the valley of the shadow of death. We experience danger. We have enemies. There are places of scarcity. For some, the tables are empty and the cups only half full. We know fear. The forces of anxiety can scatter us, or herd us together so tightly that we are at risk of suffocating or being trampled if anyone panics. We stray from the paths where God seeks to lead us. We become weak and tired. We know grief and despair. Sometimes we wonder how we can keep going in the face of difficult challenges and overwhelming obstacles.

Yet, even in these dark valleys of fear, danger, suffering or despair, we need fear no evil. The Lord is our shepherd. God's shepherding care enables us to walk safely through the valley, secure in the promise that God's goodness and mercy shall follow us all the days of our life, and we shall dwell in the house of the Lord forever. God is present with us, blesses us, and gives us the gift of life. No matter where you go, you are not alone. God is always with you. We may not always recognize it. It may not look like what we expect. The menu may even surprise us. Yet, still, God sets a table before us. And God sets that table in the presence of our enemies. The table is set, not so that we can taunt our enemies by eating in front of them, but so that together we can taste God's banquet of reconciliation and peace. The rules of hospitality in ancient Mediterranean culture insisted that those who had dined together shared a common bond, and that they must hold to a truce and not attack each other until a few days after the meal was over. To dine with an enemy was to treat that person as a friend. God, our good shepherd, leads us to the banquet table, where we taste the sweetness of God's love, where our thirst for forgiveness is quenched, and where we feast on the fruit of peace, love, and hope.

As people of faith, whenever we walk through the valley of deepest shadow, we recognize that we also stand in the shadow of the cross of Christ. As our good shepherd, Jesus has taken the full weight of human experience, with all of our suffering and pain, upon himself, bearing it with us and for us. As we live in the shadow of the cross, we also proclaim the promise of Easter. God our shepherd stands among us with strength and courage. God our shepherd leads us with compassion and love. God is always bringing life from death. Christ is our good shepherd, who walks with us, guiding us, directing us, and making all things new. God's goodness is unwavering. Our good shepherd's love for us is steadfast and unending. This is the faith that carries us onward, through the dark valley, into the green pastures, beside the still waters, where goodness and mercy follow us all the days of our life. The Lord is our shepherd! Amen.

– Julie A. Kanarr

Hymns
Opening: Have No Fear, Little Flock
Sermon: The King of Love My Shepherd Is
Closing: Lead Me, Guide Me.

May 3, 2015

5th Sunday of Easter

Lessons

Revised Common Lectionary (RCL)	Roman Catholic (RC)
Acts 8:26-40	Acts 9:26-31
Ps 22:25-31	Ps 22:26-28, 30-32
1 Jn 4:7-21	1 Jn 3:18-24
Jn 15:1-8	Jn 15:1-8

Speaker's Introduction for the Lessons

Lesson 1

Acts 8:26-40 (RCL)

Guided by the Spirit of God, Philip met an Ethiopian on the road from Jerusalem to Gaza. Philip joined the stranger in his chariot, discussed scriptures written by Isaiah, and introduced him to Jesus. When the man from Ethiopia requested to be baptized, Philip baptized him.

Acts 9:26-31 (RC)

Barnabas helped the Christians in Jerusalem set aside their fear of Paul by telling them of Paul's vision on the Damascus road and Paul's advocacy for Jesus in Damascus. Immediately the Christians in Jerusalem accepted Paul into their fellowship.

Lesson 2

Psalm 22:25-31 (RCL); Psalm 22:26-28, 30-32 (RC)

This is the thanksgiving portion of an overall psalm of lament. These verses focus on the praise and worship of God by the community expanded to include all the families of the nations.

Lesson 3

1 John 4:7-21 (RCL)

Love is at the heart of the Christian experience. Love is from God. If we are born of God and know God, we love like God loves. If we love God, we love each other.

1 John 3:18-24 (RC)

Real love finds expression in action. Jesus expressed love in laying

down his life for others, for us. We know that we abide in Christ
when we obey his command to believe in him and to show love
toward one another.

Gospel
John 15:1–8 (RCL/RC)
Jesus identifies himself as the true vine of God. Believers in Jesus are
the branches of that vine. The best evidence of people's union with
the vine is their good works, by which God is honored and with
which God is pleased.

Theme
God's love flows into us and empowers us for loving one another.

Thought for the Day
God's love for you is so strong that it can never be exhausted.

Sermon Summary
The commandment to love one another invites us into relationship with
God and with one another. God's love empowers us for mission. God's
love continually recharges us to reach out to share God's love with others.
Our love for God becomes visible through our love for one another.

Call to Worship
One: Come, let us turn to the Lord,
All: Who has made the world and all that is in it.
One: Come, let us give praise to our God,
All: Who acts in love for all humankind.
One: Come let us bow down in worship,
All: And proclaim God's love to all generations.

Pastoral Prayer
Almighty God, your infinite love surrounds us. We ask that your love may
abide in us, and that we may reflect your love in loving others. Be with
those who are in need. Bring comfort to those for whom love is a stranger
and who long for community. Bring healing to fractured relationships and

peace to human divisions. Hold close those who are ill, those whom death draws near, and all who are grieving. All this we pray in the name of Jesus our Savior. Amen.

Prayer of Confession and Assurance

God of unconditional love, we confess that we have not fully loved one another as you have loved us. We have ignored the needs of those around us. We have tended to our own comfort and convenience at the expense of others. We have not forgiven others as we have been forgiven. We have shied away from the hard work of reconciliation and of seeking understanding with those who differ from us. Melt the hardness of our hearts, that we may be renewed in your love. Assure us of your pardon that we may know the power of your forgiveness. We pray in the name of Christ our Savior. Amen.

Prayer of Dedication of Gifts and Self

Gracious God, in your love you have given us all that we have. You are the vine, we are the branches. Receive these fruits of our labor, which we dedicate to your glory. Use us and these gifts that we offer, that we may be signs of your love in and for the world, through Jesus Christ our Savior. Amen.

Hymn of the Day
Lord of All Hopefulness

In the text from 1 John we read that "we abide in him and he in us" (1 Jn 4:13). What stands out in this text is the the word *abide*. Stay connected to, remain rooted in, hold fast to the vine. Jan Struther's "Lord of All Hopefulness" imagines this abiding in the ordinary moments of our days. "Be there at our waking. Be there at our labors. Be there at our homing. Be there at our sleeping." Her text is a prayer that God fill our days with bliss, strength, love, and peace. SLANE, an Irish folk melody, fits the text impeccably.

Children's Time: Let Us Love One Another

(Have a small token for each child: a cookie, a bookmark, a sticker, and so on.)
As the children gather, share the token gifts with them. Watch for responses and encourage them to verbalize any feelings. Explain to the children that you enjoy their company. You have brought a treat or token today because you care for them, and by sharing, you can show them your love. Ask the children what they might share with you sometime. Help them to understand that sharing is a way of caring.

In the Bible reading today we hear about loving one another. One of the things that Jesus taught his friends was that they should love one another, just like Jesus loved them. True love is like sharing a gift; it is giving ourselves to others in a way that will be helpful and kind.

Let's pray: Dear God, thank you for loving us and teaching us how to love each other. Be with us every day and help us remember that love comes from you. Amen.

The Sermon: Love Is from God
Scripture: 1 John 4:7-21

The author of 1 John calls us to "love one another, because love is from God" (1 Jn 4:7). This command to love one another is more than just a sweet, sentimental suggestion spoken to those who don't really need to hear it. The scriptures are not complacent about love. Love, though easy in theory, can be difficult in practice. No matter whether we are new to faith or longtime Christians, we never reach the point where we have mastered God's love. The Great Commandment, to love God with all one's heart and strength and mind and to love one's neighbor as oneself, is a lifelong endeavor for God's people.

The author of 1 John engages in an earnest plea for us to love one another. Whether our starting point is indifference or hatred, the author of 1 John calls us to love. Where we already experience love, we are called to even greater love. We are called to love more fully and to love more widely. This commandment comes to us as a word to draw us deeper into relationship with God. It is a word to connect us with our brothers and sisters in Christ. God loves us into loving others. This love propels us outward to share God's love with the world. Loving God and loving neighbor are intertwined; one cannot separate one from the other.

God's love abides in us. God's love comes into our lives to stay. God is love. Wherever we experience love, God is there. Love is a signal of God's presence. God's very being is love. God reaches out to us in Christ. God's love flows into us, and out through us, back to God, and over to the lives of our neighbor. Love calls us into a new reality. Love moves us beyond our resentments, criticisms, and jealousies. It calls us to let go of our long-standing grudges against those who may have slighted us, who disagree with us, or who didn't do our bidding.

Love melts away our impatience, our indifference, our self-centered-ness, and yes, even our denials and betrayals. Love transforms us. We are rooted in God's love, claimed as God's beloved sons and daughters, and named as Christ's friends. We are drawn into community with God and with one another. We are called to love one another in the same way that God loves us.

The author of 1 John is insistent that our lives are indicators of God's love. It is like the connection between a lightbulb and its electricity source. Lightbulbs need electricity in order to function. Whether from a battery or from current flowing through wires, lightbulbs need electricity. If the power goes out or the battery dies, the lightbulb won't shine, even if there is nothing wrong with the bulb itself. If a wire breaks or becomes discon-nected, the electricity won't flow and the bulb won't shine. If electricity is present, the wiring is intact and the bulb isn't broken, the light will shine whenever the switch is turned on. The power itself is hidden from our view. You can't see it, except through what it does. If you want to know whether the power is on, look at the lightbulb.

The lightbulb can't shine on its own. It doesn't generate its own elec-tricity. Its power comes from an outside source. Likewise, love doesn't just generate from within us. Love comes from outside, from God. Love is en-ergy, God's energy, flowing through us. God's love, hidden and unseen, is made visible in our lives as we love one another. Our love for one another is the sign that God's love is present. The Gospel uses the metaphor of a vine and its branches bearing fruit to express this same relationship. As the branches, we bear fruit because we are connected to the vine. We draw our energy from the vine and express it by bearing fruit. As branches grow, they both strengthen their connection to the vine that sustains them and expand further outward. As branches grow, they produce more and more fruit, the visible sign that the branch is healthy and connected to the vine. Our call is to share Christ's love by loving one another. God is love. Those who abide in love abide in God and God abides in them. Love is more than a feeling. Love is not passive. God's love for us is active. It is bold. It is fierce. It casts out fear. It is like the love of a protective parent who will not allow anything to bring harm to her beloved offspring. It is the love of a friend who is willing to lay down his life for another. It is the love of the brother or sister who is able to forgive. God's love reconciles enemies. God's love unites us. God's love flows through us and becomes visible as we love another.

God's love is poured out generously and is freely poured into us. Christ's love comes to us as a gift. You don't need to earn it, and you don't need to worry about losing it. God's love for you is certain. It is unshakeable. It is unwavering and it is unbreakable. God loves you, no matter what. Love isn't just a feeling. Love is not merely emotion. Love is action. Love is expressed in caring, in compassion, and in service. God's love for us is most clearly visible in Christ. Jesus loves us fully, laying down his life for us. So it is that our lives are opened by Christ's love. Let us receive that love as a gift. Let us abide in that love. Let us share that love. And let us love one another, for love is from God. Amen.

– Julie A. Kanarr

Hymns
Opening: Alleluia! Jesus Is Risen
Sermon: Jesu, Jesu, Fill Us with Your Love
Closing: Love Divine, All Loves Excelling

May 10, 2015

6th Sunday of Easter

Lessons

Revised Common Lectionary (RCL)	Roman Catholic (RC)
Acts 10:44-48	Acts 10:25-26, 34-35, 44-48
Ps 98	Ps 98:1-4
1 Jn 5:1-6	1 Jn 4:7-10
Jn 15:9-17	Jn 15:9-17

Speaker's Introduction for the Lessons

Lesson 1

Acts 10:44-48 (RCL); Acts 10:25-26, 34-35, 44-48 (RC)

Peter is summoned to the home of Cornelius, a Roman centurion; preaches the gospel for the first time to Gentiles; witnesses the descent of the Holy Spirit upon all who are present; and offers baptism to the first non-Jewish converts to Christianity.

Lesson 2

Psalm 98 (RCL); Psalm 98:1-4 (RC)

The psalmist evokes a "new song" to God for marvelous acts and steadfast love (*hesed*). The choir consists of all creation, human and natural, who rejoice in God's coming as righteous judge.

Lesson 3

1 John 5:1-6 (RCL)

The author sings of the love of God in obedience to God's commandments as the faith that conquers the world.

1 John 4:7-10 (RC)

The author draws readers a portrait of God, whose essence as love is revealed in the act of God sending God's Son into the world.

Gospel
John 15:9-17 (RCL/RC)

As he prepares for his crucifixion, Jesus offers the assembled disciples the key to their life together. Once he is gone, they are to love one another.

Theme

Christ calls us to be his friends and share in his love for the world.

Thought for the Day

The love of a friend is stronger than life itself.

Sermon Summary

Jesus names us as his friends. As Christ's friends, we have been invited into partnership with Christ in carrying out God's mission of love for the world. We are challenged to consider what it means for us to be Jesus' friends, and to take on his character in our lives.

Call to Worship

One: We gather in the name of God, our creator, redeemer, and sanctifier.
All: Sing to God a new song!
One: With all of creation, we rejoice in God's abundant care and mercy.
All: Sing to God a new song!
One: Befriended by Christ, we open our hearts to God's love.
All: Sing to God a new song!
One: Led by the Spirit, we lift our voices in worship and praise.
All: Sing to God a new song!

Pastoral Prayer

Gracious God, we praise you for the friendship you have shown us in Jesus. As you have chosen us to be your friends, empower us to be your ambassadors in the world. Give us courage to stand up on behalf of those whom the world hates. Give us strength to live as your friends who know and do your will. Come alongside those who are in trouble. Be the companion to those who are lonely, strength to the weak, and hope for the grieving. We pray in the name of Jesus, our friend and savior. Amen.

Prayer of Confession and Assurance

O God, we confess that we have not lived up to your calling to live as your friends and to continue your work in the world. We have failed to love all others as you have first loved us. We have struggled to see ourselves as your beloved friends. We have not cultivated our relationship with you. We have looked to our own interests at the expense of others. Forgive us for all that we have said and done that has brought harm to others. Forgive us for the ways that we have not trusted in you or lived according to your will. Yet, in all of our failures, help us to know the power of your love that continues to support us and lift us up, giving us assurance of your pardon. We pray in the name of Christ. Amen.

Prayer of Dedication of Gifts and Self

God of abiding love, your mercies are new each morning. Your abundant grace springs up to sustain us with your generosity as you provide for the needs of every living creature. Help us to see our place within your creation, as your friends and as stewards of all that you have made. We offer our lives to your service, and dedicate these gifts to your purpose. Use us and all that we bring to care for others, to carry forth your mission, and to share in your redeeming love for the world, through Jesus Christ, our friend and savior. Amen.

Hymn of the Day
No Greater Love

Today's Gospel lesson conflates a number of Johannine themes: abiding in Jesus' love, completeness of joy, loving one another as Jesus loved us, no longer servants but friends, Jesus choosing us, our appointment to bear fruit. Each of these leads to different musical choices. However, for those "wanting it all," there is Michael Joncas's "No Greater Love," a work whose text is this very pericope. The refrain is meant for all to sing; the chant-like verses, however, are intended for a cantor or choir. A fine traditional choice is Somerset Lowry's "Son of God, Eternal Savior," set to In Babilone.

Children's Time: Jesus Is Our Friend

(Talk with the children about friendships. Do they have many friends? Do they have any really special friends? What do they like to do with their friends? Talk about friendships you had as a child and friendships you have now. Especially talk about friends who accept you exactly for who you are, friends you can tell anything to, friends with whom you can wonder and dream, friends you can argue with but still be friends afterward.)

Jesus is our friend. Jesus is like our best friend. He will never stop loving us. We can tell him anything in our prayers. We can wonder about things, we can be ourselves. We never have to worry about Jesus not liking who we are.

Jesus wants us to be that kind of friend with others, too. He said, "I have loved you, and I call you my friends. I want you to do what I have taught you. And most of all, I want you to love one another."

It's not always easy being friends with people. But Jesus shows us that we can find ways to love others, no matter what, just as he does.

Let's pray: Thank you, God, for giving us friends and teaching us how to love. You shared your love for us in Jesus. We love you. Amen.

The Sermon: Friends, Forever!
Scripture: John 15:9-17

What qualities do you look for in a friend? Social media sites have expanded the definition of "friend" to encompass not only friends and relatives, but also acquaintances and even those who are only tangentially connected to you. Because of Facebook, those who are the friends of the friends of the friends of your friends can be called your friends, too. So it probably isn't too hard for us to draw up a list the characteristics of a good friend. What is a friend? A friend is someone who is loyal, compassionate, and caring. A friend is someone who is fun to be with, willing to do things with you and for you. A friend is someone who accepts you for who you are. At the same time, a true friend is willing to be honest with you and gently tell you those hard things and uncomfortable truths that you really need to hear. A friend is someone who knows your strengths and weaknesses. A friend is someone who won't take advantage of you. A friend is someone you can turn to when you need help, someone who will look to you for help in return. A friend is someone who is resilient and forgiving, and is willing to give you a second chance. A friend is someone who really knows you, yet likes you anyway.

Friendship is a powerful relationship. In today's Gospel reading, Jesus proclaims that we are his friends. Jesus doesn't say, "You are my servants." Nor does he say, "You are my followers, or my flock, or even my disciples, family, co-workers, colleagues, teammates, neighbors, or acquaintances." Jesus says, "You are my friends." For some, thinking of Jesus as a friend is a familiar, comfortable, and comforting idea. It may even evoke the sentiments of the hymn "What a Friend We Have in Jesus" with its message that Jesus is one that we can turn to and rely on when we're having a hard time. For others, the idea of God as a friend – not judge, master, or lord – has the power to open us up and draw us into a closer and deeper relationship with God.

Thinking of God as a friend can break through associations of God as some distant, authoritarian deity who is fault-finding, aloof, or unapproachable. When we think of God as a close friend, a "best friend," then prayer becomes personal conversation, offered in trust and confidence, without fear or worry about being misunderstood or about getting the words right. When we think of God as a friend, we experience God's grace for us. God is a friend who knows us and loves us anyway.

We don't really need to be told to love our friends. That comes naturally. Rather, where we need encouragement is in living in such a way that our friends can see and know that we truly love them. We are invited to think not only in terms of Jesus being a friend of ours, but also to explore what it means that we are friends of Jesus. Jesus draws a sharp distinction between being a servant to a master and being a friend to a friend. The role of the servant is to follow instructions, conforming to the master's plan about how things should go, following the master's rules, and being rewarded for doing it right, or punished for doing it wrong. Servants find their security in having what is expected of them spelled out very clearly. They may not have a full understanding of all that the master is doing, but they are given a detailed description of their job, and they don't have much choice in the matter. In contrast, a friend is a willing partner who shares in understanding the "big idea." A friend is entrusted and empowered in working together side by side to accomplish that shared vision. Friendship is characterized by freedom, trust, and responsibility.

Jesus' word to us that we truly are friends of God has radical implications for us in the way that we live our faith and do ministry together. It moves us away from a self-centered religious posture that measures our faith commitment in terms of cost-benefit analysis of what we put into it compared to what we get out of it. To be friends of God changes how we hear words like *evangelism*, *stewardship*, and *mission*. As friends of God, we are invited to share in God's generosity. That's stewardship!

When we see ourselves as friends of God, we live as God's friends in the world. When we see ourselves as friends of God, we hear Jesus' words "love one another as I have loved you" as an invitation for us to share in the values held by our divine friend. That's mission! Friendship begins with words of introduction and invitation. Friendship is about connection and sharing. As God is always seeking new friends, we are encouraged to be intentional and not shy about inviting others into friendship with God. That's evangelism! As friends of Christ, we are invited to share in his life and mission.

Because God's love and friendship is so vast, there is always room for more. Friendship with God is not an exclusive club limited to just a few. God seeks to be friends with everyone. There is no limit to God's friendship and love. God keeps reaching out to make new friends. God is friends with you and will never unfriend you. Christ never stops looking for new friends, and never stops inviting us to grow and deepen our friendship with him. Amen.

– Julie A. Kanarr

Hymns
Opening: Bind Us Together
Sermon: Lord, Whose Love in Humble Service
Closing: O Christ the Same

May 14, 2015

Ascension Day

Lessons

Revised Common Lectionary (RCL)	Roman Catholic (RC)
Acts 1:1-11	Acts 1:1-11
Ps 47 or Ps 93	Ps 47:2-3, 6-9
Eph 1:15-23	Eph 4:1-13 or 4:1-7, 11-13
Lk 24:44-53	Mk 16:15-20

Speaker's Introduction for the Lessons

Lesson 1
Acts 1:1-11 (RCL/RC)

After reminding readers of the actions, teachings, death, and resurrection of Jesus, Luke reports Jesus' promise of the Holy Spirit to the disciples and his ascension into heaven.

Lesson 2
Psalm 47 (RCL); Psalm 47:2-3, 6-9 (RC)

While "God has gone up with a shout" likely triggers the choice of this psalm for Ascension Day, its underlying theme of God's universal reign provides Ascension's cause for joy and hope.

Lesson 3
Ephesians 1:15-23 (RCL)

Paul offers a prayer for believers at Ephesus, calling upon God to grant them knowledge of God's power, working in Christ's resurrection and ascension.

Ephesians 4:1-13 or 4:1-7, 11-13 (RC)

As with most of Paul's epistles, this is a practical message that provides direction for the lives of God's followers.

Gospel

Luke 24:44-53 (RCL)
Appearing to the disciples just before his ascension, Jesus instructs them to remain in Jerusalem until they have received the promised gift of power from God to bear witness to the good news of repentance and forgiveness of sins.

Mark 16:15-20 (RC)
In the longer ending of the Gospel, Mark (as recorded by some early manuscripts) reports Jesus' postresurrection appearance to the disciples, his commission to preach the good news, and his ascension into heaven.

Theme

The ascension invites us to see how Christ remains present out in the world.

Thought for the Day

When you wonder where Christ is now, look into the eyes of your neighbor.

Sermon Summary

At the ascension, the disciples stood staring into the heavens, looking up to see where Jesus had gone. God redirects their gaze outward into the world and forward to the future. We are invited to look with God toward the world, bearing the good news of God's love.

Call to Worship

One: Christ, as you have lived for others,
All: Draw us together as your church.
One: Christ, as you have risen from the dead,
All: Raise us up to life in you.
One: Christ, as you have ascended into glory,
All: Send us forth to share your love.

Pastoral Prayer

Living God, as Christ ascended into heaven, we praise you for the blessing of your eternal presence. When we are only aware of your absence, help us to recognize that you are still among us. Help us to see how you still seek to unite us in love and draw us closer to you. Bring strength to the suffering, healing to the ill, and hope to the grieving. Empower us to be your body in the world. We pray in the name of Christ. Amen.

Prayer of Confession and Assurance

Ever-living God, we confess to you all the ways that we have lost our focus on you and your unending love for us. We have turned away from loving you with all our heart and mind. We have refused to love our neighbors as fully as we love ourselves. We have chosen greed over generosity, indifference over compassion. For all that we have done, and for all that we have failed to do, we seek your pardon and ask your forgiveness. Teach us your ways and guide us into your path. Fill us with the assurance of your pardon, that we may know the depth of your love and the confidence of your forgiveness, through Jesus Christ, our Savior. Amen.

Prayer of Dedication of Gifts and Self

Loving God, you have poured your love into us, filling us with your Spirit and sustaining us with your gifts. Open our hearts to know that everything we have comes to us through your abundance. We dedicate our lives and these offerings, the fruit of our labor and the efforts of our time, to your service. Direct our gaze that we may look outward in mission and ministry, loving you and serving our neighbors in your name. Amen.

Hymn of the Day
Hail the Day That Sees Him Rise

Concluding the first part of the Luke-Acts narrative, the scene of Jesus' ascension is simple but visually powerful. Jesus lifts up his hands to bless his disciples one last time, and as he does so he is transported to heaven. Charles Wesley's "Hail the Day That Sees Him Rise," from 1739, is a hymn written also for today. Originally a work ten verses in length, none of them is used today in an unaltered form; even the "Alleluia" after each line was added in the middle of the 19th-century. Robert Williams's LLANFAIR brings out both the majesty and the might of Wesley's text.

Children's Time: Jesus' Ascension

(Bring in a shallow white bowl filled about halfway with water, a pepper mill set on a coarse grind, and liquid dishwashing soap.) Do you ever lie on your back to watch the clouds? What shapes do you see? It's fun to imagine while we watch the clouds.

Forty days after Easter, Jesus' followers saw something wonderful in the clouds. But it wasn't something they imagined. It was real. It was time for Jesus to return to God, his Father, in heaven. Jesus gathered his followers and said, "I will send you the gift of the Holy Spirit. The Holy Spirit will go with you as you tell people about my life, death, and resurrection. Tell everyone this good news, to the ends of the earth." Then Jesus was lifted up, and a cloud took him out of their sight.

(Gather around the bowl. Have a child add pepper to the water.) Let's pretend that the pepper is all of Jesus' followers, including us. Jesus said that we should go to the ends of the earth. Watch what happens to the pepper when we add a drop of soap to the water. (Add one drop of soap in the center of the bowl.) Jesus wants us to spread out just like that pepper and go everywhere to tell all people about his love.

Let's pray together: Dear Jesus, help us tell all people, near and far, about your love. Amen.

The Sermon: Don't Look Up, Look Out
Scripture: Acts 1:1-11

Today we celebrate the festival of the Ascension of Our Lord. Jesus had been with his disciples for 40 days following his resurrection. He appeared in their midst as the crucified one, now risen from the dead. During that time, he had taught them. He had addressed their doubts, eased their fears, and breathed peace into their troubled hearts. He had walked with them, opening their hearts to understand the scriptures. He had eaten with them, making himself known to them in the breaking of the bread. But now he was leaving them. As he ascended, he promised that they would soon be filled with the power of the Spirit and sent out to be his witnesses throughout the world.

As the risen Christ ascended, the disciples stood gazing into heaven, necks craned to watch that spot where they had seen Jesus last, hoping for one final glimpse. Perhaps they stood reminiscing, remembering the good old days when Jesus had been with them. Perhaps they were thinking about what might have happened if things had been different. They had been hoping that this would be the moment when Jesus would restore the kingdom to Israel, so that they would live in that blessed messianic age, where all wrongs would be righted and they would live happily ever after. But that wasn't what was happening. They stood staring up into the heavens, mouths wide open in amazement. They were amazed. They were surprised, confused, wishing that he hadn't gone, and hoping against hope that he would come back, soon.

Then the disciples hear a voice asking them why they are standing around, looking up into the sky, toward heaven. The voice startles the eleven out of their fixation on the past. They are called away from their reminiscences, their secret yearning to return to the good old days. They are startled out of their hope that somehow they could see Jesus again if they peered into the clouds long enough. The voice tells the disciples that they looking in the wrong direction.

Discipleship does not mean standing around and staring into heaven, looking up out of this world. Discipleship does not mean looking to the past, wishing that the good old days were here again and talking about how much better things used to be. The disciples are not to stand looking with their heads in the clouds trying to pinpoint that spot where God might be found. The disciples learn that their job is not to stand around staring up toward heaven looking for God, but to look with God toward the world, bearing the good news of God's love. Their call is to be Christ's witnesses: "In Jerusalem, in all Judea and Samaria, and to the ends of the earth" (Acts 1:8).

We are invited to look with God at the world, to proclaim the good news of Jesus' death and resurrection. Jesus' promise rings in their ears and in ours: "You will be my witnesses in Jerusalem, and in all Judea and Samaria and to the ends of the earth." The disciples are being prompted toward the next phase of God's mission, to set their sights on the question of "What's next?" They return to the city to pray and await the promised Holy Spirit who will empower them for their mission in the world. At the ascension, we see the disciples poised at the beginning of that mission. Like runners taking their place at the starting line, they are ready. They are on their marks. They are getting set. And at Pentecost, they will hear the word "Go!" with the Spirit poured out on them, giving them language to proclaim the good news to people of every nation. As the book of Acts unfolds, that mission carries the good news of Christ from Jerusalem to Rome. The good news of Christ flows out into the world, to the very heart of the Roman Empire to the ends of the earth, and to us.

The disciples' experience becomes our pattern of life as the church. The disciples came together in the days and weeks after Easter, first wondering "what happened," then trying to figure out "Now what?" Like them, we, too, are gathered together in the name of Christ. Like them, we may have questions and doubts. Like them, we may be wondering where God is, and looking in all directions trying to find God. We may be caught up in nostalgia, looking with fondness to the past and wishing we could re-create it. We may be wondering about what's next for us, and may be looking in every direction for guidance.

As disciples of Jesus, our job is not to stand around staring toward heaven, trying to figure out where Christ has disappeared to. Our job is not to worry about when he's coming back, or to stand apart from the world, biding our time by staying out of trouble until we die and are united with Christ. As disciples of Jesus, we are sent into the world in Christ's name. We are sent to continue the ministry of Jesus. We are sent to be witnesses. We are sent to care for others, to stand with the poor and to feed the hungry. We are sent into the world to seek righteousness and justice, to be peacemakers, to be merciful and compassionate, to proclaim God's love, to bear witness to truth, and to give our lives away in friendship toward others. We are sent into the world to live as Jesus lived, and to love as Jesus loved. We are sent into the world with the mission to be the ongoing presence of Christ's body in the world.

We are sent into the world, yet we are not sent alone. We are not sent on our own or left to our own devices. We are sent, remembering all that Jesus has taught. We are sent with the blessing of the risen Christ, who remains among us. We are sent with the promise of the Spirit, who equips us with love and empowers us for service.

– Julie A. Kanarr

Hymns
Opening: Lord, Be Glorified
Sermon: Christ Is Alive, Let Christians Sing
Closing: Go, Make Disciples

May 17, 2015

7th Sunday of Easter

Lessons

Revised Common Lectionary (RCL)	Roman Catholic (RC)
Acts 1:15-17, 21-26	Acts 1:15-17, 20a, 20c-26
Ps 1	Ps 103:1-2, 11-12, 19-20
1 Jn 5:9-13	1 Jn 4:11-16
Jn 17:6-19	Jn 17:11b-19

Speaker's Introduction for the Lessons

Lesson 1

Acts 1:15-17, 21-26 (RCL); 1:15-17, 20a, 20c-26 (RC)

Luke describes how the earliest disciples replaced Judas among the 12. As we listen to their process, might it be useful to consider the way that we choose wise leaders in our congregations?

Lesson 2

Psalm 1 (RCL)

The psalmist confesses an orderly world of reliable cause and effect, where the righteous flourish and the wicked dissipate like chaff in the wind.

Psalm 103:1-2, 11-12, 19-20 (RC)

In this psalm, David sings of personal mercies he has received; then he calls on creatures to praise the Lord.

Lesson 3

1 John 5:9-13 (RCL)

The writer of this passage claims that those who believe in Jesus have eternal life. How does that invite us to live? What do we understand is asked from us in response to that gift?

1 John 4:11-16 (RC)

These verses remind us that loving others is a commandment, not an option for Christians. We are challenged to ask ourselves how we live that commandment in the world. Can others see God abiding in us?

Gospel
John 17:6-19 (RCL); John 17:11b-19 (RC)
Listen as Jesus says that he is glorified in us! What have we done lately to glorify him and what could we do this week to show others his glory? How can we honor his love of us?

Theme
Chosen by God and led by the Spirit, we are equipped for service.

Thought for the Day
The question is not whether you have been called by God; the question is where and how God is calling you.

Sermon Summary
Like Matthias, we are equipped by God for ministry in our daily lives. As we discern our particular calling, we are led by the Spirit and guided by the community of believers. God provides each of us with ways to serve and bear witness to Christ's love.

Call to Worship
One: Bless the Lord, O my soul.
All: May all that is within us bless God's holy name.
One: Let us praise God with our heart and mind and voices.
All: And come into God's presence with joy and gladness.
One: God's steadfast love endures forever.
All: May all that is within us bless God's holy name.

Pastoral Prayer
Loving God, we thank you for the witness of all of your faithful disciples in every generation. We give thanks for those who have been teachers, mentors, leaders, and pastors for us. Help us to discern our calling to ministry in our daily lives. Help us to call forth the gifts of all of your people and to nurture one another in discipleship. Guide us to do your will, to show your love by reaching out to those who are hungry, those who are ill, and those who are in any need. We pray in the name of Christ. Amen.

Prayer of Confession and Assurance

O God, we confess to you that we have not followed your will. We have not fully embraced your call to us to live as your disciples in the world. We confess that we have not always graciously welcomed the ideas of others. Though you have called us to collaboration, we have often chosen competition. Though you have called us to a new future, we have felt threatened by change. Though you have called us to discern your will, we have chosen to follow our own way. Open our hearts that we may receive the promise of your forgiveness and the assurance of your pardon. Open our lives to be receptive to your will, that we may walk in your paths, and know the everlasting presence of your love and mercy. In the name of Christ we pray. Amen.

Prayer of Dedication of Gifts and Self

God of abundance, you have called us to lives of ministry and service. You have filled our lives with your gifts and drawn us into community with you and with one another. We dedicate our lives and these offerings that we have gathered for your service. Pour your Spirit into us. Bless us so that we may be a blessing to others and carry out your will and purpose. We pray in the name of Christ our savior. Amen.

Hymn of the Day
Come and Find the Quiet Center

Shirley Erena Murray, a New Zealand hymn writer, wrote this text for a Presbyterian Women's Conference with the theme of making space. Just as the disciples needed time and space to pray for guidance, so do we. Prayer is a means of finding that space; the place where we empty ourselves so that God can fill us anew with wisdom and courage to move forward on our pilgrimage. The tune associated with this beautiful text is BEACH SPRING. Use the simplest harmonies possible to avoid "the chaos and the clutter" often found in harmonically busy hymns. One or more of the stanzas of this hymn make a meaningful introduction or conclusion to a congregational prayer.

Children's Time: Prayerful People

I'm wondering if you can tell me, what do you think it means to pray? *(Affirm responses.)* Prayer is talking to God. We can pray in many ways. We can pray in any place and at any time; like right here and right now! Let's pray! Everyone stand up. Let's begin with thank you prayers. I'm going to say, "Thank you, God, for" and then touch something. You finish the prayer by naming whatever I touch. Thank you, God, for *(touch your ears).* The children should say "ears!" *(Continue by touching your mouth, eyebrows, head, elbows, shoes, and so on.)*

(Keep up a brisk pace for this prayer.) Now let's sit down. Let's think about something that is making us sad. Make a little box with your hands and whisper your sadness into your hands. Rub your hands together. Now raise your hands up high and let your prayer go up to God.

(Walk with the children to another area of the church. Invite a child to offer a prayer there. Repeat this in another area before moving back to the original place.) Whenever Jesus' disciples had a problem or a difficult choice to make they gathered together and prayed. Here is one of their prayers. Let's join hands and pray it together: "O Lord, you know every heart. Show us the way. Amen."

The Sermon: Called, Blessed, Sent
Scripture: Acts 1:15-17, 21-26

Matthias is not one of those disciples we hear much about, except for how he was chosen. After Jesus' resurrection and ascension, Luke tells us, the disciples gather together in Jerusalem. They are waiting for what's next. But their group is incomplete. They feel the hole left by Judas's betrayal and his ignominious death. They feel the absence of their beloved Jesus. Meanwhile, they have gathered together in an upper room, following Jesus' instructions to remain in the city and wait.

This is an interim time. It is the time between the ascension and Pentecost. As they await the new beginning, they wonder about what shape it will take. They are brimming with hope and expectation. It is a time for prayer and worship. It is a time for sharing the stories of Jesus, for teaching and for learning. It is a time for remembering and looking forward. It is a time for discerning how God is leading them into the future. As their numbers grow, it is a time for discerning the collective gifts that God has given them for ministry.

In this interim time between the ascension and Pentecost, the early church goes through a call process because Judas' death had created an apostolic vacancy. Instead of 12 apostles, there were only 11. This call process is both Spirit-led and Spirit-driven. They prayerfully select two candidates from among the community of those who had been following Jesus from the beginning. Their names are Justus and Matthias. Next they draw lots, and Matthias is chosen.

The call involves both community discernment and Spirit-led action. Both are important. The Spirit involves the community of the faithful in the process. The community doesn't act on its own, apart from the Spirit's direction. There is no campaigning. They consider whose gifts might best equip them for this ministry. They don't just ask for volunteers and accept the first one to offer. They didn't choose on the basis of popularity or influence. This is more than a human election; it is a divine call. It isn't a matter of luck or chance. It wasn't a random choice. The process of casting lots was understood to be a way of discerning God's will. Matthias's selection as the new 12th apostle is truly a call from God. In that way, Matthias becomes a model for all of us.

We don't hear much about Matthias afterward. Like the majority of the other apostles, Matthias carries out his ministry away from the limelight, in relative anonymity in comparison to people like Peter, James, and John. Yet even though he had been present from the beginning, without the kind of recognition that the Twelve received, Matthias is not an insignificant bystander. Matthias becomes one among the countless faithful generations of servants of God. Even as he is numbered among the Twelve, he becomes one of many who proclaim the gospel and work in God's vineyard. Matthias has been called by God to use his gifts in service. Even though we do not know the specifics of his story of ministry, he has been called to continue in Jesus' teaching, fellowship, and prayer. Matthias has been called to bring healing, to proclaim justice, to feed others in Christ's name. Ministry happens through him, but is not about him.

And then there is the other guy, Justus. He was one who was not chosen. He, too, had been present from the beginning. All we know about him is his name: Joseph called Barsabbas, also known as Justus. Even though he wasn't numbered among the Twelve, he also was numbered among the faithful. Acts keeps telling the stories of the outsiders coming in, and the insiders going out. In the next chapter, the Spirit propels all of the disciples out at Pentecost to share the good news, speaking in the languages as the Spirit gave them utterance. And then there is Saul, the persecutor of the church, transformed into Paul, minister of the gospel. All of these people respond to God's call to ministry: Matthias, Justus, Paul, and countless others, including those women and men whose names are not recorded.

Whenever we think we are on the sidelines, we are invited to remember the story of the call of Matthias. No matter who we are, we are called by the Spirit in our baptism to lives of vocation and service. God chooses you for service and vocation. Open your eyes to recognize your gifts, and be courageous to put them to use. Open your eyes to recognize the gifts in others. God doesn't waste anybody. By being chosen as the 12th apostle, Matthias plays a role in the early church's preparation to be sent out in mission to the whole world. God uses Matthias in ways that he may have little understood or imagined.

God also uses us, in ways we can little imagine, in order to do God's work in the world. Through the Spirit, we are called to ministry and mission. The Holy Spirit equips and sends us in ministry, in mission. We are part of a community called to prayer and discernment. We are challenged to help each other identify our particular gifts and to encourage one another in ministry. Through the Spirit, God provides the Christian community with all the tools we need for doing God's mission. Sometimes the Spirit raises up leaders from within, like Matthias. Sometimes the Spirit brings them in from outside, like Paul. And sometimes the Spirit calls forth from us gifts that we may not have even realized that we have. And like Matthias and Justus and countless others whose names we do not even know, we are called, and blessed, and sent to share the good news of Jesus. Let us go in peace to love and serve the Lord. Amen.

– Julie A. Kanarr

Hymns
Hymn: We Are Called
Sermon: Will You Come and Follow Me
Closing: Listen! God Is Calling

May 24, 2015

Day of Pentecost

Lessons

Revised Common Lectionary (RCL)	Roman Catholic (RC)
Acts 2:1-21 or Ezek 37:1-14	Acts 2:1-11
Ps 104:24-34, 35b	Ps 104:1, 24, 29-34
Rom 8:22-27 or Acts 2:1-21	1 Cor 12:3-7, 12-13 or Gal 5:16-25
Jn 15:26-27; 16:12-15	Jn 20:19-23 or 15:26-27; 16:12-15

Speaker's Introduction for the Lessons

Lesson 1

Acts 2:1-21 (RCL); Acts 2:1-11 (RC)

The apostles, gathered in Jerusalem, receive the gift of the Holy Spirit, which enables them to speak in other languages and empowers Peter to explain to skeptics how that gift was foretold through the prophet Joel.

Ezekiel 37:1-14 (RCL)

Ezekiel's dream conveys a message of hope based on the amazing power of God to bring breath and new life to dry bones. This message brought hope to a dejected people in the midst of a long exile in a foreign land, and it brings hope to us today.

Lesson 2

Psalm 104:24-34, 35b (RCL); Psalm 104:1, 24, 29-34 (RC)

The psalm celebrates the diverse manifestations of God's workings in creation, underscoring that the Spirit is God's agent of bringing life and renewal to all.

Lesson 3

Romans 8:22-27 (RCL)

Paul describes the Holy Spirit as that which intercedes with God on behalf of human beings, who wait in hope for redemption.

1 Corinthians 12:3-7, 12-13 (RC)
Paul addresses the nature of spiritual gifts – apparently an issue to the church in Corinth – as multifaceted, but all of equal value to the whole body of Christ.

Gospel
John 15:26-27; 16:12-15 (RCL/RC)
Jesus tells the disciples, gathered in the upper room on the last night of his earthly life, about the coming of the Advocate, the Spirit of truth, who will guide them once he has gone from among them.
John 20:19-23 (RC)
After Jesus appears to the disciples on the evening of the resurrection, Thomas, not present to see him, declares his disbelief, until he can see Jesus for himself.

Theme
By the power of the Holy Spirit, God makes all things new, including us.

Thought for the Day
Pentecost is the promise that as people who have been transformed ourselves we can bring transformation to others.

Sermon Summary
Scripture provides wonderful stories of prophecies, visions, and dreams of people and a world made new by living in God's way. God is still gifting people with the power to live God's dream and bring God's transformation to the world.

Call to Worship
Scripture tells us of how, time and again, God's Spirit has been poured out upon God's people, renewing, re-creating, and reinvigorating the community of faith.

On this Pentecost Sunday, we come to this place and time of worship confident that God is with us. The Holy Spirit will be our guide, our comfort, and our truth.

With the universal church in all its history and diversity, we pray:
Come, Holy Spirit. Refresh and renew us in hope, peace, joy, and love.

Pastoral Prayer

How blessed we are, God, to be Pentecost people – men and women,
younger and older, with all our diversity of strengths and limitations and
with a variety of gifts and talents – each of us experiencing and responding to the touch of your Spirit and the love we know in your Son. As
your Pentecost people we share a passion to make Christ's love known. As
your Pentecost people we claim the power of your Spirit working in and
through us. As your Pentecost people we live with the purpose of bringing
Christ's transforming love to the world. Amen.

Prayer of Confession and Assurance

Again today, God, we will hear that "when the day of Pentecost had come
the disciples were all gathered together. And suddenly a sound came from
heaven like the rush of a mighty wind… and they were all filled with
the Holy Spirit." Help us be aware that you are present with us, as real
to us here on this Day of Pentecost as to those first disciples in ancient
Jerusalem. Give us a sense of expectation and excitement in our gathering
together. By your Spirit empower us to better understand one another so
that as individuals, communities, and nations we can avoid misunder-
standings that so often lead to distrust, anger, and conflict. Help us to live
in the assurance that your Spirit gives us new beginnings and that your
love is always available to your people.

Prayer of Dedication of Gifts and Self

Creating and giving God, on this Pentecost Sunday we claim the blessing
of your Holy Spirit at work in us as individuals, and as a faith community
brought together in the name of your Son, our Savior Christ. We thank
you that by the Spirit we are being made one in heart and mind and love.
Because your Spirit is working within us we want to share what we have to
help others. In bringing this offering we express our willing participation
in Christ's ministry. Accept us, with our gifts, for his sake. Amen.

Hymn of the Day
On Pentecost They Gathered

Just as there are many preaching themes found in today's readings, so are there a number of hymns appropriate to the occasion. Tanzanian Wilson Niwagila's "Gracious Spirit, Heed Our Pleading" sounds great with drums. David Haas's "Send Us Your Spirit" is an excellent contemporary choice, as is Marty Haugen's driving "Send Down the Fire."

Jane Parker Huber's "On Pentecost They Gathered" is a traditional hymn that stands out because, unlike many others, it so clearly refers to the events of Pentecost. MUNICH, the German chorale harmonized by Felix Mendelssohn, adds a sense of jubilation to Huber's text.

Children's Time: A Birthday Surprise!

(Bring a box fan with an extension cord, a large pillar candle, and matches.) In today's Bible story, Jesus sends a surprise party for the disciples. Before Jesus ascended into heaven he said, "Wait in Jerusalem and you will receive the gift of the Holy Spirit." One day, while the disciples were waiting, a sound like a strong wind filled the house. *(Turn on the fan.)* Suddenly divided flames appeared in the air over each disciple's head. *(Turn off the fan and light the candle.)* The disciples watched in wonder and surprise as these beautiful flames flickered over their heads.

The sound of wind and the flames announced Jesus' gift of the Holy Spirit, a birthday gift for Jesus' church, the Christian church. The Holy Spirit helped all the disciples speak other languages. They rushed out into the streets of Jerusalem and told everyone about Jesus, each speaking in a different language, so that everyone could understand. Three thousand people believed and were baptized. With the gift of the Holy Spirit, the church began.

Let's sing "Happy Birthday to the church." *(Sing, then all blow out the candle together.)*

Let's pray together: Dear Jesus, thank you the gift of the Holy Spirit. Help us, every day, to share your story. Amen.

The Sermon: Living the Dream
Scripture: Acts 2:1-21

Medical researchers tell us that everyone dreams. This is part of our shared human experience. Most people average from three to five dreams per night that last for a few seconds or as long as 20 minutes. The succession of images, ideas, and sensations occur, involuntarily in the mind. There is a whole field of study, called oneirology, related to analyzing the content and purpose of dreams. Our dreams apparently act as a kind of release mechanism that lightens the load of stimulation our brains accumulate during our waking hours. Most of us have wondered why it is that our pleasant dreams seem so fleeting but our bad dreams stick with us. However we assess them – good or bad – our dreams convey a message.

The prophet Ezekiel had a vivid dream, and its message is as important to us today as to the people of ancient Jerusalem and Judea in the midst of their Babylonian captivity. Ezekiel was himself one of these exiles, and in this dream he stood in a valley of dry bones. He recalls the dream in vivid detail: "There were very many [bones]... and they were very dry." With God's prompting, Ezekiel preached to these bones, declaring that God would restore them to life. With restored flesh and muscle, with life breathed back into them, these bodies would be knit together and these rebuilt and alive-again people would be a restored nation.

Ezekiel's dream conveyed a message of hope based on the amazing power of God to bring breath and new life to dry bones. This message brought hope to a dejected people in the midst of a long exile in a foreign land.

We 21st-century North American Christians can sometimes feel like we are strangers in a foreign land. The social landscape has shifted and the church is no longer guaranteed a place of influence in the community. We may feel displaced and discouraged. Our faith may have gone dry. How good it is that on the 50th day after Easter we come again to the Day of Pentecost. Today's scripture readings from Ezekiel 37 and Acts 2 remind us of the Holy Spirit being gifted to the church and of the difference this makes to its life and work.

Luke's description of a noise from above like the rush of a mighty wind and the appearance of what looked like tongues of fire and the unexpected ability to speak in other languages seems as amazing and as dream-like as Ezekiel's vision of new life for dry bones.

Peter stands up and raises his voice to cut through the clamor, and he does this by reminding them of another dream. He quotes the prophet Joel who dreamed of the day when God's Spirit would again be poured out. The result would be that men and women, younger and older, will also dream and prophesy and see and understand signs of God's transforming power at work, bringing new life to the world and all that is in it, on it, and above and beyond it.

Ezekiel and Joel and Peter weren't the last to be aware of the Spirit working in them to prophesy, or to see visions, or to dream dreams. They weren't the last to claim a God-given power to be transformed themselves and to bring transformation to others. The change, the new way of living, will be as obvious and as powerful as a strong wind and a mighty flame.

Rev. Mark Lewis, a former moderator of the General Assembly of the Presbyterian Church in Canada, once preached a sermon in which he describes a strange dream that had a profound effect on him. In this dream he had a vision in which his life is compared to an item in an *Antiques Roadshow* of the soul. In the course of this dream he thinks of all the things he has, all the possessions and achievements that he values. Near the end of the dream he is shown how little these things matter but how much his life and his faith and his feelings are valued by Jesus the Christ.

He says, "I awoke with joy and peace and with the prayer that I would remember the message of the dream. And as you go through life searching for your treasure, I recommend that you put less emphasis on your possessions and your accomplishments, and instead fill the sky with the sound of your joy in a new way of living,"

This experience of transformation and renewal is found in the traditional spiritual practice of some Native American or First Nations peoples who build a sweat lodge, a circular wooden frame covered with hides and blankets that when finished is like a cave. Heated rocks are placed in a central pit inside the lodge. Those participating in the cleansing ceremony crawl inside and sit around the pit. The lodge quickly becomes hot and sweaty. The leader burns some sweetgrass and sage on the rock. The fragrance helps participants concentrate on praying that God will send visions and dreams to help people live in a new and better way.

The witness of scripture and of a variety of spiritual practices is that God's Spirit offers a prophecy, a vision and a dream for each of us to live by – an experience of new flesh and breath that brings new life to dry bones, an experience of the presence of God that leads to a new under-

standing and appreciation for the good news of the gospel: in Jesus Christ
and by the power of the Holy Spirit, God makes us and all things new.

– Gordon Timbers

Hymns
Opening: Come, O Spirit, with Your Sound Like a Wind
Sermon: Spirit of the Living God, Fall Afresh on Me
Closing: Filled with the Spirit

May 31, 2015

Trinity Sunday

Lessons

Revised Common Lectionary (RCL)
Isa 6:1-8
Ps 29
Rom 8:12-17
Jn 3:1-17

Roman Catholic (RC)
Deut 4:32-34, 39-40
Ps 33:4-5, 6, 9, 18-19, 20, 22
Rom 8:14-17
Mt 28:16-20

Speaker's Introduction for the Lessons

Lesson 1

Isaiah 6:1-8 (RCL)

This lesson recounts the call of the great prophet Isaiah. He has a fantastic vision of God's glory against which he interprets his own insignificance. God has another idea, however, and calls him to serve.

Deuteronomy 4:32-34, 39-40 (RC)

Moses appeals for the people's obedience because of the previously recounted saving acts of God. He exhorts his people to faithfulness because God is above all other gods, and concludes by pointing to the gifts of home and land, once yearned for when they were enslaved.

Lesson 2

Psalm 29 (RCL)

A sevenfold "the voice of the Lord" underscores the power of God evidenced in the imagery of a storm.

Psalm 33:4-5, 6, 9, 18-19, 20, 22 (RC)

The praise of the Lord is the subject of this earnest prayer.

Lesson 3

Romans 8:12-17 (RCL); Romans 8:14-17 (RC)

Paul makes a case to the congregation in Rome that our relationship with God makes us God's adopted children, worthy of the trust and courage that this tie implies. He reminds us that the adoption is legal. There are two witnesses: our own sighs and the Spirit's.

Gospel
John 3:1-17 (RCL)
Nicodemus, a member of the religious elite, comes under cover of darkness to speak with Jesus as he could not in the company of his peers. Jesus engages him in a conversation about being born again of the Spirit.
Matthew 28:16-20 (RC)
Following Jesus' direction, the 11 disciples went to the designated mountain. Jesus met them there and issued the Great Commission to go into all the world, baptizing and teaching. His charge is bolstered with the promise that he will be with us always.

Theme
God is always more than our language can express.

Thought for the Day
The concept of the Trinity invites us to find new words and responses to express the fullness of God's activity in us and our world.

Sermon Summary
The story of the young Isaiah hearing and responding to the call of God is paired with the story of the elderly Nicodemus conversing with Jesus about life in the kingdom of God. These stories offer us the comfort and the challenge of new life that is possible with God.

Call to Worship
The writer of Psalm 29 invites us to join with the heavenly beings to ascribe to the Lord glory and strength. Ascribe to the Lord the glory of his name: worship the Lord in holy splendor.

To the God who creates and provides, we sing our praise and thanksgiving. To the Son who reveals our purpose and ministry, we bring open hearts and minds. To the Spirit who makes all things new, we lift our souls in anticipation and joy.

Let us worship God!

Pastoral Prayer

Loving and gracious God, we are blessed by the beauty of your creating activity in the world and people around us. We thank you for making this world an earthly home for us; thank you for sending Jesus to show the fullness of your mercy and love; thank you for the presence of the Spirit to support and guide us.

As stewards of your creation we want to serve others in ways that make a positive and lasting difference. Mobilize us for meaningful ministry in prayerful use of our time and money and resources that your will may be done.

Prayer of Confession and Assurance

How do we name you, God? What words can we use to describe who you are and what you do? How do we define our relationship with you and what this means for our relationships with one another? We ask these questions in the awareness that our human language is limited and inadequate, but still we come to you in prayer, because we want to give voice to our hopes and needs as well as to our praise and thanksgiving.

God, you reveal yourself to us in a multitude of ways, and on this Trinity Sunday we celebrate you as creator, savior and sustainer. In the assurance of your presence with us may we live each day with a joyful willingness to convey your blessing by all that we say and think and do.

Prayer of Dedication of Gifts and Self

We come before you, God, with open hearts and open hands, ready to receive and ready to give. Aware of our blessings we seek to be a blessing to others through words and actions that express care and compassion. Through this offering may we and others experience the generous love of our Creator, the amazing grace of our Savior, and the intimate and abiding friendship of the Holy Spirit. Amen.

Hymn of the Day
Here I Am, Lord

Also known as "I, the Lord of Sea and Sky," this well-known hymn was written by Dan Schutte in 1981. Its words are based on the prophet's declaration in Isaiah 6:8. Found in most Christian hymnals, it is one of

the most familiar hymns today and has been translated into more than 20
languages.

Children's Time: Three-in-One
*(Ask for three volunteers and assign each a number: 1, 2, or 3. Have this
group of three stand in a circle and hold hands.)*
Child 1, raise both your hands. Now lower your hands. Child 2, raise your
hands. Now lower your hands. Child 3, raise your hands. Now lower your
hands. What happens when they raise their hands? *(One hand of each of
the other children in the group raised too.)*
    *(Now name Child 1 as "Father," Child 2 as "Son," and Child 3 as "Holy
Spirit." Repeat the activity, saying, "Father, Son, and Holy Spirit" instead of
"one, two, three." Note again how all are connected.)*
    Today we remember the Holy Trinity. Trinity means three. God's
love for us comes in three different ways: God the Father *(touch the head
of Child 1)* created the earth and planned for the cycle of the seasons and
day and night. God the Son is Jesus *(touch the head of Child 2)*, who came
to earth to teach us about God's love. God the Holy Spirit *(touch the head
of Child 3)* is with us, helping us to love God and love others. God is all
three of these together. Where does a circle begin? Where does a circle
end? Like a circle, God's love is never-ending.
    Let's pray: Dear God, thanks for loving us in three terrific ways
– through creation, through Jesus, and through the Holy Spirit. Amen.

The Sermon: New Life Promised and Provided
Scripture: Isaiah 6:1-8

Good educational practice provides opportunities for learners to review
and consolidate their understanding of the material under study. In the
flow of the church year, Trinity Sunday is a kind of "summing up" Sunday.
It gives us an opportunity to review what has been covered since the start
of the church year in our recalling the birth, life, ministry, and death and
resurrection of Jesus Christ. The observance of Pentecost last Sunday
celebrated the gift of the Spirit to the church for all time as it continues
Christ's ministry. And now today on Trinity Sunday we use the familiar
formula describing God as "Father, Son, and Holy Spirit" to celebrate God
who creates, redeems, and gives new purpose and meaning to all creation.

Because there is such scope and breadth to this review of God's activity it is helpful to have some anchors in the specific details in today's lectionary readings from the Hebrew Scriptures and the Gospel of John. The verses from Isaiah 6 begin by telling us that "in the year that King Uzziah died" the prophet was given a vision of an interaction with heavenly beings that overwhelmed him with an awareness of the holiness and majesty of God. The reading from John 3 begins with the information that on a certain night, a Pharisee named Nicodemus, a leader of the Jews, came to Jesus with questions that led to a conversation about new life in God. These stories are grounded in place and time. This grounding helps us to latch on to them to give ourselves an opportunity through them to see God's creating, saving, and sustaining purposes in our own lives.

The ancient prophet is given a vision that enables him to see and understand that God is once again taking the initiative to give the people another start in their relationship with God. The opening words of chapter 6 give the context: "In the year that King Uzziah died . . ." Uzziah, who reigned from 792 to 740 BCE, had been a good and powerful ruler. His death precipitated a crisis as Assyria gained influence during this time of political transition. Israel was weakened. The leaders and people allowed themselves to be influenced by the Assyrian culture and religion, distancing them from God.

In the midst of this time of spiritual darkness, Isaiah had a vision of God in glory, a visual representation and reminder of God's power and might that had benefited God's people in times past. The activity of the seraphim, in their constant praise and worship, is a visual representation and reminder of the people's need to revitalize their own praise and worship of God.

The prophet, in his role of representing the people, responds to the revelation of God's glory with a personal confession and he also speaks on behalf of the whole Israelite faith community: "Woe is me! I am lost, for I am a man of unclean lips, and I live among a people of unclean lips." This confession of a lack of faith is in sharp contrast to what Isaiah sees in how the seraphim give fervent and continuous praise to God.

The wonder and amazement of Isaiah's vision is only enhanced by what happens in response to this honest and humble confession. Isaiah's admission and anguish at being a person of "unclean lips" is met by a visual representation and reminder of the grace of God as the seraph takes a live coal from the altar and touches Isaiah's lips with it and says: "Now that this has touched your lips, your guilt is departed and your sin is blotted out." Even without asking for it, God's grace and compassion is freely given. Isaiah, and by extension Israel itself, is given another experience of the love and mercy of God. New life is promised and provided.

Isaiah sets the example for grateful response. God asks, "Whom shall I send, and who will go for us?" When Isaiah says, "Here am I; send me!" he is voicing words of willing acceptance of God's invitation to new life in a new way of living.

There are some interesting parallels between this story from the ancient Hebrew Scriptures and what we read from chapter 3 of John's Gospel. Israel is again under the political and cultural influence of a powerful empire. Fear of the Romans has compromised religious practice and corrupted social relationships. People are suspicious and mistrustful of one another. The darkness of the situation is represented by the nighttime visit of Nicodemus, a Pharisee and leader of the people. The implication of this visit is that like so many others he is fearful and confused, but like Isaiah with his vision of an encounter with God, so Nicodemus has an interaction with Jesus in which he is given another vision of the new life that is possible with God.

Questions and answers are part of both stories. In the midst of God's glory and transcendence, Isaiah responds to God's question, which is really an invitation to take up the offer of new life in God. In the quiet and intimacy of their meeting together, Jesus answers all Nicodemus's questions, and here too, there is comfort in God's promise and challenge in the invitation to be "born from above."

This passage doesn't tell us how Nicodemus responds to Jesus, but we do see him again near the end of John's Gospel when he is brave enough to ask Pilate for permission to bury the body of Jesus.

What makes these two stories so appropriate for us to hear on Trinity Sunday is the fullness of the portrayal of who God is and how God interacts with us. God is holy and transcendent, the one to whom we are to offer unceasing praise and worship. God is also immanent and personal, touching our individual lives and giving us new purpose and meaning in our daily living. God is intimate in hearing our questions and gentle in encouraging and challenging us to make new beginnings in the assurance that God will be with us.

We need God to be all these things, and we express both our need and our response in the names we give to God: Father, Son, Holy Spirit; Creator, Savior, Sustainer; Maker, Friend, Presence.

Every day we live we have opportunities to broaden and deepen our experience of God's love and grace. These experiences invite us to find new concepts and vocabulary for our interactions with God. What names or descriptions could you offer to express the fullness of God's presence and activity in your life?

– Gordon Timbers

Hymns
Opening: Glorify Thy Name
Sermon: Bring Many Names
Closing: Thou Whose Almighty Word

June 7, 2015

2nd Sunday after Pentecost (Proper 5)
RC/Pres/UCC: 10th Sunday in Ordinary Time

Lessons

Semi-continuous (SC)	Complementary (C)	Roman Catholic (RC)
1 Sam 8:4-11 (12-15) 16-20 (11:14-15)	Gen 3:8-15	Gen 3:9-15
Ps 138	Ps 130	Ps 130:1-8
2 Cor 4:13—5:1	2 Cor 4:13—5:1	2 Cor 4:13—5:1
Mk 3:20-35	Mk 3:20-35	Mk 3:20-35

Speaker's Introduction for the Lessons
Lesson 1
1 Samuel 8:4-11 (12-15) 16-20 (11:14-15) (SC)

Israel calls on Samuel to demand a king and Samuel resists. God directs Samuel to give them what they want and to warn them what the consequences will be.

Genesis 3:8-15 (C); Genesis 3:9-15 (RC)

Adam and Eve attempt to hide from God, and the ensuing judgment declared upon the deceiving serpent.

Lesson 2
Psalm 138 (SC)

A song of thanksgiving for God's hearing of the psalmist's plea for help, which ends with a petition to God not to forsake "the work of your hands."

Psalm 130 (C); Psalm 130:1-8 (RC)

A powerful lament that nevertheless urges patience in God, in the image of a watchman in the night who keeps vigil for the rising of the sun.

383

Lesson 3
2 Corinthians 4:13—5:1 (SC/C/RC)
The writer urges the community to not lose heart, in spite of outward difficulties, trusting in God's never-failing grace.

Gospel
Mark 3:20-35 (SC/C/RC)
The story of Jesus' family seeking to "restrain" him frames Jesus' encounter with a delegation of scribes who charge him as being in allegiance with demonic powers.

Theme
What does it mean to be a "brother or sister of Jesus Christ"?

Thought for the Day
By Jesus' definition, his is an open family – all who desire to do the will of God are welcome!

Sermon Summary
References by Jesus to Satan, Beelzebul, blasphemy, and a radical definition of family bring indications of the opposition Jesus is facing in his ministry. This passage calls us to remember Christ's ultimate victory and recommit ourselves to him by doing the will of God as his "family."

Call to Worship
We are called to give thanks to God with a whole heart, to be thankful for God's steadfast love and faithfulness. In gratitude we remember that though God is great and glorious, God is not far removed from us. God, in Christ, and by the Holy Spirit, walks this life with us. God saves and delivers us. God's purposes are fulfilled for us and through us. With joyful praise and boundless thanksgiving let us worship God!

Pastoral Prayer
God, we hear and respond to the commission to love and serve you by loving and serving your people. We thank you that by your grace and

through Christ we are all part of your family. Help us to not take this gift for granted or deny its blessing to others. We pray with and for those in need and together we ask that you would make good your purpose for us. By your Spirit guide us to find and build partnerships in ministry that will witness to the unity that is ours in Christ Jesus our Lord. Amen.

Prayer of Confession and Assurance

God, we hear the psalmist declare that though we walk in the midst of trouble, you preserve us and stretch out your hand to deliver us. The psalmist voices the promise that you will fulfill your purpose in us and that your steadfast love endures forever. We claim this promise, God, in the awareness of our own need and with a desire to minister to the needs of others. Guide us to mend the brokenness and overcome injustices that afflict relationships between individuals, communities and nations, especially the ways in which we ourselves contribute to difficulties, discord, or divisions.

Convince us again, God, of the good news that Jesus, filled with the Holy Spirit, invites us to share his mission and ministry. Assure us again, God, that we can be of the same mind and same Spirit with Christ in the new family of his sisters and brothers.

Prayer of Dedication of Gifts and Self

We thank you, God, for your faithfulness and for the assurance that you are with us. God of all peoples and nations, God of all cultures and communities, we claim the promise that all who draw near to you will feel you draw near to them. Bless us and bless these gifts we bring for ministry that we, and our gifts, will offer the love and acceptance of Christ. Amen.

Hymn of the Day
Once to Every Man and Nation

As noted in the sermon, Mark's quoting of Jesus' "a house divided against itself" was itself quoted in a speech by a then unsuccessful candidate for US Senate from Illinois in 1858, Abraham Lincoln. Lincoln's accompanying insight was that he did not think the problem of slavery would pass until "a crisis shall have been reached and passed." The abolitionist James Russell Lowell had 14 years earlier written a poem entitled "The Present

Crisis" that framed his abolitionist sentiment in starkly biblical imagery. A portion of that poem became the hymn "Once to Every Man and Nation." Its strongest musical setting is to the powerful Welsh tune TONY-BO-TEL (EBENEZER).

Children's Time: We Are Family

In our Bible reading today, we learn about what it means to be a part of God's family. In the time of Jesus, most children grew up to do the same kind of work that their parents did. Children of bakers or blacksmiths grew up to be bakers and blacksmiths themselves. You probably remember that Jesus grew up in the family of a carpenter. I'm sure that most of the people who knew Mary and Joseph believed that Jesus would grow up to be a carpenter.

But that is not what happened. Instead of staying in Nazareth and taking over the carpentry shop, Jesus became a traveling minister. That didn't mean that Jesus' own family had forgotten about him. In fact, they seemed to be very concerned about him. His family may have thought that Jesus was working so hard that he wasn't taking good care of himself. Just like your parents want to make sure that you get good food to eat and plenty of rest so that you don't get sick, Jesus' family may also have been worried about Jesus' safety. They knew that he was getting into trouble with some of the nation's leaders. Some of those leaders did not like Jesus and were trying to have him arrested or even killed.

When Jesus' family arrived in Capernaum, they wanted to take Jesus back home to Nazareth. But Jesus told them that his life was different now, and that his family was different, too. He said his family had grown, and that everyone who does God's work belongs in the same family.

That larger family is what we are part of in our congregation. And just as in the Bible story, Jesus calls us his brothers and sisters, because we are doing what God wants us to do, like Jesus did.

Let's pray: Dear God, help us to love everyone in our family. Help us to know that Jesus is the best friend that anyone could ever have. Amen.

The Sermon: Focus on the Family
Scripture: Mark 3:20-35

This Sunday fits in between two prominent cultural celebrations of family, with Mother's Day in May and Father's Day later in June. Today's Gospel reading also has a "focus on the family," but it is in sharp contrast to the popular and generally positive presentation of "family" that we often see in greeting cards and television specials. These verses also give a very different presentation of Jesus – not at all the "gentle Jesus, meek and mild" that is such a popular, but such a limiting, image of him.

We're all familiar with the soft-toned pictures of Jesus that show him sitting quietly with a group of well-scrubbed and well-behaved children, or cradling a cuddly little lamb in his arms. But what Mark gives us here is a picture in vibrant color, with actions and vocabulary that startle and surprise us today, just as they did his contemporaries.

In first-century Palestinian culture the family unit was the foundation block for society as a whole. The family unit provided security for those born into it. Orphans and widows were particularly vulnerable because they had lost a vital link to the protection of a larger family. Then, as now, people derived their personal social standing from their family.

Family honor is still a life-and-death matter in Middle Eastern culture. We hear news stories of the dire consequences to individuals who are thought to have brought shame on their family. Jesus hits a nerve when he speaks sharply to his own family members who seem to have been embarrassed by him. When his family heard that he had attracted another large crowd around him, "they went out to restrain him, for people were saying, 'He has gone out of his mind'" (v. 21). When told that his mother and siblings were standing outside, calling for him, Jesus defines his true family not by blood relations but by "whoever does the will of God" (v. 35).

We may find it difficult to deal with what seems like a rift between Jesus and his mother and siblings who have expressed opposition to his ministry. Opposition also comes from his extended faith family. Jewish religious leaders also declare that Jesus is "out of his mind." They characterize this by saying, "He has Beelzebul, and by the ruler of the demons he casts out demons" (v. 22). Both expressions of family opposition come from the same point of irritation that Jesus is not behaving as they both would wish. He is not acting as one of them.

A quick review of the preceding chapters in Mark's Gospel shows that Jesus is indeed "different." Even after John had been arrested (1:14-15), Jesus continues to proclaim the message that the kingdom of God was at hand and called on people to repent, to turn their lives around. He drew attention to himself by hanging out with the wrong sorts of people and created more notoriety by healing lepers and freeing those held by unclean spirits. He publicly restored health and mobility to those who have been paralyzed, and he questioned the laws related to observing the Sabbath. Complaints about him have escalated to the point where Jesus is accused of being possessed by an evil force, "Beelzebul, the ruler of the demons."

Beelzebul was the name of an idol worshiped by Israel's long-time adversaries, the Philistines. "Beel" is a Greek form of Baal, the Canaanite god of the Hebrew Scriptures. To link this name to Jesus was to accuse him of being no better than this idol.

But Jesus is not without a creative and powerful response. He spoke of a "kingdom divided against itself." Eugene Peterson's translation of this passage in *The Message* is very helpful. "Does it make sense to send a devil to catch a devil, to use Satan to get rid of Satan? A constantly squabbling family disintegrates. If Satan were fighting Satan there soon wouldn't be any Satan left."

Jesus is saying that if he wasn't changing people's lives by the power of Satan, then it must be by the power of God. The question to his accusers then is, why would they oppose what he is doing by calling it the work of the devil? In verses 29-30, Jesus speaks very strong words that stand in sharp contrast to the promise of forgiveness in verse 28. He declares that there is such a thing as an unforgivable sin. Back in verse 23 we read that Jesus has called his accusers, family and scribes alike, to hear what he has to say about blasphemy against the Holy Spirit, what he calls "an eternal sin" for which there is no forgiveness, and he particularizes this in verse 30: "for they had said, 'He has an unclean spirit.'" The sin against the Holy Spirit is an act of defiance against God in calling the work of the Holy Spirit the work of the devil, rejecting God by rejecting the one sent by God.

There is nothing meek and mild about Jesus here, or about what he is saying. The words are as jarring for us as they must have been for his mother and his siblings – and for the religious leaders. It is hard for us to hear this warning, because it makes us wonder if we have committed this unforgivable sin of being defiantly rebellious against God. John Mark

Hicks suggests that this does not equate to some inadvertent remark about the Spirit, or one's unbelief at some point in their life, or to a willful sin in their past. Rather, it is a persistent rejection of Jesus as the herald of the kingdom of God. The condemnation continues as long as that rejection continues.

We can be relieved to know that our wrestling about these things is in itself a sign of the Holy Spirit at work within us. The unforgivable sin is to knowingly reject God's love and forgiveness. Turning back to the words of today's Gospel reading we could say that those who try to thwart God's will for healing and wholeness are the ones who are "out of their minds" and of "an unclean spirit." Those who join with Jesus in doing the will of God are a new family, what the NRSV names "The True Kindred of Jesus." Those who are actively and willingly living in God's way are the new community of faith, people who are demonstrating God's reign in the world, breaking down Satan's kingdom by building up the kingdom of God.

– Gordon Timbers

Hymns
Opening: Praise Our Maker, Peoples of One Family
Sermon: Brother, Sister, Let Me Serve You
Closing: In Christ There Is No East or West

June 14, 2015

3rd Sunday after Pentecost (Proper 6)
RC/Pres/UCC: 11th Sunday in Ordinary Time

Lessons

Semi-continuous (SC)	Complementary (C)	Roman Catholic (RC)
1 Sam 15:34—16:13	Ezek 17:22-24	Ezek 17:22-24
Ps 20	Ps 92:1-4, 12-14	Ps 92:2-3, 13-16
2 Cor 5:6-10 (11-13), 14-17	2 Cor 5:6-10 (11-13), 14-17	2 Cor 5:6-10
Mk 4:26-34	Mk 4:26-34	Mk 4:26-34

Speaker's Introduction for the Lessons
Lesson 1
1 Samuel 15:34—16:13 (SC)
The Lord regretted Saul's kingship and sent Samuel in search of a replacement. After disguising his search with a believable story, Samuel goes to Bethlehem to find Jesse and his sons. There he anoints not the oldest or most prominent, but David, the youngest.

Ezekiel 17:22-24 (C/RC)
Ezekiel prophesies about the coming Messiah by using the cedar tree as an image. Begun as a mere cutting, the mighty tree will welcome all to its branches, and all will know that God is the Lord.

Lesson 2
Psalm 20 (SC)
This psalm that asserts God will help his "anointed" (likely a royal psalm) makes the intriguing judgment that military might (chariots and horses) is not cause for pride (self-assurance).

Psalm 92:1-4, 12-14 (C); Psalm 92:2-3, 13-16 (RC)
This psalmist confidently declares God's praise day and night in the wisdom tradition that asserts the wicked perish while the righteous flourish with vitality ("full of sap").

June 14, 2015
3rd Sunday after Pentecost (Proper 6)
RC/Pres/UCC: 11th Sunday in Ordinary Time

Lesson 3
2 Corinthians 5:6-10 (11–13), 14-17 (SC/C); 2 Corinthians 5:6-10 (RC)

The writer of 2 Corinthians explains that as long as we live in time and space, we are, in some ways, separated from Christ. At the same time, we are never really apart from him. In Christ, our world is bigger than the one we see.

Gospel
Mark 4:26-34 (SC/C/RC)

Jesus explains the nature of God's reign. As the mustard seed begins small but grows to a sturdy bush, so God's reign might not look like much now, but in time, all will find a home there.

Theme
The kingdom of God grows within and beyond us and even despite us.

Thought for the Day
Mark 4:30 gives us a valuable invitation to consider: With what can we compare the kingdom of God? What parable will we use for it?

Sermon Summary
Two familiar parables challenge us to find new interpretations about how the rule of God grows in us and around us. We are also invited to actively look for God's rule growing and taking root in unexpected people and places.

Call to Worship
As we gather for worship we want to have our hearts and minds open and receptive to the Spirit of God speaking through scripture, hymns, sermon, and prayers as well as through silence and reflection. As a community of faith we come together to worship God, the giver of life. With praise and thanksgiving we anticipate an outpouring of God's grace that we will experience as hope, peace, joy, and love. Let us worship God!

Pastoral Prayer

Creating and loving God, we thank you for life in the world you have made and for the ways in which you sustain this earth and all that is in it. We are also grateful for your willingness to receive our prayers, trusting that you will enfold them into your care and compassion. We pray for places and situations of conflict that your peace might prevail. We pray that for places suffering from natural disasters there would be a generous response for rebuilding and redevelopment. May our words and actions be agents of your healing grace. Amen.

Prayer of Confession and Assurance

How good it is, God, to hear Jesus speak of how your kingdom grows because it is yours: the earth produces of itself. Jesus also declares that the kingdom of God spreads and grows, impossible to stop or control. It is good to learn that Jesus spoke the word to his disciples, as they were able to hear it, and that he explained everything to them. We are like those first disciples. We also have limited or preferred understanding, and we also need to broaden and deepen and expand our awareness of your Spirit at work. We thank you for the assurance that you lead and guide us into fuller understanding and increasing participation in the ministry and mission of our Lord Jesus Christ.

Prayer of Dedication of Gifts and Self

Loving God, we continue our worship by acknowledging and expressing thanks for our many blessings. We return thanks by bringing an offering of ourselves and of our resources. We give because we can, and we give because we want to continue Christ's ministry in actions that bring hope and healing, growth and renewal, in Jesus' name. Amen.

Hymn of the Day
God, Who Stretched the Spangled Heavens

Jesus was one of the great parable tellers of all time, using them to help his listeners imagine God's kingdom. Musicians, hymn writers, and other artists share in this creative task when they forge words and ideas that help us ponder what being a Christian looks like today. In "God, Who Stretched the Spangled Heavens," Catherine Cameron prods us to think about just that. We share creative powers with God, she declares, and asks God to guide us in using these powers to "serve others" and "honor you." This outstanding text makes HOLY MANNA sound like it was composed yesterday.

Children's Time: Planting Seeds

(Bring a planter filled with potting soil, zinnia or marigold seeds, a watering can with water, and wet wipes. Choose a location outside where the children can watch the seeds grow.)
(Place a seed on your palm.) Look at this little seed. God has a plan for this seed. What will happen when we plant it? *(It will grow into a flower and the flower will produce many more seeds. Those seeds will grow into flowers.)*

Jesus wanted all of his followers to spread the good news of his love. He said that his followers are like seeds. We grow strong in God's love, then we tell others the good news of God's love. And so the message continues to spread and grow, like a garden planted with many, many flower seeds.

Let's all plant one seed. *(Have each child use one finger to poke a hole in the soil and drop in one seed. After all have planted a seed, smooth over the soil. Wipe off dirty fingers. Water the seeds.)* I'll put this planter *(name the location you have chosen)*. You can watch your seeds grow into big strong plants. And you can grow big and strong in God's love by telling others about Jesus.

Let's pray: Creator God, help us to grow big and strong, like beautiful flowers, so we can share the story of your Son, Jesus. Amen.

The Sermon: Freed to Be All That God Wants Us to Be
Scripture: Mark 4:26-34

This week's Gospel reading presents some interesting challenges both to preachers and those listening to sermons on this text. One problem is that we've likely heard (and preached on) these verses many times before. It is hard to hear these familiar Bible stories with freshness because they are like old friends. We recognize them and think we know all about them. These parables are perhaps too familiar to us.

A second challenge is that they are what they are – parables. We've come to understand the parables of Jesus as "teaching stories." We can readily recall how Jesus used everyday objects like a coin, a sheep, a flower, or a seed to make a point that applies to our life of faith. A danger is that we may think of these "teaching stories" as short and snappy object lessons and fail to find the deeper wealth of meaning and interpretation. We may just see the object and not fully appreciate how Jesus is using it.

It helps to remember that Jesus spoke these parables some 2000 years ago in a prescientific culture. Farmers would have understood the need for water and warmth and weeding, but the process of growth would seem like a miracle, a gift of God. The parable of the growing seed in verses 26-29 gives a straightforward, nonscientific description of a familiar process and its expected outcome. The earth (somehow) produces of itself. Seeds are planted in a field; they grow from the time the first shoot pokes through the earth to the stalk and stem and branches and finally the fruit, ready for harvest.

This sense of the miraculous is also linked to the second familiar parable, the story of the mustard seed, which is very small, but when planted it can grow to become a shrub big enough that birds can make nests in its branches.

A familiar interpretation would be to see these well-known and well-loved parables as stories about how the kingdom of God grows within us as we are transformed and made new – spiritually fruitful – and all of this happening by God's initiative and in God's timing. In each parable, the image of seeds makes the point that in God's way of doing things, grace abounds. The fruit is greater than the seed. With God, more happens than we can make happen on our own.

Beyond this, verses 26-29 make the point that God brings the growth in God's timing. This is an important reminder to those of us who may be impatient or inclined to action for action's sake. This reminder certainly had an application in the first-century context of a nation and people under the political, economic, and social control of a foreign power. This reminder about change coming in God's timing was a warning to those first-century Israelites who wanted to accelerate the coming of the kingdom of God, and they wanted to do this by engaging in armed conflict with the Roman occupation forces.

The reminder is an assurance that just as "the earth produces of itself, first the stalk, then the head, then the full grain" (v. 28), so the coming of God's rule in all its fullness is a work in progress that is not of our doing. God is at work. Change is coming. The oppressors will be brought low and the oppressed given freedom. Just as a planted seed is growing and developing, unseen and active, so God is active, bringing in God's kingdom. The growth of God's kingdom is visible, just as we can see a plant sprout and grow. We are partners in reaping the harvest and claiming the blessings but the gift and initiative is from God.

With this insight and awareness we can look again at verses 30-32 and consider that they may be saying something very different than the familiar platitude that great things often come from humble beginnings. Bible scholars like Professor David Lose encourage us to go beyond considering parables as tame teaching stories. In a blog (June 17, 2012) on this text, Lose says that parables are meant to overturn, to deconstruct, to cause frustration, and for those who stay with them, the parables bring transformation.

Sharon H. Ringe also challenges our domestication of this parable by reminding us that even though mustard is indeed an herb with medicinal properties and one that is useful for flavoring and preserving food, the mustard bush of this parable is actually a garden pest. It would never be sown on purpose because it grows all too readily on its own. From the proverbial small seed, it grows into a bush several feet high that tends to grow and spread where it is not wanted. Those branches that are big enough to safely hold bird nests do indeed attract birds, but the birds may then further spread the seeds and bushes to other places where farmers do not want them.

This more radical image for the reign of God could be interpreted as a message that the well-organized military might of the Roman Empire would be subverted by the power of a very different kind of kingdom. The growth of the kingdom of God would be propelled by the uncontrollable power of the Holy Spirit, illustrated by tiny seeds that sprout huge shrubs that give shelter to birds, who in turn scatter more seeds, and so the growth continues, unstoppable.

Seeing the mustard seed and bush differently can give us a different perspective on the meaning of this parable. More than declaring that something small can produce something great, this parable also declares that the kingdom of God proclaimed by Jesus is not something under human control. Seeds have been planted. Growth will come, and it will come in ways that will startle and surprise. The growth of the kingdom of God will not be restricted to neatly laid out plans and programs, nor will it be limited by those who would try to build fences to either contain it or keep it at a distance.

This is a wonderful word of hope to those who feel themselves bound and constrained by the powers of this world. Change is coming. This word of hope also challenges those of us who have freedom, health, and resources to be participants in God's kingdom as agents of change and transformation.

These two parables are stories that teach about growth, not of plants or shrubs, but of how we grow as we live in relationship to God and to one another. As the kingdom of God grows with us, we are freed to be all that God wants us to be.

– Gordon Timbers

Hymns
Opening: Blessed Jesus, at Your Word
Sermon: One More Step along the World I Go
Closing: Teach Me, God, to Wonder

June 21, 2015

4th Sunday after Pentecost (Proper 7)
RC/Pres/UCC: 12th Sunday in Ordinary Time

Lessons

Semi-continuous (SC)	Complementary (C)	Roman Catholic (RC)
1 Sam 17:(1a, 4-11, 19-23) 32-49	Job 38:1-11	Job 38:1, 8-11
or 1 Sam 17:57—18:5, 10-16		
Ps 9:9-20 or Ps 133	Ps 107:1-3, 23-32	Ps 107:23-26, 28-31
2 Cor 6:1-13	2 Cor 6:1-13	2 Cor 5:14-17
Mk 4:35-41	Mk 4:35-41	Mk 4:35-41

Speaker's Introduction for the Lessons

Lesson 1

1 Samuel 17:(1a, 4-11, 19-23) 32-49 (SC)

At Socoh, the Philistine army massed to fight Israel. Their bravado was incarnate in the giant, Goliath. David, yet a young man, offered to take him on, rejecting normal protection offered by his king. David slew Goliath with a sling and a stone in the name of the Lord of hosts.

1 Samuel 17:57—18:5, 10-16 (SC)

We learn of the deep friendship between David and the king's son, Jonathan, as well as Saul's growing madness.

Job 38:1-11 (C); Job 38:1, 8-11 (RC)

After experiencing grievous losses, Job challenges God to hear his lament. From a whirlwind God responds, clarifying that God's wisdom and will is far beyond what humans can comprehend.

Lesson 2

Psalm 9:9-20 (SC)

Part of an acrostic psalm (along with Psalm 10), these verses assert God as stronghold even as they invoke God's gracious intervention with those who cause the psalmist suffering.

Psalm 107:1-3, 23-32 (C); Psalm 107:23-26, 28-31 (RC)
The psalmist witnesses God's deliverance of those who "went down to the sea in ships" by the God who stills the storm and quiets the sea.
Psalm 133 (SC)
The psalmist extoles the virtures of unity.

Lesson 3
2 Corinthians 6:1-13 (SC/C)
The writer of this text points out the distortions that have been attached to those who have been in ministry with the Corinthians. The writer appeals to the Corinthians to open their hearts to the word, so that they might know the day of salvation.
2 Corinthians 5:14-17 (RC)
Defending the ministry of reconciliation with the Corinthians, the writer appeals to them to see themselves as new in Christ and to no longer regard others from a human point of view.

Gospel
Mark 4:35-41 (SC/C/RC)
Jesus and his disciples left the crowds and set out in a boat for the other side of the sea. However, a great windstorm arose and threatened to swamp the boat. When Jesus calmed the wind and waves, the disciples were left to wonder just who he was.

Theme
Christ is with us and within us.

Thought for the Day
The picture of Jesus asleep in a storm-tossed boat reminds us that his Spirit is present within us, ready to come awake in us.

Sermon Summary
The power of Christ to calm the storm reassures us that we can turn to Christ in our times of need. We can also realize that the power of Christ's presence is alive within us, and when we are awake to this reality we can minister effectively, whatever the circumstances.

Call to Worship

One: The psalmist declares that "The Lord is a stronghold for the oppressed, a stronghold in times of trouble.

All: We will therefore give thanks to God and tell of God's wonderful deeds.

One: God rules the world with righteousness and demands justice of the nations.

All: We will sing praise to God with joy and thanksgiving.

Pastoral Prayer

We thank you, God, for your promise to hear and help your people. Today, and every day, is an acceptable time to celebrate our salvation. We pray that in our intentions and actions in ministry we would put no obstacle in anyone's way. By our patience, kindness, and Christlike love and caring may we come to oneness with ourselves and others, bringing blessings to this world and its people as agents of your peace and justice. Let our words and actions declare the truth that new life has begun by your saving work in our world. Amen.

Prayer of Confession and Assurance

Sometimes, God, in those moments when we are perplexed or anxious, when we are in pain ourselves or hurting because of the suffering of others, we can feel ourselves alone with our concerns. With the fearful disciples we question: Do you not care? When we find ourselves being tossed about by the storms of life, we need to see Christ present with us. We need his presence to come awake and alive within us. We need to realize again that the Jesus who rebuked the wind and said to the sea, "Peace! Be still!" speaks those same words to us, telling our anxious hearts and troubled minds: "Peace! Be still!" Wherever we are, whatever our situation, may some spark of faith within us rise up to meet Jesus, who is there with us in the middle of the storm.

Prayer of Dedication of Gifts and Self

God, in presenting an offering as part of our worship we are bringing something of what we have achieved or been given, and we offer it back to you as the source from whom all good things come. We pray that these gifts would be used through the church to declare and demonstrate the amazing grace of our Lord Jesus Christ, the extravagant love we know of you as our creator, and the intimate friendship of the Holy Spirit, alive and awake within us and ministering through us. Amen.

Hymn of the Day
Jesus, Savior, Pilot Me
The earth's oceans, seas, and other large bodies of water hold a certain mystique for us. We are impressed by their size, respectful of their depths, aware of their wildness. It is no wonder that when a great windstorm arose on the sea, threatening to swamp their boat, the disciples were scared to death.

In "Jesus, Savior, Pilot Me," Edward Hopper likens our life journey to crossing a tempestuous sea, where "unknown waves" hide "rock and treacherous shoal." Jesus is the one who guides us; the one who says to the waves, "Be still"; the one who leads us safely to the other shore, saying, "Fear not, I will pilot thee."

Children's Time: Jesus Is in the Middle of the Storm
What are you afraid of? *(Accept responses. Add your own.)* How many of you are afraid of storms? Today's Bible story is about a time when Jesus' disciples were afraid.

Please help me tell this story by making sound effects. Now, let's imagine that we are Jesus' disciples. We are sailing in a boat, gently rocking on the Sea of Galilee. *(Rock back and forth.)* Jesus is sleeping in the back of the boat. It begins to sprinkle. *(Snap your fingers slowly.)* It changes into a steady downpour. *(Rub palms of hands together in a circular motion.)* Then the storm hits. *(Slap palms loudly on legs.)* The wind howls. *(Say, "Ooooo." Continue to slap palms on legs.)* The boat is in the middle of a storm. Waves splash over the sides of the boat. The boat is filling with water. It's going to sink. "Wake up, Jesus, we're going to die!'" the disciples cry out. Jesus wakes up. "Peace! Be still!" *(Stop slapping palms.)* And the storm stops. "Who is this?" the disciples wonder. "Even the wind and the waves obey him."

Who stilled the storm? *(Jesus did!)* Whenever we are in the middle of a storm or we're frightened, we can remember that Jesus is with us, watching over us.

Let's pray: Thank you, Jesus, for watching over us in scary times. Amen.

The Sermon: Christ Awake in Us
Scripture: Mark 4:35-41

Because the Gospels of Matthew, Mark, and Luke all include a version of what happened on that stormy night out on Lake Galilee, we can assume that this is a very important story. And, looking at Mark's Gospel in particular, it is important to note where this story is placed. It comes right after Jesus has been teaching his disciples about the kingdom of God and their part in it. Mark says, "On that day" – the day on which Jesus had told the two parables about seeds growing in their own time and about the fast-spreading mustard bush – "when evening had come," Jesus and the disciples got into a boat to cross to the other side of Lake Galilee. There is immediacy between what they had just been taught and what they would soon experience out on the water.

The parables of the growing seed (4:26-29) and the mustard seed that becomes a large bush (4:30-32) present two familiar images of the reign of God. The first parable teaches that one way of looking at the kingdom of God is to see it as a process of growth as natural as a planted seed sprouting, growing and producing fruit ready for harvest. The second parable teaches that the rule of God will spread and grow like a wild bush that cannot be held back or contained by earthly plans, programs, or powers. With these images in our minds, Luke then takes us off the land and onto the waters of Lake Galilee, familiar territory for the Galilean fishermen among the disciples. We are given the scene of Jesus in a little fishing boat with his disciples. A sudden storm blows up and even the experienced fishermen among them become fearful. The boat was being swamped, and there was Jesus, asleep! The disciples wake up Jesus with their question: Don't you care that the boat is being swamped and we're all about to perish?

If they were afraid then, they were likely even more afraid when they saw what Jesus could do in answering their question. Verse 39 gives us the amazing picture of these fearful men in their little boat with the wind blowing and waves rolling, and then Jesus woke up and rebuked the wind, and said to the sea, "Peace! Be still!" Then the wind ceased, and there was a dead calm. It isn't difficult to picture these men, wide-eyed in awe and wonder, asking: "Who then is this, that even the wind and the sea obey him?"

As with the familiar parables about a seed sprouting and mustard plants spreading, we can go deeper with this familiar story and gain some new insights and understanding. And one way to do this is to go back a bit in the story, move away from the familiar image of Jesus commanding the wind and waves and get another perspective on the sleeping Jesus, surrounded by fearful disciples in a rocking ship on a stormy sea.

The sea is the geographic location for this gospel story. It speaks of something as familiar to fishermen as the land is to farmers. Water and wind can be empowering – but they can also be dangerous, as we know from the realities of floods and hurricanes that can wreak devastation as they displace people and destroy property. This image of storms of life threatening to swamp us is an all too familiar experience. Illness, financial insecurity, our own mistakes, and the negative actions of others all affect us as individuals, as communities, and as nations. Abundant as our human and natural resources may be, and with the blessings of personal freedoms and democratic institutions, our country still has its troubles in dealing with natural disasters, cultural shifts, and the effects of political and economic forces. It seems that our ship of state has hit some stormy seas and we humble citizen-sailors are being tossed about by the roaring wind and the rolling waves.

Theologian Frederick Buechner has a wonderful ability to help people see the grace of God at work in their daily lives. He brings that perspective to this familiar Gospel passage when he writes, "Christ sleeps in the deepest selves of all of us, and whatever we do in whatever time we have left, wherever we go, may we in whatever way we can call on him as the fishermen did in their boat to come awake within us and to give us hope, to show us, each one, our way. May he be with us especially when the winds go mad and the waves run wild, as they will for all of us before we're done, so that even in their midst we may find peace … we may find Christ" (C.F. Buechner, *Secrets in the Dark: A Life in Sermons*).

The element of grace that we claim from this story is not just that Christ commands wind and waves to be still, bringing quiet amid chaos. Wonderful as this is, there is something even more amazing for us as we encounter the storms of life. We can recall the image of the kingdom of God growing as naturally and purposefully as a planted seed sprouting, growing, and producing fruit. We can recall the image of the kingdom of God as the work of the Holy Spirit, as prolific and unstoppable as the rapid spread of wild mustard. And this same power and presence of Jesus Christ is asleep and available within each of us. In the face of the storms of life we can come awake again to the reality of Christ present with us, not just as a power to whom we turn in times of need. Christ is present within us. The presence of Christ, alive and awake within us, gives us the power to respond to whatever storms are currently raging and to minister to those around us.

In the smooth sailing and in the stormy seas, in our prayers and sermons and songs in church, in our words and actions in our communities, wherever we are and whatever we are doing, Christ is awake and alive in us and the kingdom of God comes near.

Thanks be to God. Amen.

– Gordon Timbers

Hymns
Opening: Through All the Changing Scenes of Life
Sermon: Eternal Father, Strong to Save
Closing: For the Healing of the Nations

June 28, 2015

5th Sunday after Pentecost (Proper 8)
RC/Pres/UCC: 13th Sunday in Ordinary Time

Lessons

Semi-continuous (SC)	Complementary (C)	Roman Catholic (RC)
2 Sam 1:1, 17-27	Lam 3:23-33 or	Wis 1:13-15; 2:23-24
	Wis 1:13-15; 2:23-24	
Ps 130	Ps 30	Ps 30:2, 4-6, 11-12a, 13b
2 Cor 8:7-15	2 Cor 8:7-15	2 Cor 8:7, 9, 13-15
Mk 5:21-43	Mk 5:21-43	Mk 5:21-43 or 5:21-24, 35-43

Speaker's Introduction for the Lessons

Lesson 1

2 Samuel 1:1, 17-27 (SC)

At Ziklag, a messenger comes to David to report the defeat of Israel's army and the deaths of the king, Saul, and his son Jonathan on Mount Gilboa. This text is David's lament over Saul and Jonathan.

Lamentations 3:23-33 (C)

With words of comfort and hope, the poet appeals for patience and a long view of God's work in our lives. God is faithful. God's love never ceases.

Wisdom of Solomon 1:13-15; 2:23-24 (C/RC)

This text works out the theological difficulties behind the fact that we all die. Asserting that God did not create death, the author goes on to point to the envy of the devil as the cause of death.

Lesson 2

Psalm 130 (SC)

Sometimes known as the De Profundis from the opening words in Latin, this psalm of lament opens with a sobering plea and closes in quiet hope with the psalmist waiting for the God who redeems.

Psalm 30 (C); Psalm 30:2, 4-6, 11-12a, 13b (RC)
The psalm sings the story of one whose lament and pointed protest to God has been turned around, so that mourning has become dancing and the night turned to day.

Lesson 3
2 Corinthians 8:7-15 (SC/C); 2 Corinthians 8:7, 9, 13-15 (RC)
One of Paul's great mission projects was to gather a collection for the poor in the Jerusalem church from the Gentile congregations he mentored. This was a concrete way for him to demonstrate to the skeptical leaders of the Jerusalem church that they were all one in Christ.

Gospel
Mark 5:21-43 (SC/C/RC)
Having just left the country of the Gerasenes because the people were afraid of him, Jesus lands before a great crowd by the sea. A religious leader's daughter and an unclean and outcast woman both are beneficiaries of Jesus' healing.

Theme
Jesus' care extends to all people.

Thought for the Day
Take this story as a kind of parable about those powerless, marginalized people who come to Jesus seeking help and healing. More than healing, they receive life.

Sermon Summary
A woman in pain comes forward out of the crowd and touches Jesus. She is healed. Let this biblical story be for us a parable of Jesus and his care for us. Jesus exudes life; life for those who live in the shadow of death, particularly those whom the world does not acknowledge in their pain.

Call to Worship

One: Hope in the Lord! For with the Lord there is steadfast love, and with him is great power to redeem.

Many: This I call to mind, and therefore I have hope: the stead-fast love of the Lord never ceases, his mercies never come to an end.

One: They are new every morning; great is your faithfulness.

Many: "The Lord is my portion," says my soul. "Therefore I will hope in him."

Pastoral Prayer

Lord Jesus, giver, preserver, and restorer of life, we pray this day for all those who are sick in body or mind, who languish on beds of pain, or keep the long night vigil, praying for dawn to come, seeking relief from their suffering, an end to their illness.

We pray for those among us who care for the sick, those in this congregation who care for children who are disabled, or for parents who are old and infirm, or who make their living in hospitals, nursing homes, or convalescent centers.

Help us to see all healing as a gift of your grace. Enable us to embrace health and life as precious gifts of God. Strengthen us in our patience and perseverance in times of sickness. Make us feel the pain and misfortune of others as keenly as we feel our own. Amen.

Prayer of Confession and Assurance

Healing One, we admit that many of our ills are but the effect of our own wrong or willful choices. We tend to think we are invulnerable. When we are well, we easily forget to appreciate and care for the life you have given. Then, when sickness comes upon us, we cry out to you, "Why me?" When, as church, we become insular and exclusive, we reject our mission and you who desires through us to heal division and prejudice, to heal loneliness and grief, to heal sick bodies and souls. We confess the weakness of our faith when we pray tentatively, when we pray not believing that all things are possible for you. And when we pray defining what we expect the answers to be, we are not trusting in your wisdom. Forgive us, we pray. Amen.

As the psalmist affirms, it is God "who forgives all your iniquity, who heals all your diseases, who redeems your life from the Pit, who crowns you with steadfast love and mercy, who satisfies you with good as long as you live." Thanks and praise be to God!

Prayer of Dedication of Gifts and Self

God of all who suffer, your compassion reaches out to all who are distressed. In our caring, we make this sacrificial offering for the restoration to health and freedom of those held captive by oppressive powers. May these gifts be the means of bringing encouragement, hope, and release into new life, we pray. Amen.

Hymn of the Day
O Christ the Healer, We Have Come

Mark reports in generous detail the predicaments of Jarius's daughter and the woman with a hemorrhage. To the astonishment of all, Jesus heals both. Yet, Mark infers through both instances that one's faith in Jesus' power to heal is of paramount importance. F. Pratt Green's "O Christ, the Healer, We Have Come" provides words to our yearning to be healed, both on a personal level and in the communal or societal dimensions of our lives. W. Walker's tune DISTRESS matches the depth of this remarkable text.

Children's Time: Healing Touch of Jesus

Who has been sick at some time? What did you do? *(Affirm responses, including things like stay in bed to let your body rest and heal, go to the doctor or hospital, take medicine.)*
(Tell today's Gospel story to teach the children that God expects us to reach out to Jesus when we or another need healing, not as the last thing, but the first thing we do.) To pray is to reach out to touch Jesus, just like the woman who believed that Jesus' power could heal her. God loves us and desires to help our bodies, our hearts, and our minds to heal when any part of us is sick.

Let's pray together. You can repeat each phrase after me.
Dear Jesus,
Thank you
for always loving us
and promising to be near.
Help us remember
we can always reach out to you.
Your love will be there for us.
Amen.

The Sermon: From Death to Life
Scripture: Mark 5:21-43

Sometimes the most important things that happen to you in life are the
intrusions. You are on your way somewhere, with an agenda, a clear, direct
purpose in mind, and you get distracted. Something else comes up that
demands your attention, and that "something else" turns out to be more
important than the journey on which you originally launched.

I know that lots of laypeople complain that preachers do not manage
their time very well. Sometimes it seems to take us too long to get things
done. Try to have some sympathy with us. We get distracted. We have
set aside a morning to prepare a sermon, but here comes someone with a
need, an immediate problem, and we drop everything for this intrusion.

Today's Gospel is a story about a woman who was an intrusion. Here
in this section of scripture, Jesus is about important business. In the verses
just before she intrudes (vv. 21-24), a leader of the synagogue, an important and impressive man, persuades Jesus to make a house visit on his
ailing daughter. Just after this woman's intrusion, the story of the man at
the synagogue is resumed and finished (vv. 35-43).

On the way to do something very good for an important person and
his daughter, Jesus gets distracted. A woman appears. She intrudes from
the margins. Of course, on the margins is where lots of women have been
through most of history. Historically, these women have not had a place in
the "big story." They have been there on the margins, living quietly. They
take what they can of the leftovers of history. But they don't get to make
history. They don't get mentioned when the final account is given of what
really happened in the world.

Still, this woman pushes forward. She demands to be noticed. She intrudes into the story. We don't know this woman's name. We know nothing of her family circumstances. All we know is that she is a woman whose body is in trouble. She is a person in pain.

For 12 years she has been hemorrhaging. That is a lot of blood to lose, a lot of life to be lost. We also learn that she had "endured much under many physicians." In frantic pursuit of well-being, she has spent her days in waiting rooms, in emergency rooms. She has filled out those endless insurance forms and waited. She has been poked at, tested, discussed, humiliated, lost her dignity, and still she suffers.

Now she has nothing. Medicine has done all it could for her, and to what end? She is poor. Now she has no hope, no hope it would appear except for Jesus.

Now, without hope, at the end of her rope, she makes one last effort to live. She reaches out, she pushes out from the margins to move toward the power.

Can you see her hand moving out to touch Jesus? You know the picture by Michelangelo of the creation of Adam in the Sistine Chapel? There, the Almighty, God the Father reaches out to touch the listless, the lifeless body of Adam, to give him the spark of life.

Here, the action moves in a different direction. Here, the woman reaches out to Jesus. Her lifeless, bloody finger reaches out toward Jesus, toward life.

She had said to herself, "If I but touch his clothes, I will be well."

This is one of the strongest images of faith I know of in the New Testament. Her hand, reaching out from the margins of the crowd to where she had been pushed by her poverty, her pain, her gender, reaching out to touch Jesus, the Lord, the giver of life.

She reaches out and receives the life for which she had hoped. Immediately (one of Mark's favorite words, *euthus*) she is healed. For the one pushed to the margins of life, there is great life.

Now Jesus speaks. You can't tell from the tone of his voice if he is upset with this intrusive woman, or anxious because some of the power has left him, or compassionate toward this hurting person. Perhaps he speaks because he wants to know who this person is with such faith that she demanded such a blessing.

His disciples appear to have little concern to identify the woman. Jesus is different. He wants to know who she is.

Perhaps this is one of the most healing moments in the whole story. This woman who was an unknown, identified only by her bleeding and her pain, is now going to be known, known by face, by name, in all of her particularity and individuality.

Again, this woman takes matters in hand. She steps up and identifies herself. This tells me much about her.

The woman trembles. After all, she has made a bold, decisive move, a move that all of her upbringing and her cultural norms tell her is inappropriate. She is pushed out from that location on the margins where society has relegated her. She is pushed out toward Jesus. She had been told to be the merely passive recipient of whatever life there was, and had boldly reached out and seized life for herself. She has touched the center of power from her pain. Now, will she be severely disciplined?

Jesus speaks to her. He recognizes her as a partner in the creation of new life. He doesn't criticize or scold her.

He addresses her, not as "you patient," or "you recipient of the health care system." Tenderly he calls her "daughter." It is an intimate designation that honors her, that places her within the family, the family of God.

He praises her action: "Your faith has made you well." Note that Jesus doesn't even claim to have healed her. Rather, he gives her all the credit. She had faith that Jesus could heal her. Yet she also had faith in herself. She had refused to accept the relegated position to which society had assigned her. She was determined to be someone more than simply a person in pain and helplessness. She had faith in Jesus, but she also had faith in her own capacity to reach out and touch, to receive the power.

And so Jesus blesses her, "Go in peace." Go in wholeness, go to live life in its fullness. Your faith has made you well. Her reaching out has been confirmed in his reaching back toward her.

Mark goes back to the big story, the story about the daughter of the leader of the synagogue. Life will also be given there, but we still can't help being more impressed with the life that is given to this once sad woman. This woman becomes a way of knowing who Jesus is. We have learned something about her, but she also, through her action, has revealed some important things about Jesus.

Can this be your story? From what I can tell, there is a great deal of bleeding, much hemorrhaging going on. Life is ebbing away from us,

June 28, 2015
4th Sunday after Pentecost (Proper 8)
RC/Pres/UCC: 13th Sunday in Ordinary Time

day by day, and I am saying that only because I am over 60! We, like the disciples, stand by and watch people get pushed to the margins, relegated to hopeless situations, powerless, weak, and in pain.

Too easily we say, "She is beyond all hope," or "You just have to adapt and accept your present situation."

But here comes this story of this pushy, intrusive woman, intruding into our settled arrangement, reminding us that in Jesus Christ, there is a power let loose in the world, which is there for us.

In whatever pain you suffer, however caught or trapped, will you reach out to that power? Will you let him speak to you? Will you let the life that God intends for you, flow toward you?

This is the faith that makes us whole.

– William H. Willimon

Hymns
Opening: Here in This Place
Sermon: There's a Wideness in God's Mercy
Closing: Blest Be the Tie That Binds

July 5, 2015

6th Sunday after Pentecost (Proper 9)
RC/Pres/UCC: 14th Sunday in Ordinary Time

Lessons

Semi-continuous (SC)	Complementary (C)	Roman Catholic (RC)
2 Sam 5:1-5, 9-10	Ezek 2:1-5	Ezek 2:2-5
Ps 48	Ps 123	Ps 123:1-4
2 Cor 12:2-10	2 Cor 12:2-10	2 Cor 12:7-10
Mk 6:1-13	Mk 6:1-13	Mk 6:1-6

Speaker's Introduction for the Lessons
Lesson 1
2 Samuel 5:1-5, 9-10 (SC)

David enters sovereign leadership through divine calling recognized by the tribal elders. Covenantal relationship is accompanied by the edict to remain pastoral: be a shepherd to the people.

Ezekiel 2:1-5 (C); Ezekiel 2:2-5 (RC)

Ezekiel's call sets him on his feet. He is forewarned: many will reject what he has to say, yet he is to declare, "Thus says the Lord."

Lesson 2
Psalm 48 (SC)

This psalm celebrates God's close connections with and defense of Jerusalem and the temple mount of Zion in its midst.

Psalm 123 (C); Psalm 123:1-4 (RC)

A terse, beautiful, and powerful supplication to God that blends trustful reliance with frank expression of having had one's fill with a contemptuous situation and scornful people.

Lesson 3
2 Corinthians 12:2-10 (SC/C); 2 Corinthians 12:7-10 (RC)

The church wrestles with competing hallmarks of leadership: outwardly expressed ecstatic power and the acceptance of finitude. Paul chooses the less spectacular so that Christ may be known.

412

Gospel

Mark 6:1-13 (SC/C); Mark 6:1-6 (RC)

Jesus' hometown questions the validity of his leadership because it is more than was expected. In response, Jesus sends out the disciples with new leadership responsibilities.

Theme

Jesus' way is a narrow way that not everyone wants to walk.

Thought for the Day

He warned his disciples that they might face rejection. He was, they were, we are sometimes fated to be "prophets without honor."

Sermon Summary

Being a Christian, a prophet, a truth teller in the name of Jesus means learning to make proper distinctions between our ways and God's way, our truths and God's truth.

Call to Worship

One: Who are we who gather this summer Sunday?

Many: Who are we who gather this summer Sunday?

One: We are those besieged by the messages and values of the world, but who choose to live instead by God's truth.

Many: Why do we come here?

One: We come to worship God, the source of life, to hear again the words of Jesus, to discern his way, and find grace to walk it.

Many: How are we enabled?

One: We attend to Christ's teaching, contemplate the symbols of the gospel story, and pray to be strengthened by the Holy Spirit for faithful life and witness in Christ's name.

Many: Why do we come here?

One: We come to worship God, the source of life, to hear again the words of Jesus, to discern his way, and find grace to walk it.

Many: How are we enabled?

All: We attend to Christ's teaching, contemplate the symbols of the gospel story, and pray to be strengthened by the Holy Spirit for faithful life and witness in Christ's name.

Pastoral Prayer

Lord Jesus, you speak to us, but not always in words that we want to hear. Like the prophets of Israel, you speak the truth to us, whether it is truth we want to hear or not. Keep talking to us, gracious Lord. Keep working with us. Keep telling us the truth about ourselves and our world because our best hope is in your truth. Keep enabling us to be prophets, speakers, and doers of the truth. Use us to do your will in this world and strengthen us when we, like you, suffer rejection and resistance. Although we are unworthy disciples of your gospel, by your grace we have hope in being much more than we could be on our own. Amen.

Prayer of Confession and Assurance

Holy God, your truth challenges us to see the reality of who we are in our sinfulness. Our thoughts are not your thoughts, nor our ways your ways. We adapt too easily to the broad way of the world rather than the narrow way of Christ. Because we fail to keep clear the difference between being loyal citizens of an earthly nation and citizens of your realm, we easily lose the perspective of Jesus, go along with the world, and worship at the wrong throne! You call us to be salt and leaven, to speak and live the gospel we confess; but we are reluctant, self-protective witnesses. Forgive, O God, our failure, to be your courageous, truth-telling and truth-living prophets. Amen.

We have received God's word of assurance through the prophet Isaiah, who declared that when we confess our sin, God will abundantly pardon. This truth has become reality for us in Jesus. We can trust it, and begin again to live in accord with God's will and purpose.

Prayer of Dedication of Gifts and Self

Commissioning God, you count on us to be bearers of the truth of your word and your love in this fear-filled world. The task is daunting and discouraging. But we would be faithful prophets, for we know the hope that

414

is in Christ, for us, and for all humanity. We bring these gifts of monies, symbols of the offering of ourselves as your truth tellers and hope givers. Amen.

Hymn of the Day
The Church of Christ, in Every Age

Jesus sent disciples out two by two, instructing them to travel light and giving them the power to heal. Lo and behold, their mission was a success! They cast out many demons, and anointed with oil many who were sick and cured them. "We have no mission but to serve," declares Fred Pratt Green in "The Church of Christ, in Every Age." Perhaps those first Christian missionaries we hear about today were driven by such an ideal. William Knapp's WARREHAM is a fine melody for this text, with a steady sense of flow to the phrases and a triple meter that captures well the stress of the words.

Children's Time: Having Faith in Someone

(Think of a time when you did not feel you could accomplish something and another person's faith in you helped you achieve it. If nothing comes to mind, try to recall an occasion that happened to someone you have heard about.) Today's Bible story is about a time Jesus went back to where he had grown up. Some of the people in the town gave him a bad time. They probably said things like: "Who does he think he is? He grew up here; he is no better than the rest of us!" It can be hard for people to accept it when someone they have known before changes – or even just grows up. The story goes on to say Jesus wasn't able to do much there, because people didn't have faith in him.

What does it mean to have faith in someone? *(Affirm responses, including to believe he or she can do something, to feel good about him or her, to know he or she is going to be successful.)* There was a time when someone had faith in me *(or someone you know. Tell the story. Include your feelings about the event as well as the facts.)*

It really makes a difference when you know someone is on your side, doesn't it! It makes you want to try to do your very best; it can give you the strength you need to do something that may be very hard. When someone has faith in us it can make a big difference. The nice thing about having an experience when someone encourages us to do our best, is that we also will feel more like having faith in someone else. When someone is worried about a test for which they have really studied and thinks they are going to fail, we can help them to believe in themselves. We can tell them they can do it and help them to relax so they will remember the answers.

Let's pray: Loving God, thank you for having faith in us and helping us to do our best, even when we are not sure we can. Help us to remember to help others have faith in themselves and to never say things that make people feel bad about themselves. We pray in Jesus' name. Amen.

The Sermon: Prophets, Santa Claus, and Flags
Scripture: Mark 6:1-13

In today's Gospel we have a not-too-unusual occurrence: Jesus has preached, at his hometown synagogue no less, and the congregation has rejected what he had to say. If you know anything about the story of Jesus, you know that rejection tended to come with the territory. One can understand perfect strangers reacting negatively to the teaching of Jesus. But these are his own family and friends. When it comes to accepting Jesus, to receiving his words and following his way, even being his own family and friends is no guarantee of a good hearing or an enthusiastic following. Then, right after this, Jesus sends out his followers. But before sending them out to do his work, he warns them: the going may get rough. Don't be surprised when people reject you because of me, he tells them. Be prepared to shake the dust off your feet and head off to another town if one town rejects you. So today's Gospel is a vivid reminder that following Jesus is not always easy.

Along the way, Jesus is forever correcting and surprising us with how odd, how very different is following than we first imagined. Jesus impresses us with how against the grain his way is when compared to our ways. Something about Jesus and his message struck hard against the received wisdom, the common sense, the universal values of his day – and of ours. His way – the gospel way to life – is narrower than we often appreciate. One reason why we get together on a weekly basis, tell these stories, and examine these texts is so that we may more clearly discern his way and see the difference between his way and our way.

A former student of mine at the divinity school was telling me that she had a rough year at her first parish. This surprised me because I heard that she had been well-received when she arrived last year. "What was it that was causing the trouble?" I asked her. "Santa Claus," she said.

"Excuse me?" I said.

"My church is in danger of running me off because of Santa Claus," she continued. "Last December, they told me that they had a tradition in the church of having Santa Claus appear at the worship service on the second Sunday in December. 'The kids just love it,' they said. 'In fact everybody loves it. It really gets us in the Christmas spirit.' I did what you told me in class," she said. "I tried to move into this carefully."

"Well, that's an interesting liturgical tradition," she said. "But I don't really believe that Santa Claus has any place in a Christian sanctuary. Most of us with young children feel like we've got such a struggle going on with Christmas, the commercialism and all, I don't think we need to do anything else to get our children any more into the Christmas spirit. Santa Claus is fine, but he is not Jesus. It's just so hard for the church to get its message across, with all the Christmas commercial hoopla, I don't think we need to be confusing things, blurring the issues, by having Santa Claus visit us at church."

Then she told me, "I think they may kill me over this!"

I personally can see her point. And I like the way she made it. One of the purposes of church is to get us together in order to keep clarifying the Christian way. We are bombarded every day by thousands of messages – mostly in the form of advertising – that proclaim a worldview, a way of living, and a system of values that are not Christian. So we get together at church and try as best we can to keep things clear. But it isn't easy, for we are always in danger of confusing our ways with his narrow way. But there are those moments when church becomes a place of clarification.

Jesus experienced rejection because his way was narrow, odd. He warned us that if we were going to be faithful to him, we ought to expect rejection as well. Indeed, if we gather as the church and there is never any dissonance, any abrasiveness about what we do, then we ought to begin to worry. We have to "test the spirits" because not all spirits are the Holy Spirit.

We open the scriptures and we ask the preacher, "Is there any word from the Lord?" because we have spent all week listening to the cacophony of other words that are not God's words.

I was once at a large conference of pastors. After the lectures, Alan Storey, a pastor from South Africa, led us in worship. Alan stood up before us, handed out the bulletins, and walked us through the service. Then, at the end of the instructions, he said quietly, "One more thing as we begin our service. Could I just say, as a visitor to your country from another place, that I wish you would consider removing the American flag from your sanctuary? I was shocked when I entered this church today and found your country's flag so prominently positioned near the altar. That would not happen in my church. My church law forbids us to have flags and other secular political paraphernalia in our services. I wish you would think about this and how this flag clashes with the symbols of our faith. Of course, I am from South Africa. And we've learned the hard way about the difference between the ways of God and the ways of the world."

We sat there in awkward silence and then went on with the service. What do you think about that? Does the American flag have a place in our Christian sanctuary? I fear a confusion of symbols.

To Christians, symbols are big. We sit here today surrounded by symbols of our faith. We take symbols seriously because we know the ways that these symbols form us. The symbols don't only speak about our deepest commitments; they form our deep commitments.

Should a flag be in church? I expect, when we hear somebody like Alan Storey, we think to ourselves that, "Well he's from South Africa. We're different. We live in a democracy. Our country is good. We're innocent."

I hope none of us would say such sentiments openly, because they are not true. Our country has blood on its hands. The souls of countless African slaves, of slaughtered Native Americans, and others would rise up and accuse us if we made such an arrogant statement about our country. Like any nation I know of, our country has blood on its hands, and is far from innocent.

Time and again in scripture, the great competitor for our allegiance to God is our allegiance to the nation. Much of the time, when Hebrew prophets condemn false gods and idolatry they're talking about the false trust we put in kings, in armies, and the mechanism of the state. It is not enough to say, "We fortunately live in a democracy where we don't have a king, where the people are king." Democracy puts us in an even more spiritually demanding situation. Once, we went to war for the king; now we go to war and kill for ourselves. The government has become our protector from the cradle to the grave, our main source of meaning, that to which we look in life for salvation.

We ask too much of the government. We sacrifice too much for the nation. Don't tell me that we shouldn't be careful about bringing the objects of national devotion into our Christian sanctuaries. Just yesterday, people in the United States celebrated the Fourth of July, the birth of our beloved nation, a nation that has been so good to so many. On the Fourth of July we celebrate our Declaration of Independence. Independence is not a biblical word. Independence is what government promises us, if we will just serve the government.

In today's Gospel Jesus gives his disciples orders and expects them to follow his instructions. As Christians, our Sunday morning goal is not independence, but rather dependence upon the will and the righteousness of God. We Christians are weirder than we often admit. I hardly ever come to this Sunday in the year, the Sunday after July 4, that I don't remember my visit, about 30 years ago, with my family to a very large church in California – a church with lots of glass and a huge TV audience. During the service we sang "America the Beautiful," "My Country 'Tis of Thee," and a lot of the songs that one might expect on a Sunday celebrating July 4. And then we came to the sermon.

The preacher at that church was away that Sunday, spreading the gospel in Hawaii, we were told. They had a guest preacher, Charles Colson. A lot of you are old enough to remember Charles Colson of Watergate fame, the trouble that he got into, and the time that he served in prison. My mother, who was sitting next to me, said in a voice loud enough to be heard by a number of people near us, "I haven't come here to church to hear some jailbird preach."

I said to her, "But he has had a conversion experience; he has given his life to Christ."

"That's what they all do when they come before the parole board," she said. At any rate, Charles Colson began to preach.

"This is quite a congregation that is arrayed before me," he said. "I wish you could see yourselves and how magnificent you look on this beautiful Southern California day. I wish all of those watching TV could see what a grand and glorious place this church is. Quite a contrast from where I preached yesterday. I preached not in this grand church, but in a little cinder block building at the Los Angeles Prison Farm. There I preached, not to this fine assembly, but to murderers, rapists, and thieves. And you do know with which group Jesus was more at home." Then he proceeded to attack us for our materialism, our greed, our insensitivity to the plight of the poor.

My dear mother leaned over to me and said, "I hope Mr. Colson is having a good time preaching here because he will never be invited back." The greatest service Christians have to render this nation is to be a critic, a visible reminder that God, not nations, rules the world; that we have a loyalty that qualifies every other loyalty. Jesus Christ is Lord, and he intends to rule, to reign, whether we like it or not.

– William H. Willimon

Hymns

Opening: Called as Partners in Christ's Service
Sermon: We Meet You, O Christ
Closing: Sent Forth by God's Blessing

July 12, 2015

7th Sunday after Pentecost (Proper 10)
RC/Pres/UCC: 15th Sunday in Ordinary Time

Lessons

Semi-continuous (SC)	Complementary (C)	Roman Catholic (RC)
2 Sam 6:1-5, 12b-19	Amos 7:7-15	Amos 7:12-15
Ps 24	Ps 85:8-13	Ps 85:9-14
Eph 1:3-14	Eph 1:3-14	Eph 1:3-14 or 1:3-10
Mk 6:14-29	Mk 6:14-29	Mk 6:7-13

Speaker's Introduction for the Lessons

Lesson 1

2 Samuel 6:1-5, 12b-19 (SC)

Dancing with exuberant abandon before the Lord, David and all the house of Israel bring the Ark of the Covenant toward its new home in Jerusalem.

Amos 7:7-15 (C); Amos 7:12-15 (RC)

Amos, who says that he is but a farmer and "no prophet, nor a prophet's son," is sent to the shrine at Bethel, the king's chapel. There his prophetic message of judgment is opposed by Amaziah, Bethel's priest.

Lesson 2

Psalm 24 (SC)

The sweeping affirmation of all creation belonging to God moves next to rightful response to such a one, joining liturgy to ethics in a seamless whole that echoes the message of the prophets.

Psalm 85:8-13 (C); Psalm 85:9-14 (RC)

These verses affirm trust that salvation remains God's purpose, and the covenant gifts of love and faithfulness, righteousness and peace will again grace the land and people.

Lesson 3
Ephesians 1:3-14 (SC/C/RC)
Here is a well-developed image of believers as God's children, as adopted through Jesus Christ and made heirs of all the promises of God's mercy.

Gospel
Mark 6:14-29 (SC/C)
The dramatic story of the execution of John the Baptizer at the birthday party of Herod comes as an interlude between the sending out of the disciples in mission and the feeding of the five thousand.
Mark 6:7-13 (RC)
Jesus calls and sends the twelve disciples, two by two, with authority to engage in mission, along with directions for the journey.

Theme
We are in God's hands, and that our great calling is the work we first saw in Christ: to reconcile all the broken things.

Thought for the Day
Paul's vision changes the way we view church, ourselves, and the world at large.

Sermon Summary
Drawn from a variety of nationalities and backgrounds, the church of Jesus Christ is a community where divisions break down and God is parent of us all.

Call to Worship
One: God has a dream, a great uniting dream where all God's people know we are one in Christ.

Many: God has a vision, a cosmic vision of reconciliation on earth and in heaven.

One: As Christ's church we are called to be bearers of the vision, dream catchers for God.

**Many: But we dimly see what God sees. We need our vision
sharpened, our minds enlightened, and our hearts enlarged.**
One: Let us be open to the moving of God among us as we sing
hymns of praise, pray, and listen for God's living word to us this
day.

Pastoral Prayer

Lord, we come to church for many reasons. We come to recover our
vision. The everydayness of life sometimes overwhelms us all. Often we
lose our purpose and our way. Speak to us, today, through the hymns,
the prayers, and the holy scripture, that we might be stirred to dream the
dreams and do the deeds you have for us. Grant us wisdom, grant us courage for the living of these days. Amen.

Prayer of Confession and Assurance

Dear God, we confess that we are far from a united Christian community.
We are a fragmented people because we have created division by the way
we regard one another in the church and in the world. We seem to have
lost your vision that delights in differences within one essential, spiritual
unity. We have committed sins of prejudice, judgment, and self-righteousness. Forgive us for failing to be the incarnation of love that Jesus exem-
plified from his birth to his death, reconciling us to you. May we thus
become reconcilers in his name. Amen.

In Christ, God made known "the forgiveness of our trespasses, according to the riches of his grace that he lavished upon us" (Eph 1:7-8).
In Christ we are made one on earth and in heaven, a forgiven people freed
to praise God together with our lips and lives. Glory to God and to Christ
Jesus!

Prayer of Dedication of Gifts and Self

Caring God, all over the world there are those of your family in desperate need this day. With you there is no distinction regarding who should
receive help, for all are worthy in your sight. It is in your Spirit that we

make our offering, committing ourselves and resources to your vision of an earth and heaven where all people are one in love and mercy, justice and kindness. Amen.

Hymn of the Day
You Are the Way

In addition to filling us in on the gruesome demise of John the Baptist, the big issue here is Jesus' identity. Herod, ever superstitious, thinks Jesus is John come back from the grave to haunt him, while his advisors guess Jesus is Elijah or some new prophet. George W. Doane's "You Are the Way," inspired by Jesus' words to Thomas, is a direct, powerful affirmation of who Jesus is. DUNDEE, with its unvaried rhythm and straightforward harmony, is the tune that best expresses Doane's text.

Children's Time: Love Can Change the World

(Have the children look at each other and at the congregation to note any differences they can identify.) We each look and sound different. We each behave and feel differently.

(Ask children to mention some ways in which we are the same.) God made us and understands us in our differences, but loves and cares for us all the same. We and all creation belong to God. God wants us to think of each other and treat each other with love, because we and all people in the world are members of God's one family.

Let's pray together: Dear God, no matter how different we are from one another, we are all your precious children, and you love us. Help us to be loving toward others too and to make your world a better place, day by day. Amen.

The Sermon: It's the Music
Scripture: Ephesians 1:3-14

Robert Fulghum, popular writer and teller of tales, shares an experience that moved him greatly. He writes that every year he spends a week in Weiser, Idaho, a tiny place that is hard to find on a map. Only 4000 people live there. Little happens in that town except once a year when it becomes the home of the Grand National Oldtime Fiddlers' Contest. On the last week in June, people descend on that little village. Fiddlers come from Pottsboro, Texas; Sapulpa, Oklahoma; Caldwell, Kansas; and some from as far away as Japan. They come to play, sing, and have a good time. He writes that once, fiddlers were pretty straight country folk. The men had very short hair, their wives stayed home and cooked, and everybody went to church on Sunday. But through the years the fiddlers' convention has changed. Long-haired hippies began to show up. People with tattoos and leather jackets came on motorcycles. And some of these strange-looking people were wonderful fiddlers.

Fulghum asked one of the old-timers what he thought about the new crowd joining them. The old man said, "I don't care who they are or how they look. If you can fiddle, you're all right with me. It's the music we make that counts." Fulghum said that under the stars, with 1000 people picking, singing, and fiddling together, he looked out on fat and skinny, young and old, hippies and straight-laced, people of just about every color. He said it was such a moving sight he came back year after year. He played his banjo next to a Weiser policeman. As they picked, the old policeman winked at him and said, "You know, sometimes the world seems like a mighty fine place" (*All I Really Need to Know I Learned in Kindergarten*).

When Paul wrote this letter to the Ephesians from a prison cell, he wanted his friends in those little house churches to capture a vision. He wanted them to see that in the middle of a fractured and divided world, there would be a church where all could come despite their very real differences. There they would find a place of safety and wholeness for all. What we find at the beginning of that letter in Ephesians 1:3-14 is really an overture of all that will follow. All the themes that we find in the six chapters of this book are embedded in these elevan verses. John Mackay has called these words "truth as melody."

Like the fiddlers in Weiser, Idaho, it was the music they made together that mattered. It made no difference who they were or how they looked. All was subsumed under the larger goal of their music.

The church was so taken with this vision it became part of the liturgy of the early church. Into their prayers, songs, and sermons the words of Ephesians can be found. They were much like the civil rights foot soldiers of the '60s who gathered in little black churches to pray and sing until they found a power that kept them going despite fear of death, loss of jobs, fire hoses, bombings, and a world that did not understand.

Paul's overture has three stanzas. These three stanzas form the vision for any real Christian community. In verses 3-6 we are given first a hymn to God. Paul knew that whatever power those little beleaguered churches possessed was not of their own doing. They would never be overwhelmed by the powers and principalities when the focus of their singing was directed toward God. It was only when they moved away from this vision, relying on their own resources that they would flounder and fail.

So the vertical dimension is primary. Israel's faith is reflected in their first prayer book, the Psalter. Around a vision of praise, lament, thanksgiving, and doxology – all addressed to God – Israel found its center. That center lifted their eyes beyond the harshness of their days, the impossibilities of their world, and they found strength to go on. And so they began their worship with God. And when they gathered to sing "Holy, Holy, Holy," something swept them up into a larger purpose than they had ever known before.

In *God's Order*, John Mackay wrote that the wonder of this music is when we see God as Father, the world is an orphanage no more. We are not left to some sort of cosmic solitariness. We are connected to one another. We are brought into the circle called family. This is what Paul saw in his great vision.

The hymn moves from the vertical to the horizontal. In verses 7-10 not only do we know this is a hymn sung in praise to God, but this is a hymn to the world as well. Paul keeps faith with John 3:16 in this stanza. God really does love the world. Heaven touches earth. This father knows and loves all his children.

Paul's vision says that in Christ we have been delivered and we have found forgiveness.

Wheeler Robinson told the story of a man who stood in the back of a sanctuary as the choir was practicing the 23rd portion of the mass: "Lamb of God that takes away the sins of the world, have mercy upon us." And he said a man came in and stood next to him, listened to the wonderful petition sung in Latin, and began to moan, again and again, "Oh, God, if only he could! If only he could!" And with that he ran out of the church. The music we make together says we can all be redeemed and forgiven. For the vision was that in Christ, not only would there be no north or south, no east or west, but more.

All things in heaven and earth are united once and for all. "He has made known to us the mystery of his will, according to his good pleasure that he set forth in Christ, as a plan for the fullness of time, to gather all things in him, things in heaven and things on earth" (Eph 1:9-10). No more pecking order. No more we and they. No more them and us, but one great fellowship of love throughout the whole world.

But even this global stanza does not end the hymn. In verses 11-14 the hymn becomes personal. Note the pronouns: "We have also obtained an inheritance, having been destined . . . we who were the first to set our hope on Christ." "You had heard the word of truth." "The gospel of your salvation." "This is the pledge of our inheritance toward redemption as God's own people." From behind bars Paul knew this gospel spoke a personal word, a word to the heart.

In the second chapter this man in prison, cut off from friends, family, and work – under sentence of death – writes a personal word that flows directly from these verses: "So then, remember that at one time you Gentiles by birth, called 'the uncircumcision' by those who are called 'the circumcision' – a physical circumcision made in the flesh by human hands – remember that you were at that time without Christ, being aliens from the commonwealth of Israel, and strangers to the covenants or promise, having no hope and without God in the world. But now in Christ Jesus you who once were far off have been brought near by the blood of Christ" (2:11-13). The words continue a few verses later, which are as beautiful an oratorio as the church has ever sung: "So then you are no longer strangers and aliens, but you are citizens with the saints and also members of the household of God" (2:19).

In *Traveling Mercies*, Anne Lamott, after years of drug and sexual addiction, suicide attempts, and great depression, tells about one Sunday when she heard the sounds of gospel music coming from a little church across the street. The building was not much to look at. It was just a little ramshackle building with a tiny cross on top. But, she said, the music forced her to stop and listen. She heard words of gospel songs she remembered from her childhood. Week after week she would come back, stand outside the doors, and listen. After many weeks she got up the courage to move to the doorway of the church and listen to the songs. The choir of five black women and one white man was making glorious music. The congregation of 30 or so seemed to radiate kindness and warmth. She began to go back about once a month, always slipping out before the sermon. She grew to love many things about the church, their care for one another, their community mission program, the way they welcomed strangers. But she writes, "It was the singing that pulled me in and split me wide open." She got the courage to walk inside, sit in the back, and let the singing envelop her. That music, she said, was breath and food. She writes,

> Something inside me that was stiff and rotting would feel soft and tender. Somehow the singing wore down all the boundaries and distinctions that kept me so isolated. Sitting there, standing with them to sing, sometimes so shaky and sick that I felt like I might tip over, I felt bigger than myself, like I was being taken care of, tricked into coming back to life.

It was always an exciting time when those little house churches received an epistle from Paul. But when those little isolated congregations received this letter from prison, they listened with more intensity than usual. The president of the congregation would open the letter and begin to read.

There was no poor mouthing or woe-is-me in this letter called Ephesians. Neither was there a Pollyanna optimism. What they heard was simply music written from the heart of an old man out of years of faith experience. It was a hymn about the father of them all. It was a hymn about a world without barriers or divisions. And most of all it was a song that touched the hearts of all those who needed a vision and a hope.

When the church sings this great song, not only does the world seem to be a mighty fine place. We begin to look at even the hard things of life, not with despair, but with eyes of grace, wonder, and faith.

–William H. Willimon

Hymns
Opening: My Life Flows On (How Can I Keep from Singing?)
Sermon: We Who Would Valiant Be
Closing: We Are Marching in the Light of God/*Siyahamba*

July 19, 2015

8th Sunday after Pentecost (Proper 11)
RC/Pres/UCC: 16th Sunday in Ordinary Time

Lessons

Semi-continuous (SC)	Complementary (C)	Roman Catholic (RC)
2 Sam 7:1-14a	Jer 23:1-6	Jer 23:1-6
Ps 89:20-37	Ps 23	Ps 23
Eph 2:11-22	Eph 2:11-22	Eph 2:13-18
Mk 6:30-34, 53-56	Mk 6:30-34, 53-56	Mk 6:30-34

Speaker's Introduction for the Lessons
Lesson 1
2 Samuel 7:1-14a (SC)

Nathan, the prophet, reveals to King David the wishes and plans of God concerning David's reign and his kingdom. David need not build a house (temple) for God. Instead, God will build a house (dynasty) for David.

Jeremiah 23:1-6 (C/RC)

Through Jeremiah, God warns the leaders of Judah who have not shepherded the people but scattered them. God promises a messianic ruler who will rule according to God's plan and restore the kingdom.

Lesson 2
Psalm 89:20-37 (SC)

This portion of the psalm provides an extended explication of the Davidic covenant – a covenant that, in the verses following these, is sorely longed for.

Psalm 23 (C/RC)

The so-called shepherd psalm, traditionally attributed to David, celebrates trust in God's providence and leading – even in shadowed places and among enemies.

Lesson 3
Ephesians 2:11-22 (SC/C); Ephesians 2:13-18 (RC)
Old divisions between Jews and Gentiles have been bridged through Christ. Because of Christ, both groups are also reconciled to God. All Christians are being built into a holy temple and a dwelling place for God.

Gospel
Mark 6:30-34, 53-56 (SC/C); Mark 6:30-34 (RC)
Mark's story of Jesus' welcome to the disciples as they returned from their mission of healing and teaching, followed by the narrative of the crowd seeking Jesus and the miraculous feeding.

Theme
The church is a new family, formed, called, built by God out of formerly feuding and fractured humanity.

Thought for the Day
If you are here in church today, following Jesus, it is because you have been put there by God in Christ.

Sermon Summary
From those who were divided – Jews and Gentiles – a new household has been formed, a new people called the church. To be in the church is to be a member of an alternative community, a new people with values, views, and virtues different from the world in order that the world, through Christ, might be saved from itself.

Call to Worship
One: We are a new creation of God, built upon the faithfulness of those who have gone before, with Christ as head and cornerstone.

Many: We are a people built by God and being built, a people reconciled and being reconciled, a people yet becoming who God in the Spirit enables us to be.

One: Let us be at peace; let us be in unity, as we rejoice and give thanks for the inheritance we share by adoption.

Pastoral Prayer

Lord, once we were no people, diverse, separated, walled off from one another. Now, by the great mercy of Jesus Christ, we have been brought together in the church. Old boundaries, old walls have been overcome, bridged. We, who were once strangers, have become family.

Help us, O Lord, in our life together, to demonstrate to a fractured and hurting world that Jesus really makes possible the existence of a people who are able to live by their convictions, who are able to live as sisters and brothers in all that we do and say. To the glory of your name. Amen.

Prayer of Confession and Assurance

Creating and re-creating God, we ask this day for your forgiveness when in pride we forget we are your building, your household, your children called, chosen, included, and grafted by love and grace into your family. We credit ourselves with much spiritual knowledge and wisdom as if by our own choosing and doing, our own effort and expertise we form the church, when the truth is that apart from you we are nothing, can do nothing. We confess also that within the new household of your making, we have yet to be whom you intend. We have yet to love and live in the peace and harmony you desire, as sisters and brothers in your family. Forgive us, we pray, and cleanse us from the residue of self-trust, self-will, and self-serving we have brought with us from the world. May we be a contrite, expectant people, continually made new by grace. Amen.

We who were once far off have been brought near in Christ, who by his sacrifice made us no longer strangers but friends. God has forgiven us of our sin and embraces us as beloved children; we are adopted in love into a glorious new family, the church of Jesus Christ.

Prayer of Dedication of Gifts and Self

Loving God, you have cared to make us your family, cared to show us your love, given us your guidance, and provided for us according to our need. We make this offering in gratitude and pray that you use us and these gifts of your church today to further the gathering, redeeming work of Christ in the world. Amen.

Hymn of the Day
Jesus Christ, May Grateful Hymns Be Rising

We read today of Jesus' concern for the large crowds that had gathered to hear him. Despite the weariness he and the disciples feel, their compassion for the sick and weary who come to them overcomes the desire for a private retreat. Gratitude for mercies like those described partially motivated Bradford W. Gray (1898-1991) to compose this hymn about the crowds in urban areas for a 1954 Methodist conference. The poetry asks God for the strength to serve the needs of those who come to our churches, and to move us with the mercy of Christ for all whom we serve. CHARTERHOUSE by David Evans (1874-1848) was Gray's choice and has been paired with the text since first published.

Children's Time: The Church Is a Family

What is a family? People who live together? Not always. People who love each other in a special way? Yes. We each have a family into which we were born as a human being, and by which we were named.

But we are also members of another family – God's family. No matter what our human family background, or the color of our skin, or our age, or whether we are male or female, sick or well, we are one family called the church. God has made this so. Our love for each other and the way we speak and act tells the world who we are.

Let's pray: Thank you, God, for making us family through your great love. Amen.

The Sermon: The New Household
Scripture: Ephesians 2:11-22

They can't find the cornerstone for the United States Capitol. There was a great dedication ceremony in the early 19th century when construction of the Capitol began. But over the years, the cornerstone sank, covered by gathering debris of the ages. Now, it can't be located. They had a commission charged with digging here and there in order to find it. The cornerstone represents the history and dedication of the building, a sign and symbol of its purpose. We must not lose sight of our cornerstone, because it helps us to know why we are here. Take that as a parable on our text for this morning.

In Ephesians 2:19-22 Paul writes: "So then you are no longer strangers and aliens, but you are citizens with the saints and also members of the household of God, built upon the foundation of the apostles and prophets, with Christ Jesus himself as the cornerstone. In him the whole structure is joined together and grows into a holy temple in the Lord; in whom you also are built together spiritually into a dwelling place for God."

You can imagine what these words meant to those who first heard them, these Gentiles, Gentiles who had no part in the promises of God to Israel.

In our church youth group when I was growing up, I remember the question was often, "Will the Jews be saved?" That question is not really a biblical, New Testament question. Romans 11:29 is clear: the gifts and the calling of God are irrevocable. God has made a promise to preserve and to love Israel and God keeps God's promises.

No, the big New Testament question is: "Will the Gentiles be saved?" What about those who do not have the scriptures, who know nothing of the words of the prophets, the promises of God to Israel? What about them? What about us?

Yes, says Ephesians, by an amazing act of God in Christ, the promises of God to Israel are brought even to the Gentiles. Thus the writer to the Ephesians says in 1:5 that we outsiders, we Gentiles, have been destined by God "for adoption." Through grace "that he lavished on us" (1:8). What a great phrase; we have been brought close to God through Christ.

We can only be in God's family through adoption. No one comes in here naturally; Christians are made, not born (said early church leader Tertullian).

We, who weren't in the family, have "obtained an inheritance." We weren't in the will, Gentiles as we are. Now, we're heirs to a fortune. By the "seal" of the Holy Spirit we are marked as "God's own people" (Eph 1:11, 13, 14).

In chapter 2 Paul continues, "Remember that you were at that time without Christ, being aliens from the commonwealth of Israel, and strangers to the covenants of promise, having no hope and without God in the world." You were (in a great phrase) "far off." Now we're close, the wall is down (2:12, 13, 14).

Which brings us to the scripture that is our word for this Sunday.

The writer uses an architectural metaphor. Note that the verbs are passive. He doesn't say, "You decided to join the church." The writer says, you were "built," you were "joined together," you were "built together spiritually" (2:22). Your relationship to this new family is not something you do. It's something done to you: grace.

Note that the passage begins with political talk – talk of aliens, citizens. These people have exchanged their citizenship in one country for that of a new country. If you thought that being a Christian is something that comes naturally, the natural, normal thing to do, think again. Nobody comes in here by birth. You have to be adopted, transferred into, built into this household.

I think that right there, this text seems most strange to us.

My parents never worried about whether I would grow up Christian. It was the natural, normal thing to be Christian. I woke up a few years ago and realized that, whether my parents were justified in believing that, no one believes that today. The world in which Christianity was normal and natural has ended. I find among us a new awareness that our children will not necessarily grow up into this faith.

Being Christian is no longer the normal, natural thing to be. Our children spend up to 30 hours every week in front of a screen. They are in church a maximum of a couple of hours per week. When watching television, texting, posting, posing for selfies and more, they are being bombarded with images of success, of the good life, of the goal of humanity that may be at great variance with how the Christian faith defines these matters. Suddenly the church, and its teaching, witness, worship, and work become important as a way of instilling in us and our young a way counter to the world's ways.

Years ago, a Catholic theologian spoke of "anonymous Christians," people who were good and sincere, but who did not formally embrace the Christian faith. They were sort of Christians at-large, anonymous Christians, even though they did not know that was who they were.

They may have been good people, but they were not Christians. To be a Christian is to be someone who self-consciously follows, or is attempting to follow, the way of Christ; someone who is attempting to let the story of Christ form and guide his or her life.

A church without boundaries, with no borders, without distinctive marks is hardly a church. Thus today's scripture from Ephesians speaks of the church as a building, a house, a place. Perhaps there was a time when it was enough, in our culture, to be merely sincere, to have a warm feeling in your heart at the mention of religion, to try to do the best that you could in life, in a wholesome sort of way.

Now, things have changed. We are beginning to feel, as North American Christians, like aliens, like missionaries in the very society that we thought we had created.

In such a time, this text from Ephesians begins to make sense again. The church is an identifiable new family. It is bigger than that which we normally call "family," for it is made up of all those diverse people whom Jesus has called to follow him. Think of being a Christian as if you are taken out of your human family and made a member of the family of God, the "household of faith" as the writers calls us. It's a house with Christ as its cornerstone, that stone upon which the whole house is built, that foundation upon which everything else rests.

I hope that you take comfort in this. Too often we are guilty of presenting the Christian faith as something that we do or decide. Listen to us when we talk of "when I gave my life to Christ," "when I asked Jesus to come into my heart." It's all about me, my, myself.

But note the passage from Ephesians speaks of us in the passive tense and God in the active voice. It is God who has called us here. God made a decision for us. God has built us as parts of this new household. God has broken down the dividing walls between women and men, between the races, and the ages, and social classes. If you are here in church today, following Jesus, it is because you have been put there by God in Christ.

I say this is a comfort because it reminds me that, when all is said and done, my relationship to Christ is – thank goodness – not just a matter of what I feel or do or say, but what God in Christ, through the church, has done. I don't always feel, act, or speak like a Christian, but that's not the point. The point is that I have been called forth to be part of this strange, wonderful, new, divine experiment in human family called "church."

Haven't you found this true yourself? How many Sundays have you come here empty, not really believing anything for sure? Then, through the music, or the reading of scripture, or the singing of hymns, or maybe even the sermon, you have felt faith growing strong in you?

I was once asked, "Do you think it is okay to say the words of the creed, even when you have trouble with some of the things that it says?"

It is not your creed; it is the faith of the church. Sometimes, when we say the creed, you are anything but sure of your faith. But the great thing is that it isn't your creed. On those Sundays, the church is saying it with you, for you, until that time when you are able to say it for yourself.

Sometimes we pray a prayer of confession here. You may not feel like confessing your sin. Fine. We'll do it for you. We'll confess and perhaps you will sense our confession as your confession, and you will join us in Christian honesty about sin. This is what was meant by the church in saying, long ago, that the church was a "means of grace." By that we meant that the church was a human means through which God gets to us and does for us that which we could not do on our own.

In such moments, you give thanks to God that you were fortunate enough to have been invited, called, built, joined into this household. You have not been left on your own, so far as your faith is concerned. You're part of the family, the family of God called church.

People, we are up against something! And you are right to expect the church to give you the skills, the insights you need to resist the world and its lures.

So today we hear, "You are no longer aliens" – alienated from God. But some of you are learning today that by being close to God, you are aliens from this society, at odds with some of this culture's dominant values. You have been joined to a new family, a new household.

With Christ as our cornerstone, we are a new people, a visible building for all the world to see that Jesus makes possible a viable, visible alternative to the way the world gathers people, a new people by water and the word. Amen.

–William H. Willimon

Hymns
Opening: Sing Praise to God, Our Highest Good (Who Reigns Above)
Sermon: Like a Tree Beside the Waters
Closing: We Are Your People

July 26, 2015

9th Sunday after Pentecost (Proper 12)
RC/Pres/UCC: 17th Sunday in Ordinary Time

Lessons

Semi-continuous (SC)	Complementary (C)	Roman Catholic (RC)
2 Sam 11:1-15	2 Kgs 4:42-44	2 Kgs 4:42-44
Ps 14	Ps 145:10-18	Ps 145:10-11, 15-18
Eph 3:14-21	Eph 3:14-21	Eph 4:1-6
Jn 6:1-21	Jn 6:1-21	Jn 6:1-15

Speaker's Introduction for the Lessons
Lesson 1
2 Samuel 11:1-15 (SC)

> King David schemes to have Uriah killed so that he can take his wife as his own.

2 Kings 4:42-44 (C/RC)

> Elisha uses a little food to feed many hungry people.

Lesson 2
Psalm 14 (SC)

> The psalmist condemns the folly of conceiving a creation without a creator. Such ones can make mischief, but they will ultimately come up short – for God sides with the poor and the righteous.

Psalm 145:10-18 (C); Psalm 145:10-11, 15-18 (RC)

> This last of the acrostic psalms proclaims an A to Z compendium of God's gracious deeds and character, with these verses in particular rendering thanks for God's faithfulness, providence, justice, and availability.

Lesson 3
Ephesians 3:14-21 (SC/C)

> The writer to the Ephesians prays that these new Christians might "have the power to comprehend . . . the breadth and length and height and depth" of the love of Christ.

Ephesians 4:1-6 (RC)

The writer of Ephesians urges the church and its members to live in ways worthy of the call of Christ.

Gospel
John 6:1-21 (SC/C); John 6:1-15 (RC)

A large crowd follows Jesus, attracted by his powerful signs. Their interruption of retreat with need occasions a miraculous sign of Jesus' power and mission.

Theme

The risen Christ comes among us, not simply to meet our needs but to rearrange them in order to reveal himself to us.

Thought for the Day

We live in a society that encourages us to put ourselves at the center of our world. Yet, church is where we gather to put Jesus at the center.

Sermon Summary

In church, sometimes we get more than what we were looking for. We get the Christ, the one who is looking for us that he might call us, change us, transform us.

Call to Worship

One: Paul said that God made all nations to inhabit the whole earth, and he allotted the times of their existence and the boundaries of the places where they would live, so that they would search for God and find him – though indeed he is not far from each one of us.

Many: For in him we live and move and have our being. For we too are his offspring.

One: Let us together seek God, the divine creator of us all, and worship the Lord with true devotion.

Pastoral Prayer

Lord, we come with so many needs. Some among us are sick and in pain or love someone who is sick and in pain. We have tough decisions to make and come seeking help with those decisions. Our families are not what they ought to be, and we need help. We have so many needs. Yet amid all of our questions, our pains, and our tribulations we have one great need: to be near you, to know your will for our lives, to love you as we ought. Come near to us, Lord. Speak to us, even when what you have to say to us is different from what we expected. Be with us. That is our greatest desire. Amen.

Prayer of Confession and Assurance

Lord Jesus, as your followers, we know you care about the needs of all who look to you for help, about all who suffer in body, heart, mind, or spirit; you care about us. But we confess that, like the crowd around you, we sometimes follow because of what we want you to do for us, not that we may know and respond to what you want us to do for you. And when in your wisdom we are not given what we think we need, not healed or helped as we expect, our faith grows dim. Worthy as every true need is, we confess how often we fail to seek first your will, to wait silently and receptively before you, fully exposed to your Spirit. Forgive us our sin, we pray. Amen.

Jesus has promised that when we seek with all our hearts, we will find him for whom we look. When we sincerely confess our sins and desire to live a new life, we are enabled to hear the word of forgiveness Christ brings. We are freed from guilt, and become new creations by grace.

Prayer of Dedication of Gifts and Self

Caring God, we are making this offering because we have been touched by your compassion and challenged to give of ourselves for the meeting of others' needs; whether of soul or body. Receive and bless these, our gifts, that the poor may be assisted, the sick attended, the oppressed freed; that those who do not know Christ find in him the eternal answer to their longing. Amen.

Hymn of the Day
You Satisfy the Hungry Heart

In the symbol-rich world of John's Gospel, it's impossible to miss the eucharistic connotations in today's reading. There were only five barley loaves and two fish to feed 5000 people on that mountain, yet the meal lasted until everyone was satisfied. Omer Westendorf's "You Satisfy the Hungry Heart," set to Robert Kreutz's BICENTENNIAL, is a beautiful choice for this text. As John's Gospel does, Westendorf and Kreutz's hymn makes clear that Jesus' meal is meant to alleviate much more than physical hunger. This is a deeply satisfying hymn deserving wider usage.

Children's Time: Following Jesus' Way

(Before worship starts, hide a small but unusual object somewhere near the space where you will talk with the children; for example, a large button.)
Who has played the old game Hide the Button or a version of it? The one who does the looking may be guided toward where the small object is hidden by another who helps the searcher find it by saying, "Getting warmer or cooler, hotter or colder." *(Play a short version of this game.)*
We come to church looking for Jesus our Lord, our teacher, and our friend. Our church teachers, ministers, and friends help us find the one we are looking for, and they help us to grow to love Jesus more and more, and to learn how to be obedient followers of God's way.

Let's pray together: Dear Jesus, help us to be followers of your way. And when we get lost, remind us that we can ask for help. Amen.

The Sermon: What Are You Looking For?
Scripture: John 6:1-21

"When Jesus realized that they were about to come and take him by force to make him king, he withdrew again to the mountain by himself" (Jn 6:15).

Believe it or not, we spend a fair amount of effort selecting the hymns that we sing on Sunday morning. We try to key the hymns to the assigned scripture lessons for the day, the season of the church year. But we also, believe it or not, take into account what you like in your hymns. We ask ourselves, "Do they want to sing this hymn?" It makes a big difference what sort of music you like. I must say, that is probably one main reason why some hymns are selected for singing on Sunday: Does the congregation like this hymn?

While that's a fair question, isn't it interesting that we rarely ask an even more basic question: Does God like this hymn?

Of course, that's a frightening question; frightening not only because there are bound to be many answers, many of them conflicting, but also because it is such a basic question. And it's frightening because the scriptures note that Jesus drove away about as many people as he attracted. Jesus obviously based his ministry on more substantial questions than, "Do the people like what I have to say?"

This brings me to today's scripture from John. It's a story about Jesus, but first it is a story about a crowd. "A large crowd kept following him," says John (v. 2). Can there be a surer sign of success than this? Who can argue with numbers? Look at the bottom line – a large crowd. Jesus has become popular.

Then John tells us why they were following Jesus. "They saw the signs that he was doing for the sick" (v. 2). Jesus has healed the hurting multitudes. If there is one indisputable, uncontested good that we have, it is health. Great crowds are following Jesus because they see his signs. He heals them. He meets their needs.

Curiously, Jesus does not continue to meet their needs. Next verse: "Jesus went up the mountain and sat down there with his disciples" (v. 3). Even a dedicated do-gooder like Jesus needs a break, a temporary respite from meeting people's needs.

Jesus looks up from his mountain retreat and "saw a large crowd coming toward him" (v. 5). Having a bit of fun with Philip, Jesus asks, "Philip, how much money do you think it would take to cater a meal for such a crowd?"

Philip replies that six months' wages might provide a snack for them, but not much. A kid is found who has a few loaves and a couple of fish. Jesus commands the people to sit. He takes the lad's food, gives thanks, and they all eat their fill. Jesus is the compassionate one who feeds the hungry, hurting multitudes.

Now, you've probably already heard that sermon. Jesus is the compassionate one who meets our needs. And after all, isn't that why we're here? We are here hoping to have our needs met by Jesus.

Please note, however, that this story does not end with Jesus' feeding of the multitudes. The people are naturally impressed. "This Jesus must be quite a prophet of God who has come into the world!" they exclaim. Surely Jesus is gratified by their exclamation. At last, they appear to have gotten the point. After so much rejection, at last the people see who Jesus is and proclaim him Lord. At last, the Jesus movement is getting somewhere.

No. Jesus rejects their acclamation. Next verse: "When Jesus realized that they were about to come and take him by force to make him king, he withdrew again to the mountain by himself" (v. 15).

That's curious. Right at the point when people have at last accepted Jesus, have acclaimed him Lord, he nervously withdraws, departs the crowd to be alone.

Why? Why did he withdraw precisely at the point when his coronation was being arranged?

The people need bread. Jesus has given them bread. They acclaim him as king. What else could Jesus want?

Do you remember, at the beginning of Jesus' ministry, how he was tempted in the wilderness? Satan met Jesus and offered him this world and heaven too. "Make stones into bread," said Satan. Jesus refused.

Isn't bread good? Isn't feeding the hungry self-evidently good? Why did Jesus refuse, and why, when he did feed people, was he so put off by their calling him king?

Something in Jesus recognized that he could not meet the needs of so many people who were clamoring after him without at the same time denying who he was called by God to be. In the wilderness, Satan tried to transform Jesus into a wonder worker. Jesus refused. Now, Jesus has given bread and when the grateful crowds attempt to crown him king, Jesus withdraws. When the crowds find him the next day, Jesus rebukes them for caring only about their bellies. They ask for a sign from Jesus, perhaps hoping for another free meal. But Jesus refuses, and launches instead into his famous "bread of life" discourse, where he identifies himself with what they truly need. Many of his disciples say, "This teaching is difficult," and many of them no longer follow Jesus after he stops giving them bread but now says that he is their "bread from heaven" (v. 60).

Jesus refused to do for the crowds what they wanted, as if to do so would be forsaking his vocation. "Jesus, what will you do for us?" must be subsequent to the prior question, "Jesus, who are you and what is your mission?"

I confess that I think most of us show up at church to get help making it through the week, to obtain a sense of inner peace, to receive guidance in making difficult decisions that are before us. Yet note that this story, which at first seems to be about us, before it is done is a story about Jesus. We come to church thinking mostly about ourselves, but then the scripture talks mostly about God.

That's why I think this story is told to us. When will we ever learn? Christianity, following Jesus, is not merely another helpful, means of helping us get what we want. Rather, following Jesus is the means whereby God gets what God wants. Jesus cannot be enlisted as another helpful therapeutic device to enable us to get what we want before we meet Jesus. The gospel implies that we do not know what we want, what we need before we meet Jesus. How well this was understood by the atheist Nietzsche:

> Christianity is a system, a whole view of things, thought out together. By breaking one main concept out of it, the faith in God, one breaks the whole: Nothing necessarily remains in one's hands. Christianity presupposes that man does not know, cannot know what is good for him, what evil; he believes in God, who alone knows it (quoted by Kenneson and Street, *The Selling of the Church*).

I once heard William Sloane Coffin say that he did not know how you attracted people to the gospel by appealing to their essentially selfish needs and then ended up offering them the unselfish gospel of Jesus.

John says that Jesus performed a great miracle, feeding hungry people, but not so much a miracle as a sign, something that points beyond itself to something greater and more important than the sign. The bread blessed and given for the people was a sign that God was among them, not among them as fulfillment of all their hearts' desires, but present as Jesus.

This God was even greater than their hunger. This God was there to be worshiped, to be obeyed, to be followed, even when the following did not appear to meet their needs.

Let us listen and learn.

– William H. Willimon

Hymns
Opening: I Come with Joy
Sermon: Come and Find the Quiet Center
Closing: Let All Things Now Living

Monthly Prayers for Church Meetings

by Charles Somervill

These 12 prayer devotionals, with a time for celebrations and concerns, are intended for beginning and ending your church meetings with prayer. They take about five minutes and follow the church year.

August 2014
Opening Prayer
God of life and love, it is good to be here together. You give us the gift of fellowship that we may celebrate with one another, but we often are preoccupied with other matters. Calm our hearts now that we might find the peace of your new world and discover our purpose within Christ service. Amen.

Bible Reading: Matthew 14:22-33

A Time to Share Celebrations and Concerns
(Ask those present) As we begin, are there any celebrations you want us to know about? *(Pause.)* How about any needs or concerns you would like to share? *(Pause again; then begin the prayer.)*

Prayers for Needs or Concerns
Let us take a moment for silent prayer. *(Silence, then continue.)* God of all creation, we thank you that you have shared your image and vision with us. We confess that sometimes as we see the mounting storms of life, we wonder if we are up to the task. We witness the misery and pain of others and look for a quiet harbor to shut out their voices. Yet you call us out and set our feet in your path so that the needs and concerns of others may become ours. Forgive us when we falter and guide us with your Spirit that we may once again walk with you and share your mission. In Jesus' name we pray. Amen.

(The meeting may now be called to order.)

Prayer of Adjournment and Lord's Prayer

At day's end, we must place our hands in yours, O God. We have no other way to turn. You have the power to transform our lives and to put your Spirit within us. Send us out as your disciples remembering the manner of prayer that Jesus taught, saying, "Our Father . . ."

September 2014
Opening Prayer
Forgiving God, we open our meeting focused on how we are summoned together in Christ. Take away the sharp edges of disagreement that may sometimes arise among us. Help us to see each other as bearers of your grace sharing in your mission. Move us toward the gracious fellowship that we treasure in Jesus Christ. Amen.

Bible Reading: Matthew 18:15-20

A Time to Share Celebrations and Concerns
(*Ask those present*) As we begin, are there any celebrations that you would like others to know about? (*Pause.*) How about any needs or concerns you would like to share? (*Pause again, then begin the prayer.*)

Prayers for Needs and Concerns
Let us take a moment for silent prayer. (*Silence, then continue.*) God of fellowship and reconciliation, we thank you for those closest to us, for family that extends beyond our homes to those in this room and in our congregation. Even so, we realize how this very closeness leaves us vulnerable to one another. We often suffer more hurt from friends and other Christians than from strangers. At those times, we are tempted to withdraw from fellowship and go our separate ways. But then we remember how the disciples you chose also experienced conflict with each other. By your grace, they reclaimed and strengthened their fellowship. Make it so with us now. Give us the spirit of reconciliation and the joy of ministering to the needs and concerns of others within and without your church. We ask this through Jesus Christ who makes us one. Amen.

(The meeting may now be called to order.)

Prayer of Adjournment and Lord's Prayer
O God, as we leave this room move us beyond a passive life of doing no harm to actively seeking your ways of peacemaking. Remind us once again of how we are to live as citizens of your world in the prayer that Jesus taught us, saying, "Our Father . . ."

October 2014
Opening Prayer
God, give us courage and strength not fashioned from our own convictions but grounded in your grace. We know that we possess only partial knowledge and each of us falls short of doing your will. --But in this meeting grant us your Spirit so that our deliberations may be based less on group consensus and more on Christ's leading. We pray as always that the same mind that was in Christ Jesus may be in us also. Amen.

Bible Reading: Matthew 22:15-21

A Time to Share Celebrations and Concerns
(*Ask those present*) As we begin, are there any celebrations that you would like others to know about? (*Pause.*) How about any needs or concerns you would like to share? (*Pause again, then begin the prayer.*)

Prayers for Needs and Concerns
Let us take a moment for silent prayer. (*Silence, then continue.*) Great God, we thank you that you have placed us in your hands and allowed us to come to you in prayer even with questions and doubts. Jesus, we look at you and wonder about our priorities. You call us to pick up our cross and follow you. We know that you cared about nation and family. You wept over Jerusalem who refused your care. You commended the care of your mother to an apostle even as you were dying. And yet when we hear your words of forgiveness from the cross, we discover that your grace is more than a priority but an embodiment of who you are. As your disciples we realize that it is not nation and family but your cross that defines who we are. Fill us now with your Spirit so that our prayers may go beyond our priorities. Lead us into a grace-filled life involved in the lives of those in need just as your cross joins our lives with yours. Amen.

(The meeting may now be called to order.)

Prayer of Adjournment and Lord's Prayer
Pull us together, God of grace, that we may leave this meeting with each of us seeking your wisdom. Give us patience and forbearance and deliver us from pride and arrogance. Help us to be Christians who not only meet together but also rejoice in the love that unites us. Keep us always in the peace of Christ who brings us together in prayer saying "Our Father . . ."

November 2014
Opening Prayer
God of all, as your gathered disciples we commit ourselves to you before all other loyalties. Refresh us now and alert us to your presence that we may serve you gladly. Channel us through your Spirit so that we may be attuned to the mission for which you have called us. Amen.

Bible Reading: Matthew 25:31-40

A Time to Share Celebrations and Concerns
(*Ask those present*) As we begin, are there any celebrations that you would like others to know about? (*Pause.*) How about any needs or concerns you would like to share? (*Pause again, then begin the prayer.*)

Prayers for Needs and Concerns
Let us take a moment for silent prayer. (*Silence, then continue.*) Thank you. God, for calling us to active service so that we may be keepers and caretakers of one another. Enlarge our compassion to those strangers we see in need of our assistance. Open our hands and not just our hearts to the hungry, to those in prison, to the ones suffering illness or death, and to the desperately lonely and friendless. We give you praise for ministering to us in times of crisis. Help us to remember what our ministry through Christ can do as we pass it on to others. Amen.

(*The meeting may now be called to order.*)

Prayer of Adjournment and Lord's Prayer
O God, as we leave this place we ask that the Spirit of Christ and Christ's words may be at work in our lives. Prod us with your Spirit to go beyond our comfort zone and become actively engaged in alleviating poverty and injustice. We ask this in Jesus Christ who has taught us to pray saying, "Our Father . . ."

December 2014
Opening Prayer

Wondrous God, as we meet together, we celebrate the very special time and place that you chose for revealing yourself in Jesus. Thank you for the inspiration of Christmas and the generous spirit of this season. Guide us into your presence that we may know the joy of following your star and doing your bidding. Amen.

Bible Reading: Luke 2:8-14

A Time to Share Celebrations and Concerns

(*Ask those present*) As we begin, are there any celebrations that you want to share? (*Pause.*) How about any needs or concerns you would like to mention? (*Pause again, then begin the prayer.*)

Prayers for Needs and Concerns

Let us take a moment for silent prayer. (*Silence, then continue.*) Most gracious, good, and loving God, we praise you for coming not only to the wise ones of the East but also to lowly shepherds in the fields. You filled their ears with the singing of angels and you bless us even today with the sounds of Christmas. Help us to capture the meaning of peace and goodwill and to share it with those in need. Open our purses and pocketbooks to those without shelter, to the homeless, and to those lacking the means to get by. Bless those who are suffering from illness, the death of a loved one, or loss of hope. As you have given us the spirit of Christmas, we commit ourselves to living in Christ and singing your praises throughout the year. Amen.

(The meeting may now be called to order.)

Prayer of Adjournment and Lord's Prayer

O God, sometimes in this harried time with the noise of shopping malls and music celebrating little but reindeers and snow, we lose sight of the real Christmas. As we leave this meeting, bring us back to the manger and rekindle our spirits so that once again we may kneel in worship and adoration of the Christ child. We ask this in Jesus Christ who has taught us to pray saying, "Our Father . . ."

January 2015
Opening Prayer

God of forgiveness and renewal, we look again for a fresh start in this new year as we gather together. Refill us with your Spirit so that what we do now may reflect your will and purpose. Move us beyond our lack of faith and slowness of heart to an eager anticipation of what we can do in this time and place through Christ who strengthens us. Amen.

Bible Reading: Mark 1:14-20

A Time to Share Celebrations and Concerns

(*Ask those present*) As we begin, are there any celebrations you want to share? (*Pause.*) How about any needs or concerns you would like to mention? (*Pause again, then begin the prayer.*)

Prayers for Needs and Concerns

Let us take a moment for silent prayer. (*Silence, then continue.*) God of all worlds that are, we discover you once again on the other side of our Christmas celebrations. You remind us to leave behind the trash of our misdeeds and immediately follow you. In your pathway we are grateful for new beginnings through your forgiveness and guidance. We ask that you show us opportunities for helping others we may have turned away from in the year gone by. Through your Spirit open our hands and our hearts to those afflicted from illness, loss, poverty, or their own misjudgments. Keep us from arrogance that assumes we are morally better from the least of these for whom we pray. Re-create us in the same mind that was in Christ Jesus. Amen.

(The meeting may now be called to order.)

Prayer of Adjournment and Lord's Prayer

O God, you are with us in our comings and goings, in our successes and failures. As we depart from this meeting, we know that in your loving persistence you are not through with us yet. Keep us in the thoughts and prayers of one another in that same spirit of prayer Jesus taught us saying, "Our Father . . ."

February 2015
Opening Prayer

Gracious God, we open our meeting with prayers for our church. In this season of repentance and restoration, bring us together so that we may truly be one even as you and the Father are one. Release us from the distractions of hidden agendas, past hurts, and resentments so that we may joyfully claim you as our common Savior and follow together as your disciples. Amen.

Bible Reading: Mark 1:9-15

A Time to Share Celebrations and Concerns

(*Ask those present*) As we begin, are there any celebrations you want to share? (*Pause.*) How about any needs or concerns you would like to mention? (*Pause again, then begin the prayer.*)

Prayers for Needs and Concerns

Let us take a moment for silent prayer. (*Silence, then continue.*) Forgiving God, you take us back when we don't deserve it. You care for us even when we have ceased caring about ourselves and others. Refresh us and re-create your Spirit within us. Sharpen our focus so that we see beyond ourselves. Give us the vision of a grace-filled life that in gratitude provides the means and nurture for those suffering in poverty, loss of direction, and of purpose. Increase our love of benevolence and make us advocates of our church's participation in programs beyond its doors for those in need. As you spoke in defense of us while we were yet sinners, let us do so for others in Jesus' name. Amen.

(*The meeting may now be called to order.*)

Prayer of Adjournment and Lord's Prayer

As we approach the Lenten season we realize more than ever how your cross draws us to you. Give us your blessing as we depart from this meeting. Remind us that we are not alone but have fellowship with you and each other. Unite us in that same prayer that Jesus taught us, saying, "Our Father . . ."

March 2015
Opening Prayer

O God, we have looked at our calendars and watches and cell phones and we are aware that the time has come for this meeting. We thank you that you are already here ahead of us ready to assist and bless us in the work of your church. During this hour, make us mindful of how we may serve you so that our lives may be synchronized with your will and purpose. In Jesus' name we pray. Amen.

Bible Reading: John 12:20-23

A Time to Share Celebrations and Concerns

(*Ask those present*) As we begin, are there any celebrations you want to share? (*Pause.*) How about any needs or concerns you would like to mention? (*Pause again, then begin the prayer.*)

Prayers for Needs and Concerns

Let us take a moment for silent prayer. (*Silence, then continue.*) Gracious God, you know how we are. We waited for the crowds to come at Christmas. We are waiting again for Easter. And then we wonder where the crowds went. We wait for the return of younger adults and the cheerful sounds of their children. In a sea of gray, we wait for the passing of those in our older generation. We despair in our waiting. But then we hear of Christians in far off nations who eagerly fill their churches and willingly give up their lives for Christ. We see you at work and once again hear your call of discipleship. Make it so with us today that we may go about your business and not be weary of well-doing. In the Easter songs of resurrection, take away our sad time of waiting and renew a right spirit within us. Amen.

(*The meeting may now be called to order.*)

Prayer of Adjournment and Lord's Prayer

Loving God, thank you for the experience of your presence and the gift of friendship with you and one another. Enrich our lives with your grace and grant us the same patience and understanding that Christ made known to us. As we leave this meeting, we commit ourselves to daily prayer in the same manner Jesus taught us, saying, "Our Father . . ."

April 2015
Opening Prayer

Breathe on our gathering, God, with your fresh Spirit. Set us in the direction of your choosing as we discover you anew in our daily walks. Open us to the witness of each other that we may grow stronger as the body of Christ. Help us this day to see new opportunities for serving you in your church and community. Amen.

Bible Reading: Luke 24:35-49

A Time to Share Celebrations and Concerns

(*Ask those present*) As we begin, are there any celebrations you want to share? (*Pause.*) How about any needs or concerns you would like to mention? (*Pause again, then begin the prayer.*)

Prayers for Needs and Concerns

Let us take a moment for silent prayer. (*Silence, then continue.*) Thank you, God, for the seven Sundays of Eastertide that continue with the joy of the resurrection and end with the reminder at Pentecost that we are not alone. In fact, we thank you for those early Christians who chose Sunday to remind us always of the first day of resurrection. Forgive us for the Sundays we have spent without joy ignoring the precious gift of your Son. With your redemption, gracious God, we commit ourselves as Christ's disciples to go forth proclaiming your word, seeking the lost and ministering to those who are suffering from hunger, lack of shelter, illness, or despair. Empower us now with your Spirit to actively engage ourselves in those things for which we pray. Amen.

(The meeting may now be called to order.)

Prayer of Adjournment and Lord's Prayer

Your power and grace enable us not only as a fellowship but also as individuals serving you throughout the week. We leave with gratitude for opening up your kingdom and revealing yourself in Christ. We pray that we may faithfully continue his work in our congregation through prayer and supplication as he has taught us, saying, "Our Father . . ."

May 2015
Opening Prayer

As we come together, God of all, put a new song within us and move us in a powerful way to proclaim your love in our witness. Set aside our trivial pursuit of status and the glittering things of this world that distract us. Create us anew in your image and guide our feet on your path as Christ's disciples. Amen.

Bible Reading: Luke 24:28-35

A Time to Share Celebrations and Concerns

(*Ask those present*) As we begin, are there any celebrations you want to share? (*Pause.*) How about any needs or concerns you would like to mention? (*Pause again, then begin the prayer.*)

Prayers for Needs and Concerns

Let us take a moment for silent prayer. (*Silence, then continue.*) God of constant mercy and forgiveness, we acknowledge the fact that we are trustees of your church and not owners. The importance of our decisions is not measured by one member winning over another but by your grace and forbearance even when we are wrong. As you provide fresh starts for us, may we do so for members who have offended us. Help us to put aside our differences and begin anew with your purpose of reconciliation and redemption. Turn our eyes to those whose needs and concerns cry out for peace, healing, and justice. Give us ears to listen and hands to provide comfort and make right the suffering of others. Move us away from the sidelines to seek the lost so that your plan of salvation through Christ may be at work within us. Amen.

(*The meeting may now be called to order.*)

Prayer of Adjournment and Lord's Prayer

Creator God, your Spirit is always fresh and sometimes surprising, but never old with energy spent. Our lives, on the other hand, need recharging and our days are soon gone. So refill us with your Spirit so that as we leave this place we might face the challenges of daily living. Inspire us with glimpses of your kingdom and keep in tune with the prayer that Jesus taught, saying, "Our Father . . ."

June 2015
Opening Prayer

Loving God, as we gather together as a community of faith we anticipate the guidance and outpouring of your Spirit. We pray that our intentions and actions will be acceptable to you and that we may join together seeking your wisdom and purpose in our lives through Jesus Christ. Amen.

Bible Reading: Mark 4:26-32

A Time to Share Celebrations and Concerns

(*Ask those present*) As we begin, are there any celebrations you want to share? (*Pause.*) How about any needs or concerns you would like to mention? (*Pause again, then begin the prayer.*)

Prayers for Needs and Concerns

Let us take a moment for silent prayer. (*Silence, then continue.*) We thank you, God, for your promise to hear and help your people. Enfold us in your care and compassion that we may be strengthened to embrace others in that same mercy and grace you have shown us. We pray that your peace might prevail in places and situations of conflict. Show us how we might become more effective as peacemakers in our homes, at work, and among nations. Open our eyes to those suffering from loss, illness, loneliness, or disasters. By your Spirit guide us that we might be of comfort and help to those very ones for whom we pray. Through Christ. Amen.

(The meeting may now be called to order.)

Prayer of Adjournment and Lord's Prayer

How good it is, gracious God, to join together with those who love you. As we leave this place we acknowledge and express our thanks for your many blessings. Thank you for the privilege of being a blessing to one another. Mold us more and more into your image so that we may be ambassadors of your grace throughout the world. Keep us in that same spirit of prayer that Jesus taught us saying, "Our Father . . ."

July 2015
Opening Prayer
God, director of our lives, you send us out in mission and bring us back in worship. We thank you for the privilege of gathering here in a free country. Grant that we may see our purpose not only as a loving fellowship but also as missionaries sent out to spread the good news of Jesus Christ. Amen.

Bible Reading: Mark 6:1-13

A Time to Share Celebrations and Concerns
(*Ask those present*) As we begin, are there any celebrations you want to share? (*Pause.*) How about any needs or concerns you would like to mention? (*Pause again, then begin the prayer.*)

Prayers for Needs and Concerns
Let us take a moment for silent prayer. (*Silence, then continue.*) God of our journey, you have challenged us to give testimony to strangers outside the church. But too many of us would rather shake the dust off our feet in embarrassment than perform the simple task of inviting others to church. And so we leave our mission to ads and slogans rather than risk the personal contact so vital in making disciples. We read about your early disciples who knew that they were sent out not in their own power and freely provided testimony and healing. Empower us with that same confidence so that we may risk telling others of you. Send us out personally to proclaim the good news as well as providing resources for those in need. Make us bold to follow in your footsteps, shaking off rejection and sharing the gospel to all who would listen. We pray this in Christ's name. Amen.

(The meeting may now be called to order.)

Prayer of Adjournment and Lord's Prayer
God, as we leave this meeting, set the tracking of your Holy Spirit within our hearts and move us in the direction of your mission. Deliver us from the timidity of hiding our identity as Christians of and making you known to others. Send us out from this place knowing that your world will become ours, even as Jesus prayed, saying, "Our Father . . ."

2014-2015 Writers

Frank Ramirez
(August 3-31; November 30;
December 7)
Frank Ramirez is the pastor of
the Union Center Church of the
Brethren near Nappanee, Indiana.
He has served Brethren congregations in California, Indiana, and
Pennsylvania over the last 30 years.
He has written many books and
articles. He and his wife, Jennie,
share three adult children and
three grandchildren. Frank enjoys
reading, writing, hiking, and other
forms of exercise.

Donald Schmidt
(September 7-October 5)
Donald is a UCC pastor who has
lived and worked in a variety of
cultures and settings. Donald and
his spouse live in Honolulu where
Donald serves as associate conference minister for the Hawaii Conference United Church of Christ.

John H. Collett Jr.
(October 12- 26)
John is executive assistant to the
bishop for the Nashville Episco-
pal Area of the United Methodist
Church.

Jeanette B. Strandjord
(October 31-November 2)
Jeanette enjoys family, preaching,
and writing. She serves as pastor of

Williams Bay Lutheran Church in
Williams Bay, Wisconsin.

Charles Somervill
(November 9-23)
Charles is author of books with
W/JK and Judson Press, retired
after serving 18 years as pastor at
First Presbyterian Church, Granbury, Texas, and continues to serve
as adjunct professor in communication at Texas Christian University.

David Neil Mosser
(Thanksgiving, Transfiguration,
Ash Wednesday, Palm Sunday)
David has written or edited 17
books with Abingdon and WJK
Press, teaches philosophy and ethics
at a Texas Community College, and
is an adjunct professor of homilet-
ics at Perkins School of Theology,
SMU, Dallas ,Texas.

Chris Ode
(December 14-24)
Chris serves as pastor of Bethel
Lutheran Church, Shoreline,
Washington. His ministry places a
special emphasis on multicultural,
inter-generational, and cross-con-
gregational collaboration.

Noelle Damico
December 25-January 11)
Noelle is a Senior Fellow at the
National Economic and Social
Rights Initiative, a human rights

organization in New York and the director of communications for the Hudson River Presbytery. For more than 20 years she has worked with people's organizations to build efforts for human rights worldwide.

Mary Sanders
(January 18-February 8)
Mary is a Lutheran parish pastor in Tacoma, Washington, has served as a volunteer police chaplain, and is married, a mother of three and grandmother of two. She does her best praying in the garden.

Deborah J. Winters
(February 22-March 22)
Deb is an affiliate professor at Palmer Seminary at Eastern University, transitional pastor, clergy coach, and cofounder of GodsPreciousChildren.com.

Andrea La Sonde Anastos
(April 2-19)
Andrea is a writer and spiritual director, currently exploring the intersection of word and symbol in fiber art. She has been a delegate to the Consultation on Common Texts, served a co-ministry, and worked in the UUA, the UCC, and the UMC as an intentional interim minister.

Julie A. Kanarr
(April 26 – May 17)
Julie serves as pastor of Christ Lutheran Church (ELCA) in Belfair, Washington.

Gordon Timbers
(May 24-June 21)
Gordon has participated in team development of congregational education and worship resources. He currently ministers with the people of Unionville Presbyterian Church in Markham, Ontario.

William H. Willimon
(June 28-July 26)
Will is a former bishop of the United Methodist Church. He serves as Professor of the Practice of Christian Ministry, Duke Divinity School, Durham, North Carolina. He is the author of many books on preaching and pastoral theology and has been chief writer for *Pulpit Resource* for nearly two decades.

Four-Year Church Year Calendar

	Year B **2014**	Year C **2015**	Year A **2016**	Year B **2017**
Advent begins	Nov. 30	Nov. 29	Nov. 27	Dec. 3
Christmas	Dec. 25	Dec. 25	Dec. 25	Dec. 25
	2015	**2016**	**2017**	**2018**
Epiphany	Jan. 6	Jan. 6	Jan. 6	Jan. 6
Ash Wednesday	Feb. 18	Feb. 10	Mar.1	Feb.14
Passion/Palm Sunday	Mar. 29	Mar. 20	Apr. 9	Mar. 25
Maundy Thursday	Apr. 2	Mar. 24	Apr. 13	Mar. 29
Good Friday	Apr. 3	Mar. 25	Apr. 14	Mar. 30
Easter	Apr. 5	Mar. 27	Apr. 16	Apr. 1
Ascension Day	May 14	May 5	May 25	May 10
Pentecost	May 24	May 15	Jun. 4	May 20
Trinity Sunday	May 31	May 22	Jun.11	May 27
Reformation	Oct. 31	Oct. 31	Oct. 31	Oct. 31
All Saints' Day	Nov. 1	Nov. 1	Nov. 1	Nov. 1

Calendars for 2014 and 2015

2014

JANUARY 2014	FEBRUARY 2014	MARCH 2014	APRIL 2014
S M T W T F S	S M T W T F S	S M T W T F S	S M T W T F S
1 2 3 4	1	1	1 2 3 4 5
5 6 7 8 9 10 11	2 3 4 5 6 7 8	2 3 4 5 6 7 8	6 7 8 9 10 11 12
12 13 14 15 16 17 18	9 10 11 12 13 14 15	9 10 11 12 13 14 15	13 14 15 16 17 18 19
19 20 21 22 23 24 25	16 17 18 19 20 21 22	16 17 18 19 20 21 22	20 21 22 23 24 25 26
26 27 28 29 30 31	23 24 25 26 27 28	$^{23}/_{30}$$^{24}/_{31}$ 25 26 27 28 29	27 28 29 30

MAY 2014	JUNE 2014	JULY 2014	AUGUST 2014
S M T W T F S	S M T W T F S	S M T W T F S	S M T W T F S
1 2 3	1 2 3 4 5 6 7	1 2 3 4 5	1 2
4 5 6 7 8 9 10	8 9 10 11 12 13 14	6 7 8 9 10 11 12	3 4 5 6 7 8 9
11 12 13 14 15 16 17	15 16 17 18 19 20 21	13 14 15 16 17 18 19	10 11 12 13 14 15 16
18 19 20 21 22 23 24	22 23 24 25 26 27 28	20 21 22 23 24 25 26	17 18 19 20 21 22 23
25 26 27 28 29 30 31	29 30	27 28 29 30 31	$^{24}/_{31}$ 25 26 27 28 29 30

SEPTEMBER 2014	OCTOBER 2014	NOVEMBER 2014	DECEMBER 2014
S M T W T F S	S M T W T F S	S M T W T F S	S M T W T F S
1 2 3 4 5 6	1 2 3 4	1	1 2 3 4 5 6
7 8 9 10 11 12 13	5 6 7 8 9 10 11	2 3 4 5 6 7 8	7 8 9 10 11 12 13
14 15 16 17 18 19 20	12 13 14 15 16 17 18	9 10 11 12 13 14 15	14 15 16 17 18 19 20
21 22 23 24 25 26 27	19 20 21 22 23 24 25	16 17 18 19 20 21 22	21 22 23 24 25 26 27
28 29 30	26 27 28 29 30 31	$^{23}/_{30}$ 24 25 26 27 28 29	28 29 30 31

2015

JANUARY 2015	FEBRUARY 2015	MARCH 2015	APRIL 2015
S M T W T F S	S M T W T F S	S M T W T F S	S M T W T F S
1 2 3	1 2 3 4 5 6 7	1 2 3 4 5 6 7	1 2 3 4
4 5 6 7 8 9 10	8 9 10 11 12 13 14	8 9 10 11 12 13 14	5 6 7 8 9 10 11
11 12 13 14 15 16 17	15 16 17 18 19 20 21	15 16 17 18 19 20 21	12 13 14 15 16 17 18
18 19 20 21 22 23 24	22 23 24 25 26 27 28	22 23 24 25 26 27 28	19 20 21 22 23 24 25
25 26 27 28 29 30 31		29 30 31	26 27 28 29 30

MAY 2015	JUNE 2015	JULY 2015	AUGUST 2015
S M T W T F S	S M T W T F S	S M T W T F S	S M T W T F S
1 2	1 2 3 4 5 6	1 2 3 4	1
3 4 5 6 7 8 9	7 8 9 10 11 12 13	5 6 7 8 9 10 11	2 3 4 5 6 7 8
10 11 12 13 14 15 16	14 15 16 17 18 19 20	12 13 14 15 16 17 18	9 10 11 12 13 14 15
17 18 19 20 21 22 23	21 22 23 24 25 26 27	19 20 21 22 23 24 25	16 17 18 19 20 21 22
$^{24}/_{31}$ 25 26 27 28 29 30	28 29 30	26 27 28 29 30 31	$^{23}/_{30}$$^{24}/_{31}$ 25 26 27 28 29

SEPTEMBER 2015	OCTOBER 2015	NOVEMBER 2015	DECEMBER 2015
S M T W T F S	S M T W T F S	S M T W T F S	S M T W T F S
1 2 3 4 5	1 2 3	1 2 3 4 5 6 7	1 2 3 4 5
6 7 8 9 10 11 12	4 5 6 7 8 9 10	8 9 10 11 12 13 14	6 7 8 9 10 11 12
13 14 15 16 17 18 19	11 12 13 14 15 16 17	15 16 17 18 19 20 21	13 14 15 16 17 18 19
20 21 22 23 24 25 26	18 19 20 21 22 23 24	22 23 24 25 26 27 28	20 21 22 23 24 25 26
27 28 29 30	25 26 27 28 29 30 31	29 30	27 28 29 30 31

Index of Sermon Texts